CUSTOMERS KNOW YOU SUCK

Actionable CX Strategies to Better Understand, Attract, and Retain Customers

By Debbie Levitt

Customers Know You Suck: Actionable CX Strategies to Better Understand, Attract, and Retain Customers

By Debbie Levitt [DeltaCX.com].
Editors are listed at the end of the book.
Cover by Mallika Fraser [https://linkedin.com/in/mallikapf/].

LEGAL STUFF:

Book Edition v1.0
First Edition/Printing: December 2022
Published by Delta CX Media [https://DeltaCX.Media]. ISBNs for this book are available on the Delta CX Media website.

Also available as an audiobook narrated by the author.

Dedication

This book is dedicated to every person hoping to fix workplace inefficiencies and improve experiences for all customers and users.

Debbie wants to thank her husband for being her best friend, duet partner, and sounding board.

Special thanks to the content editing squad who helped nudge this book in better directions. They're listed at the end of the book.

About the Author

Hi, I'm Debbie Levitt. I've been a Customer Experience (CX) and User Experience (UX) Strategist, Architect, and Researcher for over 20 years. When many people see "UX," they think "artist," but I'm not a visual artist. I have a Bachelor of Arts in Music and an MBA. The core of my work is strategic problem finding and problem solving, regardless of the industry.

My company is Delta CX [https://deltacx.com]. We're a full-service CX and UX consultancy focusing on projects, training, and consulting. We work with companies to build and elevate their CX and UX teams, practices, and collaboration with other departments and teammates. We are business designers and change agents, finding what's not working, improving processes and teams, and helping companies transform toward customer-centricity.

Clients often call me Mary Poppins; I fly in, fix everything I can, sing a few songs, and fly away to where I'm needed next.

Disclaimer: #NotSponsored

There are no sponsorships, paid placements, affiliate links, or partnerships with any company mentioned in this book. I purposefully decline all such offers so my audience knows I'm not for sale or rent. The companies and tools I like or recommend change over time. If you're wondering if I still like *that company*, please get in touch and ask.

Capital Letters

Capital letters are used to differentiate the names of departments, practices, processes, roles, and job titles from the work that is done. For example:

- Capital D **Design** refers to the process of Human-Centered Design or User-Centered Design.

- Lowercase d **designs** are the wireframes, prototypes, and other documents Designers produce.

- Capital P **Product** refers to your Product Management or Product Ownership department and teams.

- Lowercase p **product** refers to products your company offers.

Table of Contents

PART 1: INTRO

Chapter 1: Challenging Current Ways

It was just another day of trying to give companies my money.

I spent hours attempting to buy plane tickets. I selected "American Express" and spent some time typing in all the details and the matching billing address. After submitting the checkout form, a message said, "We invite you to re-enter your card information." Nothing on the screen told me what went wrong, or which field was entered incorrectly.

I know my American Express card is good, but I tried again, this time with a MasterCard. This erased the entire form, including my billing address, which would have been the same. I entered the card information and retyped the same billing address. The same message at the top of the page invited me to re-enter my card data.

I could have given up and chosen a competitor, but I wanted *these* flights. I tried a Visa card with a different billing address. An error message said my card was an invalid number. I gave up on the airline's site and purchased the flights from American Express's travel site. With that finally done, I went over to the website for Priority Pass, one of the perks from American Express. Priority Pass indicated that my account expired in May 2020. I went to the account profile area, saw an expired credit card number, and had no way to change it.

I emailed Customer Support. A reply thanked me for requesting a duplicate card. I didn't request a duplicate card, nor do I need a card showing an expired account. The email mentioned that a bot sent it, and a future email would include a survey asking how the bot did. The survey never came. I responded to the email saying I didn't need a duplicate card and asking how I update my account in their system. No reply.

Days later, I called Customer Support and learned that the system started a new but incomplete account for me. There was no way to change my old account. The Support Representative asked questions to verify me, but I got my address wrong. The Priority Pass Rep was lovely and found other information I could use to verify my identity. She gave me a 4-digit PIN the website required to finish setting up the new account. There would have been no way to do this myself, especially if a PIN from a Support Rep is required.

These aren't isolated and rare situations. You and I have so many stories like this from companies who said, "We care about customers. Our goal is to satisfy customers. We have *empathy* for customers. The customer is always right." We have stories like this from companies who made customer-centricity, user-obsession, and delivering quality part of company values. So much is going wrong.

Do your customer journey maps include experiences like mine? It's unlikely that I'm the only person that week who struggled to buy a flight on this airline's website. It's doubtful that I am the only Priority Pass customer with the wrong credit card associated with their account. Where's *my* customer journey map? Did someone decide that we should ignore the "complainers" because "they're just edge cases?" Did someone decide that we don't need to map or document customers' pain points because "customers will figure it out, or they'll contact Customer Support?"

Stories like these highlight **the struggle across multiple channels**. These aren't just digital or technology problems. These aren't just product strategy, User Experience, or Engineering problems. These aren't just Customer Support problems or call center training issues. These aren't just Sales or Marketing problems. The whole story is the true arc of my customer journey.

My experiences highlight corporate strategy problems and a lack of customer-centricity. We tend to silo customer satisfaction rather than looking at all of the interconnected stories. The call center will say, "We resolved this person's issue, and she was happy with that Agent. We have a good satisfaction rate, and that went well." Sales and Marketing will say, "The customer visited the website and completed their new account. We got a customer and made money today." Product, CX, UX, and Engineering might say, "Those changes to the website are working. Sales and Marketing reported that conversions are up." But is the customer satisfied? Do we push loyal customers to question their loyalty?

How much negative word of mouth would it take for companies to decide that fixing poor Customer Experiences is a priority? What's the Cost of Acquisition: the costs of sales, marketing, and other efforts to win a new customer? How much pain does our company need to feel before we take action to improve things for ourselves and our customers?

You hate every interaction based on a misguided corporate strategy, or someone's mega-cool idea to force or trick you into doing something you didn't want to do. You hate every interaction with a system or person who wasted your time, blocked you, and dropped you at a dead end. When we say we care about our customers – or at the very least their satisfaction and loyalty – we must follow through on those promises and show *through action* that we care. Many companies are talking about customer-centricity, empathy, and delighting users. How many companies are walking the walk?

Try It

Notice today and tomorrow how often you are frustrated, confused, disappointed, or even enraged by products, services, or experiences.

Defining "Quality"

When we release products and services that we know aren't quite right, are guesses, or will need to be fixed later, we might not all share the same definition of quality. Whether or not we are conscious of it, each of us has quality standards at every touchpoint. Your customers have quality standards for every moment they engage with you.

- You want to watch a YouTube video you're likely to enjoy, not just any random YouTube video.

- You want to stay at a hotel that meets or exceeds your standards, not just any hotel in the area.

- You have multiple choices for houses of worship or religious activities, and – if you're religious – you might not choose the closest ones. You want ones that deliver a specific experience.

- You want to talk to a friendly Support Rep who quickly understands your problem and has an easy solution they can take care of.

- You might not have even been aware of your quality standards for pizza until you had some bad pizza.

We fill our world with catchy sayings that we use as excuses when we're not building what customers would give *five stars out of five*. Many of these come from 2010s books aimed at startups.

- **"Just ship it."** Often without knowing if it's the right solution for our customers.

- **"We'll fix it later."** How often do we fix it later? When is "later," what will we have to delay, and what will it cost? Why are we releasing something we know is broken?

- **"Users will have to figure it out."** Or they will flood you with support tickets, give up, or switch to the competition.

- **"Fail fast."** There is nothing cool about failing fast or slowly when paying or trial customers suffer because of your failure. We thought it was cool when Facebook said, "Fail fast," but Facebook fails often, and in ways none of us should be emulating.

- **"Anything's better than what we have now."** And that's how we ended up with what we have now. What if whatever we do next is a downgrade?

- **"If you're not embarrassed, you shipped too late."** Is product-led embarrassment our goal? Most of us would prefer to feel proud that our product is an excellent match to customers' needs and tasks.

- **"Move fast and break things."** Only if you fix those things before the public struggles with them.

- **"It's good enough."** For the Engineering team? For stakeholders? Or for our paying or trial customers?

- **"Perfection is the enemy of good, progress, or done."** This is another flavor of "it's good enough." We should aim for the best product-market fit and experiences because our customers expect us to be *great.*

- **"You can't please everybody."** Perhaps not, but we *should* please our target customers. We must want them to be satisfied and loyal.

- **"For every X products you create, expect Y to fail."** This sounds risky, wasteful, and not Agile or Lean. Why aren't we creating more successes? Why resign ourselves or be complacent about frequent failures?

- **"Lean is the least we can do to get to the next step."** Lean disagrees. This bastardization of Lean seemed to come from *The Lean Startup* book. Toyota's original approach to Lean [https://cxcc.to/a171] – and Lean Six Sigma [https://cxcc.to/a172] – teach that Lean is about improving efficiency, reducing risk, and cutting waste.

    o "Value" in Lean is defined as customers' perceptions of what your products and services are worth to them. A stakeholder or executive does not define value.

    o Traditional Lean is about coming as close to perfect as you can the first time. The further you are from low quality and defects, and the sooner that you deliver high quality and value, the Leaner you are. "The least you can do" and "the fastest we can get this done" are the opposite of Lean, which prioritizes **efficiency and value** over speed, mistakes, and guesses. Lean trims the fat, not the meat.

    o Fake Lean is wasteful and takes us down wrong paths; we should cut fake Lean for not being Lean.

If 80% of startups fail – and many articles claim that 90+% of startups fail – why emulate startups? Models and approaches used by startups have a high likelihood of failure. [https://cxcc.to/a161]

We've been experimenting with *speed over quality* methods for years now, and it should be clear that they often don't work. Tangible evidence includes project costs, ROI (Return On Investment), Customer Support tickets, tweets, stock price, and customer satisfaction and loyalty. Low customer retention or low NPS (Net Promoter Score) also signal that what we're doing isn't working. We must stop praying to the false gods of "speed" and "give your customers broken things." All of this is high waste: not Lean, not Agile, not customer-centric.

For comparison, manufacturing failures are obvious. We *could* use the cheapest materials or a product design that has never been modeled or tested. We *could* give workers tasks that don't match their skill set. But we would see costly problems around the factory floor and during quality checks, highlighting that one or more elements in our process are broken. It's easy to see because we can hold a broken widget or see the production line slow down.

No factory would produce widgets under those conditions and *hope* customers will accept that low level of quality. Yet every day, we make poor decisions based on these hopes, and assume that our products and services are "good enough" for customers.

> *"One should not be asking the question, 'How little can we get away with?' but rather, 'How much can we afford to do to be really impressive?'"*
> *- Joe Rohde, former Senior VP of Walt Disney Imagineering*

"We Know What Customers Want"

Barely a day goes by in the corporate world where someone doesn't announce that *we know our customers very well* and *we know what they want.* If this were true:

- We wouldn't need to experiment with new ideas, run A/B tests, or bother with MVPs (Minimum Viable Products).

- We wouldn't need to run surveys or conduct research. We already know the answers.

- We would have a 100% accuracy rate when predicting which of our feature ideas are winners.

Even though time and time again, our company, leaders, and teams are bad at guessing what customers need, we continue to do it. We operate based on overconfident assumptions of what users will find valuable. Internal opinions, personal preferences, and nostalgia around "when I used to do that job" masquerade as "knowing what customers need today."

If someone declares that they know our customers or what they want, ask questions, including:

- How do you know? What data or evidence guides you or this decision?

- How recent is that information?

- Is it based on primary research like observational or interview data? Is it based on surveys and analytics?

- Who wins if two of our coworkers "know our customers" but suggest different strategies, approaches, or solutions?

Staying Open-Minded to Change

As a change agent, my job is to challenge what you know, what you *think* you know, what has or hasn't worked in the past, your goals and initiatives, processes and approaches, teams, culture, and more. I investigate, strategize, and challenge these to create the best outcomes for customers, employees, and the business. Depending upon what's going on or how it's being measured, what's "working" might not be working. **If it's working for the execs, but morale is low and customers are frustrated, it's not really working.**

I've seen too many examples of teams and lower-level managers reporting that *everything is going well: teams are efficient, and we're so Agile and Lean.* But these are often not true or are manipulations of the truth. I've seen slide presentations about how we raised our KPIs (Key Performance Indicators), but NPS is still low, and we don't know why. That's a business failure.

Since we are dealing with challenges, changes, transformations, and new ways of working, in this book, I will likely suggest some things that run against your current ideas or preferences. Please keep an open mind. Stay objective, think critically, and consider the possibilities. How you're doing things might seem "good enough," but if we want to continuously improve, we should be open to where and how we can improve.

Can We Be Customer-Centric and Agile?

We'll focus on Agile in later chapters, but let's quickly address the elephant in the room. A common response to the time, budget, and effort we would need to invest to be more customer-centric is, "That isn't Agile," "You're against Agile," or "You want waterfall." I'm absolutely *for* good implementations of Agile that prioritize customer satisfaction and value. **And we need to check our definition of Agile.**

Agile, in Short

A quick explanation for those unfamiliar with Agile. Before Agile, companies designed and built the entire product as one long project. For updates and improvements, most companies had one or two big releases annually with a few additional fixes or "patches" during the year.

Have you noticed how some of your smartphone apps update every month or so? This would be a manifestation of Agile. Imagine a non-Agile world where apps, YouTube, or Facebook released new features once or twice a year.

If you had a good UX team pre-Agile, you were confident you were releasing what people needed and that the product wouldn't need a lot of fixes. That was important since you wouldn't get to those changes for a while. If you didn't have a good – or any – UX team, it was highly risky and expensive to work for one or two years (or more), release the product, and then learn what people thought of it.

Agile represents several approaches or frameworks aiming to increase Engineers' efficiency in companies with software or digital products. Oxford's Learner's Dictionary says it's "a way of managing projects in which work is divided into a series of short tasks, with regular breaks to review the work and adapt the plans." Hypothetically, if we break larger pieces of work into smaller pieces, frequently reassess, and shift or pivot as needed, we're Agile.

Agile Manifesto Principle 1 says, "Our highest priority is to satisfy the customer through early and continuous delivery of valuable software." I have seen many fans of Agile say that the focus of that sentence is "continuous delivery": *we will make customers happy because we will deliver software fast and often.* The theory and intentions behind Agile software development focus on customer satisfaction, improved efficiency, product and service **value and quality**, and collaborative empowered teams.

But implementations of Agile vary, and often do not live up to these core ideals. Agile doesn't have matrices or frameworks that ensure that we understand customers and their tasks, their problems and needs, and build excellent executions of the best ideas to solve those. It's great when Agile organizations pay attention to customers' outcomes, realities, complaints, and needs, but Agile doesn't guarantee that we have investigated or monitored those well or at all. **Agile doesn't have QA (Quality Assurance) processes for the quality of our concept**. "Quality" in Agile is focused on coding and technology.

It's consistently impressive that people who claim to be pro-Agile love to tell me that my customer-centric suggestions "can't be done" or "are unrealistic." They say that without irony. Agile is about finding new ways of working, periodically checking processes and outcomes, and improving what we can. But when I challenge methods and processes, the walls go up, and the chorus sings, "That's not Agile."

Agile and customer-centricity can co-exist, but not easily when Agile is inflexible or we cling to the status quo.

"We can't do something like this," "This is how we've been doing it," or, "We have no idea how that can happen," must change to, "How can we make this happen, even if it's experimental first?" in mindset and action.

"We don't live in a perfect world," needs to shift to, "What's the *most customer value* we can deliver?" The world isn't perfect, but that's no reason to utilize poor processes, avoid fixing our culture, and aim for minimum viable quality or standards. We're an innovative company. We can figure out how to solve our own problems.

This book doesn't tell Engineers how to do their work; it's Engineering-method-agnostic. They are welcome to use Agile, Scrum, Kanban, XP, waterfall, or anything they like. This book is about everything else that is going on in our teams and processes that promote – if not ensure – customer-centricity.

Nobody wants to continuously deliver garbage.

Frameworks and Templates

We like things to be nicely packaged, especially if they can come with a certificate and some frameworks. We hope to accomplish our goals by filling some information into a template. Unfortunately, many templates, canvasses, and frameworks are *garbage in, garbage out*. They are only as useful or actionable as the information we add.

We try to take the complexities of business goals, customer goals, strategies, tactics, processes, and culture, and put them nicely into some boxes. **Literally "in the box" thinking.** If templates, canvasses, and maps worked, even when filled with guesses and assumptions, every company would be customer-centric. We would never experience crappy products and services. We wouldn't leave low ratings or switch to a competitor. We wouldn't need to call, email, or chat with Customer Support.

Templates, maps, and overlapping circles can be a one-way, beautifully visualized ticket to risk and waste if we lack deep knowledge of our target audiences and their tasks, behaviors, contexts, and perspectives. To break out of the box, we will need to shift away from methods and initiatives that glorify assumptions, burn internal time and resources, and have unknown or zero customer value.

Throughout the book, there are models and maps that I have invented or evolved, designed to encourage critical and out-of-the-box thinking. Those that are whiteboard-able, along with some of the exercises we do in the workshop version of this book, can be found at https://cxcc.to/miro.

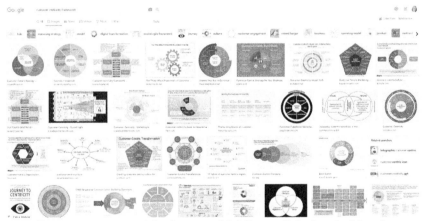

Figure 1: Googling "customer centricity framework" delivers all the interlocking shapes you could desire.

How Did We Get Here?

How did we end up with so many problems with our processes, culture, job and role definition, collaboration, and customer outcomes?

We didn't love being waterfall, we read books like *The Lean Startup* about how fast startups are, and we decided that speed was our top priority. We thought "Agility" would solve our problems. To achieve our desired speed, we lowered our standards to what internal staff decided was "good enough."

Anything that wasn't about speed became a dirty word, and nothing was worse than someone accusing you of being *waterfall*. We measured people and teams based on "velocity." We thought in sprints, forgetting that it's a marathon. We wanted to be "first to market." We fired R&D (Research and Development) because they were too slow.

We cared about the quality of our code, but we didn't care as much about the quality of our concepts or their execution. We read books and were trained on methods that could make us *even faster*: design sprints, design thinking, and "Lean" ways of creating our products and services, all based on *speed over quality*.

We claimed that everybody needed to be able to do everybody's jobs. We started devaluing specialists and experts, declaring that they were "too slow," and anybody can do their work "well enough." We wanted "T-shaped people" and "generalists" because we could constantly shift their roles or priorities as we find skills gaps.

We loved posts and articles that told us to *hire for personality and drive because skills can be taught*. We assumed that everyone could learn all skills quickly and proficiently. We imagined that our company would budget for and prioritize training those skills. We changed our entry-level jobs to block newbies; our Juniors must have 2+ years of experience, which was previously a requirement for a Mid-Level title.

We saw a lot of problems and failures, so we tried to get ourselves out of the speed trap. We started saying things like, "Outcomes over outputs," but we mostly looked at the *business* outcomes of revenue, adoption, and retention, not *customer* outcomes like satisfaction or how our products and services match customers' needs.

We changed our company values to "empathy," "integrity," and "care," but rarely lived up to them. We told our staff that we love creativity and challenging the status quo, and then we made people afraid to speak up or challenge the status quo. The people who pointed out the problem became the problem.

So here we are, going as fast as possible, often with lower-skilled generalists. We're still rejecting experts and specialists. Our processes are *speed over quality*. Our culture became high-hustle, high-burnout, and less ethical as we tried our hardest to work fast and show that *something* was going right. When customers complained or left, we ignored that, or assumed it was a signal that we needed to be even faster.

This book is not a return to the way things were. It's the next step and evolution of how we work when we want to be efficient but prioritize quality, value, and customer outcomes.

The Only Hard Data That Matters Is Yours

People sometimes ask me for "hard data" to prove that my suggestions work. Those who dislike my ideas often demand this while providing no hard data for their opposing suggestions. This is often a trap; magically, no qualitative or quantitative data is recent enough, large enough, from the right industry, or scientifically peer-reviewed enough to satisfy the request.

Even where I can provide data and success stories, that doesn't mean that my ideas will work – as they are or with modification – for every team or company. Popular and unpopular methods work in some places and not in others.

The only data that matters is yours.

X% of companies use a tool that you tried but it didn't work for your teams. That Big Company saw a Y% increase in something after implementing Technique Z. If it works for them but not for you, their "hard data" doesn't really matter. If Google or Apple does something, should you do it? If they stop doing something, should you stop doing it? We must be able to investigate and calculate our own costs, benefits, and alternatives.

What works well evolves. Companies sure that a certain technique is working might find later that it's no longer effective or producing the results it used to. If it's not working for your teams, "hard data" showing that something is popular, respected, or working for other companies doesn't change your experience and therefore might not matter. Chris Lenhart [https://linkedin.com/in/chrislenhart72/] adds, "This is precisely why boxers study videos of their next opponent. You can't just study boxing. What works on one opponent may not work on the next. You need to adapt or face the consequences."

You will need to collect both qualitative and quantitative data, and take it seriously. Not all data comes in numerical form. Customer and Employee Experiences include actions, feelings, reactions, demands, and complaints; these are all data points. When a customer says something isn't functioning correctly, the hard data of "Well, it works for me," isn't enough. We investigate and act because the complaint data set is more important than the "it works for me" data set.

A customer-centric transformation will produce a mountain of actionable data, some in numeric form, some more spoken or anecdotal. The only hard data that matters is yours. Collect, measure, and react to that data.

A Message to Change Agents

You want to be a change agent. You want to be a Low Ego Action Hero, as I call the members in my online communities. At most companies, we can only make the changes we have the authority to make. If your job isn't giving you the authority to make changes, you will have to bring your ideas and plans to someone above you who has that power. I encourage people to try to create change, even in areas where they think there might be no hope. You never know.

My main message to change agents is: ***you didn't break it; you might not be able to fix it.*** Some companies are badly broken. Some companies *know* they are badly broken, yet they resist efforts to make changes or improvements. We can only keep doing our best, and at the end of the day, look at ourselves in the mirror and know we did our best.

Being able to explain something well to people doesn't mean that you can change their minds.

If you cannot make any significant change where you work, please don't let it affect your mental health. Don't believe that you are incompetent. Sometimes the unstoppable force is against the immovable object, and we can't make the right things happen. Use your Low Ego Action Hero powers to recognize these situations early, and do what you need to do for self-care. Put yourself and your mental health first. There's only one of you, and we need you!

Chapter 2:   Terms and Models

Who Are Customers?

"Are these people customers, users, consumers, humans, or something else?" Some say that customers are the people who pay us, and users are people who don't pay us. *Someone using Facebook is a "user," but if you pay for advertising, you're a "customer."* When we divide people this way, our company might mostly or only look at where the money comes from. We will optimize for the people who pay us, and put those who don't in the periphery. Or we might build features that work against those who aren't paying us to serve those who do. A non-paying customer or someone on the "other" side of a two-sided marketplace is still a vital part of the ecosystem. Attracting and retaining them leads to attracting and retaining the revenue-generating side of the ecosystem.

To avoid that mess, I use "customer" to refer to everybody: every target user, potential customer, and current customer; every partner and reseller; every installer, maintainer, and decision-maker; anybody who can do any business with you or interact with any of your touchpoints. If you're buying something on behalf of a child or a pet, then the kid and dog are customers, too!

When we talk about our customers, we often leave out people with disabilities, diagnoses, and conditions. But "they" are us. We, our coworkers, family, and friends have trouble seeing, walking, hearing, moving, or remembering things. We know people who are dyslexic, autistic, or have ADHD, cancer, or COVID-19. We experience side effects of diseases and treatments. We struggle with depression or other mental health issues. We have broken arms. We take medication.

Yet, despite our "care" and "empathy," it's still hard to find a team at any company acting on accessibility without a lawyer, accessibility specialist, or DEI (Diversity, Equity, Inclusion) leader reminding people to care about this population. We appear unable to put our empathy into action without a voice of authority, a lawsuit, or a public scandal pushing us to action.

According to The Centers for Disease Control and Prevention (CDC) in America, 26% of Americans live with at least one disability. [https://cxcc.to/a136] 25% of Europeans do too. [https://cxcc.to/a158] How can we be sure that we have *validated or invalidated an idea* when we haven't included a quarter of our target audience? How can our product work for everyone if we never included people living with varying disabilities, diagnoses, or conditions in our research or usability testing?

When someone hears "accessibility," the typical reaction is that *we have zero or few blind customers.* If our products and services aren't accessible, you can be sure that we don't – and won't – have customers with accessibility needs. You might also hear that someone with accessibility needs can ask for help. The goal is for people to be independent. Nobody wants to find and interrupt someone else when they want to submit a form for time off from their job, order a pizza, or use our system.

Whether this is a beta version, MVP, or full release, we can't leave out accessibility or assume we'll take care of it later. As we will learn in a later interview with an accessibility expert, plugins and overlays won't solve accessibility, and might get us sued. We should care about accessibility as much as legal regulations, security, and good visual branding. Nobody would say that *we should get the beta out fast and worry later about whether or not we're easy to hack or are compromising personal data.*

Terms I Invented

Customer-peripheric (pronounced *per-IH-fer-ic*) is my adjective for the opposite of customer-centric. The customer exists in our universe, but they are not the center. They are in our peripheral vision, but not our focus.

PSE is my term for "products, services, and experiences," whatever your company sells. Customers of all types buy, use, and interact with PSE. It's a great short way to say, "Everything your company Designs, makes, builds, sells, or offers."

I replace product-market fit with **PSE-market fit**. Your customers might be best served by digital software, physical products, services, experiences, or a combination of these. Every interaction a potential or current customer can have with our company – digital, in-person, live, synchronous, or asynchronous – should be a fit and a five-stars-out-of-five experience.

CX: The "Customer Experience"

Across articles, books, speakers, and social posts, I see different definitions of CX:

1. **CX is the responsibility of the Marketing organization.** Marketing makes people aware of our PSE, and they typically run surveys that check on customer satisfaction. Therefore, Marketing "owns" the Customer Experience.

2. **CX is part of Customer Support or Customer Success.** We want to see positive Customer Experiences with our Support Representatives. These teams are aware of where people have problems or concerns, leading some to say that Support and call centers are the core of CX.

3. **CX is helping people buy and feel good about buying.** That sounds like a customer-peripheric definition of the Customer Experience. Buying is a very narrow slice of a potential or current customer's journey. We could run into questionable ethical decisions when we overfocus on "helping" people buy.

4. **CX is where "what's good for the business" overlaps with "what's good for the customer."** That sounds good initially, but what about the areas where there isn't overlap? What about when "what's good for the business" is bad for customers? These customer-peripheric experiences and touchpoints are still part of the Customer Experience.

5. **CX is the complete end-to-end Customer Experience.** Before Customer Support helps you and before you consider buying, there are **our PSE**, the main reason you are in our ecosystem. Our Marketing department may or may not have been

involved in how potential customers got there.

- o CX considers the whole journey and all target audiences' tasks, sub-tasks, and interactions with our company. **This is the CX definition used in this book.**

CX is everything that touches your customer, or your customer can touch. CX is omnichannel, omnidevice, and omnitouchpoint. Every moment is a chance to bond with your customer or possibly alienate them.

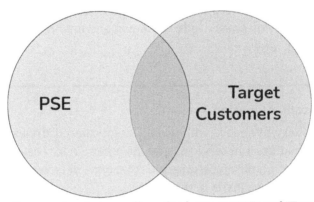

Figure 2: Venn diagram showing a small overlap between "PSE" and "Target Customers."

In the above Venn diagram, the overlap between PSE and customers is small, indicating that we have many products and features that don't serve users or meet their needs. The diagram shows that we have a lot of customers whose needs aren't addressed by our PSE. The PSE that don't match our users' needs are risks we need to mitigate or waste we should eliminate. Customer needs that we are not aware of or not addressing are missed opportunities and could create risk. We're leaving money on the table.

Figure 3: Venn diagram showing a large circle for "Target Customers" and a smaller circle inside the larger circle labeled "PSE."

Why doesn't the Venn Diagram of our PSE and customers overlap like the above diagram? All PSE serve customer needs. Unknown and unaddressed customer needs are opportunities for our future PSE.

Try It: PSE-Customer Overlap

Prepare a virtual whiteboard with two different colored circles next to each other. Label one circle "products and services" and the other circle "customers" or "customers' needs." These are our "blank" Venn diagrams that don't yet overlap. Make sure you have one set for each person you invite to the exercise.

Get the cross-functional team into a meeting. Ask them to resize and overlap their circles based on how much they think our current PSE overlap with customers and their needs. Will anybody create a circle inside a circle, as seen above? Will the circles have minimal overlap?

Initiate a discussion about how much our PSE serve our customers, what the optimal Venn diagram would look like, and how we work on improving our PSE-market fit.

Whether or not we invest time, money, or qualified professionals in our PSE's design, **there will be a design**. We should make sure it's a great match to customers' definitions of quality and value.

Whether or not we invest time, money, or qualified professionals in our QA, **there will be QA**. Bugs exist and will be found, probably by angry customers tired of dealing with broken stuff that your company decided was "good enough."

Whether or not we invest time, money, or qualified professionals in making our products fully accessible for every disability, diagnosis, or condition, **there will be customers with accessibility needs trying to use your PSE**.

Design, QA, and accessibility can't be sprinkled on later or hoped for. They are components of the Customer Experience. You choose whether they will be great, or a source of complaints, frustration, and attrition.

"CX" and "UX" Are Interchangeable When Done Well

The term User Experience was created in the early 1990s by Don Norman. It originally meant everything we now mean by CX. In a video explaining this original definition, Don uses the example of buying a computer in the early 1990s. [https://cxcc.to/a115] The User Experience included researching different models, going to a computer store, checking out the options, asking people you trust what they recommend, wondering if the computer will fit in your car to bring it home, the purchase process, and beyond.

While people with UX job titles often have tasks including making interfaces visually attractive; planning, conducting, and analyzing research; and designing digital interfaces, that's not all UX is *when UX is done right*. Whether you call your team or staff "CX," as I recommend, or "UX," as has been common over the years, these are people with various specialties performing the tasks that will facilitate everyone in our company becoming more customer-centric. CX practitioners should be strategic problem finders and problem solvers. In later chapters, we'll look at their processes, tasks, and roles.

When done right, CX is UX and vice versa. When CX and UX are done right, they are part of the Brand Experience (BX). Brand Experience is commonly defined as people's thoughts, feelings, and opinions in response to interacting with your PSE and company. It's how people perceive the value you offer or deliver, and how that's associated with your brand.

No matter what we call any of these, it's all about the X – the experiences.

Voice of the Customer (VOC)

VOC is about collecting feedback from target and current customers everywhere they express themselves. Directly speaking with customers (primary research) might be involved. But VOC is often secondary research or indirect communications with customers including publicly available information like tweets, social posts, online ratings, and app reviews. This is combined with internal information like complaints and themes from Customer Support channels, survey data, and satisfaction scores. Analyzing this feedback helps bring to light what is on customers' minds, where they have pain points, and potential priorities for our company to address.

VOC adds color but often doesn't reveal *why* something is happening or *what* to do about these pain points. Your VOC program should be augmented by observational research so that we have examined and understood who, what, where, when, why, and how. We can then prioritize customers' unmet needs and our opportunities to better serve them.

The Four Horsemen of Bad CX®

Figure 4: A hand-painted portrait of The Four Horsemen of Bad CX: Frustration, Confusion, Disappointment, and Distraction.

The Four Horsemen of Bad CX are Frustration, Confusion, Disappointment, and Distraction. These jump out at us during observational studies and interviews. We see and hear them in Voice of the Customer (VOC) data. We check for them during usability and other testing with real and archetypal customers. We want to ensure that customers have an easy, intuitive, and efficient experience.

Noticing The Four Horsemen in our PSE is one way to start a conversation about the quality and value of the current PSE or potential solution. It's simple language that anybody can use. As soon as we notice anything that is or has the potential to be frustrating, confusing, disappointing, or distracting, we should have some serious team conversations about *not* releasing PSE that we already know will need to be fixed later.

Cost of Poor Quality (COPQ)

A great model for examining and calculating the actual costs of our guesses, mistakes, and failures is the "Cost of Poor Quality" from Lean Six Sigma.

Internal costs might not be evident to those outside our company. They include:

- Bad partners or suppliers.

- Delays.

- Failure and root cause analysis.

- Rework and retesting.

- Downtime.

- Low morale.

- Training.

External costs are likely to be experienced by customers, and sometimes seen by the public, including:

- Complaints and support tickets.

- Bad word of mouth, including social posts and reviews.

- Environmental costs for physical objects and products.

- Repairing goods and redoing services.

- Returns, recalls, and exchanges.

- Safety incidents and lawsuits.

Your company has had – and probably currently has – disaster projects: time wasted, money burned, customers frustrated or leaving, Customer Support receiving more tickets than usual, and low morale. To calculate the Cost of Poor Quality for one such project, start with what the company spent internally, including all the time it took multiple teams. How about Marketing costs and Sales efforts? Did anybody write training on these features? What did it cost us to delay and fix things? Work with someone from Customer Support to see what complaints, tickets, or issues they have about this project's features. Work with Sales to find numbers on customers who canceled or downgraded. Can we figure out the costs of MVPs, especially failed MVPs? Did our PSE include physical parts that were low quality? What is the environmental cost when customers need a replacement part or a dongle? Check VOC data for reputational damage; unhappy customers can be vocal micro-influencers.

The Cost of Poor Quality can be used in every project for risk identification and mitigation before and after problems and failures occur. Quantify this as best as you can, and examine root causes to understand what mistakes really cost us and how to improve for the future.

Conversely, the Cost of Good Quality (COGQ) has two types: prevention and appraisal. These cost us money but are clear investments that are highly likely to improve our company, PSE, and outcomes.

Prevention includes:

- Better planning.

- Improved vetting of suppliers, staff, or vendors.

- Training staff.

- Improving ways of working and processes.

Appraisal includes:

- Internal audits and assessments of PSE and processes.

- Continuous testing and iteration on PSE before they go to the public.

As we invest in improving customer-centricity, we should estimate or calculate the costs of poor quality, fixing that poor quality, and improving internal and external quality. Proactive improvements plus investments into prevention and appraisal will help us avoid the Cost of Poor Quality.

Deceptive Designs (Formerly Known as "Dark Patterns")

When a company wants to force or trick people into doing something they wouldn't normally do – or wouldn't want to do – we call these "deceptive designs." [https://deceptive.design] The most common examples include companies that add something to your shopping cart, trick or force people onto email mailing lists, or make it difficult or impossible to cancel or downgrade a service or subscription.

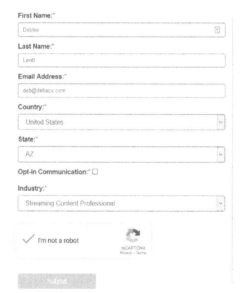

Figure 5: Screenshot of a contact information form before downloading a free software driver. The checkbox for opting into "communication" is a required field.

The above screenshot shows a form I had to fill out before downloading a free software driver. I had no choice but to "opt-in" to "communication." Is that ethical? Am I still "opting" in if it's not optional? What are the terms and conditions? Is this customer-centric and based on my needs and tasks? Did someone decide to force people onto the mailing list while claiming they had *empathy* for users, and they *really kept customers in mind*?

I posted this example to LinkedIn, and two people quickly commented that this absolutely was not a deceptive design. One was a Client Account Executive and the other was a Senior Strategic Planning Analyst at a company on Forbes' Digital 100. Between the two of them, they said this was a great "sales strategy." They advised that I could not unsubscribe, and must stay on the mailing list forever because that was the deal. They disagreed with my concern over privacy and GDPR (General Data Protection Regulation, the EU's data protection and privacy laws). They said it's not an issue because it's "clearly marked," and I wasn't "forced" to fill out this form. They told me that this is a "fair exchange of goods." The driver is a good, and I can trade my information and privacy for that good.

They were ready with many excuses they have probably made repeatedly in meetings that decided on something customer-peripheric, deceptive, or unethical. They *did* admit that it was "not consumer-friendly," but still firmly believed that this was an excellent way to increase the company's Sales and Marketing audience.

Are your Strategists recommending tactics and strategies that they *know* aren't consumer-friendly? This advice is risky, can lower customer satisfaction, and can limit PSE value. Customer-peripheric deceptive designs are everywhere and will live on as long as your ethics, values, processes, and lack of accountability allow.

Once we talk about deception and questionable ethics, it's easy to find multiple examples from Facebook (Meta). In March 2022, it was revealed that Facebook had recently fixed a "bug" that was giving an algorithmic lift to hate speech, nudity, pornography, violence, and Russian state media. [https://cxcc.to/a152] Facebook claimed it was a ranking failure they first discovered over two years prior (in 2019), but didn't have a significant "impact" until October 2021. The "bug" was fixed roughly ten days after Facebook publicly announced on 1 March 2022 that it would stop showing Russian state media. Facebook was still showing this propaganda – if not raising it in their algorithm – for some time after that pledge. [https://cxcc.to/a153] It appears that Russian state media got a bump for months before Russia invaded Ukraine, and continued getting that bump for two weeks after the February 2022 invasion.

A Facebook spokesperson said the bug "has not had any meaningful, long-term impact on our metrics." Super. Congrats on your metrics. How about the impact on humans who saw the content? What about the effects on societies due to the increased visibility of Russian state media?

Suppose your company had a "bug" that "accidentally" shows people sex, violence, and political propaganda. Wouldn't you put your best Engineers on that problem 24 hours a day until the "accident" was completely resolved? Would you allow this bug to continue for six months? Would you be complacent because a former member of your "Civic Integrity" team didn't notice any "malicious intent" behind this bug? Were Facebook Engineers incapable of fixing this bug for six months?

Let's call this what this is: a controlled experiment.

Six months was enough time to study the impact of this harmful and often unwanted content on humans and their behavior within the Facebook ecosystem.

Deceptive design can be lawsuit worthy. Harry Brignull [https://linkedin.com/in/harrybrignull], who coined the original term "dark patterns" and its revised name "deceptive design," provides expert witness testimony and other evidence at trials related to deceptive digital practices and interfaces. The following legal document includes some of his testimony in a class-action suit against Noom. [search https://cxcc.to/a116 for "Brignull"]

"Noom employs on its website, in its app, and in email communications with users [exploitative and deceptive patterns that] work together to exploit human mental biases to create an environment in which a reasonable user (1) can become automatically enrolled in a recurring, non-refundable premium subscription as a result of signing up for a free or low-cost trial without any idea that they have done so; and/or (2) is unable to (or unaware of the need to) cancel that subscription, increasing the length of time that the user is subscribed and contributing to Noom's revenue stream."

Noom agreed to a $56 million USD settlement.

Chapter 3:   Interview: Ethical Design

Trine Falbe is an experienced UX Designer with a wide background in digital design. For 20 years, she's been driven to create value for people. She is a consultant, author of *The Ethical Design Handbook* [https://ethicaldesignhandbook.com/], speaker and educator, and the founder of the Ethical Design Network, where ethical-minded Designers from across the world come together to discuss how we can Design ethically. Find out more about her work and Ethical Design training on her website trinefalbe.com.

Debbie: How do you define customer-centricity?

Trine: Customer-centricity is having a focus on whoever uses, consumes, interacts, or anything in between with your product or your service. You must genuinely focus on them beyond looking at them as "consumers," genuinely interested in their perspectives and the problems they have that your product or service should solve for them.

Debbie: What is Ethical Design?

Trine: The overarching definition is: *growing businesses, services, and products from a principle of fairness and fundamental respect towards everyone involved.* It's not a siloed activity; it goes across the entire organization. Fundamental respect means that you respect their privacy, their freedom of choice, and their time and effort. But it also means that you respect the people who build the business, who build success in the products and services.

To respect them fundamentally, you need to instill proper governance, autonomy, working conditions, and decision-making. Ethical Design is about creating products that rest on sound principles like non-deceptive and trustworthy Design. Ethical Design and ethics tie into customer-centricity in the way that you – as a company or as a professional – hold yourself accountable for providing value. Ethics, providing value, and being transparent are key.

Debbie: It's very easy to spot some publicly-known controversial, unethical decisions. What are some subtle or sneaky ways companies do unethical things?

Trine: Some of the more subtle examples are very often tied to data usage, especially outside of the European Union because in the EU, we have GDPR, and companies have to comply with those restrictions. But outside of the EU, I'm noticing that the cookie consent popups make it super hard to not accept the terms and conditions. Sometimes it's impossible to say no to cookies. I make a point of never agreeing to cookies beyond the necessary cookies. I visited a service the other day where I couldn't do that. They didn't make that possible for me, and it made my blood boil. It's even harder for audiences that are vulnerable in some kind of sense to protect their data privacy.

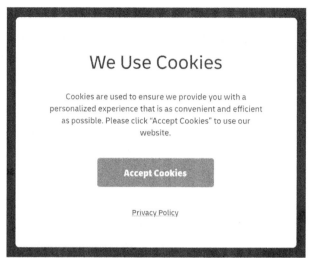

Figure 6: Screenshot from DHL's American package tracking website. There is no way to not accept cookies or control which cookies you accept.

Debbie: It's a deceptive design move by making the granular selection of cookies so awful and complicated that you just want to say "yes" to all the cookies to make it go away.

Trine: Unethical design happens on different levels. It can be the result of actual hurtful intent. It can also be due to a lack of knowledge. Maybe the team that created this thing used a deceptive design pattern because they were lazy and doing whatever was fastest. But it could also result from someone not knowing how to create something differently.

I tend to blame the tech giants for standardizing deceptive design. When you see new Designers, Developers, or Researchers entering the industry, and they look at best practices, where do they look? They look at the biggest platforms, which aren't necessarily super ethical in how they approach their business and customers. But they've set the standards.

Debbie: Bad things other companies are doing end up as precedent. *Super famous company did this, so it must be OK for us. Let's just get the lawyers to write something in the terms and conditions.*

Trine: Exactly. *If it works for them, it will work for us.* Ethical Design is about looking at your own decisions and saying, "Why are we making this decision? What are the potential consequences? Is it because of standards? Or super famous Company X is doing it? Should we do something else? Do we want to do something else?" Ethical Design starts in the decision-making process.

Debbie: To me, one of the most blatantly unethical things about cookies is where they claim that companies have a "legitimate interest" in tracking what you're doing.

Trine: Why is it legitimate? Is it because their business will profit more from it? Why is it legitimate to me? In 99 out of 100 cases, it's because it benefits the business. That's the opposite of customer-centricity: only caring about the business interest. UCD [User-Centered Design, explained later] has the whole notion of establishing and identifying business needs, customer and user needs, and then finding that sweet spot in between.

Ethical Design doesn't mean that you are a nonprofit or not making money. We live in a commercialized world. I don't belong to the group of people who genuinely believe that the commercialization of products is automatically evil and bad. But we have to create businesses that fundamentally respect the people that they sell to and the people that they employ. I don't mind a business making tons of money if they do it in the right way. I salute them if they are able to do that.

Debbie: What about the perspective that says, "By tracking Debbie in these subtle, hidden, lesser-known ways, we're ultimately giving her what she wants. This is proactively helping connect people with products and services they're genuinely interested in?"

Trine: I assume that's the reasoning used by companies using behavioral tracking and marketing. One question they forgot to ask themselves is, "Does Debbie want our help? Did Debbie ask for our help?" And the answer is no; she did not. Therefore, it's unethical.

Respecting people's privacy is not just about not collecting their data unless they say "yes," but also thinking about whether they have freedom of choice. At one of our Ethical Design events, Tiziana d'Agostino [https://linkedin.com/in/tizianadagostino/], who specializes in behavioral psychology and UX, said that for nudging to be ethical, it has to have actual freedom of choice. There are so many gray zones in nudging because we can also discuss whether someone needs to lose weight or needs to get in shape. If objective parameters say that this is apparent, does that give us the right to invade their private space and say, "Hey, we have this product that could help you." We should and must have absolute freedom of choice.

Debbie: We had a few days here in the house where we talked a lot about almonds. I didn't Google or research almonds. I didn't do anything on my phone or computer related to almonds. But we talked a lot about almonds because we had a house guest who was deathly allergic to almonds. Within about a day or so of scattered almond discussion, Instagram was showing me ads for almonds.

My thoughts were, "Thing one, get out of my life. Thing two, they obviously missed the context." The context was: *we can't give this person almonds*. You would think that if they understood the context, I would have gotten ads for soy milk. But instead, I got, "Go buy almonds," the opposite of what I needed.

Trine: Companies pay for their brand to be exposed to you. It's funny that, in this case, it had the opposite effect. But this happens all the time. I have a Facebook account that I don't use very often. I make sure to never log into Facebook when I search online. One day, I was mistakenly logged into Facebook, and I bought a face product from a website. I had said "no" to cookies, but maybe they were using Facebook pixel or something. The next time I visited Facebook, it was full of ads for face creams. I had already bought the facial product somewhere else. You're too late. All the money these brands spent on showing me ads went to waste. And I'm not sorry.

Debbie: I still hear people saying that we should make a product that is addictive, and we should read books teaching us how to do that.

Trine: It's definitely not ethical because the principles are usually to identify weakness. *Get customers by finding a weak spot, tap into where people are weak, and take advantage of that.* Being customer-centric and being focused on Ethical Design are very much a mindset. The mindset of finding weakness or "creating addiction" is the opposite. *We have this product; how can we shove it down people's throats to the greatest extent possible and make the most money? How do we make them susceptible to our product?* It's the complete opposite of trying to figure out what value can we bring to people, what problems are they struggling with, and how can we – in a respectful and meaningful way – help them solve that problem.

Debbie: When I ask people to name a product or service they've been unhappy with, they could talk my head off for a week. When I ask them about a product or service they love that really fits their needs, it's hard for them to think of something. Yet many companies pretend they're on people's lists of what they love.

Trine: Very few companies are on that list. And the reason for that is that we remember bad experiences with twice as much emotion as positive ones. It's the reason why people can talk about bad experiences to a much greater extent than positive experiences. It's just the way that the human mind works, but companies tend to ignore this.

Product is what we see. It's where ethical or unethical Design manifests. I don't expect all companies to be on the highest level of the scale of Ethical Design. If you, as a company or as a professional, improved based on where you were last year, that's fantastic.

I'd much rather look at incremental change and incremental improvement. That's what a transformation is. Transformation takes time. It's the long haul. As long as you progress, that's great. We can't grow things rapidly. Rapid or exponential growth often leaves lots of victims along the way. We won't have these victims if we choose responsible growth. It's extremely important to look at the consequences of the strategic decisions we're about to make. *Who have we not thought about? Which target audience haven't we included?*

Debbie: I remember a SaaS system with a policy of not letting you export your data. Their perspective was: *if we make it easy for people to leave, they'll leave.* How can a company catch themselves in that moment where they're dreaming up something that sounds good in the meeting room but might be evil?

Trine: There have to be people who are allowed to raise a red flag. Company governance has to allow and promote autonomy, including the autonomy to raise a red flag. I know a Designer who works at a company with incredible governance. They told me a story that a relatively new employee noticed something that they were deeply concerned about. They raised that red flag to their manager, and everything stopped until they had investigated that concern. A relatively new, non-senior employee was allowed and encouraged to raise a red flag, and was taken seriously.

A business cannot prevent bad decisions if they don't let their employees raise red flags and take them seriously. Governance is absolutely key in making that happen. We've all been in a meeting room where a decision has been made, and you're like, "This doesn't sit well with me." But you didn't have the autonomy to say, "Hey, wait a minute." You knew that the consequences of saying, "Hey, wait a minute," to your manager or a superior would be significant.

As a CEO, you cannot possibly know everything that goes on in your Engineering, UX, or Marketing teams, but you can have opinions on things. And that's where it goes wrong. If opinion trumps professionalism, that's where the deep problems are. To mitigate or reduce these types of mechanisms, top management needs to understand what they know and don't know, and trust their employees to a much greater extent. We could also mitigate a lot of these things with measurements.

Debbie: Should companies have an ethics department? Is there an Ethics Officer?

Trine: It depends on the size of the organization. Typically, as organizations grow, they become more hierarchic. A startup starts with a small team, completely flat. As the company grows, it starts dividing into silos.

I generally don't promote the "Ethics Officer" because it's a function that's not tied to a specific department. I advise a governance model that specifically includes ethical decision-making. You could also have someone with a mandate who has a red flag in their hand and is allowed to raise that red flag. They answer up to top management.

These things should be defined in the corporate manual and culture. It's important to verbalize and formalize these types of things. Without that, an employee can raise a red flag, but someone will dismiss it. The employee would be able to say, "It's part of our process. I am allowed to do this." It's very important to give that kind of power to employees.

Debbie: When it looks like unethical companies succeed, what's the incentive to be more ethical?

Trine: It's not the first time that I get that question. There are a handful of reasons why it makes sense for a company to move more toward Ethical Design.

One reason is the megatrends. We're seeing a significant increase in consumers who turn their backs on companies whose values don't align with theirs. Salesforce does reports every year. In the last one, they surveyed 8,000 buyers and consumers. 61% had turned their backs on a company whose values didn't align with theirs. [https://cxcc.to/a124] That's not just a megatrend; that's a smack in the face.

Second, it's possible to run a business on sound ethical principles. It's good for employees, and it's good for employability. We're seeing an increase in professionals who genuinely want to use their powers and their skills to do good. Instilling Ethical Design principles increase the number of people who will want to work for you, and they will stay longer.

There's also significant proof that Ethical Design makes happier employees. Proper governance means we're providing more value to customers. Most professionals would rather provide that value than use deceptive design. [https://cxcc.to/a125]

PART 2: CUSTOMER-CENTRICITY

Chapter 4: What Is Customer-Centricity?

Before we can strategize and plan how we move customers from the periphery to our central focus, let's align on what customer-centricity is, and why we should invest time and effort in a transformation.

Definitions of Customer-Centricity

Customer-centricity puts the Customer Experience at the center of strategies, goals, initiatives, projects, and more. Gartner, a large international consulting firm, says:

> *"Customer-centricity is the ability of people in an organization to understand customers' situations, perceptions, and expectations. Customer-centricity demands that the customer is the focal point of all decisions related to delivering products, services, and experiences to create customer satisfaction, loyalty, and advocacy."*

Gartner's May 2022 article, "How to Know Whether You're Really Customer-Centric," offers three indicators of customer-centricity [https://cxcc.to/a107]:

1. "You engage and listen to customers about the good, the bad, and the other. You acknowledge those whose needs best match your company's current products or services. Too often, we only hear customers when they validate our worldview, plans, or internal bias. Talking to customers is not the same as listening to customers."

2. "You admit that your products and solutions will not solve every customer problem. There is always one more thing to do, and you will do it for the customer."

3. "You change your internal structure, adjust compensation, or reallocate resources in the face of customer needs."

It's easy to become complacent by finding *some* way your company fits these three indicators. "Remember that time we ran that survey? We engaged customers! We listened to people whose needs match our products. Check this one off! Close this book! We are customer-centric!"

It's also easy to recognize that you're *not* matching these indicators but then have no idea what to do. How can we tell if we are talking or listening to customers? Or neither? What if we're listening but taking the wrong actions? What does it look like to change internal structure due to customer needs?

Augie Ray, Vice President of Customer Experience at Gartner, included this in his article, "Being Customer-Centric (Probably) Doesn't Mean What You Think It Means" [https://cxcc.to/a117]:

Are you and your organization customer-centric? Do you:
* *Prioritize lasting customer satisfaction, loyalty, and advocacy equally with short-term sales and profit?*
* *Approve projects that deliver long-term improvements to customer relationships as quickly and frequently as you do with short-term ROI?*
* *Evaluate and measure investments against how it improves your customers' lives or business as much as your margin, costs, or marketing ROI?*
* *Reward, praise, and promote employees who improve customer outcomes as often as those who deliver company-centric results?*
* *Analyze your customer data to find the verifiable connection between your existing customers' satisfaction or perception, and their lifetime value to your organization?*
* *Measure loyalty as much through leading attitudinal measures of customer intent as through lagging indicators of customer purchase behavior?*
* *Seek to constantly improve your customers' Voice of the Customer feedback and not merely beat your competitors' scores?*
* *Listen for and resolve the barriers your employees face that prevent them from offering customer-centric products, services, and experiences?*

Large and small consulting firms are promoting the ROI of CX. They have webinars, slide decks, and reports on how leaders need to create change and drive strategies and initiatives that better match customers' needs and goals. Forrester, another large international consulting firm, is also pushing Customer Experience. Their site says:

"As a Customer Experience (CX) leader, you rally your organization around customer needs. You dismantle old ways of working and build new ones through the introduction of CX-focused disciplines that drive up efficiencies, competencies, and ultimately deliver business results."

Customer-centricity isn't anti-revenue, anti-business, or against lifts in metrics. It's about finding ways to boost what the business wants to improve *while* putting real customers' needs and opportunities first. It's about creating positive business outcomes *because* we created positive customer outcomes. Customer-centricity is the strategy and actions that flow from our promise to create PSE that inspire customer satisfaction and loyalty.

CX is the table (#CXIsTheTable) and every department sits at the table. Everybody at this table needs customers to survive. Everybody at this table hopes for more and more humans who will pay us, buy from us, license our system, consume our content, interact, and engage. Everybody at this table needs people who will sign up for our platform, read our notifications, and try our suggestions. Everybody at this table might need partners and resellers.

Customer-centricity means that every domain's perspectives are important, empowered, and have autonomy. When we have pressure from managers and stakeholders, it's easy to forget that we work for **potential and current customers**. They are impacted by our decisions: the good, the bad, the hasty, and the uninformed. When customers leave, or a down economy blocks new customers, we lay staff off and terminate jobs. Everyone at our company, including executives and the board, answers to customers.

11 Pillars of Customer-Centricity

I've created **11 Pillars of Customer-Centricity** as a framework of behaviors and values. These pillars guide the decisions and actions of everyone from top executives and leadership to teams and individuals.

1. **Evidence-based decision-making.** Business strategies, goals, and initiatives are based on what we've learned about current and potential customers. Research first and often. Guesses and assumptions are signs that we need more research and knowledge. Decisions should be led by unbiased and current evidence.

2. **Quality and value are defined by customers.** We shouldn't be *hoping* for value or guessing what might be valuable. We should reject methods and approaches that require us to strip value down to the least we can get away with.

3. **Customer-focused, not competitor-focused.** Competitors are often getting it wrong. They're already working on their next thing. Why would we steal their current thing? That's not disruptive or innovative, and could be a mismatch for

our target audiences.

4. **Task-oriented, not feature-oriented.** Task-oriented design will be explained later in great detail.

5. **We are continuously checking for PSE-market fit.** There is no "product greatness" if PSE are not a great match for customers' tasks and unmet needs. If every feature or aspect of PSE doesn't match these, or if a feature or PSE work *against* customers' needs, we should stop and question why we would knowingly build something with poor PSE-market fit. If we are surprised later by poor PSE-market fit, we will need to take a closer look at our ways of working and our approach to risk identification and mitigation.

6. **Teams are given the time and budget to do their best work.**

7. **Ethics, diversity, equity, and inclusion.** We can't be customer-centric if we are not invested in all of our customers. Everything we produce must be accessible to everybody. We aren't customer-centric when we trick customers into actions they didn't mean to take, or work from stereotypes or assumptions about user groups.

8. **Real accountability, including actions and follow-through.** More about this later in the book.

9. **Critical thinking and speaking up are rewarded.** People feel and are empowered to do their best work, challenge the status quo, make evidence-based decisions in their domains, and raise red flags.

10. **Customer experiences and business metrics are both improving, together.**

11. **Quality over speed.** Save time by doing smart and efficient work. Stop burning time and money on cycles of guessing and fixing it later.

Customer-Centricity in ISO Standards

ISO is the International Organization for Standardization. They create and publish standards in areas including food safety, health, environmental management, IT security, and quality. "Customer Focus" is Quality Management Principle #1 of ISO 9000 and 9001. To quote the PDF on Quality Management Principles [https://cxcc.to/a105]:

"The primary focus of quality management is to meet customer requirements and to strive to exceed customer expectations. Sustained success is achieved when an organization attracts and retains the confidence of customers and other interested parties. Every aspect of customer interaction provides an opportunity to create more value for the customer. Understanding current and future needs of customers and other interested parties contributes to sustained success of the

organization."

The document lists the key benefits of "customer focus" as:

- Increased customer value and satisfaction.

- Improved customer loyalty.

- Enhanced repeat business.

- Enhanced reputation of the organization.

- Expanded customer base.

- Increased revenue and market share.

As additional benefits and ROI, I would add:

- Lower costs and more success in attracting and retaining customers.

- Improved morale and higher employee retention rates.

- Increasing your company's value or attracting more investment.

- Time and money saved due to:

    o   Lower utilization of Customer Support channels.

    o   Better and earlier risk identification and mitigation.

    o   Creating a better PSE-market fit earlier than we generally do now .

ISO quality standards list the key actions you can take as follows:

- Recognize direct and indirect customers as those who receive value from the organization.

- Understand customers' current and future needs and expectations.

- Link the organization's objectives to customer needs and expectations.

- Communicate customer needs and expectations throughout the organization.

- Plan, design, develop, produce, deliver, and support goods and services to meet customer needs and expectations.

- Measure and monitor customer satisfaction and take appropriate actions.

- Actively manage relationships with customers to achieve sustained success.

These seem obvious, but there's a good chance that our company is doing few of these well or at all. Bonus question for ISO 9000 or 9001 certified companies: are you adhering to or living by these standards and suggested actions?

ISO standard 9241-210 is about Human-Centered Design, which is defined as:

"An approach to interactive systems development that aims to make systems usable and useful by focusing on the users, their needs and requirements, and by applying human factors/ergonomics, and usability knowledge and techniques. This approach enhances effectiveness and efficiency, improves human well-being, user satisfaction, accessibility, and sustainability; and counteracts possible adverse effects of use on human health, safety and performance."

Usability is defined as *the extent to which specified users can use PSE in a specified context of use to achieve specified goals with effectiveness, efficiency, and satisfaction.* Context is key. Where is the user? Are they doing something else while trying to use our PSE? What type of environment are they in? Who else is there? Are those people a distraction? Collaborators? Does our customer have disabilities, diagnoses, or conditions? Contexts of use are one of many important elements we learn about during generative research, which will be explained in the "Customer Intelligence" chapter.

ISO 9241-210 includes principles outlining what should be done to be "Human-Centered":

- PSE Design is based on an explicit understanding of users, user groups, and their tasks, environments, and their resources.

- Relevant users and user groups are involved throughout Design and development.

- Design is driven and refined by evaluation, and uses relevant users as part of the evaluation method.

- PSE Design addresses the whole User Experience.

- The team involved in HCD includes multidisciplinary skills and perspectives.

Human-Centered Design and User-Centered Design

Human-Centered Design (HCD) and User-Centered Design (UCD) are terms I use interchangeably, though I tend to say UCD more often since I hope it focuses on our users and customers rather than leaving teammates wondering who I mean by "humans." I will not try to rename it "Customer-Centric Design (CCD)." HCD has ISO definitions and standards, so it doesn't need a rebrand from me or anybody else. HCD's ISO definitions and standards work for UCD.

HCD and UCD have customer-centricity in their names. This is Design with a capital D, an entire process, not just the tasks that some people associate with the word "design," such as sketches, wireframes, and visual branding. UCD has multiple phases of work, including research, content strategy and content design, information architecture, interaction design, testing, visual design, and continuous monitoring after PSE release. Each phase has multiple specialized tasks that can be done. CX and UX professionals must approach this process strategically, deciding which tasks are needed, how long they will take, in what order they will be done, and what resources are required.

UCD is fluid and is often cyclical. For example, testing CX designs often leads to iteration: another round of information architecture and interaction design work. We should test again before we can call this completed. In this way, each iteration helps CX professionals spiral their way to the best design solution.

You also hear, "**Learn, build, and test**." This is baked into UCD, which starts with research and learning. Models that start with **build** are missing a lot of early learning we should do if we care about building the right things for our target audiences. It's also why when CX or UX professionals are asked to guess during the **build** phase and "make some screens," often without important qualitative data from research or testing, it's another high-risk adventure likely to lead our project down the wrong path. It's the Lean sin of *underutilized talent* when we only budget enough time for CX to guess at screens when there is so much risk-mitigating science and technique in UCD.

You might also hear, "**Discover, define, design, validate, and iterate**." You might see "Double Diamonds," "Triple Diamonds," and new variations claiming to replace them.

Every customer-centric and Design model or process can be superimposed onto the phases and tasks of UCD.

Some derivatives, like the original Double Diamond, are still close to UCD. Some derivatives, like design thinking, are quite far from UCD. Design thinking will be discussed in a later chapter. Ultimately, you can't go wrong with the original UCD since it's flexible and strategic, adapting to each project based on our staff, budget, timing, and desired customer and business outcomes.

If a Product Manager, Engineer, or executive has an idea, it should still be run through the User-Centered Design process. Everybody is sure they have the perfect solution for our customers, but we don't know which idea is the best match until it's tested with real or archetypal users. This is not done with surveys, A/B testing, or releasing the fastest, minimally viable sliver you can get out there. We Design our solution based on sound research data, and use testing to confirm that we solved the original problem in a way that matches how our target users think and behave.

We can also avoid arguments or decisions based on the loudest opinion when we shift toward standardized processes that shepherd value and check ideas for quality.

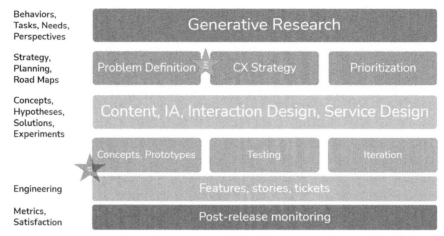

Figure 7: A visualization of UCD based on what phase we're in. As an example, an orange star says, "You are here," near problem definition and CX strategy. A black star says, "Not yet," near concepts, features, and stories. Explained below.

The above simple visualization is a reminder of the best order for our UCD process. When we need to know more about customers' behaviors, tasks, needs, and perspectives, it's time for generative research. Afterward, we move into a phase focused on strategy, planning, and roadmaps. This is where we utilize what we learned from our research to define one or more problems, develop our overarching CX strategy, and prioritize the unmet needs and opportunities we discovered. The upcoming "Common Research Mistakes" chapter will examine where companies tend to go wrong in conducting research, skimping on it, and how it's utilized.

Next in UCD, we move into a phase focused on concepts, hypotheses, solutions, and experiments. CX's key tasks include content strategy, writing, information architecture, interaction design, and service design. CX works on concepts and prototypes, running these through rounds of testing, and iterating and improving based on test results. Once we're sure we have a five-star solution, it can move to Engineering or the next appropriate step if you are a service-based business. Once the PSE have been released, we need to continue our qualitative and quantitative research to monitor metrics, satisfaction, and new pain points or opportunities.

Many teammates would like to start with solutions and ideas, but the above visualization reminds us that designing potential solutions is later in the process. Our "solutions" are guesses if we have not completed generative research, problem definition, CX strategy, and prioritization of problems and opportunities. We cannot hope to solve a non-understood problem experienced by people we haven't learned much or anything about.

We also must have a clear CX strategy for our project or PSE. Very often, when people in a variety of different work roles tell me stories about wild and disaster projects, I ask what the plan or strategy was. 100% of answers have been, "We didn't have one." It's easy to run in all directions when we're unsure where the finish line is or our plan to get there.

Later in the book, we will cover CX strategy.

Value-Led

Will we be a product-led, engineering-led, or sales-led organization? Will we be values-led, as in led by our company values?

We will be value-led: how much value we can frequently create for potential and current customers.

Wouldn't that be a product-led organization? Being product-led is supposed to be about attracting and retaining customers through high-value PSE. Some "product-led" companies decide on features based on guesses, assumptions, or things they want to push people to do. That might be product-led, but it wouldn't qualify as value-led. How to execute on being value-led is throughout the book.

A highly qualified and experienced UX Researcher from my community was recently laid off after his company announced internally that they would be "product-led." Some companies define "product-led" as allowing anybody to do research, no matter their skill level or experience, and no matter the quality of the research or its outcomes. We'll cover this in detail in the "Common Research Mistakes" chapter. But being product-led should inspire us to grow research teams, not lay off our best Researchers.

We might say we are a sales-led organization, but ultimately, we are selling PSE, which must be an excellent PSE-market fit. Sales will struggle with turning trial customers into paid, turning leads into conversions, and retaining and growing existing customers when our PSE are low value and fail to meet target audiences' standards.

Some clients have told me that no matter what they do, their organizations don't understand Customer or User Experiences, and it's hard for them to shepherd change when they use terms like "CX" or "UX." **CX is the best term here**, but if it's causing misunderstanding and blockers, consider calling your customer-centric transformation your "Total Quality Process," "Product-Market Fit Initiatives," or "Value-Led Transformation."

All roads lead back to CX, value, and how we turn a deep understanding of customers' unmet needs into five-star PSE.

End-to-End Customer Journeys

To explain the end-to-end customer journey, let's imagine a chain of hotels. The customer's journey starts with a **trigger**, a reason to need a hotel or book a stay. Triggers include a *why* and sometimes the *what* as well. Potential customers might need to attend a conference or wedding, or perhaps this is a vacation or business trip.

The trigger sends the potential customer into what I call "**orbit**." Potential customers are circling possible vendors or solutions, and narrowing down to the ones that might be selected. After the orbit, they will choose nothing, your competitor, or you. The orbiting stage is your opportunity to attract their business.

It is critical to uncover potential customers' decision-making processes. Though these process steps appear beyond our control or realm, they are often where we find interesting revelations about customers and how we can improve their journeys. For example, if we find that there are collaborators or approvers involved, it might be wise for us to consider features related to facilitating that collaboration or approval.

Let's imagine that today, the orbiting potential customer is in our **ecosystem**. They might be on our website or using our app. They might need to contact Customer Support for help. They might need to reference a wedding invitation, conference website, or work travel policies. They might need to ask their partner to check out possible hotels. They might require a manager's official approval before booking a room. Any of these might pause or end their time in our ecosystem, and send them to the next **action**, even if that action is *waiting*.

When we don't understand the whole end-to-end journey, we sometimes imagine that the potential customer is a "tire-kicker" if they don't book a room. We say they bounced or abandoned. We act like something must have gone wrong because the customer was ready to book a room but didn't. This assumes that the task was *to book a room*. Perhaps today's mission was to find good hotels near an event or get pricing for three hotel options so someone else can decide or help decide. To the user, that task is complete. As we research and map journeys, we must remember that in some cases, the journey includes customer tasks that don't make us money or directly involve us.

The last phase of the end-to-end customer journey includes the **actions** that are part of this task but happen after the user leaves your ecosystem. They might make a final hotel decision or wait for purchase approval. They might search for more rooms and check out competitors.

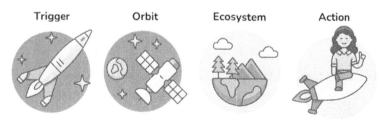

Figure 8: Visualization of the four high-level stages of a customer's task: trigger, orbit, ecosystem, and action.

Booking the hotel room is not the end of the Customer Experience or the only journey we must consider. The customer will eventually arrive at your hotel. They're back in your

ecosystem with a new set of tasks. They will see your hotel, smell it, and meet the front desk and other staff. They'll have to find, assess, and experience their room and its amenities. They might eat at your restaurant or drink at your bar. They might have problems during their stay and need to speak with front desk managers, maintenance, housekeeping, and other people they directly interface with. All of these are tasks or sub-tasks along a larger journey.

Eventually, their stay at your hotel is over. They form opinions of how the checkout process went. They may tell friends or colleagues about their experience. They might leave an online rating or review, write an email to the company, or answer a survey about their stay. They might positively or negatively generalize their experience at one hotel to the entire brand. These are some of the things that can happen after they leave your ecosystem.

Now the end-to-end journey is truly complete. A journey can have multiple tasks and sub-tasks. Customer-centricity will require us to understand all of them and in what order they're likely to happen.

Our ecosystem is omnichannel, omnidevice, and omnitouchpoint. If you lose someone in one channel, you probably lose them in all channels. A customer unhappy with your hotel is unlikely to visit the website or use the app again. A customer frustrated with your website might not book your hotel. Every touchpoint is an opportunity for connection or disconnection.

A common customer journey mapping mistake is looking at the journey only through the business's eyes.

> **"First, I became aware of Company X,"**
> **said no customer ever.**

Potential customers start with a need or task that **triggers** them to research or **orbit** options. Their journey doesn't begin at "awareness" and end at "advocacy." Maps showing the "customer journey" from awareness to advocacy are not *customer journey maps*; they represent an acquisition process or funnel. It might be how we perceive our relationship with the customer, but it's not how they perceive their relationship with us.

Very often, even beautiful customer journey maps primarily focus on the time people are in our **ecosystem**. Maps might start with a Google search or the tiniest sliver of the **orbit** stage. Make sure you map the full end-to-end journey including tasks and sub-tasks from customers' perspectives, as learned through research.

Customer-Centricity Is What Customers Would Choose for Themselves

Customer-centricity requires us to focus on target audiences' needs and the experiences they would choose for themselves. This is easiest to illustrate with an example of a popup interrupting a website visitor's task to ask if they would like to join

our mailing list. Zero customers would have chosen a popup interrupting their task.
Here are some other things zero customers would choose for themselves:

- Anything in the terms and conditions that would allow this company to reveal or sell individual users' data.

- PSE designed to make people feel hooked or addicted.

- Interrupting the normal use of free or paid PSE to try to push users toward an upgrade or higher-priced tier.

- Popups and overlays interrupting user tasks for chatbots or support.

Objectively considering what customers would choose for themselves is one good litmus test for what is customer-centric and what might be customer-peripheric. But to take this perspective, we must have excellent qualitative research and deeply understand our users and their perspectives, needs, and tasks. We must have granular and detailed insights into the existing customer journey and its sub-journeys and steps. This is our customer intelligence.

Try It: What You Would Choose for Yourself

As you experience various PSE from multiple companies, consider which moments or experiences you would not have chosen for yourself, but the company chose for you.

Will Customer-Centricity Lead Us to Create PSE Our Company Shouldn't Create?

Some people claim that customer-centricity is bad and wrong for every company. The argument typically sounds something like, "Customer-centricity will lead us to PSE that won't work for our business model, but we'll build the PSE anyway even if it destroys us because, customer-centricity." I've never heard of customer-centricity destroying a company, and when I ask people who say this for examples, they don't have any. This appears to be a slippery slope argument that's lacking even cherry-picked examples.

It's rare that companies are observing target audiences, asking the right questions, truly listening, and building what people need. It's hard to imagine a situation in which these were executed well but it meant failure for the business. It's easier to imagine the situations in which these were executed poorly, or we *thought* we knew what people wanted, but we were wrong, and the wrong solution brought business failure.

Opening this discussion on LinkedIn led to only one type of example: the PSE-market fit was "excellent," but the pricing was off. There was a demand, there was an unmet need in the market, the company researched this well, built something fantastic, and then overcharged for it, leading to low adoption.

This would still mean that the PSE-market fit wasn't quite right since you didn't have an audience willing to pay what you wanted or needed to charge. Early strategic decisions around PSE can help us avoid Designing, engineering, and releasing something that's not a viable business move.

Customer-centricity doesn't mean that an enterprise SaaS business should start producing cotton candy if they learn users like cotton candy. Better and deeper understanding of our target customers might reveal an opportunity to take PSE in a new direction, consider new target audiences, or consider a merger or acquisition. But these must be approached strategically, ensuring it's the right move for the business and likely to be successful.

Will Empathy Make Us More Customer-Centric?

One of the hottest buzzwords is "empathy." *You need to have more empathy, create empathy, and use a customer journey map to increase empathy.* Empathy originally meant "feeling what others feel," or at least genuinely seeing others' worlds through their eyes without your biases, assumptions, prejudices, or perspectives. Most of the time someone mentions empathy, they mean, "I'm thinking about our customers," or, "I care about our users." That's not empathy; that's possibly sympathy.

We can skip the debate on the meaning of empathy and whether it can be "created" in a business workshop or from a customer journey map. **Empathy isn't enough**. Even the *sympathy* of, "It's a shame that customers are struggling with this," isn't enough. Caring or thinking about customers isn't enough.

We know it's not enough because having customers in our hearts or minds doesn't guarantee that we truly understood them or took the right actions for them. It doesn't guarantee that we were customer-centric or made real users our focal point. And there's only so much sympathy or empathy we can say anybody had if we didn't get the time, budget, or resources to significantly improve our PSE.

As an example, my bank imagined a woman in her 40s has kids, so they sent me "back to school" ads and promotions. When I get ads for PSE for kids, back to school time, and wishes for my "very special Mother's Day," I know the segmentation driving these messages – based on age and gender assumptions – is lazy and not personalized. I'm 50 now and purposefully never had children, so these messages and ads are irrelevant, poorly targeted, and annoying. These companies use what I call "lazy marketing segments" or "lazy buckets." They waste money advertising the wrong things to the wrong person.

Messages about children and Mother's Day could be upsetting or devastating for anybody who wanted children but ended up childless. How could we show that person "back-to-school" ads? It's almost cruel. If we truly understood our customers and had empathy for them, we would never show a message or ad about "your children" to someone who never had children or tragically lost a child.

We're not being honest when we throw the word "empathy" around. Here are reminders of how hollow empathy is at our workplaces:

- If we saw customers' realities through their eyes, perspectives, and beliefs, and felt what customers feel – or at least cared about what they feel – **we wouldn't hand them minimally viable PSE, something we rushed out, or something we already know needs fixes later.**

- When an "empathetic" leader or stakeholder hears that customers have struggles or pain points, do they **immediately allocate teams, budget, and time to make sure that customers never face these problems again**?

- If we believed the articles passed around about how much great leaders need to have empathy, **we would get rid of our toxic leaders**. If your company has "empathy" as a corporate value, but you have not fired toxic staff, then empathy appears to be unimportant for your company and certainly not a value. Bonus negative points to the companies who promote toxic leaders.

- **Do we have empathy for our staff?** Our staff struggle, often work unpaid overtime just to keep from falling behind, and are put under the toxic leader we keep shuffling around the company.

    o To gaslight and guilt trip people who want to work well-defined hours, 2022 brought us the unacceptable term "quiet quitting" to describe someone who isn't going "above and beyond" or working outside of humane hours. Where's the empathy there?

    o I receive at least one message each week from someone asking me how to handle a narcissist or malignant narcissist coworker, manager, stakeholder, or leader. The stories are about people who can never be pleased, have to be right, work to make others look wrong and bad at what they do, steal credit for work, and step on others thinking this is the path upwards. What is your company doing about these people? They and their obvious behavior aren't secrets.

- Especially in America in 2022, more **marginalized communities ask if anybody can *truly* empathize with their lived experiences and realities after a survey or one-hour research session**. These groups are rightfully concerned that we are falling back on stereotypes while calling it "empathy."

    o Are you making "lazy bucket" assumptions that *Black women in their 30s do or need the same things*? Are you *not* a Black woman in her 30s, but you say you have "empathy" for her and see her world through her eyes?

- **Do you know anybody at your company who is racist, sexist, ageist, ableist, or homophobic?** Does anybody believe those people will change with some training or a team workshop? Do they say they have empathy? Do we believe them?

- **Have you ever experienced poor PSE, and said or thought, "This company needs more empathy?"**

Try It: Walk in My Shoes

You've gotten to know me a bit. You read my short bio. You've been hearing my perspectives for 50 pages. Can you walk in my shoes? Can you feel what I feel?

Ultimately, customer-centric **actions** based on deep knowledge of people, contexts, and tasks will be more effective than the too-often meaningless use of the word "empathy."

Having examined empathy, what's an empathy map, and can it help us be more customer-centric? An empathy map typically has four quadrants: *says*, *thinks*, *does*, and *feels*. Some templates combine *says* and *does*, which is interesting since, in observational research studies, we may find people saying and doing opposite things. Some map templates combine *thinks* and *feels*, which might make sense since it's the portion of the map where the most guesses and extrapolations happen. Some templates include extra sections for *sees* and *hears*.

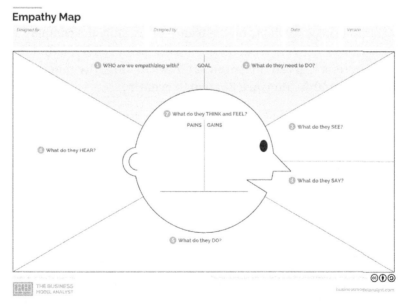

Figure 9: Common empathy map template. This one is from BusinessModelAnalyst.com.

Empathy maps are problematic. First, you are not guaranteed that they were made with any empathy, nor are you guaranteed that they will create any empathy. Second, what are the sources of our data? What did we observe during research studies versus what are guesses, assumptions, or an attempt at role-playing? For example, if we place,

"This is ridiculous! I hate using this," in our quadrant for *thinks*, how do we know our user thought that? If they said that, we should place it in the *says* quadrant. How can anyone know what someone else is thinking? This sounds egotistical, arrogant, and overconfident.

The same is true for *feels*. Empathy maps often indicate the user is "worried" or "excited." How do we know that? If the user said that, I would suggest putting a direct quote in the *says* quadrant. The number of times someone has told me that I looked or sounded worried, angry, upset, hurt, or frustrated when I wasn't feeling any of those reminds me that people are generally bad at guessing what other people feel.

We also can't know for sure what anybody sees or hears. Just because something was communicated or offered doesn't mean that someone noticed it, parsed it correctly, or understood it. You might see an empathy map saying that the user "sees" the discount code on the top of the screen. Yet some studies show that users don't always notice information above a website's logo and main navigation.

If we remove *thinks*, *feels*, *hears*, and *sees* from the empathy map; only *says* and *does* are remaining. An empathy map is an artifact Researchers *could* make, though anything outside of documenting what a user said or did is likely to be presumptive. I prefer to share what users say and do with video clip montages centered around specific themes. For example, *here are six people struggling with our checkout*. Or *here are seven minutes of some positive and negative experiences with our hotel's front desk staff*. Video clips, audio recordings, and direct quotes from potential and current customers are more powerful than an empathy map that might end up filed away and never referenced again.

The goal is to bring everybody on the team – or possibly the company – closer to what real Customer Experiences are from the customers' perspectives, unfiltered and not paraphrased. Therefore, **given the potential flaws in empathy maps and how they are unlikely to be actionable, they are not worth creating.**

Artifacts

Documents that can be created from CX tasks are called "artifacts." It sounds like they were unearthed from another era, but it's a common word you will hear. It's used interchangeably with "documentation."

Will Innovation Make Us More Customer-Centric?

The definition of "innovation" is: *a completely new method, approach, product, or service*. Innovation is neither a small improvement to your current PSE nor a variation of what your competitor is doing; this is more likely an evolution. True innovation is a revolution. This raises critical questions about our attempts to brainstorm innovations:

- **Did we start with good knowledge, research insights, and data?** Or did we start with guesses, assumptions, and pre-decided solutions?

- **Are we calculating the actual cost of innovation workshops and exercises?** Include staff time for hours or days away from their usual work to participate in these sessions, the cost of professional facilitators, and tools or resources we purchased.

- **Have we kept track of which innovations were created during these workshops?** Are we truly innovating in 100% of workshops? 50%? None? Track the percentage of innovation exercises that lead to actual innovations, especially ones that made it to market.

- **What were target customers' reactions to our innovations?** Finding that rare gem of true innovation doesn't mean it was a good match for our customers' needs and tasks. Was the project successful, and how did we measure that success? What was the ROI?

- **Are we pressuring teams to innovate when our PSE aren't getting some of the basics right?** Think about some interactions and experiences that made you uninstall an app or stop doing business with a company. Was it ever because the company wasn't innovative enough? Unlikely. It was probably because it was difficult to accomplish something you thought should be simple, especially a task you would do frequently.

- **How do we monitor impact, success, and failure?** Very often, a release is celebrated, we wipe our brows, and then get to working on something else. We must pay attention to outcomes, consequences, and customer feedback.

The pressure to innovate is self-imposed. Inventing something completely new and patenting it, if possible, is exciting, but if we cannot deliver simple and intuitive solutions for the real problems and pain points that our customers experience, what are we doing?

Many companies are semi-obsessed with "innovation," but nearly zero of these companies have R&D (Research & Development) teams, who are typically responsible for most of a company's innovation. Some organizations disbanded their R&D department thinking they were too slow or unnecessary, or "anybody can research or design." We want to innovate, but we no longer employ those who usually create most of a company's inventions or giant PSE leaps into the future. For those thinking that the MVP and experimentation replace R&D, we'll cover that later in the book.

Many individuals and teams admire – if not idolize – Apple. In 2021, Apple spent nearly $22 billion on R&D, an increase of approximately 17% from 2020's $18.7 billion spend. [https://cxcc.to/a119] Apple spends more on one day of Research & Development than most companies spend in five years. Few companies are on Apple's scale, but we can calculate this as a ratio to revenue. Apple's 2021 revenue was $378.4 billion. Nearly 6% of revenue was spent on R&D. Could your company budget 6% of your revenue for R&D and the Customer Experience?

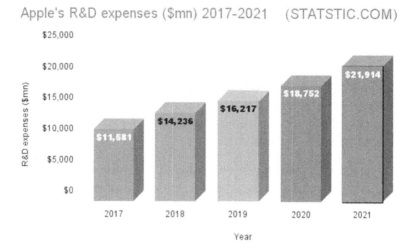

Apple's R&D expenses ($mn) 2017-2021   (STATSTIC.COM)

Figure 10: Bar chart from statistic.com showing Apple increasing R&D spending every year from 2017 to 2021.

If you do not have an R&D department or team, your new CX department will serve that purpose. If you have an R&D department or team, your CX department should partner and collaborate with R&D. A later chapter will examine building or rebuilding your CX department.

People like to quote Apple execs, but then they don't emulate Apple at all. Apple doesn't rush out MVPs. Every time Apple releases something, they tell you it's perfection. *This is all you need. It's the pinnacle of hardware or software. It does precisely what you want.* Such statements don't accompany MVPs and experiments. These are statements made by a company that is confident in its PSE-market fit, having extensively researched and spent time on cycles of Design, iteration, and refinement.

If You Want to Be More Like Apple, Be More Like Apple, But Make Sure It's What Apple Really Does

A Product Manager told me that his project didn't need usability testing; the VP two levels above him said that Apple doesn't do usability testing, so we don't need to either. I shared my screen, opened LinkedIn Jobs, searched for open UX Researcher jobs at Apple, and showed that Apple is looking for the same usability testing skills that the Product Manager's company looks for in UX Researchers. *Yes, Apple does usability testing.*

Will Experimentation Make Us More Customer-Centric?

Experimentation is an area that is surprisingly customer-peripheral at many companies. As we will learn in the upcoming interview with Craig Sullivan, key mistakes center around prioritization, incorrect methods, lack of research, and burning cycles of work on guesses and random ideas.

A culture of experimentation should be a culture of de-risking our PSE through intelligent experimentation. We must also remember that releasing PSE to the public – as a real release or as an experiment – should not be the first time a concept is tested. We have our UCD process to evaluate and improve concepts before a large or small population struggles with them.

You have probably witnessed a variety of bizarre experiments that would not have happened if the company had any accountability. Would the possibility of a performance improvement plan, demotion, or having your budget cut inspire decision makers to choose public-facing experiments more carefully? Without this accountability, teams can fearlessly run in all directions knowing that even if it ends up a complete waste later, there are no consequences. Accountability is key to reducing risk, waste, and customer dissatisfaction.

I have seen two companies in two different industries test removing most of the buttons and options from a page to drive people to the one action they wanted people to take. If you want to lift the metric related to more people moving to the next step of the funnel, removing anything they can do other than moving to that next step can work. But is it a good Customer Experience? Was anybody held accountable for this manipulative experiment? Was there backlash when people couldn't find the other buttons and options they needed or were used to?

Some teams love experiments that test whether a deceptive design will achieve our business goals and KPIs. Spoiler alert: these absolutely can work, but you create added risk, and might end up in unethical territory. *Can we make more people join our email mailing list by automatically putting them on that mailing list without telling them?* Yes, you will grow your email mailing list. But how many people:

- Mark you as spam or report you for abuse?

- Complain that you violate regional privacy laws like GDPR?

- Unsubscribe upon receiving your first email?

- Never open your emails or click on any links?

- Spread negative word of mouth because they didn't like being added to a mailing list?

How many of these unpleasant questions or statistics are in Marketing's presentations? Or do we only report the number of people we added to the mailing list? Customer-centricity requires us to find the balance between Marketing wanting to grow the email mailing list and customers not wanting to be forced or surprise-opted into an email mailing list.

Chapter 5:   Interview: Purposeful Experimentation

Craig Sullivan has been blending Experimentation, UX, Analytics and Customer Research for over 13 years, powering growth for companies like Google, Amazon, Spotify, Eurostar, LEGO, John Lewis, Facebook, and Red Bull. He has helped over 500 clients to unlock the latent value and growth inside their products or services.

Using a mixture of Experimentation, Data, User Research, Lean, Agile, and Cultural Change, he's gained them over £5 billion in incremental revenue. Fixing digital leakage is his specialty, a plumber who fixes the flow of revenue and customer delight.

Find him on Twitter as @OptimiseOrDie or on LinkedIn [https://linkedin.com/in/craigsullivan/].

Debbie: How do you define customer-centricity?

Craig: It's about a deep immersion into customer problems and friction. A lot of companies spend almost all of their effort obsessing over the tiny percentage of customers who actually convert. On most e-commerce sites, it will be rare to see a double-digit conversion rate. Most averages are around 2-5%. Basically, you're saying that if it was a retail store, you're sitting in the back of the store watching crowds of people come in, but 97%, 98%, 99% of them walk out of the store without buying a thing. Wouldn't you want to spend all your time asking *them* questions? Wouldn't you want to intercept them outside and ask what we've done wrong?

We must supplant our internal narratives, thoughts, assumptions, and cherished notions with raw and unvarnished customer feedback. We need to actively seek out negative feedback to worry about it, explore it, venture into it, quantify it, to understand it absolutely, utterly, and completely. When you have the continual feedback loops in place, you can start to understand where the gaps are. *What's the problem for that 97% who don't do what you want?* Then you can go about solving those problems.

Debbie: We often see slide decks that take unwelcome news and present it in the sunniest possible way. "Hey, satisfaction scores are still low, but we converted 0.1% more."

Craig: There's often a vacuum here. The customer doesn't have a seat at the table. They don't have a voice. They're not represented. People are not using customers' contexts, device setups, and innate characteristics to figure out how to design a product for them. There's no connection there. We can talk about data like NPS or various UX metrics, but these are abstractions, not reality. Some abstractions are useful to give us a good summary, but they also hide a lot of the underlying raw data. Different research methods give us different levels of abstraction.

I remember a meeting with 15 senior people from [famous streaming platform]. They had asked me to help them with UX and experimentation stuff. About an hour into the meeting, it began to dawn on me that there was something horribly wrong. I said, "I'd like to go around the table and ask all of you when was the last time that you looked at some customer feedback. When was the last time you watched a customer using a product, listened to a customer, or watched a video of a customer doing something?" They all thought about it and almost all of them said, "Never." *Never in the time that they had been at their job!* I was flabbergasted. I said all their job titles out loud, and I said, "There's no customer. You've not even looked at any customers. You're not connected with them at all. You've put all this insulation and abstraction between you and the customers."

Debbie: Many companies think experimentation is, "Hey, a bunch of people at our company have ideas. Some might be crappy, and some might be good. Let's have Engineering build all of them and release them as live experiments."

Craig: All tests need prioritization and filtering. It's OK for people to have ideas and OK for us to look at all of them. It's just not OK to turn them all into experiments. Not all of them can be run as experiments. What we need to ask is: *what's the best tool in our toolkit to use in this specific context and situation based on what we need to find and figure out?* The answer isn't always to A/B test. The answer isn't always to do user research. You need to match the problem with the right toolkit, which will be different at different times in the product development lifecycle.

Debbie: A client trying to increase conversions made web page changes and measured if people got to the next step. Getting to the next step started to seem more important than the actual conversion. The next time I looked at their page, they had stripped almost everything you could do off the page other than go to the next step. They said, "Now we can show that people are moving through the funnel."

Craig: You can use a lot of these hacky techniques. They've been around since the early days of CRO (Conversion Rate Optimization) and experimentation. You could take a stick to people in Oxford Street and shove them through a shop doorway, but it's not going to make them stay inside the store. Yes, you've shifted the conversion, but you've moved the problem further down the line. It doesn't help at all.

I've seen this before where people will think that if you have too many form fields, that will make conversion drop, so we'll just remove all the fields. The classic example was a booking site for entertainers: musicians, clowns, whatever you wanted at a kid's party. They took away the comments field, thinking *fewer fields to fill in*. But the comments are where the freaking useful stuff is! Like, "I'd like to check that there won't be any swearing during the show because it's a heavy metal band for my nine-year-old metalhead son's birthday."

Free or cheap A/B testing tools have been like giving everyone lightsabers. You're just going to end up with a whole load of people with arms chopped off in hospital. We gave tools to lots of people that don't know how to run controlled experiments properly, so they just try stuff. I've seen it all. Tweaking stuff that's got no basis or hypothesis. A cosmic particle passed through the Marketing Director's brain, a random neuron fired, and we ran an experiment on our live website.

Debbie: "Our research has determined that our target customer needs a little more encouragement. We're testing adding 'good luck' to the page."

Craig: I've seen some stuff like this. Tiny, tiny little tweaks. I remember a dodgy ticketing company that's always in the news for scalping tickets. They had a cart icon with burning flames saying something like, "Our website is under heavy load. You better hurry up and purchase!" I told them it was possibly the most self-harmful thing that I've ever seen. Why would you say that your website is on fire, and why would that encourage people to buy?

Debbie: "We're bad at running servers! Please buy from us!" I remember refreshing a client's product page in a private browser and getting a different variation every time. I took screenshots of what seemed to be an A/B/C/D/E/F/G test, but each variation wasn't a slight change. There were completely different page layouts.

Craig: If you're mixing multiple ideas in the test, there's usually no clear hypothesis or critical thinking behind the experiment. Therefore, the results are going to be questionable.

Often people focus so much on the experiment. But it's the selection of ideas, the prioritization, and the research that goes into the ideas. You're more likely to get cracking ideas for tests and experiments if you're doing good-quality generative user research. That will absolutely stone-cold give you the best tests you can ever run. Diary studies, user testing, customer interviews, and listening to people can yield huge pivots in business strategy. Like, "OMG, we're totally doing this all wrong," or, "These people need an entirely new product that we hadn't even thought of before."

Experimentation is often seen as a way to tune the product. But experimentation should be seen as one of many tools that are available to you to optimize innovation, business value, customer value, societal value, supplier value, partner value, etc. If you don't work out what your experiment is doing to those metrics, you're talking about the short-termism of a lot of experimentation. "Wow, we increased the conversion rate massively, but our returns rate is now triple what it was before." That's a business loss. You caused business harm. If you ran that experiment and didn't collect the impact it had on returns rate or customer satisfaction – or any metrics which would actively go against your big story of success at increasing conversion rate – then you're just running the experiment wrong.

It would be like running a drug trial and saying that we only want to hear from people who feel better. It's like covering one eye and saying, "I can see perfectly well with one eye," but it's not stereoscopic vision. You don't have perspective or parallax. So the data person covers one eye and says, "My data is perfectly good. I don't need to measure what happens on the website because I know we fixed everything." And another person is saying, "I don't really need to know if this solves the problem we were trying to solve. Or whether there's a decent market fit. I'm not interested in that stuff. I'm going to throw sh*t at a wall and see if it sticks." From their perspectives, both of them are perfectly correct.

If I'm creating a postcode lookup system, I can design the interface. I can take that into a lab. I can iterate on it and wash it largely free of defects with several user testing sessions. At the end of that series of iterations, I know I have a good product that almost everyone should have few or no problems using. But I still don't know if it will work at scale because behind that address lookup is a database of 60 million addresses. There are 10 million user searches for addresses per month that access that database. All of my user testing cannot prepare me for what will happen when those inputs are exposed "in the wild" to the underlying database.

Usability tests can't predict what will happen at scale when 200 million people are going to use that address finder over the next two years. But I can measure that, and it's when you blend the techniques – generative qualitative research, quantitative data, and experimentation – that it becomes very powerful. In some people's minds, you only do one of these, but in my world, I get to play with all three.

You could grab an idea, throw it at people, experiment, and randomly iterate your way to a product. I call it "drunken Agile." You go out and get drunk, and then set out for home. You're zigging and zagging on the pavement. If you're spending a lot of time on velocity, you're going to high-speed zig-zag across the pavement, and the distance to walk home has gone from one kilometer to 15 kilometers. You're having a great time! You think you're going really fast, but it's going to take you 15 times as long to walk home because you're not going in the right f*cking direction most of the time.

I've seen so many companies fall into this trap of drunken velocity. I tell them they shouldn't be doing A/B testing right now. They should be doing iterative user research. One startup I worked with persisted in spending vast amounts of time A/B testing rather than getting their product-market fit right. They ran out of cash after seven months.

Many people persist with this idea that randomly trying stuff will get them to a better product-market fit. All these growth hackers can't answer one question, which is, "How did the startup grow if they had too little traffic to run A/B tests?" The answer is that they got the product right and then grew to the size where they *could* run tests.

Debbie: But that advice doesn't create cool books about startups.

Craig: The best startups I've seen spent a lot of time with customer research and knowledge that finds gaps in the product-market fit *before* they build prototypes, experiments, MVPs, or pilots. The companies hoping I can fix their problems are the ones where they never did that stuff up front. It's basically User Experience debt.

We talk about technical debt. UX debt is the same. You're saying, "I'll worry about that stuff later. We're just going to build it now." It's like accepting, "We're going to build a new car model, but we'll worry about the airbags, safety, and crumple zones later." No, they're an intrinsic part of the product. You shouldn't design a whole car without knowing that stuff. But we imagine that we'll iterate the car. When you think about it like that, you realize that would be the wrong way to design a car. Or any product.

Debbie: What about the MVP?

Craig: That's another thing responsible for the idea that we don't need user research or a UX Researcher, and that data will tell us everything.

Debbie: "My idea is so good we should just do it. It doesn't matter what anybody says because this idea is great. I'll pay developers for weeks or months to build it."

Craig: Ego is the biggest problem in product design today. The cherished notion, the assumption, the "I know our customers" or "I've worked in Marketing 20 years," the presumption that a few people can mind read potential future customer behavior.

Let me give you an example: If you're working for Ferrari, you will not catch the Race Director or CEO messing directly with the "product." They're not wandering down to the engine bay, and whilst the guys are working on it, sticking their hands in there, moving things around, and offering advice. They say, "I trust you. You know what you're doing with the car. You're all Engineers. You know how to increase the performance of the car. I need you to get two seconds off the lap time. I'll let you work out how to achieve that."

But this is not what happens with digital stuff. Opinions, cherished notions, ego, and assumptions take the place of user insight, research, or actual customer knowledge. There's a lot of theater going around. Design Thinking Theatre. SAFe Agile Theatre. Experimentation Theatre. If it feels like you're faking it, then you probably are!

Debbie: New topic: we still have a universe filled with popups that mostly want us to join the mailing list. Nobody wants to join your mailing list.

Craig: This contributes to a problem I call "viewport stacking." The Marketing team and others at a company are looking at their website, but not at what it looks like for the customer's first visit. They get a cookie message and have to say *no cookies*. They get a sale banner. There's often some discount code in the header. They get a banner saying, "Please install our app on the app store," and then they get this "join our mailing list" thing slapped on top.

By the time this all loads, it takes ages to get rid of all this crap off the front of the website. I looked at [famous retailer's] website recently, and their cookie message has no border between that and the header. When you read the website, it looks like the cookie message has something to do with their spring promotion.

A website visit might be the first touchpoint with your brand. And the "first viewing experience" is overloaded and sub-par. You have to keep clearing stuff off, and then the live chat pops up, and maybe more floating modals. On mobile, many of these floating controls end up obscuring critical site functions or navigation. Sure, you can chat to support, but you can't use the menu. You can't *add to cart* because there's a giant box floating above "Add to Cart."

Figure 11: Screenshot of Remo.co mobile homepage as an example of viewport stacking. Pinned to the bottom of the browser is a language selector; a bottom navigation with links to the FAQ, live chat, and demo; and a support chat icon. A "Virtual Event Platform" popup then appeared with an auto-playing video. I had 4 layers of stuff over the site I was trying to use.

Debbie: Getting back to experimentation, can you tell us some *good* reasons to test?

Craig: The main one is so that you know if something worked or not and what the magnitude of that impact was. Same as running controlled trials anywhere else: you want a reliable and trustworthy answer, not your colleague's opinion.

Here's one example of a good one. At Autoglass, we wanted to understand the psychology of where people were when they had damaged glass and were looking to get it fixed. We did some contextual diary studies, but we also paid a very good Researcher to do one-to-one interviews with people who had broken glass that needed repair. Those interviews led to a deeper understanding of the customer. We essentially explored the psychology of the consumer as they went through this phase of resolving the problem.

We discovered that this damage is a very distressing thing for the customer. They're completely freaked out and worried. They might be in a car on the side of the road. Maybe they have kids. Maybe they are a woman on their own. Maybe someone needs to drive their parents around and worry about the danger to the car occupants. But people in the company had no idea how distressing this was for customers.

We discovered another thing: when we asked people what the process would be to get their glass fixed, nearly everyone said to us that first, they would call their insurance company. They would then have to wait on the phone for quite a while, an estimated 30–40 minutes. They would then get to talk to someone from the insurance company, give them the policy details, and the Rep would look it up. The Rep would give them an authorization code. They would then call Autoglass, give us that code, and we would process their repair or replacement.

Except that's not what happens at all! We had deals with all the insurance companies to do this stuff directly. The lightbulb moment for this was huge. It led to a whole series of experiments around marketing and advertising. It was that core piece of knowledge that drove it: *people don't realize that they don't need to call their insurance company first.* So, we ran some experiments based on acting on a piece of knowledge that we had earned from good-quality research.

When we thought about the photography on our site, we checked competitors' websites around the world. They had pictures of auto repair shops and manly guys with big sheets of glass. People doing stuff with drills. It was all very technical. Our first thought after doing that user research was that this is not what people want to see. Maybe it should be someone like their mum, ready to make them a cup of tea and chat it through. "Don't worry, Craig. Sit down. I'll help you sort it all out."

I began to experiment with imagery. One of the first things I noticed was that body language made a difference. Defensive body language postures made a big difference. How about natural, open body language? We also discovered that natural smiles made a big difference. We tested stock photography compared to photos we took of our employees and offices, which won hands down every time over stock photos.

I also ran experiments testing female images against male, and I found that the female outperformed the male considerably, even when there was a predominantly male audience on the site. *Hmm, interesting.* The more countries I tested, the more I found that the female images worked better. Eventually, most markets in Western Europe other than Spain had a female image on the homepage. I spoke to my contact in Spain and sent him a picture of a woman who worked in the call center. He said to me, "She's ugly. She's so ugly I would never use this lady in any marketing." I asked what images they had, and they were all shots of oiled-up Rafael Nadal types carrying heavy equipment around the workshop.

I suggested that we put it to a test. My 45-year-old call center lady, who looked like somebody's nice Spanish friendly mum who would sit them down and get them a cup of tea – she wiped the floor with all the hunky Rafael Nadal types by 22%. People generally don't want to have sex with the auto repair guy. They want the windshield repaired and someone to sort it all out and make sure that the paperwork is done so they get back on the road quickly. We understood that emotional connection and especially that the model, their body language, and their eye gaze all made a difference.

Even when we found that the female image worked better, television adverts had a male guy as the lead. *Maybe we should make the new website lady the face of our TV advertising?* So, they made a TV ad with her, which was absolutely awesome. It did incredibly well, especially in conjunction with her image on the website. The best bit of all is that none of us knew what would happen next: we got flooded with applications from women who wanted to become repair technicians.

This all came from one user research study. Sitting down and asking people about their problem – the problem that our whole business, website, service, and every employee working for it was supposed to be solving. That's where some of the best experiments come from.

Debbie: What about product quality?

Craig: It's my biggest ongoing problem over the last 20 years. *What has the worst impact on product quality?* It's a toss-up between two things: not testing with users ever and not making the product work on the devices and the setups that their customers own. I continuously have to point out to companies that either their product is broken, or some function doesn't work on a device. It might be search, navigation, the checkout form, or the "contact us" page. All of these things can be broken.

The first problem is that most companies do not have a proper data-informed list of what they should test. Remember when companies had messages on their websites saying, "This site only works in Netscape Navigator?" You have to support what your customers actually have. Otherwise, you are leaving money or engagement on the table. When I asked one team about their testing list, they said, "Uh, yeah, we test it on Firefox."

I also find that even if companies have a device testing list, which is rare, they don't then buy the hardware to give to the teams. They're spending millions of [British] pounds on building adverts and changing site features. Yet their teams are not given the key lens through which the customer sees their product. *Does it work on a Mac laptop? iPhones? Android? Windows? Chrome and Edge?*

Most companies don't know because they've never tested it. Even if they test it, they don't look at all the different viewports. They'll say that the iPhone in their pocket is a proxy for all the iPhones that everybody in the rest of the world has. But there are a lot of mid-size and small, 4.7-, 5.4-, or 5.5-inch iPhones kicking around. If you only test on the 6.1-inch ones, your site will probably work on 6.1-inch iPhones, but it won't work on any of the other f*cking iPhones.

Many of these companies I'm working with are designing products that cut themselves out of major parts of their market because the products don't work for the devices, screen sizes, and viewports people have. Nobody thinks, "Hey, we spent $350,000 on Facebook ads this month. Has anyone checked to see if our ads render on iPhones, where 80% of our revenue comes from?" No, no one's ever checked, and the ads are broken. Do you know who the winner is? Facebook. Facebook's and Google's business strategy is based on you doing something suboptimal with your marketing efforts. If companies increased their level of efficiency with online ads, Facebook's and Google's profit margins would drop.

In another example, we saw that pageviews for a product list on a mobile site went up massively just on iPhones starting on one single day. I asked in the meeting what happened that day. "Oh, we launched a new site design. It was awesome!" Then I asked them, "What would make the pageviews on your product list page go up nearly three times on that day?" The answer was, "Maybe people liked browsing our new design so much that they just browsed lots and lots of products." I replied, "Nope, nice try, but that's not true. Think about it." They tried various guesses, but they didn't know.

I suggested that we look at what happened on Androids on the same day. It was a flat line that didn't change. Windows? Flat. Mac? Flat. Only iPhones had the pageviews increase massively. I told them, "That was the day 12 months ago when you broke the filter and sort controls for all iPhones." In the middle of the meeting, I told everybody to take out their iPhones and go to their list of 900 products. *Try it out.* None of them could filter. The only way to look at their products on an iPhone would be to go through *every page* of products, 16 products at a time.

We knew demographically that the customers with the most money coming to their site were people with iPhones. I summarized, "So the most valuable customers that you have on your platform have been unable to filter your products for the last 12 months." After they fixed that issue, they didn't tell me the amount of money they'd saved, but the quote I got was, "F*Ck me, Craig, fixing that one bug made us more than the CRO team of 8 people made us in the last two years."

The customer is not the canary in your User Experience coal mine. This is your job. It's not the customer's job to tell you that you've gotten it wrong. It's your job to make sure it hasn't gone wrong like this. Are you sure you want to move fast, break things, or ship product that contains massive defects across large swathes of your customer base?

I had a meal company with a payment page issue costing them several hundred thousand [British] pounds each month. There was a travel site where if you tried to book a journey with two cities, the return leg of the journey would break on about half of the devices. It was costing them about £800,000 a month. There was a ticketing site that was losing £900,000 a month.

My favorite was a jewelry site, where paid search traffic was just bouncing off the site. Hardly anyone was buying. Almost everybody left. Looking at the data, people who landed on a product page pinged off this site like a ping pong ball hitting a giant marble obelisk. *What the heck is going on? Do people not like the product pages? Do they suck?*

We tested it. We went to the site, and I noticed that when I put my finger on the screen to scroll, it zoomed the product image. You couldn't scroll. There was a tiny little region of the header that you could snag to get down to the "Add to Cart" button, but that region was hard to find. It meant that most people could not scroll the page. That was costing them £1.2 million a month. Nobody had checked it. They spent all this money on advertising without even having a look.

That would be my dearest wish from Santa. *Santa, please make people do more testing.* I know it's boring, but it's actually really important.

Debbie: What do you think companies are messing up most often?

Craig: One of the biggest things missing from how Design was done 20 years ago is context. Context is everything. *Is the user wearing contact lenses? Running for a train? In a weird lighting situation where it's part shade, part light? Do they have a slow data connection? Where is the customer? What are they doing? What's the urgency, their motivation? What problem are they trying to solve? What's the temperature or weather?* All of these things make a difference.

The most perfect example of this is airline apps. Almost all of them show you the same thing on the home screen when you open them, regardless of the time or context. *What should the app show me three days before my trip? Two days before? One day before? As I'm approaching the airport? As I'm past security? As I'm boarding the plane?* Imagine one app that maps onto all of these contexts. But airline apps don't dynamically handle context, and that's the problem. You can put the boarding card on the home screen. Great, but I'm not even at the airport yet. We have phones that know where I am, but you're still showing me something I don't need, and you know it.

Debbie: I was traveling 100,000 miles per year before the pandemic. I couldn't believe how many taps it took me to get to the boarding card when I needed it. And when I got to the airport, I wanted to know where the check-in or agent desk was. The app doesn't know that. But the airport knows that we always assign this flight to check-in desk 217.

Craig: Or you have to congregate like 50 meerkats around the airport screen waiting for it to refresh to show the gate number for your check-in. You're thinking, "But this data is in the IT system. The airport is showing it on a giant screen. Why isn't this in the app? And why isn't it telling me when I arrive at the airport? It knows I'm here. We have GPS!"

For two decades, user context in product design has been largely missing. When someone puts in the effort, it's truly magical and incredibly useful.

Chapter 6:   Customer Intelligence

Strategies and decisions are only as good as our customer intelligence, which is only as good as the research that we have done. That research is only as good as:

- **How we planned the research.** Did we collaborate across and within cross-functional teams to ensure that our study will address the unanswered questions, guesses, and assumptions that we and our teammates have? Did we include questions that work *against* research best practices?

- **Which method(s) we chose.** Common customer research methods include observational and field studies, in-depth interviews (one participant at a time), focus groups (many participants at a time), diary studies, card sorts, tree tests, moderated or unmoderated usability testing, surveys, Voice of the Customer data, digging into analytics, and Googling to find other peoples' research.

    o   Did we use the best methods to answer our specific questions versus whatever would be fastest or cheapest?

- **How we recruited.** What types of participants we selected, where we found these people, and how many of them completed the study.

- **How the moderator or interviewer conducted the sessions.** Did they remain neutral? Were they solution-agnostic? Did they use any faces, words, tones of voice, or body language that changed how participants behaved?

- **The quality of our questions.** Did we make mistakes like asking people to predict their future behaviors, limiting people's choices to answers we hope to hear, or asking leading or biased questions?

- **How the data is analyzed and synthesized.** Did we include enough time for thorough research analysis? Did we take the time to watch or listen to our session recordings? Did we find the correct patterns and themes without missing important patterns and themes? Or did we make mistakes, like fitting the data into the themes we hoped to hear?

- **How actionable our research insights and artifacts are.** Do staff and teams know what to do next because of solid evidence and suggestions?

- **How well our research insights answered our original questions?** If we conducted research but are still left wondering *why* – or other questions – we might not have done our research well.

- **How well we separated flukes from important findings.** If only one person said something, is it an insight? Or an edge case? Or something else? Research specialists will know what to do in these situations. "The more people said this, the truer it is," is not the case for CX research. Amazing insights can come from a single person who noticed or experienced something others missed.

- **How well we prevented research from being a self-fulfilling prophecy.** Teams often embark on "research" hoping to validate a concept, prove an idea is good, or support something a stakeholder believes. This "research" is highly biased and nearly always invalid.

The more expertly all of the above are done – and the more we avoid mistakes – the better and clearer our findings and insights will be. With so many tasks and sub-tasks in research, it is easier to get research wrong than to get it right. But it is also easy to have confidence – even falsely – that our research is "good enough" simply because *some research occurred.*

The above list contains some of the differences between "research" and "great CX or UX research." Please do not call poorly planned, executed, or analyzed research "user research," "customer research," or the like. Perhaps it's "market research." If it doesn't meet the standards of being called CX, user, or market research, it might be invalid and shouldn't be a source on which we base strategies or decisions.

In a customer-centric organization, everything comes from research. You might currently base nearly everything on surveys and handfuls of customer calls. We might be complacent because it sounds like good research was done. But I challenge you to question if the research various staff and teams have been conducting is good enough, and how it can be five stars of excellence. Research is not something that we simply check off a list and declare done. If it is not expertly done to high standards of quality, our findings, insights, decisions, and projects could suffer from inaccuracies. Research fuels our customer intelligence and – in some ways – our business intelligence. Knowledge from research feeds our business strategies, goals, and initiatives, guiding our PSE priorities and direction.

We work from what we know.
And when we don't know, we work from what we guess.
This is where risk and waste creep in.

If we have processes that allow or even encourage this risk and waste – especially if we have a culture that does not want people raising red flags or questioning the status quo – then we have a system that continues cycles of risk and waste. A customer-centric transformation should snap us out of this.

Research, knowledge, and data around and from target audiences inform and prioritize at all levels:

- Business strategies and goals.

- KPIs, OKRs, and initiatives.

- Products, services, experiences, innovations, projects, and experiments.

A later chapter on common research mistakes will go more deeply into pitfalls and how to avoid them.

Beware of the Clickbait

The unfortunate likelihood of poor research planning, execution, or analysis has led some people to write articles claiming that *research hurts more than it helps.* You might also see articles discussing *which is more destructive: bad research or no research.* Those aren't our only two choices, despite how it might sound in articles and videos.

As we reach for social media likes, followers, and monetary gain, clickbait is increasingly prevalent. Media titles warn against customer-centricity, research, Design, utilizing specialists or experts, and the importance of PSE strategy.

Many of these articles and videos use an inflammatory headline to get your attention, but then prove the point that is opposite to their headline. One article had a title of, "User Research is a Waste of Time," and a subtitle about how it'll kill your product and company. The body of the article said that research was important and sometimes vital, but you shouldn't give this research work to newbie Designers who aren't educated or experienced in research. The key message in this style of clickbait is often, "Research is good, but bad research hurts more than it helps."

If headlines and sub-headlines don't match the points the author makes, it's clickbait. If we stop at the headline and assume that is the author's point, we might miss the true message in the text or video.

Three Collaboration Points

There are three key phases during CX research studies where Researchers should collaborate with the cross-functional team and stakeholders. It would be even better to involve leaders and executives so that everybody has a direct line of sight into our potential and current customers and their experiences.

1. **Planning.** Before speaking to customers or sending out surveys, research must be properly planned. The planning phase is an excellent time for Researchers to check in with teammates and stakeholders to learn their unanswered questions, guesses and assumptions, information that might be outdated, and anything else the group hopes to learn from the research.

   o This can be a meeting, or you can try something asynchronous like sharing a virtual whiteboard and allowing everybody to post notes with their questions, assumptions, what they think they know, and knowledge requests.

- o This is a cousin of a FOG exercise, where we identify facts, opinions, and guesses. It's a variation of an idea I saw used by Helen Page [https://linkedin.com/in/helen-page-a6a19918/]

- o Researchers decide the best way to work these into the research plan and how to phrase questions to participants.

- o Researchers can also use internal knowledge gaps and desired research outcomes to pick suitable methods and participant profiles.

- o During the planning phase, the Researcher should learn what types of documentation teammates and stakeholders prefer to receive at the end of the study.

2. **Session observation.** The cross-functional team and stakeholders should watch as many research sessions as possible: joining a live video call, watching from the other side of a two-way mirror in a lab setting, or reviewing video or audio recordings. Observers gather first-hand information by directly seeing and hearing participants.

- o Observers joining live can send private messages to the Researcher if there is a topic they would like to see probed further.

- o Live and asynchronous observers should also share their notes with Researchers, who may incorporate these during the research analysis phase.

3. **Insights, actionable suggestions, and artifacts.** The Researcher should debrief with the team about what everyone heard or observed. Since reporting and documentation will include actionable suggestions, the Researcher should discuss with the team their suggested PSE strategies or changes, based on what research revealed.

- o They should also share their final documentation and artifacts with the cross-functional team and stakeholders. These should be stored online and easily accessible to anyone who would like to learn more about the study, its outputs, Researchers' suggestions and advice, and later outcomes related to the study or project.

Generative Qualitative Research

Generative research **generates** knowledge and data about people, contexts, and how they interact with systems and other people. We use it to learn more about users, their tasks, behaviors, perceptions, mental models, preferences, decision-making, and habits. We might observe how they perform a task, but the goal of generative research is not to assess the usability of the PSE; it is to learn more about our target audiences and their behaviors. Evaluative research, which will be explained later in this chapter, encompasses the methods used to **evaluate** our PSE.

Generative research might be conducted as part of a project, or it can be unrelated to any particular project or area of our PSE. For example, research into customers' attitudes around pricing is an interesting generative study that is probably unrelated to a single project, and would end up touching multiple parts of our PSE. Some people might refer to generative research as "exploratory" or "discovery." Those terms are acceptable, but it's all still generative research.

There is more later about how long generative research can take, but it varies. It's an average of 1-3 months, and rarely shorter than one month, though I have seen it run longer than 3 months. My company spent four months on a study for Etsy in 2020 that included observational sessions with 71 participants. Projects that require weeks or months *can* be Agile if we plan for the time good research requires.

Common types of generative studies include:

- **Observational.** We watch someone do something live: online and remotely with a shared screen, in person in the environment where people usually perform this task, or in a lab setting.

- **In-Depth Interviews (IDIs).** These are conversations with one individual participant at a time.

- **Diary Studies.** A diary study asks a participant to track an experience over time as they attempt or accomplish the task steps. They are asked to journal their experience as it happens or at pre-decided times.

    o Imagine you want to learn more about how people shop for a used car. We could interview them, but they might not remember every step they take in order and what could be improved at each step. A diary study might require car shoppers to report whenever they search for cars online, visit the dealership, discuss cars with friends, or perform any step of a car shopping task.

    o While there can be flaws with self-reporting, a diary study can be a more complete picture than we would get from an interview, and more feasible than trying to have a Researcher observe all of these steps and conversations.

Correct Number of Research Participants

For quantitative studies, there are ways to calculate how many participants you need for statistical significance. While some of these calculations are complex, Survey Monkey offers a simple online calculator. [https://cxcc.to/a138] You need to know your population size (how many people fit into the target audience), what confidence level you want (99% would be best, but many studies use 95%), and what is your margin of error (often 5% but you can go lower). Confidence level represents the probability that your participants represent your intended audience.

Assuming a target population of 20,000 people, how many completed survey responses would you need for statistical significance?

- At 95% confidence and a 5% margin of error, 377 completed responses.

- At 99% confidence and a 5% margin of error, 645 completed responses.

- And if you want to be really accurate, at 99% confidence and a 2% margin of error, 9,084 completed responses.

Notice that the more accurate you want to be, the more of your population you need to survey. The less accurate you don't mind being, the more you allow fewer people to speak for everybody. This is also why recruiting is so important; when fewer people speak for the population, we want to ensure they are the population's best representatives. If you allow the survey to be completed by the first 400 people who click on the link, how are we sure that we have the right demographics, roles, or audience? If we have 20,000 people or more using a feature on our site, and we collect 77 survey responses, this ranges from non-scientific to potentially invalid.

What about participants for qualitative research? I've often heard staff and leaders at all levels deciding – before qualitative research was done – that it can't possibly be of any value because we're only talking to "a few people." I have also noticed that **when Product Managers, Engineers, Business Analysts, Marketers, and other non-CX staff want to speak to "a few people," this is deemed valid and worth our time.** We should call this double standard what it is when we see it.

Qualitative research such as observational studies, in-depth interviews, and usability testing requires fewer participants than surveys and other quantitative research. The best practice for generative research is to have 8 to 12 participants per persona or target segment, plus a group of people with various disabilities, conditions, and diagnoses. For example, if you have four target segments, your research should include 32 to 48 people, plus your group with accessibility needs.

For evaluative research, the best practice is to have at least five participants per persona or target segment, plus your group with accessibility needs. You would select new participants in each additional research or testing round. You would not do three rounds of evaluative research with the same five people unless you are stuck and cannot find any appropriate subjects outside of those five (uncommon but possible).

It is also a requirement that these participants be correctly recruited to ensure that they fit in the persona or segment they represent. This is one reason why CX Researchers rarely grab whoever they can find in a coffee shop. If your local coffee drinkers do not match our target audience, they are the wrong people to include in research, even "quick" research. And speaking to only "a few customers" wouldn't match qualitative CX research standards for the number of participants and what groups they fall into.

Additionally, in both generative and evaluative research, it's often better to include non-customers. They have fresh perspectives, and don't yet have workarounds, biases, or PSE familiarity.

We should ensure that our qualitative and quantitative Researchers are given time, budget, resources, and access to customers and non-customers who fit desired study participant profiles.

Task Analysis and Optimized Task Flow

Task analysis is done after qualitative research, such as observing and interviewing users. You can't do a great task analysis based on surveys or what we guess about people. Even diary studies can leave out steps or workarounds that the user thinks aren't important to mention. If we had observed these people, we would have noticed these missing puzzle pieces.

Task analysis starts with a Researcher creating a flow diagram detailing every step they observed participants taking. This is the *what*: what does our target group do, step by step? The Researcher then adds notes to each step indicating the **tools**, **knowledge**, and **workarounds** users employed to accomplish or improve that step. This is the *how* of each step. For example, the user checked the sticky note they keep at their desk (workaround and tool), they went into photo editing software first (tool), or they asked a coworker where to find a form (workaround and lack of knowledge).

Knowledge gaps, the difference between what we assume people know or understand and what they *actually* know or understand, are most easily found during observational research. We see people using workarounds, getting stuck, or giving up. As an example, my company observed participants shopping for custom printed items. Some websites asked for a PMS color, which is a number unique to the Pantone system. One woman typed "navy blue" into the Pantone field. She understood the word "color," but didn't understand that the system was looking for a numeric value. This has the potential to lead to dissatisfaction. Her knowledge gap might delay her order if Customer Support contacts her to clarify the exact color. Her knowledge gap might lead the vendor to guess which shade of navy blue she wants, and risk customer dissatisfaction with the printing color.

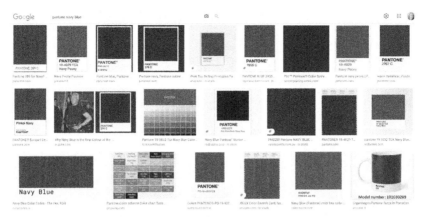

Figure 12: Google search results for "Pantone navy blue." There are many different Pantone numbers here. Who knows which shade the participant wanted, especially if she is trying to exactly match her company's brand colors?

Next to each step of the task, Researchers add sticky notes representing **issues** and **concerns**, anything that might be an **obstacle** to this step. These are not issues that our company has internally. For example, in a study with small online sellers, my company found that some people trying to upload photos of their items thought they could drag and drop the photos. The company had never built a drag-and-drop feature, so this produced confusing and disappointing results. This confusion is an example of an issue or concern that might make this task step inefficient or a negative experience. Additionally, knowing that you *can't* drag-and-drop was **knowledge** that not all participants had.

These stories are excellent reminders of things we would not have learned from a survey. Even participants documenting their process for a diary study might have said something like, "Then I upload my pictures." Without seeing how they do that, attempt to do that, or struggle doing that, we lack the true detail of their workflow and experience.

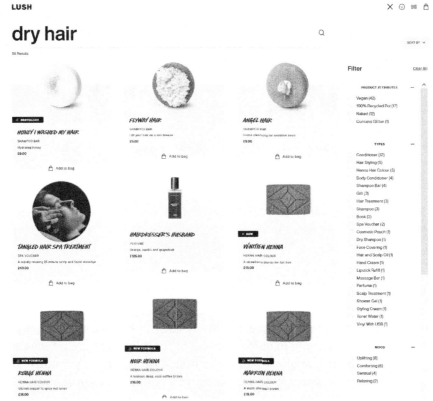

Figure 13: Screenshot from the Lush.com website. If I want to solve my dry hair, which products are best for me? A search for "dry hair" produces everything Lush offers for hair. Results included shampoos, a spa treatment voucher, perfume, hair coloring products, and apparently every shampoo, conditioner, and hair styling product Lush offers. Which is best for dry hair? I will have no idea unless I visit each product and read more. Task analysis and designing for knowledge gaps would consider why people search and why some customers want more from Lush than just moods and scents.

Documenting the **tools**, **knowledge**, **workarounds**, **issues**, **concerns**, and **obstacles** gives us six new categories where we can find behaviors, themes, preferences, unmet needs, insights, and opportunities. We want to improve the process steps, but we can also improve each step's parameters, details, blockers, and dependencies.

Once the *current state* task analysis document is complete, Researchers create an "optimized task flow" document by looking at where the system can take workload off the user. This allows our Researchers to be strategic partners, examining current Customer Experiences and considering how those can be streamlined, improved, and made easier.

Creating the optimized task flow isn't just reducing user steps through automation or making the system perform task steps. It is also intelligently and deliberately architecting our systems to account for what we expect people to reasonably know or remember. Build knowledge *into* the system. Deliberately architect and design for moments where people use outside tools or workarounds, and where they run into obstacles. This is called "knowledge design," and is an essential technique for CX Architects and Designers to learn and utilize.

Returning to the project where people shopped for custom printed items, our observational research asked people to start from any website. We gave them a hypothetical budget of $1,000 and said they needed 125 customized water bottles for an event. Many people grabbed a real or smartphone calculator, and divided $1,000 by 125. They determined they could spend $8 per item, but were surprised when they were over budget at the end of the task. Only one participant did the math and then realized she didn't actually have $8 per item. She estimated that she had only $6 per item because this type of e-commerce website tends to add setup fees, shipping, and tax later. She was right! Not only did we observe the calculator used as a **tool**, but we also learned that only one participant had the **knowledge** necessary to anticipate costs and stay within budget.

For the interaction design phase of the project, we added an "enter your budget" area to the product page. The system would then deduct taxes, shipping, and setup fees, and tell you how many of this item you could afford. As you changed color, shipping speed, and other parameters, the number of items you could get for that budget changed. Not only did this solve multiple problems and fix the **tool** and **knowledge** dependencies, but we invented something no competitor was doing. We saw 20 competitors during our research, and nobody had a way to enter your budget and see how many you could get. *This is innovation.* You can start to see how task analysis goes far beyond what we tend to know now from our surveys or A/B tests.

Task analysis artifacts can look simple or complex, but ultimately, they are an excellent way to map research insights and set later steps of the project up for success. Visualizing complexities, inefficiencies, and blockers helps us strategically optimize the workflow to remove friction.

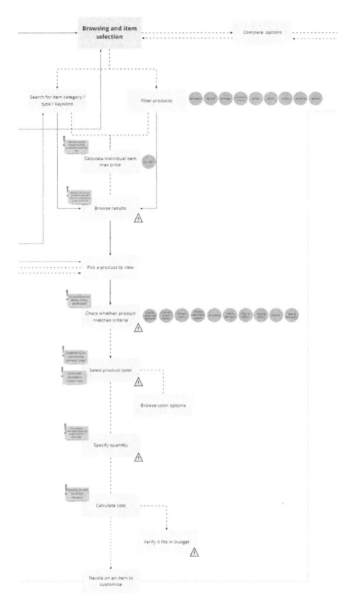

Figure 14: Screenshot of part of our large, complicated task analysis for the custom printed items project. It looks like a flow chart. Green sticky notes show the steps of the task as users search, browse, and compare items. Orange notes are obstacles and issues faced at certain steps. Purple notes are tools, knowledge, and workarounds. For example, common filters people used to narrow down items required the knowledge of what might get them closer to the best items for their needs. Yellow emergency triangle icons indicate steps where the user might give up or end the task, possibly prematurely.

Task Dimensions™

Task Dimensions is my working title for a model presented by Larry Marine [https://linkedin.com/in/larrymarine/]. These will appear in our task analysis document as parameters related to task steps. Even if you don't work in CX or UX, anybody can use these terms (and The Four Horsemen of Bad CX from an earlier chapter) when they notice customer-periphery in PSE or difficulty in user task steps.

- **Manually intensive.** Does a task or flow have many steps or a lot of manual work?

- **High cognitive load.** *"Don't make me think!"* as Steve Krug popularized. People don't want to have to figure things out or make sense of your mess. Did this task step require a lot of thinking or mental processing?

- **Error-prone.** Did we observe users – even confident users – making mistakes? It's not enough to give people an error message and hope they solve their problem. It's not enough to give people a tooltip, hope they read it, and hope they get things right. Great CX design keeps people from ever making that mistake in the first place.

- **Knowledge dependent.** Is there something we assumed a user knew, understood, or remembered that they didn't?

  o Have you ever gone online to pay a bill requiring your account number? You probably didn't have it memorized and might not have had it handy. Now you must stop what you're doing, find an old bill, and find that account number. The account number is a knowledge dependency.

  o Knowledge design techniques consider the information people are likely to have, know, or remember. Perhaps you could match their account by their phone number or email address, which they will likely know.

Task Dimensions and The Four Horsemen of Bad CX are examples of the **friction** we try to remove for our target and current customers. Their journeys are full of obstacles and frustrations that make their tasks inefficient and more difficult. Customer-centricity means creating friction-free PSE.

A Friction-Filled Adventure with Apple

I was trying to publish this book to Apple Books. I don't use Apple devices, and I wasn't sure if I had an Apple account. The Apple site told me that to create an account, I needed to download iTunes. This seemed unnecessary, but it gave me no other choice. After trying to create an account in iTunes, I learned I already had an account for my email address. Did I really need to download iTunes to learn that?

iTunes sent me to Apple's "I Forgot" site, and I reset my password. It then asked me to sign in. I got my password right, but my security questions wrong. Despite feeling confident, I did not know my own dream job or the first name of my high school best friend. When I went through the "I Forgot" process again, this time to reset my security questions, I landed at a dead end.

Figure 15: Screenshot of Apple page with an error message but no action I can take next.

The web page told me that Apple doesn't have "sufficient information" to reset my security questions. There was nothing I could do next: no link, no button, no "contact us." Finding similar stories in Apple forums, it looked like I needed to call Support to resolve this.

The Support Rep was completely unfamiliar with my situation, as if nobody had ever called Apple unable to reset their security questions. I was put on hold multiple times so they could ask their Supervisor what to do. Finally, they just transferred me to their Supervisor.

The Supervisor explained that Apple's new login was "completely automated," so automated that no human can intervene. Support can't help me reset a password or security questions. They can only tell me to go to the "I Forgot" website and follow instructions.

The Supervisor explained that the automated system sees someone who resets their password and their security questions back-to-back as fraudulent. The system doesn't consider when my last login was, or that forgetting my login details in that amount of time might be normal. Additionally, the error message on the above page doesn't match reality or the knowledge the system has; I can't reset my security questions because I look fraudulent, not because Apple lacks information.

The Supervisor suggested that I wait 24 hours for the fraud flag to fall off my account.

But she warned that there was a good chance I would not be able to reset my security questions. She said I might not be able to get back into this account, Support can't help, and I might need to start a new account. This sucks for me, but I can't imagine someone losing all of their photos, documents, or music because they can't access their Apple account, and no Support Rep can help.

If this book isn't for sale on Apple Books, you know that friction won, and I gave up. If this is what it's like to log into an account, I don't look forward to what the process must be like to enter a book's metadata, pricing, and images. What if I get locked out of my account again? I don't trust that Apple Support will be able to help me.

Why bother with something that is manually intensive; high cognitive load; error-prone; full of frustration, confusion, disappointment, and distraction; and makes me feel like I'll never have the knowledge I need to get this done well?

For video lessons on task analysis and knowledge design, see the Delta CX YouTube channel "Micro Lessons" playlist for videos featuring Larry Marine. [https://cxcc.to/a176]

What about Jobs To Be Done (JTBD)? Everything that it promises – customer-centricity, aligning teams on strategy and direction, remarkable customer outcomes, and more – can also be accomplished through task analysis. Both rely on the quality of your qualitative research; each produces different artifacts. Some authors and trainers suggest that research is optional for JTBD, which companies might love to hear, but this is bad advice. Research and customer intelligence are often a company's most significant weakness, a problem which is not solved by avoiding or minimizing good research.

I find that task analysis provides more actionable details that reveal insights and opportunities. You can try both artifact styles (JTBD or task analysis) to see which is more meaningful, actionable, and helpful at all levels of your organization.

Defining the Problem(s)

The problems we plan to solve not only drive PSE initiatives but should also shape a larger CX strategy. *Doesn't problem definition start from strategic initiatives?* It can, but if we have customer-peripheric strategies, beware the path you're headed down. Circle back and check your business strategies: were they guided by recent evidence and detailed customer problems? Strategies might need rethinking or iteration based on fresh information.

As an example, consider the COVID-19 pandemic. Companies had strategies and initiatives in place when the whole world changed. Some companies cut back and laid people off, but didn't conduct new research on target audiences and their changing needs and perspectives. Fresh evidence and data would have revealed new and changing customer problems, which *should* have helped companies redefine strategies, goals, and initiatives.

Missed Opportunity: Car Shopping During the Pandemic

A few months into the 2020 pandemic, a famous American luxury car brand requested a proposal from me and some other Researchers. The car brand wanted to understand how their target customers' car shopping needs were changing during the pandemic.

We planned a thorough research study to answer open questions quickly, and track some participants for months to watch how attitudes and behaviors changed over time. Our proposal was around $140,000. Our research would have to help them sell 20 more cars to break even. The brand responded that they loved the proposal, and it was exactly what they wanted, but what could we do for $40,000? We declined the project.

Understanding your target audiences and their problems is vital in prosperous times, but it is even more essential during economic downturns and regional catastrophes.

To get everybody on the same page about customers and their needs, we can create problem statements. These are not user stories, use cases, or descriptions of solutions or features; they are solution-agnostic. Problem statements should address who, what, where, when, why, and how. They do not include every detail we have about the situation, but are designed to be brief summary statements.

Continuing from the story at the beginning of the book, let's pretend that we conducted proper qualitative research on customers' experiences with Priority Pass. Let's imagine that we now have detailed knowledge around customer struggles when the credit card associated with their Priority Pass account expires. Our problem statement could be:

- When a customer's credit card expires, Priority Pass closes their account. We create a new account for the new credit card, but the account isn't active until the customer gets a code from Support staff. Our system does not automatically update credit card information, nor do we offer a way for the user to update their credit card information. This creates frustration for customers and taxes our Customer Support teams, who currently walk people through setting up the half-created Priority Pass account.

Another problem statement example (for an unrelated issue) is:

- We require potential customers to verify a home address with us. We only accept utility bills, bank statements, and driver's licenses as proof of this address. Many people are not named on utility bills, have no driver's license, live in campers or boats, or are digital nomads. Some people have a post office box or old address on their bank statements, or no current bank account. Customer Support tries to help these people, but is blocked by our policies. We tend to lose these customers as we cannot verify them.

Problem statements can be used in our prioritization efforts: *what is the most important customer problem that we should solve first?* Problem statements can also be used as an internal check for our proposed solution. If our concept does not solve the problem statement, we might be solving the wrong problem, or our work is not yet done.

Don't offer a problem statement in a vacuum. Make sure the cross-functional team has insights and artifacts from research such as maps, journeys, video clips, and user definitions or personas. You can also include evidence-based use cases, each marked as "required" or "nice to have."

Share All Information

There is an immediate power imbalance when only one person or domain has the information the cross-functional team needs. For example, at companies where CX Designers are treated as order takers, they often get drips of information on an as-needed basis. Designers might be told to design something that does X and Y. Designs satisfying X and Y are rejected with, "What about Z?"

Nobody ever said Z before today. Why not? Is it a priority or a "nice to have?" Is Z evidence-based, or is it a stakeholder request? What is the source of this use case, and is it valid? Perhaps Z is an assumption but not necessarily a customer reality.

Rejecting designs for missing an unstated use case looks like a power play. Give all teammates all information as that information is known.

Customer Journey Maps (CJMs)

Many companies interested in CX are looking for training, templates, and how-tos. They often find customer journey map training that says, "Here is a template, drop in what we think people do based on our existing knowledge and some surveys, and you're done." This common approach leads to mistakes including:

- **We have a CJM, but is it a *good* CJM?** We might have made mistakes including only mapping a portion of the journey, only mapping high-level moments, leaving out actionable detail, or mapping it from our internal "awareness to advocacy" or "define to conclude" perspective.

- **What is the source information?** Guessing at customers' experiences and perspectives introduces risk. As a best practice, a CJM is an artifact of qualitative research; we understand the journey because we observed as much of it as possible, asked clarifying questions, and replaced assumptions with knowledge.

- **Did we map the current and desired future states?** Many companies create a CJM and then believe that their work is done. Once you map your customers' current tasks, strategic customer-centricity specialists must map the desired future state.

- The current state map is how customers do this now. We work to simplify and improve how the tasks might flow, and then map that as a "future state" journey that better solves customers' problems.

- **Is it actionable?** A great current state CJM and its cousin, the future state CJM, help us shape business and PSE strategy and direction. If a team makes a CJM that ends up in a literal or digital drawer, never to be seen again, then the document has little value.

  - To act on a customer journey map, we must first make sure that our research and data revealed the root causes. If we don't know *why* something is happening or not happening, we are unlikely to correctly and efficiently invent the solution.

Guessing current or future state journey maps can lead us in the wrong direction. Consider this example I found in an online article about how a customer journey map can help your business. [https://cxcc.to/a162]

---

*"For example, imagine that you are designing a new experience of going through the TSA checkpoint at the airport. Your moments along the top of this user journey map might be: **Pack for Trip — Travel to Airport — Arrive at Airport — Find Security Line — Show ID to TSA — Go through Security — Find Gate — Arrive at Destination.***

Once you have your top-level journey moments or touchpoints, use your personas to go step-by-step and capture what your user is feeling, thinking, and doing at every phase. Through this process, you can begin to map the breadth of problems your user faces to identify the most prominent issues to tackle through design or innovation."

The mistakes being made include:

- **What is the source of this information?** The best CJMs are made from observational research. The second-best CJMs will come from interviews or a diary study, where people track and report their task steps and experiences over time.

  - The article quoted above simply says that you will detail the steps of the journey by "identifying the moments that a user goes through." Articles like this are typically unclear about how you should or should not identify moments or steps.

  - If the article suggested or demanded excellent qualitative research planning, execution, and analysis, companies who don't want to invest in research might avoid customer journey mapping.

- Keeping the research requirements vague gives companies permission to reduce or skip qualitative research. Articles often fail to mention how CX outcomes vary when CJMs and other artifacts are based on outdated, poor, or no research.

**Without good qualitative research analyzed correctly,
your CJM will successfully document guesses and assumptions,
and should therefore be seen as a risk, not as a source of truth.**

- **Mapping only the top-level moments might miss important task steps.** There is much more to "going through the TSA checkpoint" than finding the security queue, showing your ID, and going through security.

    - Passing through a metal detector or scanner has multiple steps including removing certain items from baggage and pockets, placing items in bins in very specific ways, removing jackets and shoes, and advising security staff of pacemakers and medical equipment.

- Starting the CJM with "packing bags" seems correct, but leaves out something important: ***knowledge*** *of the most current security policies*, which might change how you pack your bags.

    - We have seen people at the airport who didn't know they had to remove their shoes, have fewer than 100 milliliters of liquids, or couldn't bring that switchblade on the plane.

    - What do target audiences know or not know about security policies? Do they know good packing tips for getting through security quickly? Have they changed packing habits, or do they prefer to rearrange everything at the security checkpoint?

- The above quote is incorrect; **personas will not tell us what people think, feel, or do at each step of the journey.**

    - Personas are documents that explain our target audiences' unmet needs, goals, knowledge, and likely behaviors. They are target customer archetypes. Poor personas focus more on demographics and preferred brands, and leave out tasks and behaviors.

    - People commonly look at a persona and *imagine* what they think, feel, or do. At best, this "role-playing" adds bias and risk. At worst, this adds false and made-up information to our customer intelligence.

- **Does your CJM show branches or paths where groups of customers have variations of a particular step?** As a flow chart style of document, task analysis diagrams these variations well. But CJMs typically show a single path as if this is what everybody experiences.

  - The journey will vary if the taxi is a no-show, if your suitcase is overweight and costs extra, if your carry-on is deemed too large to be a carry-on, if they caught you with extra bags when the carry-on limit is one, if security goes through your stuff, if your flight changes gates, or if your flight is delayed or canceled.

  - Add additional steps if:

    - Flying internationally, which requires passport and visa checks at the departure and arrival points.

    - Nobody in the airport speaks your language or if you have a disability.

    - Traveling with a pet, child, or loved one who might need your care and attention.

- **Does the customer journey map show where customers experienced frustration, confusion, disappointment, or inefficiencies?** Does it show where they made mistakes or had trouble understanding what to do?

  - A customer journey map imagining most or all steps going well is flawed and unrealistic. Our CJM should not be the "happy path," where everything ends well for the customer.

  - Many CJMs tend to show customers starting out happy, bumping into some problems, and then finding what they need. This is oversimplified and often unrealistic.

- **The above quote makes it sound like once you create your current state customer journey map, you will absolutely know what you need to design or innovate to create better Customer Experiences.**

  - If we have not correctly defined the problems, we will not correctly define the solution.

  - Did you map the desired future state, which is what it might look like for this task to go well, if not perfectly, for the user? What if this task were fast, easy, hard to get wrong, never confusing, and didn't waste time or effort?

  - The next step is not "brainstorm the solutions." As we'll cover in a later chapter, the next step would be writing problem statements and then prioritizing the issues we want to tackle first.

Customer journey maps are just one tool or document that can put us on the road toward PSE improvements, solutions, and innovations. Flawed or guessed customer journey maps can put us on the road to risk, waste, and customer dissatisfaction. Yes, you can create a customer-peripheric customer journey map; surprisingly many are.

When people hear warnings about poorly made customer journey maps, they naturally ask for a *better template*. The CJM template, layout, or design is not what makes or breaks the document. Lovely templates are a Google search away, but they won't fix *garbage in*.

Quick Fix Versus Slow Fix: Customer Journey Maps

If a better template or toolkit doesn't yield a better customer journey map, what can we do to improve our journey mapping approach and documentation?

If a better customer journey map is made from better research, the **quick fix** is utilizing existing qualified Researchers, or hiring well-qualified Researchers as full-time employees, freelancers, or from an outside consultancy. Professional Researchers spend years learning, practicing, and improving so that they can do the work correctly and efficiently.

The **slowest fix** is to spend time training people with little or no background in observational research to do the work. We must also consider the risks of poor quality and setting a project up for possible failure when foundational research work is done by people who are not skilled at the various phases and tasks of research.

Go with the **quick fix**. Reduce risk. Bring in qualified people who will get this right the first time, and avoid going down the wrong paths. If your company currently bases or intends to base extensive strategic and tactical work on customer journey maps, it is mission critical to have them done well.

Service Design and Service Blueprinting

Imagine a very well-made customer journey map and task analysis flow chart. Bring these together and add elements of where that customer interacts with our company, both the elements they see and experience as well as behind-the-scenes people, processes, props, and technology they don't directly see. Mapping typically excludes our involvement in the customer journey.

Where did our people, tools, tech, and tangible elements interact with potential and current customers? Service blueprints include these as well as how long each step (or waiting period) typically takes. For example, many people don't buy a car on their first visit to a car dealer. There is the time they take to visit various dealers, the time they take to shop or compare online, and the time they will take to decide which car to buy. There is time between these moments where nothing car-related happens. Understanding time reveals the realities of the journey and where steps are inefficient or longer than they should take.

This is where Service Designers shine. Service blueprints map and detail where our company's people, processes, and props exist, and go well or poorly. For example, an Italian mobile phone company has vending machines in various shopping centers. If you have your government ID and a debit or credit card, you can use the machine to get a SIM card, phone number, and open an account with this carrier. A customer journey map might show that a customer chooses this carrier, finds their closest vending machine, and gets a SIM card. A better CJM from a Researcher who watched someone getting that SIM card would include important observed details, such as the times the customer needed to remove the current SIM card from their phone to read a number printed on the SIM card, and the carrier's worker using her earring as a SIM-ejection tool.

A service blueprint goes beyond the CJM to include process moments, both seen and unseen by the customer, such as someone having to:

- Fill the vending machine with new SIM cards.

- Figure out how a vending machine would validate someone's identity.

- Ensure that the machine flawlessly reads the most common forms of government IDs.

- Tie the machine's process to the next steps: cancel the customer's current mobile account, port their number, and transfer existing pre-paid credit to the new carrier.

Service design requires skills in CX research plus business design, systems thinking, and coaching, which is used to help align people and teams as well as to help them adjust to change. Service Designers must be great workshop facilitators since there are steps in the service design process where we need to meet with multiple people to check that we have mapped internal people, processes, and systems correctly. A Service Designer must also be a highly strategic problem solver to take the current state experience and map out an improved, streamlined future state service blueprint.

Service Designers research people, contexts, and systems, but often must go beyond that. They might investigate relevant societal or regional elements. They address internal strategic and financial consequences. Service Designers should be empowered to pursue and investigate all paths and players. We'll learn more about Service Design in an upcoming interview.

Evaluative Qualitative Research

Evaluative research **evaluates** a concept or design that we already have. This might be a work-in-progress or something that is live and publicly-available. It might be our PSE or a competitor's.

Evaluative research mitigates risk by keeping the wrong PSE from going out to the public. Through cycles of early testing with our target audiences, we can check for excellent usability and PSE-market fit. Evaluative research tells us if our concept or design solves real problems, is a match to users and their contexts, and if there is still room for improvement. Did we solve the original problem well or do we need to spend more time on this solution before releasing it?

Usability testing is the QA of CX and UX. We wouldn't skimp on or exclude QA testing for our code; why rush out untested product concepts? Usability testing helps us validate, invalidate, and improve concepts. Research and testing help us know what users find high-quality and valuable.

For digital PSE, Engineering shouldn't start coding the design until one or more rounds of evaluative research tell us that the concept and design are five-stars-out-of-five and ready to go. Every time Agile says that *we want feedback from users, we want to learn if the product is going in the right direction, or we want to know if users find value in the features*, the answers come from CX research, both generative and evaluative. Qualitative questions are answered by qualitative research.

Evaluative research methods include:

- **Tree tests** – The participant sees a hierarchy representing the areas and sub-areas of a website, app, or digital system. We ask target audiences where they expect to find information or perform a task. We can determine if our suggested hierarchy needs improvement based on how quickly and easily participants are able to end up in the "right" place without making errors or doubling back.

- **Usability testing** – Researchers present participants with a prototype, dev build, or live PSE. Participants are given a task to perform, and Researchers observe where the current concept or design is easy and efficient to use. Errors, inefficiencies, Task Dimensions, and The Four Horsemen of Bad CX are indications *not* that the participant is unintelligent or needs more training, but that our design should be considered buggy and has room for improvement.

A common flaw in usability tests relates to the quality of the prototype. If this is a digital experience, we cannot realistically test a participant's experience with sketches on paper or a prototype that they cannot move through as naturally as they would on a finished product. These interactively-unrealistic prototypes are often called "click-through" prototypes or models. Click-throughs typically allow a participant to tap or click to move to the next step or another screen, but the user cannot execute normal aspects of their task, such as typing into form fields.

Document the risk of testing an unrealistic prototype. Additional risks occur when Researchers abandon best research practices and provide guidance to stuck and confused participants on what they should do. Guiding participants makes your test invalid.

Stepping Stone: Usability Testing

Companies reluctant to spend time or money on research can start with some evaluative research, often usability testing. It is relatively fast and inexpensive to run, and when done right, it surfaces bugs in concepts and designs. This allows us to fix these bugs before we waste Engineering cycles or unleash buggy PSE on the public.

Sometimes usability testing shows that our idea is not a good match for our target audiences. I once observed a study where all participants had a reasonably good time moving through the prototype. We noticed only a few minor changes we should make. But without being asked, seven out of the eight well-recruited participants volunteered that they would never use a service like this. These people were archetypal members of the target audience, and they declared that they did not need this service. Congratulations on having a decent design, but it sounds like the overall concept or feature is not a match to the target audience. This company should have pivoted or questioned some of its strategies, but it didn't, and unfortunately went out of business a few years later.

Once we can establish the positive outcomes that usability testing delivers, we can try to get others interested in also trying generative research. If testing can help us fix mistakes while we are Designing, consider the mistakes we will never make when we are guided by insights and customer intelligence from generative research. This would save time and money, and reduce risk.

Chapter 7:   Interview: Service Design

Jan Wardecki is a Service Designer with a strategic mindset and solid facilitation and design research skills. He firmly believes that taking a holistic and Human-Centered Design approach is vital for businesses to thrive and grow.

He works in the UX Centre of Expertise at the Digital Transformation Department in the BNP Paribas Bank Poland. He drives enterprise-scale design efforts for different business lines to identify and explore new opportunities to set the ground for digital transformation and innovation. Utilizing a combination of Service Design, User Experience Design, and co-creative methodologies, he delivers business value and customer satisfaction.

He is also the co-founder of the Service Design Network Poland Chapter, and is an SDN Accredited Service Design Practitioner. [https://linkedin.com/in/jan-wardecki-service-designer/]

Debbie: How do you define customer-centricity?

Jan: It's a very holistic approach in which we are listening to customer needs and trying to respond to them, putting the customer at the center of our thinking.

Debbie: Before you were in Service Design, you were a Product Manager. Did you have that customer-centric view as a Product Manager?

Jan: I gained it later when I realized that a well-organized backlog according to business needs will not necessarily give us product success. I was working on an internal product for students at a huge private university in Poland. It was an internal digital software platform for checking grades, engaging with students, and trying to build a huge digital marketing and communication platform. The KPIs were around reaching the students to let them know we have additional offers.

Suddenly, I realized that we have to listen to the students. I realized that we must understand the needs by conducting user research and later usability testing. We discovered a lot of pain points during the research phase. We developed different personas based on university students' years.

I also realized that we should combine business objectives with customer needs. It was eye-opening for stakeholders! And for me! It was mind-blowing to think about the end-users while building the software.

Then I learned about customer-centric approaches, Human-Centered Design, and other stuff. I took post-graduate studies in User Experience Design and Service Design. I learned that the most important thing is how we deliver the Customer Experience by organizing a whole company or organization around value. Then I became more interested in combining this with business processes. That was the first evolution of my career toward Design.

Debbie: There are probably many people reading this book who are starting from a position of what the business wants. *How can we make the business numbers look good and stakeholders happy?* They assume things will work out OK for the customer.

Jan: Exactly. I didn't want to be the guy dealing only with business needs. I took different approaches for a long time. I was trying to figure out how to use business analysis to understand customers. Business Analysts get requirements from stakeholders, but in the end, they are often not achieving any results in terms of a good product, something that fulfills customers' needs but also is usable.

Debbie: Service Design confuses many people. They think that UX Designers design digital solutions, so Service Designers design the services we offer to customers.

Jan: Service Design is the holistic and highly collaborative approach to generating value for both the service user and service provider through the service life cycle. Service Design uses the Human-Centered perspective. It's more about the business processes that mostly happen behind the scenes or "behind the stage," as we say. User Experience is more on the "front stage." Service Designers try to see the whole perspective, including digital and physical touchpoints.

Debbie: A better term might be "strategist." You're designing business process strategy, starting with mapping what the customers or potential customers experience now, both in the digital and non-digital worlds. Then you map how that can be improved. It's a very strategic job and not what most people think of when they hear "design."

Jan: I totally agree. It's not about wireframes but about investigation and research within the organization. Service Design and User Experience Design use many of the same tools but for different purposes. Both work to define and discover the true user needs and pain points. But Service Designers would also like to discover the pain points for people inside the organization, and discover – through the silos and departments in the organization – where we have bottlenecks.

For example, we had a project at our company to transform bank branches. After they designed the new branch concept, developed it, and implemented it, employees and customers thought it was innovative. However, they had some difficulties navigating through the branch. They were used to the mental model of traditional branches, developed through the years. Suddenly the bank decided to break this mental model.

Typically, you enter the branch, and you have a place to sit down. Then there are customer advisors, but we didn't have them in our branch. We had a huge open space where people were sitting wherever they wanted. It was almost like a cafe. So, we had to investigate and conduct user research in the branch, a physical touchpoint. Our User Experience specialists didn't have experience with ethnographic research, shadowing, and observation techniques.

Debbie: Was Service Design involved before the new branch design was created?

Jan: We didn't have our department yet, so we weren't involved in this process. Our department was created a year after the implementation. But then they asked us to work on it. We conducted research. We spoke with employees, and it was eye-opening because this branch was designed without thinking about the employees' needs or how they work. *What do they do during service experiences with a customer?*

Another great example was when we followed the mortgage loan application process. We conducted ethnographic research with user observations and shadowing. We noticed that the application seemed to be held for around two weeks. That led us to realize that there were difficulties with communication across departments. Thanks to that research, we learned to improve not only the product but also the processes, the back-office systems, and the whole experience. We sketched stakeholder maps, service blueprints, customer journeys, and tried to combine everything to answer user and employee needs.

Debbie: It seems like a Service Design team or department is partners with everybody in the organization. They might work with CX, UX, or Product Managers. They might look at how a Sales team does something or how the legal department gets involved. Where in the organization does a Service Design team usually sit?

Jan: We are in the digital transformation department, but I'm also part of the UX team right now. My manager is the Head of UX. We're responsible for changing the organization, but we have support from digital transformation. I think this is good, but I know that organizations around the world have different structures.

Debbie: Once you have that future state service blueprint and you've mapped what an improved business process and Customer Experience will be like, it seems like what happens next is a change management adventure. How do you turn the blueprint into action?

Jan: It depends if the organization is more waterfall or more Agile. Thanks to the stakeholder map, we can define who owns products or touchpoints. When we need to change something in a digital product, we have to think about Product Owners or the Product Manager. We'll need buy-in from the person responsible for the channel or touchpoint. In Agile, we involve the Scrum Master as a coach to collaborate on defining what will be changed. This will also affect the roadmap. We might need to work with a process team or the process owner. Sometimes we have to start with a Minimum Valuable Product or Minimum Valuable Service.

After creating our service blueprints, we often double-check them with Business Analysts, IT Architects, and others from many different departments to ensure that it's a good map. Different departments might describe this process entirely differently. We check this in a collaborative workshop. We'll also consider who should be involved in the implementation plan of our future state service blueprint. *How will we combine our initiatives into current organization roadmaps?*

It's not like we have a blueprint and it's done. We divide changes into phases. *What should we do in the first phase? Improve the Customer Experience in the front stage? Or should we think about the backstage?* We use typical prioritization approaches and workshops. We also need to be in line with KPIs. It's a very complicated process. That's why we are part of the transformation department.

Debbie: I wonder if some people will read this and say, "This sounds great, but it sounds like it takes forever."

Jan: It depends on the product and organization. It depends on what we find after framing the problem from multiple angles, which is the first phase. The second phase is initial research. After that, we can estimate the time that it will take. For example, if we know that there is a very complex product and we'll need to deal with different departments, we create hypotheses about the product, and then we can estimate time. Maybe a very simple product or process takes two weeks.

Debbie: I've often found that even when we think we know the problem, after the research, sometimes the problem looks very different. Or it's a different problem. Do you ever find that after you research, you have to look back at the problem and say, "Hold on. We thought we had the problem defined, but it's a whole other animal."

Jan: That is why we often reframe the problem after the research phase.

Debbie: The first three phases of your work might be: consider the problem or challenge, research, and redefine the problem. During this, you create current and future state service blueprints. What phase comes next?

Jan: Brainstorming and prototyping, depending on the situation or project. Sometimes after the research phase, we find some quick wins. Sometimes we go through a whole process like Double Diamond, where we will have brainstorming, prototyping, testing, and implementation.

Debbie: People sometimes think of prototyping as either a physical object, like we're going to make a model of a car we want to build, or a digital prototype, where it's a UX prototype or something coded. What other types of prototypes might a Service Designer use?

Jan: When we were investigating those bank branches and physical touchpoints, we considered that one element we could change to create better experiences was the person greeting guests in the front of the branch. The prototype could be even the process. We can imagine these changes and then check with the internal person who owns this touchpoint and ask whether it's possible to implement our ideas into their services. I remember a situation when we suggested a different approach for the employee, like how to talk about bank services with customers. The sky's the limit, or the industry is the limit.

Debbie: I hope people reading this book will become interested in and excited about Service Design and Service Designers, and open jobs. How do you assess if someone's good at Service Design?

Jan: This is the funny part because it's often "invisible work." First, the person should have competencies in facilitation and communication. Facilitation is a very important skill, but it can be hard to assess in an interview. They need to be great at gathering information, analytical thinking, and critical thinking. They also need to be able to do visualization using service blueprints. They need to show how they conduct research. These are generally the skills. Candidates should be able to show their blueprints, recommendations, and the impact on the organization.

Sometimes due to NDAs, they can't show all of their work or speak to specifics. But they should be able to talk about or show some of their process, the main challenges, and the impact of the project. It's all about the strategy. You could also ask what tools they use or how they use workshops.

Debbie: It sounds like a job that's very heavy on research and strategy. And then, the facilitation piece drives some of the collaboration. You're bringing together so many different departments and domains in an organization, who will have to do some tough looking in the mirror, and possibly hear that what they're doing is not good for themselves, the customers, or the company. The facilitator probably has to help them get into a better mindset or position to be open to change.

Jan: Exactly. The crucial role is gathering people in one place, if possible. It's about connecting the dots in an organization. It's much more than thinking about one solution. You have to consider the whole organization.

Chapter 8:   Measuring Customer-Centricity

How do we track the impact of good or better CX, or how customer-centric we are? You're already doing some of that. You have leading indicators, which measure activities and outcomes that are relatively early in the customer lifecycle. You have lagging indicators, which are metrics that show later results and outcomes, often around revenue and profit. You have survey results, tweets, Customer Support tickets, app reviews, and other VOC data.

There are more things that we could measure, but our metrics and related outcomes are only as good as:

- **The metrics we are focused on.**

- **Data collection methods and tools.**

- **Data honesty.** Is the data manipulated to tell a particular story?

- **Actions taken in response to data and feedback.**

Four Stages of Customer-Centric Metrics Maturity

When it comes to the focus of our metrics, companies often progress through stages of metrics maturity. It's a spectrum with four key stops along the way:

- **Stage 1: Only tracking business metrics.** Numbers of customers gained and lost, revenue, spending, and ROI.

  o   Metrics related to customers go as far as *how often we could make how many customers do a thing we wanted them to do*: mailing list subscriptions, time on a page, clicking a specific button, and repeat purchases.

  o   Stage 1 companies are not measuring anything that would indicate quality or success from the customers' perspectives. Metrics measure business goals and successes.

- **Stage 2: Tracking business metrics and some customer metrics, but only caring about business metrics.** If the VOC data or survey scores show that customers have a lot of complaints, we find ways to rationalize or ignore those.

  o   We might manipulate and mold our data to tell a more palatable story. We add and average figures that shouldn't be added or averaged, and we announce that what we're doing is "good enough" for customers. *It doesn't matter if most of our app ratings in the last year are 1 or 2 stars; our average in the app store for the last six years is 4.4! Good enough!*

- **Stage 3: Tracking business and customer metrics, caring about both, and acting on both.** We have appropriate business and customer metrics, and we accurately track all metrics. We report honestly on them without fuzzy math and junk science.

    o   When metrics reflect that something is going wrong, we get the right teams to investigate root causes and improve our understanding of the issue before we rush to imagine solutions.

    o   We might continue to use vanity metrics such as how many people joined our email mailing list. But we take more customer-centric actions, including removing popups no customer wants. Improving desired business metrics shouldn't come at the expense of the Customer Experience.

- **Stage 4: Adjusting business metrics based on customer intelligence and knowledge of customers' needs, contexts, and tasks.** When we recognize that we push teams to create or optimize the PSE in customer-peripheric directions, we re-examine and change our KPIs.

    o   When we realize that our "more page views" metric forces project teams to create inefficient user experiences (to drive up the page views metric), we re-evaluate that metric and adjust or replace it.

Metrics around customer-centricity will show where we are customer-peripheric and how we are improving or possibly getting worse. The maturity stages remind us that poor or customer-peripheric KPIs or goals can manifest in our projects and PSE. This chapter focuses on various metrics that you can try to measure customer-centricity, internally and externally.

Short-Term Wins, Long-Term Carnage

In my article, "Your CX and UX Metrics Are Myopic," [https://cxcc.to/a148] I looked at the dangers of measuring short-term wins, as we often see in A/B testing. We might be testing a minor change and want to see if people spend more, convert more, or whatever metric we value. We see that lift, call the test a success, and we go more or entirely in on the winner.

Do we measure this metric in the longer term or across the longer end-to-end customer journey? The customer's experience doesn't stop when they check out or do that one thing you hope they will do. There are actions, sub-tasks, repercussions, and consequences that can happen later.

- What if your winning A/B test variant created higher-value purchases but led to more complaints, angry tweets, or requests for refunds? Is that variant still the winner?

- What if your B variant saw higher conversions but the customers coming through that variant were less likely to purchase again later?

- What if people moving through your B variant are doing more of what you want them to do, but are giving you lower NPS or satisfaction scores?

These can all be measured, but we rarely measure them initially or check for correlation or causation later. Anything you measure should be monitored over a longer period and longer customer journey arc. If your short-term metric winner has a negative ripple effect on a longer-term metric, we should be smart enough to watch for that possibility before we declare a variant the winner.

Types of Task-Based Experience Metrics

MeasuringU.com offers a good breakdown of types of task-based experience metrics. [https://cxcc.to/a120]

1. **Action metrics based on the ISO definition of usability.** These include completion rate, findability rate, time on task, time until failure, the number of clicks or page views required to complete a task, and the number of errors.

2. **Attitudinal metrics.** These include self-assessments of confidence and ease of use.

3. **Behavioral and psychological metrics.** These include eye tracking, facial expressions, skin responses, and heart rate. These metrics often require special equipment and specially trained experts to plan, conduct, and analyze these studies.

4. **Combined metrics.** MeasuringU has a category for combining attitudinal with behavioral. Examples include how learnable something is, how lost someone is when looking for information, an efficiency ratio (percentage of successful task completions divided by the mean completion rate), and "disasters," where a participant fails a task but still has high confidence that they were successful.

All of these are worth consideration. Many are quantitative and survey-based; remember to augment quantitative measurements with qualitative information so that you can understand behaviors, perceptions, contexts, and further details.

Action metrics such as completion rate should not be considered in isolation. A customer completing their task does not mean that it was completed efficiently, without errors, or with high satisfaction. Action and attitudinal metrics should be tracked and interpreted relative to other metrics about the same task.

North Star Metrics

Your North Star Metric (NSM) should match essential business and user goals. It measures the quality and value we deliver to users, which should lead to business growth and success.

Some well-known companies have been open about their North Star Metrics. Here are some that were made public in 2021:

- Spotify: Time spent listening

- Amazon: Number of purchases per month

- Airbnb: Number of nights booked

- Quora: Numbers of answers to questions

- Uber: Rides per week

Notice that these are leading metrics. They are up-front direct customer actions. They are not the results or outcomes from actions such as revenue or profit. You can also see this as *measuring customers' task success through this main number.*

Before someone gets a Quora answer or plays a song on Spotify, there are things we can measure, like the number of questions asked or the number of songs people searched for. Those are **input metrics**: actions or parameters we can measure, but they aren't the true mark of user success. Uber might measure how many rides are *requested* each week – a decent input metric – but a percentage of these will be canceled by the driver or the passenger. Measuring completed rides measures the accomplishment of the customer's task.

Getting an answer to a Quora question and listening to Spotify music are good North Star Metrics since they indicate user success. We can measure them and create innovations or incremental improvements that can lift these metrics. They are also tied to business success because if Quora users get answers and Spotify users listen to music, we will probably meet or exceed business goals.

Slack's NSM is active users. At first, this seems like an input metric. But Slack charges per active user. Therefore, they use an NSM around behavior – how many people actively use a Slack workspace – but it will also directly lead to revenue in paid Slack workspaces.

Notice that none of these North Star Metrics is "number of features shipped" in a certain amount of time. The NSM and most KPIs should be about moments where customers experience quality, value, and success. Customers rarely think about our teams' velocity, but they are haunted by crappy PSE. Make sure we are focused on delivering *quality over speed.*

Optimizing for Customer-Peripheric KPIs

If the North Star Metric is a mismatch to customers' tasks, perspectives, and needs, it can cause customer-periphery. We will also need to track how KPIs and OKRs manifest in team behavior and the PSE. This tracking isn't another metric; this is part of governance.

Many companies are under pressure to produce increases in quarterly or annual growth, revenue, traction, and adoption. This can make some teams desperate. They choose deceptive designs, ethically questionable decisions, and shoot for metrics like *how long someone stayed on a screen* rather than *the quality of that customer's experience on that screen* or *how well the customer was able to accomplish their tasks.*

We see this very often when our KPIs are around "engagement." The customer doesn't want more *engagement*; they want to get something done and get out of there. When we understand that people are task-based, we recognize that more time spent on a page may indicate CX problems that we should research and fix. An exception could be social, written, or visual media, where the task might be to pass the time or be entertained. The user still has tasks to accomplish, but efficiency might not be a key criterion, and time may be flexible.

Imagine a dating site or app. We could say that *how often people search through profiles* is "engagement." If frequent searches are a step *toward* task accomplishment, but are not *the* moment or indicator of success, then search frequency is more likely to be an input metric and shouldn't be a KPI or NSM. We could measure *how many people "liked" you, how often we notified you about new local members*, and the *views your profile received*. Those are nice input metrics, but they measure *activity or engagement* without measuring **success or quality**.

Teams under pressure to lift such engagement metrics might try to gamify likes or increase the frequency of new member notifications. These run the risk of being annoying or distracting, especially if we find that they do not match customers' definitions of value, quality, or success. If you've ever thought, "Why do they keep showing me [screen or popup]?" or, "Why are they trying to make me [do this other thing I don't want to do]?" you've experienced how KPIs play out in real life.

For example, Facebook's North Star Metric is active users. Given this, their system might welcome fake accounts and bots. They want those active user numbers to look big and growing. Teams might deliberately make it complex or difficult for users to delete or cancel Facebook.

What about measuring more time in our dating ecosystem? That's a nice input metric, but not a measurement of customer or business success. More time might mean that users are having trouble finding a good match, and therefore a sign of failure.

How about measuring the number of matches we send a user? This KPI might lead teams to build features that send you as many humans as possible each week, regardless of the *quality* of those matches. While some people are into quantity on a dating website, most look for quality. But if the quantity metric were our KPI, our teams might cook up features like *ignoring your search filters* or *designating people with vastly different views and lifestyles a match*. You could see a rise in metrics, usage, or engagement, but is this the *right* rise? Are we creating customer value, success, and satisfaction?

Example: OkCupid Removed a Feature

I met my husband on OkCupid in April 2017. He saw my profile, decided I lived too far away, and didn't write to me. At the time, OKCupid offered a list of people who saw your profile but didn't take action. I was checking that list for any exciting matches who were shy. I hit the life and love jackpot.

Months later, OkCupid removed that page because *if anybody saw your profile and didn't contact you, they're obviously not interested and just a waste of time.* What KPI did OkCupid have that made the "list of people who saw you but didn't take action" something to get rid of? How many people missed out on meeting their shy but perfect person?

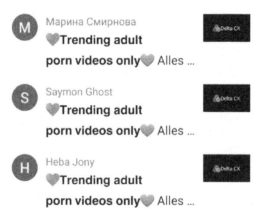

Figure 16: Screenshot from my YouTube comments where three different "people" posted, "Trending adult porn videos only," and a URL. YouTube is "smart" enough to recognize porn spam comments, especially those containing the word "porn." But YouTube rarely auto-deletes these comments or holds them for moderation. Which YouTuber would want these comments to appear under their videos? Which KPIs exist that make YouTube not auto-delete such comments? "Number of comments per video?"

There are a variety of metrics that are often goals but are probably no longer the correct targets at which to aim efforts. Consider where some of these are input metrics but shouldn't be our KPIs or North Star Metric.

- **Clicks, views, and shares.** These do not help our business strategies and desired outcomes unless we live and die by advertising, and we need to show more page views. Likes and shares are vanity metrics that don't keep us in business. These can be lovely OKRs, but metrics that aren't meaningful, actionable, and accomplishing tangible goals shouldn't be KPIs.

- **Session duration, average time on pages, and pages per visit.** Do we want people to spend more time on our screens or less time? Does more time mean they were "engaged," or having trouble getting things done? Can we shift these goals to shoot for shorter times when task-related and longer times when content-related, such as blog posts?

- **Page views.** Teams might build processes and workflows that span more pages than necessary. Rather than building an efficient process that happens on one page, or just simpler and more efficient processes, you are dragged across multiple pages. Heck, maybe even the login is on its own page so we can count one more page view this month.

-

Figure 17: Screenshot from Morgan Stanley's login flow. The only words on the page say, "We'll need to verify your identity to log in." Your only action is a "Continue" button. The page before required my username and password. There were four pages after this to complete the login, including "text me a code" and "verify the code we sent" being two separate pages. High page views appear to be a KPI.

- You might also see these slow-motion, dragged-out processes if our KPI is **more time on pages or in the system**. If pages load slowly, that might be acceptable or even a win since we celebrate when people are on pages for longer periods of time.

- **Email open rates or click rates.** These metrics may have low value since they are unlikely to signal revenue or business goals accomplished. To increase the value of these metrics, see if they can be accurately correlated to something that makes or saves the business money.

- **New or total mailing list subscribers or social media followers.** These are especially unimpressive if you mainly grow your mailing list because you force people onto it or add people without their knowledge. These metrics are also meaningless if you buy followers. Unsubscribes and unfollows can undo these metrics.

- **Leads in the pipeline.** You might find Sales doing some strange things to show more leads, even if they are poor leads unlikely to convert. That "makes the numbers," but is a waste of time.

  o A better metric might be **how many proposals you send**. Perhaps you tend to win 30% of the proposals you submit, so the KPI or NSM might be to submit more proposals, and keep watching your percentage of success.

Using our dating site example, a strong North Star Metric might be the number of messages members send each other. Like Spotify wants to measure listening time and Uber wants to measure the number of rides, a dating site may find that a critical metric leading to success and revenue is people messaging each other.

Want to dial that up and really check for quality in both directions? How about a North Star Metric around *the number of messages that receive more than one reply*? Anybody can send a message. Anybody can get a single reply, even if that reply is, "No thanks," or, "Please go away." Perhaps that conversation doesn't go beyond the first message. Perhaps one person blocks the other. Additional replies could signify a good match and potential connection between humans.

This gets us closer to dating site success without measuring obvious things like revenue. *The number of message interactions that don't end within 48 hours with one user blocking the other* signals quality and success in Customers' Experiences. The key will be to make sure that our teams don't specifically design features that push or trick people into more messaging solely to lift metrics.

Another good metric is the number of Support tickets that could have been self-service, which is a number we would want to see decrease over time. Customers hate contacting your Support center to do easy things like changing their phone numbers. Improving PSE to allow customers to handle easy or everyday tasks themselves is a win-win. Users take care of their problems – hopefully easily and intuitively – and Support spends less time on tickets that don't need an Agent's assistance.

KPIs that *aren't* leading and *aren't* about customer success can be OK *if* they are unlikely to be manipulated or drive devious behavior. One example is *cost per acquisition*. We want that cost to go down, which means that it takes less marketing and reduced sales efforts to win new customers.

Glovo's October 2022 Incident

Twenty-six-year-old Sebastian Galassi was killed in Italy in October 2022 while making a moped delivery for the Spanish company Glovo. He collided with an SUV and was run over by another car. [article in Italian from Wired https://cxcc.to/a174]

He died the next day in the hospital, the same day he received an automated text message that he never saw. In that message, Glovo fired him for not adhering to their terms and conditions. The company's system noticed that Sebastian missed the delivery deadline, triggering him to be "deactivated" – essentially fired.

We can understand that Glovo would want to inspire – if not pressure – their delivery staff to complete tasks in the shortest time possible. But with rising numbers of accidents and deaths, *at what cost?* Glovo is not alone. Delivery services worldwide are controversial for the same reasons, including their treatment of their gig economy workers.

It would be smarter to balance speed with safety. This is ultimately a service design project that should include a serious review of KPIs. Internal questions and conversations should address:

- Speed or delivery time as the main KPI might inspire people to ride or drive more recklessly – endangering themselves or others – especially if their job is on the line.
- If the technology can consider the route and transportation method, what is a short but reasonable range of time in which someone can safely make the delivery?
- How can Glovo ensure that nothing in the CX of either side of their marketplace is heartless or seeming to devalue human life? The automated text message firing of a dead man came off as cold and tone deaf.
- Can account termination include a step where a human reviews the account before automated firing?
- Does the technology count the delivery time starting when the food is ready to be picked up or when it's ordered? The delivery person should not be penalized for a slow or disorganized restaurant.
- Consider all of your customers and staff, especially in a two-sided marketplace and the gig economy. The person who placed the order that Sebastian died trying to deliver might deal with guilt or other tough emotions. Did anybody from Glovo reach out to them, and not just with a "sorry your order didn't arrive; here's a coupon?"
- Glovo apologized for the automated firing and offered to pay for part of Sebastian's funeral. Is paying for *part* of the funeral the best Glovo can do right now? Even if Glovo (hypothetically) believes its delivery staff are a revolving door of replaceable contractors, what are the best policies and procedures Glovo can create to make it seem like they care about drivers who are hurt or killed during their work?

When Customer-Centricity Shortens the Relationship

Businesses like dating websites and job boards might struggle more than the average company with North Star Metrics and KPIs. The faster a user has true success, the less they need our PSE. If you are hired for a new job after only one application, or if you find your life partner after seeing only a few dating profiles, you might be done (at least for now) with the job or dating website. This can often lead companies down unethical and customer-peripheric paths as they attempt to extend usage or increase interactions. You might hear that we need to find more ways to make our PSE "sticky" or addictive.

In these cases, you are playing a longer PSE and brand game. Customer success might mean a shorter initial relationship with the customer, but could lead to:

- **More positive and frequent word-of-mouth, ratings, and reviews.** This is the pinnacle of influencer marketing; we didn't pay anybody to broadcast or share that they like our PSE or company.

- **Being the customer's number one choice if and when they need us again.** Someone who likes their current job or partner might not stay with either forever.

- **A happy customer might find other tasks they can accomplish within our PSE.** Someone who loved finding a romantic partner on our dating site might wonder if the site is also a great place to make new like-minded friends. Thanks to our job website, someone who got hired might think of us first the next time they need to post a job.

If your business is a two-sided marketplace, fast and efficient success for one party will likely be fast and efficient success for the other party. While metrics around frequency or retention might be lower, you should see higher satisfaction scores and lower costs related to serving your customers.

Quick Fix Versus Slow Fix: Bad KPIs or NSM

I have seen executives who were aware they were measuring the wrong things or that KPIs were creating bizarre or unethical behaviors in their teams. I have seen these execs decide that new KPIs were needed, and announce that KPIs would be changing. In many cases, the exec already knew the exact KPIs they wanted to use. So why weren't these "better" KPIs in place already? Why were they still a promise of the future?

The **slow fix** is to wait until new PSE features are in place that would most precisely measure the new KPIs. I saw one company create a dependency where the new KPIs were unlikely to be official (and the harmful KPI downgraded to an input metric) until they had built and released a new B2B platform. This looked like it would take over a year, possibly two years. And they said they were Agile!

A better **quick fix** is to start experimenting with the new KPIs, knowing that how they will be measured is a work in progress. We might not yet have access to our ideal data, but what data can we get? What can we start learning through well-designed surveys? What can our analytics tools show? Are there any proxies that make sense?

Once we know that we have a KPI or North Star Metric that is customer-peripheric or influencing teams to do desperate, manipulative, or deceptive things, it's important to run with our quick fix. Continue evolving how and what you measure.

Is NPS® Customer-Centric?

Net Promoter Score (NPS) is a single survey question asking on a scale of 0 to 10 how likely you are to recommend a company to someone else. Respondents are put into buckets by the score they gave:

- "Detractors" score from 0-6.

- "Passives" score 7 or 8.

- "Promoters" score 9 or 10.

NPS is calculated by selecting a range of time and then following this formula: % Promoters - % Detractors = NPS. Passives are not part of the equation. For example, 60% Promoters minus 30% Detractors is an NPS of 30. 30% Promoters minus 60% Detractors is an NPS of -30. NPS ranges from -100 to +100.

NPS surveys rarely ask if you have already recommended us to someone else or to how many people. We have no idea if respondents will recommend us, even if they give us a score of 10. We don't know if they are satisfied. We don't know what's going wrong. We only know that they are scoring themselves on the possible future likelihood of recommending us.

NPS can be an acceptable method when matched with knowledge and action. We will need to pair it with qualitative research to learn more about *why* we got a particular score and *what* we can do to improve things. NPS on its own often isn't actionable beyond raising unanswered questions, leaving us to plan the research that will answer them.

Companies misuse NPS in a variety of ways, including:

- **NPS is just a number in a report**. Everybody hopes it looks better next quarter.

- **Low scores are rationalized or excused**. "Maybe that's normal for our industry." "Maybe our competitors have similar scores."

- **Companies with low, even negative NPS believe that *if we can win business at this low NPS, maybe we're good enough.***

- **We want to raise the NPS. But we don't plan to fix or improve the PSE problems discovered in customer feedback or surveys.** It appears that we only care about our score, but not why we have that score.

   o I saw an online discussion forum post from someone who knew why their NPS was low, admitted that their company didn't plan to fix known root causes, but wanted others in the forum to suggest ways they can improve NPS.

   o The best way to improve NPS will always be to show that you care about Customer Experiences and satisfaction by taking customer-centric action. Yes, some PSE changes are large and expensive projects. Are those projects more or less expensive than low NPS, unhappy customers, negative word of mouth, and attrition?

NPS fans often interpret high scores as a sign of satisfaction or loyalty, but are they? **100% of our current customers are susceptible to competitive offerings.** People who score us a 10 might cancel and move to a competitor. Some will jump at a lower price or when our competitor improves what they offer. Some are happy but are checking other options. **People are loyal until they're not.**

For those who love NPS, you can measure the NPS at various points of the journey. I heard about a company where NPS was close to 50, a decent score, when customers first signed the contract. When it was time to renew the contract, the NPS was nearly -30. That's terrible news. They either abandon customers during their journey or do a lot wrong while customers experience the PSE. I also saw this company average these scores to make the overall NPS look better. Do not do that. We should be talking honestly about what is going on at each step.

What can you improve if your NPS were 97? You can't rest or be complacent because you got a score you like. There are always things to fix or improve, and we must be proactive.

Stepping Stone: NPS

Surveys can be used as a stepping stone toward better and deeper research approaches. Same for NPS. We have survey results and a score, but what do we know? What should we do next? Who is loyal, who is likely to dump us, and what can be improved?

When presenting or discussing NPS results, suggest a plan for qualitative research to fill in the customer intelligence gaps.

Task and Satisfaction Scoring Systems

There are scoring systems that claim to measure customer satisfaction or the User Experience, but I find them to be poor choices. As we walk through each of the most popular ones, consider if the results are likely to be meaningful, actionable, or helpful. Also, note that many of these request future behavior predictions from people who might figure out that you're fishing for positive answers. *I have no idea how many healthy green vegetables I will eat next week, but I know my answer should probably be a high number so I sound like a healthy person.*

The **System Usability Scale** (SUS) asks users to rate statements that are written in a way that doesn't match how most people think or speak, such as:

- **"I found the various functions in this system were well integrated."** Do users know what's integrated into what, and whether that was done well?

- **"I thought there was too much inconsistency in this system."** Does the average user notice consistency or inconsistency? Do they know what we intended to be consistent?

- **"I found the system very cumbersome to use."** Do they think of systems as "cumbersome?" Do they want to admit that they struggled?

- **"I think that I would like to use this system frequently."** This asks customers to predict what they might do in the future. It also assumes that frequency of use is important.

- Five of the ten statements in the System Usability Scale are about **how easy the system is to learn**.

SUPR-Q claims to be better than SUS. Its survey questions include:

- **"How likely are you to recommend this website to a friend or colleague?"** This is NPS.

- **"I will likely visit this website in the future."** This requires a future behavior prediction.

- **"The information on the website is credible." "The information on the website is trustworthy."** Interestingly, this is focused on "the information."

  o In moderated research sessions, I often learn if the participant finds the company trustworthy and why or why not. One participant told me they didn't trust the company because they found the logo amateurish.

  o If someone can find *information* trustworthy but still find reasons to not completely trust the company, this scoring system might not capture that.

- SUPR-Q asks two questions about **how easy it is to use the website.** We know that people sometimes prefer to rate things as easy, thinking they're being polite or telling you what you hope to hear. Perhaps they feel confident that they didn't make mistakes in your PSE. Sometimes in observational studies, we watch confident users think something is easy, but then they make mistakes and have no idea they did something incorrectly.

- SUPR-Q asks two questions about **how attractive the website is**. This is not a measurement of customer satisfaction. Customers can love your branding and visual design, and still dislike your PSE or company.

The **Single Ease Question** appears after a task and asks people to rate from 1 to 7 how easy or difficult the task was. It's certainly simple, but is it too simple? If your average score this month is 4.3, what does that mean and what will you do about it?

There's the **Usability Metric for User Experience** (UMUX). Participants use a 7-point scale to rate these four things:

- **"[This system's] capabilities meet my requirements."** This implies that users have a set of requirements in their heads and are checking your PSE for how much they match those.

- **"Using [this system] is a frustrating experience." "[This system] is easy to use."** It seems strange to have these two questions back-to-back. If both get high scores, what does that mean?

    o You *can* use opposite survey questions to check if answers are consistent. But if we haven't hidden opposite questions in a longer survey, is it still a good survey technique, or does it make the survey seem awkward or manipulated?

- **"I have to spend too much time correcting things with [this system]."** The focus might accidentally be on *time*. If you had to make corrections or fix mistakes as your task went along, but you didn't feel like you spent a lot of time doing that, you might give this question a low rating. But is that a fair reflection of how error-prone the system might be?

UserZoom came up with **QXScore**, which combines a bunch of these so that you can have multiple measurable dimensions like trust, appearance, and NPS. Combining flawed questions or metrics can give you *more* data, but is it *good* data? If these scores aren't meaningful or actionable, they are probably not worth the time spent running and analyzing the surveys.

Google's HEART Framework

The "HEART" framework measures Happiness, Engagement, Adoption, Retention, and Task Success. [https://cxcc.to/a132]

- **Happiness** is about satisfaction, ease of use, visual appeal, and likelihood to recommend. This sounds like NPS and other metrics discussed above. The scoring systems commonly in use now may or may not be accurately capturing how satisfied customers are. Also, "happy" customers might still dream of or need PSE improvements.

- **Engagement** is about frequency, intensity, or interaction depth over time. This might include input metrics like logins or page views, or our North Star Metric, like the number of purchases made.

- **Adoption and Retention** examine new versus existing or current users. Adoption is a good metric, but if we are adopting without retaining, then we must look at where we are customer-peripheric.

    o We must also be careful about what qualifies as "retention." Someone returning to our website or logging in again might be a nice input metric, but it doesn't guarantee business or customer success. They might still not buy, not recommend, or be unhappy.

    o Better retention metrics might be around trial users converting to paid, how long paid users stay with us, and how existing customers grow their usage or increase the frequency of purchasing or utilization.

- **Task Success** and Time On Task can be good measurements that speak to user success, assuming that our users care about how long their task takes. Metrics related to task success are some of your most customer-centric metrics since they speak to how your CX facilitates or blocks people from accomplishing what they have set out to do.

Growth, Retention, and Attrition

Companies, especially startups, sometimes measure growth by "traction" and "adoption": how many new customers we won in a period of time. We count app downloads, trial users, and freemium customers. We might even count mailing list subscriptions or website engagement. But do any of these new customers stay with us? Over time, are they purchasing more from us?

We can measure our average Customer Lifespan: how long the average customer stays. We can calculate Customer Lifetime Value: the average annual revenue per customer multiplied by the Customer Lifespan. Even if we couldn't convince customers to increase their annual spending, we would still want to increase their lifespan.

Why are we having trouble retaining customers? Attrition is often due to one or more of these key elements:

- **Complaints, bugs, problems, and frustrations are unresolved**. Companies often prioritize new features over fixing problems. They hope they have released something "good enough" to keep users, but what we internally declare "good enough" is often not good enough for customers, especially those who are paying. Why stay with the company that releases broken PSE and deprioritizes improvements you requested, if not demanded?

- **Value proposition**. What does your PSE offer that competitors don't? Why should people try this, use it, and stay with it? How do you make customers' lives or tasks faster, easier, more efficient, or better? How have you priced what you offer?

- **Poor PSE**. There are so many ways that PSE can be considered low quality or value by customers. You can think of multiple times you started with PSE, and then canceled, downgraded, or uninstalled, probably within weeks.

  o Our company might be aggressively chasing our business goals and trying to make customers take the actions the business wants them to take. But we've put customers in the periphery. We are not facilitating their tasks or what they would choose for themselves. Our customers are intelligent people who can tell when our company didn't care what they needed.

- **Disappointing human experiences.** Even where the PSE are decent, human interactions can be deal breakers. We have all struggled with Support Reps who couldn't help us or seemed to not care, leaving us without a resolution.

    o   I once didn't renew a SaaS subscription because I hated dealing with that company's Salespeople. Every interaction with a customer is a chance to improve or hurt a relationship.

Consider the North Star Metrics we discussed earlier. Uber might count rides per month, but what percentage of those are from new customers? How many customers are repeat customers who we have retained? The company mentioned earlier, who had a -30 NPS at contract renewal time, had a strong Sales organization that could sell anything and always win new customers. But they would have to be Sales wizards since they frequently lose new customers down the road.

If we have noticeable attrition, we can't be complacent that *Sales will find more new customers*. We still need to fix our PSE, Support, or anything we find is causing dissatisfaction. This will decrease our Cost of Acquisition, which is the total our company spends to win one new customer.

Your growth strategy can't be, "We will release a steady stream of cool ideas and hope that at least some of these are good enough to attract and retain customers."

Our growth numbers can be deceptive if we focus mostly or only on adoption. Growth and retention require longer-term metrics. Growth should ultimately be measured in lower Cost of Acquisition and higher Customer Retention Rate, the percentage of customers who stay with you after a certain period of time.

Try It: Quality in the Short and Long Term

J. D. Power measures the "initial quality" of vehicles. Their "PP100" score is the number of problems experienced per 100 vehicles in the first 90 days of ownership. What about quality and Customer Experiences after 90 days? J. D. Power also measures vehicle "dependability," which examines experiences over three years of ownership.

At your company, which criteria could be used to create ratings for shorter-term "initial quality" and longer-term "dependability?" What scores would be "good enough" to create satisfaction and loyalty? Might you be able to correlate these ratings with Customer Lifespan or Lifetime Value? What types of customer-centric actions will you plan and execute to improve these scores?

Reducing Attrition with Behavior Triggers

When measuring and monitoring PSE, we look for traction, adoption, conversion, dollar amounts, frequencies, etc. What would it look like to utilize tracking and data science more proactively?

I once tried for over an hour to buy a long weekend cruise online. No matter what I tried, I got a generic error message at the last step of the checkout that offered no help or solution. I logged into my account from multiple browsers but couldn't buy from any of them. I tried different payment cards, all with credit available for this purchase. I couldn't pay for the trip in full, nor could I put a courtesy hold or a down payment on the trip. I was at a dead end on the cruise company's website, so I called Customer Support, who could only offer me the cruise at double the price. The following day, I received a cart recovery email reminding me to book now. I tried but still couldn't check out.

There are stories – often told by Marketing and Sales – when they see abandoned carts, incomplete checkouts, and ineffective cart recovery emails, including:

- "Customers like Debbie don't have enough money for a cruise."

- "Debbie just changed her mind."

- "Debbie's demographic doesn't always buy cruises on their first visit to the site."

- "We have lots of people abandoning carts. They are tire kickers and never intended to buy a cruise."

Without research to tell us what target customers' intentions or reasons are, this is speculation and imagination. What do we really know? More importantly, could we have saved any of those sales? What if we were proactive? Can we create algorithms to proactively help struggling customers *just in time*?

Consider creating what I call "Behavior Triggers." Help people before they become sad metrics. Help them before you make incorrect guesses and assumptions about their behavior. For example:

- What if the second purchase failure and error message triggered a live help chat from someone who could see (through their Support interface) what I was working on, honor that price, and help convert me into a paying customer?

  o A first checkout attempt makes me look serious and like I'm not kicking tires. The second checkout attempt is generous of me. Hurry up and save the sale! Step in when things go wrong for me a second time while we still have momentum. Once I leave, I might buy from a competitor.

- Can the system catch me logging in from more than one browser, trying to buy the same thing repeatedly?

  o Logging in from another browser indicates that I'm a serious customer trying to give you my money. Save the sale!

- Can the system notice that I'm trying multiple channels?

    o I logged in to my account, so you know who I am. I tried to buy and couldn't. I called Customer Support, who accessed my account, so you know who I am. *This customer seems way more serious about buying this as she's tried two ways to do this.* Save the sale!

Calling people you notice are struggling in your PSE would be creepy, but in digital products, you could pop up a live chat with humans (not chatbots), acknowledge they are having trouble, and offer to help. Let it peek up from a bottom corner and allow people to close it or engage. Do not pop up something large on the screen (like we often see mailing list popups), interrupting people or creating obstacles. Build your Behavior Trigger to ensure that you only poke people once per session. If someone doesn't want help but sets off the triggers more than once, don't keep bugging them.

Not every Behavior Trigger should lead to a chat popup. Here are some other Behavior Triggers that could create action in your organization:

- **Do you ever worry that a customer exporting or downloading all their data is thinking of leaving?** Set up a Behavior Trigger to notify a person or team at your company when this happens. Proactively reach out and see what that customer needs.

- **How about when someone cancels auto-renew?** That is a bad sign that they might leave. Let's not wait until they leave to learn what went wrong. Reach out and see if that customer can be helped and retained.

- **If a feature isn't being utilized as expected, this might trigger a team to spin up qualitative research.** We can learn more about why people used or didn't use this feature, and what their unmet needs are.

Someone might decide that this sounds too expensive or not worth it. *Why spend time and money to potentially convert five customers per day? They're just edge cases.* If five people per day had the problem I had on the cruise website, that's $6 million in lost sales each year. Would a $500,000 Behavior Triggers project be worth it? What if this project also decreases negative word of mouth? What about future sales lost? Someone who loved a cruise with that company might sign up for another.

What at first seems like small losses or edge cases ripple out to sales worth saving and customers we could win.

11 Pillars Survey

We can measure how we are doing with the 11 Pillars of Customer-Centricity. Form a cross-functional committee, and have everybody in Product, Engineering, and CX or UX take the survey periodically and anonymously. Calculate the scores and compare over time. The downsides to this idea include surveys often being flawed, and you might not have the same people responding over time. Self-assessment can be suffer from biases like people rating their team as doing better than it is.

The latest version of my survey can be taken online at https://cxcc.to/a133. There are 20 rating questions, and the final score ranges from 0 to 200. My survey tool randomizes the order of the first set of 15 questions and then randomizes the order of the five final questions (as they are displayed as two sets).

- Positively framed questions like, "How often did your cross-functional team track potential and current risks to the project and its outcomes?" are scored as 0 for "never," 1 for "rarely," 5 for "sometimes," 8 for "often," and 10 for "constantly."

- Negatively framed questions like, "How often did your cross-functional team prioritize the speed/velocity of work over the quality of ideas and solutions?" are scored as 10 for "never," 8 for "rarely," 5 for "sometimes," 1 for "often," and 0 for "constantly."

- The last five questions about comfort and confidence are scored as 0 for "not at all," 1 for "a little," 5 for "somewhat," 8 for "mostly," and 10 for "very."

The final two questions are open text fields. The first asks for a few words to describe the culture, allowing you to create a word cloud. I avoid using the word "values" because people usually associate company values with positive words and might not answer with negative words. The last open text field asks for suggestions and improvements.

Consider running this survey or your own variation quarterly.

CXTM™: Customer Experience Task Measurement

I'm also working on a quantitative measurement of task experience based on an intercept survey after the user has completed a discreet task. Such tasks might include registration, checkout, applying for a job, or performing a search. We can gently ask, "Hey, you just did this thing. Can we please get your feedback on how that went?"

Intercepting and interrupting are risky since you don't want to distract users from their tasks. Experiment with this and see what you can learn and measure. To be less interruptive, make sure this is a small message peeking up from the bottom corner of the page and not a large popup or modal blocking people from their next steps.

CXTM will help us know a little about how this task might go wrong, though we should still do qualitative research to ensure that we correctly define customer problems and understand their tasks. You can try the latest version of my survey at https://cxcc.to/a182.

The first question is based on UX heuristics, The Four Horsemen of Bad CX, and Larry Marine's Task Dimensions. There are eight dimensions here that people can rate as never, rarely, sometimes, often, and constantly. My survey tool randomizes the order of these dimensions:

- Confusing.

- Lacking in options or flexibility.

- Took a lot of thought.

- Unclear what to do during the task.

- Too many steps.

- Terms or images didn't make sense.

- Required information I didn't have.

- Frustrating.

It then asks if you were able to accomplish your task with choices of "yes," "partially," or "no." There is an open text field asking how this experience could be improved.

The statements are all negatively framed, which runs the risk of biasing people toward feeling more negatively about their experience than they might have. We are looking for opportunities to improve and not fishing for praise. I would rather bias people to be harsher when reflecting upon the experience than bias them toward positives like, "This was easy," "I would use this often," or, "I wouldn't need help to use this."

Score each of the eight dimensions 0 for "never," 1 for "rarely," 5 for "sometimes," 8 for "often," and 10 for "constantly." Since all statements are negative situations, the less often people experience them, the higher the score. For the question about accomplishing the task, "yes" gets 20 points, "partially" gets 10 points, and "no" gets 0 points.

Scores range from 0 to 100. You can average the scores for that individual task for a period such as monthly or quarterly. We can also calculate the standard deviation to see how varied the scores are across participants.

Having scores for individual tasks or workflows allows us to compare this over time: month to month, quarter to quarter, and year to year. Are they improving? We might also use the scoring in our prioritization.

Time to CX Resolution

Call centers have a metric called Time to Resolution, which measures the time it takes a Customer Service organization to resolve a single customer service ticket once it's been opened. It's usually an average over a period of time.

What about the real time to a *real resolution*? Measure from when we are first aware of a problem or pain point to when that has been successfully resolved and is no longer a complaint or problem *for anyone*. Measure the time between discovering that we had a bug or CX debt and releasing the real fix so that the bug or debt no longer exists. Note that the date when you first knew of the CX debt might be during Design tasks, well before the feature or PSE went live.

Every problem is different, but we can track this over time for what we consider to be small, medium, and large issues.

ROI: Modeling Success and Savings

Human Factors International has online ROI calculators you can use to model the potential ROI of a project. [https://cxcc.to/a134] One example is the ROI of increasing productivity. Let's say we have 200 staff who perform a task 10 times per day, every day. They are paid $40,000 USD per year. We plan to spend $250,000 internally on a project that will shave one minute off this task every time they do it. We anticipate that the benefits from this investment will last us three years.

The calculator shows the total gain at over $356,000, more than paying for the $250,000 project. This might be time staff can spend on something else, or it might be staff you can shift to other tasks or projects. You might be able to assign fewer workers to this task.

Another tool I find interesting is GERU.com. Aimed at Marketers, it's a funnel simulator where you can do math on traffic, conversions, and other actions that lead to revenue.

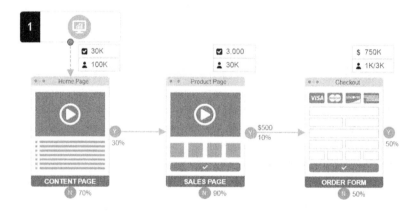

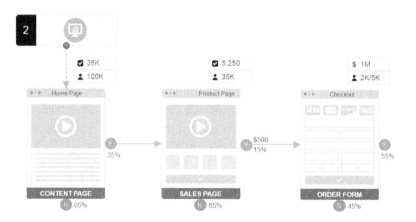

Figure 18: Screenshot from GERU modeling how conversion rates might increase and affect revenue when we improve website experiences. Explained below.

The above screenshot models the same website funnel from the home page to the product page, and into the cart and checkout. Each of the two models imagines that we are getting 100,000 home page visits per month, and not doing anything to increase that traffic. This example doesn't model the effects of improved Marketing or SEO. This models CX or UX improving our website's ability to capture people's attention, communicate the value proposition, and make purchasing easier than before.

Scenario 1 is our current experience. 30% of people hitting the home page visit the product page. 10% of people on that product page put $500 of items into their cart. This might be a single purchase, a subscription payment, or represent a longer customer value. Scenario 1 imagines that 50% of people check out. 1.5% converted. 100,000 visitors hit the site and 1,500 made a $500 purchase. This equals $750,000 in revenue.

Scenario 2 is a possible future state where we have made improvements to multiple steps in the funnel. 35% of the people hitting the home page visit the product page. 15% of those people put $500 of items into the cart. 55% complete the checkout. This nearly doubles us to a 2.9% conversion rate. 2,889 people spent $500 equaling $1,444,500 in revenue.

Scenario 2 might feel like a big jump or a distant future state. But how much time and money would we have to invest in doubling our revenue? As these figures are monthly, investing even $2 million would pay for itself quickly, and then we realize more profit.

Good OKR: Research Exposure Hours

Research Exposure measures the hours non-CX staff watch live or recorded CX research sessions. This is an excellent way for our teammates to see the who, what, where, when, **why**, and how *first-hand* without being responsible for world-class research planning, recruiting, interviewing, analysis, synthesis, or reporting.

Some people suggest that exposure hours are also used for CX Design. Is that the number of hours a Product Manager sits and watches someone do their information architecture and interaction design work? Nobody wants that.

Don't Go in the Basement!

You'll know that watching the sessions or videos affects teammates when they react like people watching a horror movie, and the next victim is about to walk right into the killer's obvious trap. Teammates will cringe and shout as people stumble through our PSE.

Chapter 9:   Interview: Startups

Karen T. or "KT" Lin (she/they/we) is a former Chief Experience Officer (CXO) of a seed-stage wellness startup where she instituted a Human-Centered prioritization model spanning all audiences (B2C, B2B, and internal/back-office ops) across a multi-channel portfolio of iOS, Android, SaaS, and API products.

Karen has over 25 years of experience designing web interfaces and 15+ years in design management consulting for Fortune 500s across web, mobile, IT, and IoT applications. She has a degree in human factors psychology and a graduate certificate in interactive design, and is also a Certified Usability Analyst (HFI-CUA) and a Certified Scrum Product Owner (CSPO). Karen is also currently training to become a certified executive coach and Kingian nonviolence trainer because she believes both are critical skills for empowering more UX professionals to stop UX erasure.

Debbie: How do you define customer-centricity?

Karen: Customer-centricity is the antidote to fragility and the antithesis of ego-centered product development cultures because it skillfully listens to, observes, continuously learns from, and adapts to the ever-evolving needs and expectations of end users.

Debbie: Companies, including startups, seem to be forgetting product-market fit.

Karen: One of the biggest traps that I see happen with startups is that founders become complacent with their early adopter traction. I call it "The Single-Finger Glove Trap." Imagine a startup discovers that they have some initial traction after creating a glove that only covers one finger. They get all excited. "Oh, this is amazing! Let's go out and now make as many single-finger gloves as possible in as many variations as possible!" Because to them, that is how you scale adoption in different markets.

That's a trap. They think they have traction, but they don't realize that their early traction is not enough to "cross the chasm" to reach the early majority. They forget they also need to scale for product-market fit while they're scaling for adoption. A lot of startups put all this money into entering different markets when they only had very loose product-market fit to begin with. Not surprisingly, a lot of them go bust quickly thereafter.

Debbie: *Because everybody surely wants a single-finger glove.*

Karen: Exactly. It's tempting to jump to conclusions, and there is also a stubbornness in not wanting to change what you had to do to get that initial traction. Founders want to double down on what they know has worked in the past instead of continually challenging the assumptions that got them that initial traction but won't be enough to continue growing.

Debbie: It sounds like we're falling into the typical cartoon of the MVP car, where you make a skateboard, then a kick scooter. You make the single-finger glove and think, "That went pretty well! Maybe we should make the glove with two fingers."

Karen: I don't fault people for being tempted to do that, but that's the trap. I'm sure that does get people success to a certain degree, but I'm always thinking about *does that really serve the needs of the public at the end of the day? How well does it serve target users' needs? How sustainable is this?* The answer is often, "You don't know until you've gotten enough traction." But the traction is a clue into the rest of the iceberg of what is really needed. And if you just stop at the tip of the iceberg, it's a lost opportunity to do more.

Debbie: What else do you see startups doing wrong?

Karen: There's also the data trap, the quantitative metrics trap of just studying our analytics of what people are doing in our app. The answers are not in your set of analytics because the answers are in what people are doing outside of your product and your app. People are maybe spending half a percent of their day in your app. If you're only looking at what people are doing during that half a percent of their day, you're not going to understand why they're doing what they're doing in your app.

Many people claim to be about "user obsession," but the default right now is quantitative data obsession. "Are people going to click on this button? If it's blue? Or if it's green? Let's try that." You're trying to squeeze some kind of efficiency out of some little thing, but you're shooting in the dark and missing what I call the "upstream" opportunities that matter way more. You won't get the answer via, "People are spending more time in the app now."

Every time I use Facebook's app or website, I click on something, and something totally unexpected happens. Then I wonder if a Product Manager saw that engagement went up because of this change, so now they're doubling down on this. They assume it's a good thing because it kept people in the app longer, but in reality, I was in the app longer because I lost my place and I'm just trying to find it again.

Debbie: You lifted the metrics. Congratulations!

Karen: But for terrible reasons that ended up creating frustration and hurting the brand and overall experience.

Debbie: I'm thinking about startups you might have worked with who claim to care about users and customers but build what the founders want. Where is the disconnect?

Karen: Follow the money. *How is this business making money? Who do they prioritize? B2B or B2C?* Some startups are using B2C users as bait to attract B2B customers. They're a two-sided marketplace, and they've decided that they make their money on the B2B side. They "care" about users on the B2C side, but only to the extent that they can generate extra value for their B2B customers.

How do you find that balance? For some of the companies that I worked with, I went in thinking, "Great, they're all about improving the UX for both sides of the market." But it turns out they were just interested in maintaining their leverage over B2C users in service of their B2B customers. They had traction and didn't want to change or evolve their model. They wanted to double down on it and then enter other verticals with a twisted value proposition.

There's a tendency for startups to think, "Build a better trap." And they treat people as if they need to be trapped into using a particular app or service. It ends up creating problems; even employees internally will feel the disconnect at a company because they are wary of the product they're building.

One of the first things I look at when I go to work for any company is *how people who work at that company feel about culture. How is the morale? Do they have misgivings, questions, or confusion about their product or brand?* If, internally, not everyone feels like, "This is great! This is working very well," that's already a red flag. If people who are being paid to work in the company feel half-hearted about their product or service, and they're paid to be there, how can you expect the general public to care when they're not being paid? At the earliest chance that they can get, these workers are likely to start looking elsewhere. It's the burn and churn that happens with users and employees at some of these companies.

Then they have to figure out how to bring people in. "Let's give everybody $10 cash just to use the app." They'll funnel a lot of money into marketing to try to get people in, not seeing the underlying issues contributing to retention and conversion problems. And that's a sign that you don't have a value proposition that sells itself. You have to spend all this money to get people in, but then you end up burning users and sometimes employees as well.

These companies are not clear on their UX strategy. Everybody's running around like chickens with their heads cut off because the latest investor or board member who joined is throwing their weight around and is demanding otherwise arbitrary changes. Different business units are demanding changes. There's input coming from everywhere, but there's no strategic way to align all these different interests and to really look at what needs to be built. So, they just try to build everything all at one time. Or end up fighting it out to see who gets their way.

That burns people out. You have unrealistic expectations and deadlines, and you're trying to squeeze your labor force to get more value out instead of looking for ways to grow that pie.

Figure 19: Email from Venmo, who will give the first 200,000 people who reply to this email $10 just for logging back into Venmo. This could cost them $2M and doesn't guarantee that anybody uses Venmo more after that login.

Debbie: Were there any baby steps or small changes you were able to make that nudged startups onto a path of being more customer-centric?

Karen: Sometimes it's very basic, like *let's do some usability tests.* It's one thing for me to come in and give recommendations based on heuristics and my expertise. But it's another thing for me to then show the proof of what's working and what's not working. I do it by collecting the evidence, even if it's finding ways to quantify the qualitative, and then telling the story in a convincing way to decision-makers. We have to speak their language and translate the problems that we see end-users having into business terms and metrics that matter to decision-makers.

Let's say people are having trouble creating an account. Find ways to estimate and quantify what is the impact on the business. *What are we potentially losing out on, and how much of a financial value can be assigned to that, even if it's an estimate?* Hopefully a scary one. At least then you can get some attention and hopefully some resources to work on getting to the bottom of the situation. If you just tell people, "This is confusing for users," it's very easy to have those insights swept under the rug.

There is very much a mentality of having to cut corners in order to keep pushing forward. But at some point, the corners that are being cut are going to come back and bite you in the rear. Whatever holes or leaks you have in your bucket now, as you try to scale and make that bucket bigger, those holes are going to also scale. You'll scale the problems as well as the benefits. I've said that to founders to get them to understand the importance of scaling product-market fit while scaling for market adoption.

It's important to make sure that there are enough processes in place and enough user feedback loops in place. That'll help close gaps at a reasonable pace as the company is growing and scaling. The tricky part is always assessing what "enough" means.

Debbie: I'm thinking about scary numbers for things. *X percent of people dropped off here. Another Y percent of people dropped off here. We charge for this, so that's $Z we didn't make this month.* But invariably, someone says, "It doesn't matter. Customers will figure it out."

Karen: Or, "They're not our target audience." Or, "They're tire kickers." We don't care about them, and we make excuses. If we can't quantify what all of this means to the business, the business won't care. It's not enough to appeal to, "Oh, we really messed up somebody's day." Can that be translated into cold hard cash?

CEOs are liable for the company's performance. They're liable to the shareholders for certain outcomes. If they're being negligent and not paying attention to what's hurting the business, or if they're doing things that cost more money or leave money on the table, then you have to find ways to frame it in that way. That will get some attention. It's just the reality of the business world.

Debbie: Do you find they respond to warnings of risk and potential failures? Or do they have to have failed?

Karen: It's a mix of both. Before there is a huge utter failure, there are a lot of little early warning signs. I look for early warning signs in reviews and complaints. *Why are people calling or emailing Support?* Go look at Customer Service logs. Look at what people's complaints are. *Are there patterns to the complaints? What is the root cause of those things? Are the complaints true?* Even if they're not true, how the customer incorrectly perceives our company can also signal problems.

I've had moments where we could clearly show customer problems, but the business decision was, "We don't want to do anything about this right now."

Debbie: Jumping to another topic, despite phrases like "empowered teams," we are still not seeing teammates treated equally.

Karen: I call it "Product Dictatorship" when companies and Product people have so much power and control that they can dictate what gets built. They don't have to answer to anybody else, and that's where we're running into a lot of problems. User-Centered Design is the antidote or antithesis to that. It's about making sure that end-users are incorporated in the decision-making process of what gets built. *What would really serve their needs?*

Many companies are missing out on real innovation because they're not taking User-Centered Design methods and applying them to their core product. UX is still off on the sidelines. More understanding of the value of UX in different parts of the organization can help you work closely with UX folks to figure out how to innovate.

Debbie: Anything else that might help readers looking to make positive changes and help their companies care more about what users and customers need?

Karen: Yes, an important strategy to consider is the nature of how businesses are structured to be very product-focused, organized around product lines, and to achieve operational efficiencies. It's very important to try to find ways to counterbalance that type of mindset with deeply understanding what users actually want. Find a way to represent that in your feature prioritization matrix so that you can balance out how the company engages and interacts with customers and end-users.

Often the biggest hurdle is a structural hurdle. The people who are making decisions about what the UX should be are thinking from a very product-centered mindset. They're not seeing end-users and customers – or sometimes the company – as a whole. Decision-makers are thinking about their own problems and which products can help them, sometimes selfishly.

That's where having what I call a "User Experience ecosystem strategy" helps. It's like a layer that sits between users and the rest of the business. There has to be a consistent holistic strategy – an overarching UX strategy – to counterbalance the Product-Centered nature of businesses.

Another point of confusion for a lot of people is that we think UX is a proxy for a graphical user interface. UX is the outcome. Design is the deliverable and the process of creating those deliverables. The impact of that Design and good UX outcomes are the results of how deeply the Product organization actually understands user needs, and how often those understandings are factored into the way they make decisions.

How good are you at deeply understanding what the needs are? Distributing and diluting UX activities and tasks only gets you superficial results. *How often are you using those deep understandings in decisions?*

Chapter 10: Interview: Customer Support and Call Centers

Sarah Freeman has almost 20 years in leadership advancing and pioneering strategic solutions that deliver Customer Success primarily in the Supply Chain Logistics, Healthcare, and Technology industries. Most recently, Sarah was Director of Global Business Services for UPS, responsible for Healthcare, Digital Access Program, Preferred, and International critical care groups in the U.S., Canada, and the Americas.

Before that, she led the organization's Information Technology Global Help Desk program. Earlier in her career at UPS, she held various leadership roles in the same-day critical contact center, emphasizing process implementation and program transformation. In 2022, she moved on from UPS, and is working on implementing transformational programs, including creating a new call center experience for her current employer.

She earned her Bachelor of Science Degree in Business Administration Management from the University of Nevada in Las Vegas, and has received several awards for innovation. [https://linkedin.com/in/sarah-freeman-adkins/]

Debbie: How would you define customer-centricity?

Sarah: It is a group of systems and processes that enable us to make sure that what we're delivering is what we promised the customer. *What are they paying for?* Everything we do should either reflect that or measure that.

Debbie: Your specialty lies in the customer support and call center universe. What would you say is the role of that department or division in customer-centricity?

Sarah: It's the folks that are facing the customer. No matter what the company is selling or what a company does for a customer, customers will reach out and want to talk to somebody about the service, about new services, or all kinds of different things. That Support role ensures that the people who make the business happen (like Salespeople) can sell the business, and Operations can move widgets around. But when it comes to talking to the customer about the promised services, it usually comes through Customer Support groups.

When you're in Customer Service, internally, you have some main stakeholders. Often that can be Sales to make sure that service issues don't become what customers constantly bring up in sales negotiations. The Customer Service department should work closely with the Sales and Marketing teams to know what we sell to the customer. *What is the business need for us to have these conversations with customers?*

Being customer-centric is twofold. You must deliver what you promised your customer, but the Customer Service organization also has to make sure that they're also delivering what's promised in service to the internal stakeholders. A good example of where that can go wrong would be: *we need to process as many orders or quotes as possible.* Maybe that's what the Sales team would want. If we don't want that extra call volume or we're trying to figure out how to send the customer to self-serve, we might not deliver what the internal stakeholders need us to do.

Debbie: From your experience, how can we best utilize the call center and Representatives as a source of knowledge?

Sarah: It used to be that you had to go to a call center to meet Representatives and have these small moments that mattered. Now we're meeting in a virtual space.

Call centers are data-rich. Most companies are capturing what happened on the call. If you have your call center knowledge, then what you do with that data is key because you'll have day-to-day customer-focused metrics there. In some companies, you have a call center buddy when you join and start onboarding.

Debbie: What are some bad call center metrics?

Sarah: Handle time is a bad call center metric. That's the average length of time spent on a call, email, or chat. It's a bad metric from the customer-centricity perspective because every customer will say that *they don't care how long it takes; you should stay on the phone long enough to get the right answer.* Handle time should really be used for staffing, forecasting, and planning, not as a metric that would be applied to the Representative.

Handle time is a lagging indicator. It's a symptom of other issues. For a Representative, handle time is like telling a person who is coughing to just stop coughing. You can't just go to a Rep and say, "Lower your handle time." There are ways that they will do that, and they won't be the ways that you or customers are likely to be happy with! You have to do your root cause analysis and focus on those leading indicators.

Handle time is also the worst to brag about. I was once going over metrics in front of internal stakeholders. We had quality issues and escalations that were the source of complaints, but someone wanted to talk about how it took 47 seconds instead of 20 for the Rep to pick up a call.

Everybody loves NPS. But customers don't tend to differentiate their journey: the phone call versus the Rep's attitude versus the service being satisfactory, etc. The customer might complete an NPS survey based on how they're feeling in the moment about the company. That shouldn't be put on the Representative they happened to deal with.

Another problem with NPS is that your calls are usually a fraction of your customers. If you have 1,000 customers, they don't all call you daily. Let's hope not! Using the NPS of a call center as any benchmark can be misleading. It would be better to find a touchpoint every customer has, which isn't in the call center.

Debbie: Sometimes it's hard for customers to tell the difference between a Rep who is not helping them or not correctly understanding their problem or complaint, and a Rep whose hands are tied because of company policies. Can the Reps feed stuff back to people like, "Look, I'm getting X calls a day about this sh*tty policy?"

Sarah: Some companies have a customer suggestion process, where the Rep needs to log the call a certain way to send it up. Maybe the customer wants to put in a process complaint. I like to have a process and procedures group or manager on the team. They should be listening to calls and checking to make sure that the processes are in control. When doing that, they should identify the pain points in the process for the customers, and look for opportunities to improve processes.

What do you do when you don't get an answer after calls or emails? You go to social media platforms and blast the company there. People look for CEOs on social media and they email the CEOs. Customers have created their own processes. Sometimes the process change happens because the CEO will ask someone to address the emails they're getting. It'll be a team of people in the call center or the C-suite's response team. I'm a big believer in empowering the frontline Rep to submit these issues. Let's look at them proactively so that the customer doesn't end up going to the top through social media.

The other thing would be to track escalations. When you ask for a Supervisor, most companies transfer you to a Senior Rep. It's usually not a Supervisor. From my company experience, they're just trying to get somebody that they can say knows the process, but gives the same answer. Until you escalate this a few more times, you don't get out of that level of Rep. But if you capture those escalations, what we had to research, and how we resolved it, it adds to the data that can help determine what you need to do to change your processes.

Debbie: It seems like Support is this sort of crutch that allows companies or teams to release lower quality stuff, knowing Support will clean up the mess.

Sarah: Some companies take the less costly way and don't log some call center calls. But in tech support, it's a given that they're logging phone calls because of this exact problem. This is masked in some companies because nobody says, "You had this many contacts come in when you did that launch, and this is how much it's costing." Call center and tech support costs should be added to the bottom line of your project. Companies should make sure that their Tech Support team is providing them with contact types by volume, and allowing them to build it into their cost plan.

There are plenty of good analytics pieces of software out there right now where you could go into the software, search for conversations around that feature or release, and you're going to then see how long those calls took, what they're saying in those calls, is the customer upset, etc. There are all kinds of data splitting that you can do. You can go in there and listen to the calls where the customer said a specific word. Fine-tune that; maybe you're looking for a cost word like every time they talk about the cost of the software. If you're looking for customers' problems, call centers are data-rich.

Debbie: How do we build better bridges between the Support teams/call centers and the teams working on products and services?

Sarah: Work with the Head of the call center. The title of the person you're looking for would have some form of "Process" or "Procedure" in it. They might be called a "Call Center Product Specialist."

Call centers are too often untapped. If your company has a "face," the call center is the voice. Representatives really do get a different perspective than most in the company. Check in with them often!

PART 3:   ROOM FOR IMPROVEMENT

Chapter 11: Investigation

As I'm typically joining companies as an outside consultant, I start transformation projects with an investigation. I interview dozens of people. At my 2022 consulting project, I interviewed over 70 people, from junior staff to C-level executives. My questions are around:

- What does this company do well or get right?

- What is this company not doing well? Where is there room for improvement?

- Relationships with other teammates and departments. Customer-centricity is often blocked because of processes and power struggles among teams.

- Is there anyone at the company – that they are comfortable naming – who they or others are afraid of? Who might be our allies in transforming toward customer-centricity? Who might be our detractors or against this type of change?

- Stories about when they had important work to do but were blocked. This will give me a sense of what type of work they deem important or high priority, and the people, processes, or policies that were obstacles.

Can you run this research yourself or have internal people do the investigation? You can try, but this is one of those cases where an outside consultant tends to be more effective. They're here temporarily to create change and they keep things anonymous. People are more likely to open up, share their secrets, name names, and tell stories. They might not tell *you* this because you are their coworker, their problem, or you have a good relationship with someone they don't like. That being said, I am typically learning what everybody already knows but wanted to sweep under the rug.

Finding Root Causes

It's easy to see the symptoms of what's going wrong, but how do we find the root causes? Internal research, some tough questions, critical thinking, deductive reasoning, and asking a lot of *why* gets us to the root cause. As an example:

- **We're not building what customers need.** Why? Where are we getting our ideas of what to build?

- **UX is told to wireframe Product Managers' ideas.** Why? Why aren't UX staff treated as problem solvers and partners?

- **Product Managers have product visions they like, and Engineering is under pressure to get this out fast.** Why?

- **Product and Engineering are often assessed by speed.** Why?

- **Teams are pressured to meet strategic corporate KPIs by specific deadlines.** Why?

- **Sales needs new things to sell so we make sweet, sweet money.**

There's nothing wrong with Sales selling PSE and our company making money. We lose our jobs when that doesn't happen. Customer-centricity isn't anti-revenue. When done well, customer-centricity should generate *more* revenue and ROI than customer-periphery.

Sales might be a root cause, but in this example, there are multiple root causes, even though some are also symptoms.

- If our **KPIs, OKRs, or other metrics** don't include measurements of the Customer Experience or are blatantly customer-peripheric, our metrics create problems that ripple out to teams, the quality of our work, and outcomes.

- **Deadlines.** Teams rush to get something ready for public release. Someone organizationally above them put a deadline in a slide deck. If we don't meet that expectation, our lower-level people will make a higher-level person look bad, and everybody is afraid of that.

- *Speed over quality*. We want teams to work efficiently, and I'm not suggesting that we take years to release PSE. But your customers will nearly always vote for **quality** over speed.

The root causes are where the fundamental changes will need to happen. It's easy to see a symptom and want to solve that. But if we are not getting to the core and causes, our plan to change might fall apart. Just like we don't want to solve the wrong problems for customers, we don't want to solve the wrong problems internally.

Find Allies and Detractors

As you research the symptoms and root causes, get to know who your allies in these changes will be, who will be the last to change (often called the laggards), and who might be passively or actively against the changes you want to make. Change management courses remind us not to bother too much with laggards. They are followers and will change when they see others changing or have no choice. I'm focused on the allies, but also the detractors.

At most companies where I am consulting, I can tell by my third day there who in the organization are the problems. They pressure others, they micromanage, and they create fear. We can't ignore them. They might passively be against this or try to sabotage the efforts. In a few companies, when I found which leaders were the problems and I started saying something, I was surprised by my employment ending early. This is another good reason to bring in an outsider to break the news; you don't want to risk someone sabotaging your job.

We must stay vigilant, know who we're watching, and document anything we see that looks like detractor behavior. This will be important if we need to answer to or report on why the change didn't happen as planned, why it took longer, or why it was derailed in a particular part of the organization. If our detractors are part of that reason, we will want to have kept good notes and have screenshots of conversations.

You will also need to use critical thinking. *Why would any detractor want to see the company slightly or entirely fail when the goal is improved customer-centricity?* I don't ask the detractor these things as it can seem aggressive or confrontational. There aren't any great reasons to be against customer-centricity, so I start with a hypothesis that this type of transformation works against the detractor in a more personal way.

I always wonder four things about the detractor. Will improved customer-centricity efforts or my report on what's blocking us from being more customer-centric:

- Change how detractors are paid?

- Change how they are assessed?

- Change how they are admired, respected, or rewarded?

- Bring to light any of their toxicity, bullsh*t, manipulations, or other inappropriate behaviors?

For example:

- If the detractor is from Sales, they might be worried that something we change will decrease their sales success or lower their commissions.

- If the detractor is from Engineering, they might be concerned that being more customer-centric means slowing projects down. Engineers are often assessed by speed, so they might imagine that slower projects could make them look bad.

- If the detractor is from Product, they might be concerned that they will lose their "golden child" status. Product Managers are sometimes credited with most of the success of our PSE. That would change if Product, CX, and Engineering had more equal voices and shared the recognition more equally.

- Stakeholders behind some of our most wasteful projects might be detractors when they realize that their pet projects are less likely to happen in a more customer-centric environment. We are not stakeholder-centric.

- Toxic narcissists might be detractors, period. But more specifically here, they might worry that calls for process changes and real accountability shine unwanted spotlights on them.

  o If they're good at reading people, they'll also notice that they can't manipulate or bully me, which leaves some of them desperate and ramping up their strange behaviors.

My technique is to find a place in casual conversation to ensure that each detractor knows I'm their ally, and that while there will be changes, these changes will benefit them.

- Creating more of what customers want should help Sales sell more efficiently.

- Creating more of what customers want should improve Engineering's efficiency because it will reduce risk and the time spent on bad ideas, changes, and later rework.

- We'll be grateful to our Product Managers when we create more of what customers want. Projects should go more smoothly, and advocates for customer-centricity will feel more aligned to a shared PSE vision.

- We welcome project ideas from stakeholders, but we will have to check these for user value and prioritize them accordingly.

Typical Findings and Insights

Before I can plan changes or a more extensive transformation, I am looking for everything that might hold a company back or block them from being more customer-centric. Some are obvious or known, some are harder to spot, and nearly all are the things we're sweeping under the rug.

I typically find and report professionally but bluntly on what I find. Most companies exhibit most if not all of the following:

- There's **no overarching CX or PSE strategy** other than "chase KPIs the execs want to see lifted."

  o What is our strategy to become or stay #1 in a highly competitive global or regional market? What is our strategy to improve customer satisfaction and loyalty? How will we staff up and allocate the budget to follow through on those initiatives?

- **Company strategies, KPIs, and initiatives are customer-peripheric.**

  o Facilitating a positive customer and Brand Experience will lead to revenue and business success. But we chase what can most directly make money, even if that means using deceptive designs, tricks, sneaky terms and conditions, and other ethically questionable decisions.

  o Customer complaints and fixes that we know the PSE need are delayed or deprioritized – sometimes forever – because a leader doesn't see how improving Customer Experiences will pay off in revenue, word of mouth, retention, or Brand Experience.

  o Sometimes the pressure a Sales team is under trickles down to the rest of the organization. Sales must attract and retain customers, so they might want some control over the PSE they are selling. This can lead to skewed strategies or KPIs that help Sales reach goals, often short-term goals. Be careful of how Sales pressure and short-term wins can affect the metrics the whole company is asked to focus on.

- **(At least) one or two high-level leaders, C-level executives, or business owners create most of the morale problems and company culture toxicity.** They receive promotions because they successfully make the business money or "make the numbers."

  o These toxic people are often feared, disliked, and the partial or complete reason people have been quitting or are flight risks. They often operate in defiance of company values.

  o In many cases, most of the organization knows how difficult these people are, but they have never been held accountable. The company is afraid that the success these leaders create will be hard for someone else to reproduce.

  o Often, the people working under the toxic leaders behave similarly. The difficult leaders hired them. The workers noticed the success and respect the toxic leaders seemed to have, and thought that operating the same way would win them success and respect.

  o Remember that you can find and hire people capable of creating fantastic CX and revenue successes without being toxic jerks, narcissists, or bullies. If these negative people stand out at your company, you've done a great job hiring, and can potentially replace toxic ones with people that match the positive culture you want to create. If the toxic people fit in at your organization, you have a long road ahead to replace the leadership, redefine values, and completely change the culture.

- **Stories about Costs of Poor Quality and disaster projects.**

  o These stories contain details of the money we burned, customers we alienated, and what it took to fix some of our problems or public backlashes. Yet we rarely learn from these. Companies tend to keep doing the same things repeatedly, ignoring how that didn't work last time. We are endlessly optimistic that this time, it'll magically be better.

  o We're in a poor-quality cycle, and either nobody has the authority to change it, or nobody wants to be the one to speak up and challenge the system.

- **CX or UX is badly misunderstood.** They're seen as grunt staff, the pair of hands documenting someone else's ideas and solutions. The people who make buttons bluer.

  o CX and UX leaders are not invited to general leadership meetings that other managers and leaders attend. Or they are invited but don't present because they're not seen as equals to other teams.

- **There is a disdain for or disbelief in qualitative research**, especially if the company has already disbanded an R&D (Research & Development) department or team.

  o These companies don't see deep and current customer intelligence as a competitive advantage and a great way to avoid risk and waste. It's seen as slow and unnecessary.

  o Involving current customers, trial customers, potential target users, and people using our competitors in observational studies or interviews is seen as a waste. Research isn't seen as an investment or a required step to set PSE and projects up for success.

  o In many cases, companies would rather rely on surveys since they are fast and cheap to run, no matter how flawed they usually are or how easily manipulated they can be. We do just enough research to figure out what we can probably sell to customers. We run surveys and focus groups, and ask people, "If we built this idea, would you want it?" We are left wondering why users do or don't do things, which leads to...

- **An over-reliance on solution-by-workshop and Aspirologies** (explained in a later chapter). Many companies will schedule frequent workshops when they don't understand potential or current customers, their needs, tasks, habits, motivations, decision-making, perspectives, or preferences.

  o Up to 50 people are invited to guess why users aren't doing what we want them to do. Everybody can then brainstorm and guess how we will solve these guessed-at problems.

- o The costs of wasted time and taking people away from important work add up. But more importantly, these workshops create extensive risk for the related projects. The more guesses about our customers, their needs, and their whys that we layer on each other, the more likely we are to guess incorrectly and release PSE that don't match users' needs.

- **Copying and playing catch-up with one or more competitors.** *Competitors seem successful or their features seem cool; let's do what they're doing.*

  - o That's not innovating or disrupting.

  - o We also don't know if the feature we want to copy works well for our competitors. They might be working on optimizing, changing, rethinking, or removing it. While we try to look like what they have now, they are already working on their next thing. We will always be behind if we are not more customer-centric and working to surpass competitors.

- **It's a feature factory.** Qualitative research isn't seen as an essential investment, and teams are guessing what PSE we should build. If someone's idea sounds good, we build it.

  - o It often goes out to the public as an A/B test or controlled experiment where a percentage of live users will see the variation or new feature.

  - o Teams look at one metric in the short term to judge if this feature is a winner. This is often a metric of revenue generation or user engagement, but we don't check metrics around positive Customer Experiences or task accomplishment.

- **A two-sided marketplace focused mainly on the side they think makes them the most money.** A two-sided marketplace must focus equally on both sides since attrition from even one side could mean a small or large disaster.

  - o I've seen a famous e-commerce platform more focused on buyers than sellers because of the commissions made when an item is bought.

  - o I've seen multiple job platforms more focused on the people posting the open jobs over the people searching and applying for the jobs because of the money made when jobs are posted.

  - o YouTube is a two-sided marketplace. You need content creators constantly posting new videos that content consumers can watch and interact with. YouTube might make money from ads and commissions, but it needs both sides of the marketplace to be active to be successful or profitable.

- **People are tired of hearing promises of change.** Given the disorganization and poor morale at the company, leaders have often tried to retain their staff with promises of change and exciting future visions. We handed out t-shirts or stickers with our values or a catchy phrase on them, but promised changes rarely happened the way the staff needed them. The changes might not have happened at all.

    o My interview participants will sometimes tell me in one sentence that they have "change fatigue," and in many other sentences that "things aren't changing here." This tells me that they have what I call **"promise-of-change fatigue."**

    o People often weren't even sure what the promised changes were. "They said they would work on that," or, "They said that would be improved," are non-specific promises. What are we changing? What does this look like now, what is the desired future state, what will it look like to get there, and how will we know we're on the right track? If you believe in transparency, then your teams and staff should know this.

- **Serious culture, values, behavior, and employee retention problems.** Current employees don't want to refer their friends to our open jobs, even when they stand to make a commission or finder's fee if we hire their friends. Few would want to see someone they care about working in this environment.

- **No accountability.** We are not holding anybody responsible for anything. Projects fail, money is wasted, customers leave, and staff quit, but nobody is in trouble. Responsible leaders or stakeholders are rarely put on performance improvement plans or held accountable.

    o Some companies don't fire bad leaders. They move them to another team or department, who now must deal with that awful person, which spreads the problem rather than solving it.

    o Companies need to define what accountability looks like and then follow through. Otherwise, there is no incentive to do or be better.

    o We must balance the "it's OK to fail here" vibe with the "you might be held accountable for problems you cause" vibe. It should be OK to fail, but what do we do to help that person not fail again? Are we watching how often that person or project fails and what that costs us? Not all failures are OK, and we must draw clear lines.

    o Do we have accountability and governance to push us out of cycles of mediocrity? For example, we might say that a Product Manager is accountable for the product strategy and outcomes. But how often are Product Managers coached or reprimanded after metrics show small or large project failures? Are they responsible for low ratings, angry tweets, and Customer Service utilization related to that PM's projects?

- o Leaders like to say that they will be accountable or responsible for their decision, but what does that mean? When customers are angry, taxing Customer Support, and leaving us for competitors, what does that accountability look like? If a leader's poor decisions cause CX and Engineering to do weeks or months of rework, how do we hold that leader responsible? "I'll take responsibility for the decision" are bold words floating away in the breeze. We need real accountability, follow-through, and governance.

- o Despite consultants and flavors of Agile reminding us to *learn and continuously improve*, we cycle around and do it all again the same way.

The problems I tend to find in my investigation and these common signs of customer-periphery **are not secrets**. We know about these internally. Our customers experience the shrapnel and ripple effects from these, even if they have no idea what's going on internally at our company. We can try to fool ourselves into thinking that we are doing better than we are, but who is truly buying that, inside or outside our company?

 Google
1 yr 9 mos

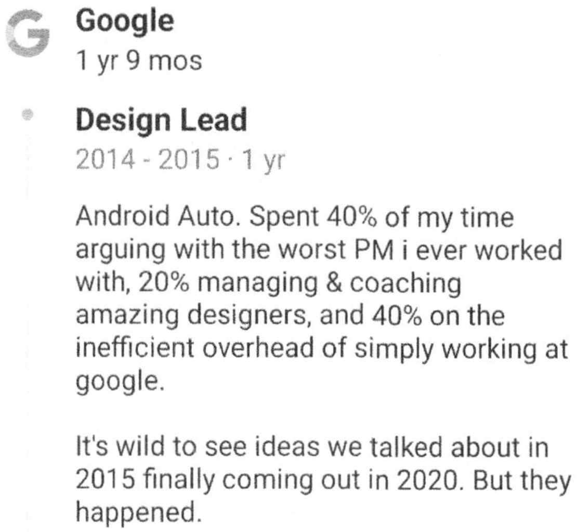

Design Lead
2014 - 2015 · 1 yr

Android Auto. Spent 40% of my time arguing with the worst PM i ever worked with, 20% managing & coaching amazing designers, and 40% on the inefficient overhead of simply working at google.

It's wild to see ideas we talked about in 2015 finally coming out in 2020. But they happened.

Figure 20: Screenshot from LinkedIn. A UX professional described a year of his work on the Android Auto project at Google as, "Spent 40% of my time arguing with the worst PM I ever worked with, 20% managing and coaching amazing designers, and 40% on the inefficient overhead of simply working at Google. It's wild to see ideas we talked about in 2015 finally coming out in 2020. But they happened."

Likelihood of Transformation Success

When I propose a transformation project, I check multiple times that the company really wants to make change, is open to hearing where their faults are, and that my team will have the authority to make change. If I see any hints that the company does not want this type of change, I either redefine the engagement or sometimes decline the project; it won't make sense to be in a "change agent" role without the proper authority.

I have also found that companies who are not feeling enough pain are not inspired to create change, even toward improved customer-centricity, and even when they are sure they want change. Executives are often selling down the hierarchy that there will be a lot of change. Staff see various consultants come and go, everybody is sent a book or they're sent to training, but the advice is rarely taken. The reality at the company, especially at executive levels, is: *why take a second look at ways of working, culture, processes, or accountability when the money is rolling in? Every meeting is a celebration of achieving our goals and making money. Why should we change? What we're doing is working!*

What's our compelling imperative for change? What's on fire? What is not going well at our company? Where are we feeling the pain of risks we ignored? What consequences and crises are we facing? The companies I've worked with who were hungry to change have many of the same problems as the companies resisting change.

People who say, "We have it under control," rarely have it under control.
If it were under control, we wouldn't spend even 10 seconds discussing it because *it's not a problem*.
If there is an "it" to control, we have a problem.

Every company has these internal and external pain points, but not every company is willing to admit them, even behind closed doors among senior leadership. The more honest we can be about where we are broken or have room for improvement, the more likely our transformation will succeed. If we have been sweeping this under the rug, we will need to do some digging and scrape away the crusty layers of "we are fine" and "we are good enough."

I also find that the more future-minded a company is, the more likely they are to be inspired to change. For example, you might be number one or two in your market now. If we are complacent, we applaud ourselves for that success, and we don't want to change much or anything because *that's how we got this success*. But if we recognize our growing competition – or the possibility that a well-funded startup could be a threat within a year – then we need to work now on strategies and improvements that can keep us a leader.

What Competition?

I noticed that a few startups competing against Company X had received massive funding from Silicon Valley VCs. I asked some of Company X's executives (privately and separately) what the strategy or plan was if these startups moved into their region or niche. They confidently told me those startups will come to Company X for acquisition.

I then asked each executive what the strategy or plan would be if those startups went to their top competitor – #2 in the market and a serious global player – to be acquired. Some executives stared at me in silence. Some executives couldn't imagine that outcome and were sure their company would be the one to purchase the startup.

Company X is unprepared for competitors' growth, and will be surprised later when their assumptions turn out wrong. They will scramble to create and enact plans.

Transformation has a better chance of success when more people, especially leaders, notice what's breaking down or not working as well as planned, including:

- Scrum Masters ask why we have so many failed MVPs.

- Project Managers examine the cost of features we guessed at.

- Agile Coaches realize that little or no innovation comes out of workshops.

- Strategists or Marketing wonder why meeting our goals is so hard.

- Support and CX report higher complaints, angry tweets, and low ratings.

- Sales struggles to win or retain customers.

- We're losing to competitors.

- "We're hearing more about the importance of CX."

- "Amazon is customer-obsessed, so we should do that too."

Any open door is an open door. Let's walk through.

Chapter 12: Common Research Mistakes

Having little, incorrect, flawed, or zero evidence can undo **evidence-based decision-making**. Poor "evidence" can drag us in the wrong direction, give us false confidence, and create risk and waste. The most common research mistakes are skipping research, skimping on it, or doing it poorly.

> *"If there's time and money to run a business, there's time and money to become informed. You wouldn't order takeout without doing research. Would you put your hand in a door, they hand you a bag, and that's dinner? You'd say, 'No, I want to read reviews. I want to talk to people. I'm investing $50 in takeout.' But we're doing a million-dollar project, and it's like, [in tone of disgust] 'Uh. We have to do research. ☹' That's ridiculous."*
> *– Erika Hall [two quotes combined and edited for brevity https://cxcc.to/a187]*

Our strategies and initiatives derive from – or are at least influenced by – our business and customer intelligence. Business and customer intelligence derive from qualitative and quantitative research data. Therefore, one of the earliest weaknesses in our critical path is **the quality of our research**.

Evidence

It's easy to say that we want evidence-based decision-making, Design, or strategies. But which "evidence" should be included or excluded? Is all data valid? Answering these questions requires critical thinking and self-awareness. We must look closely at our techniques, methods, and analysis.

Here are some critical thinking questions that can help us determine whether we should use a particular piece of qualitative or quantitative data:

- **Do we know that the data was manipulated?** We or someone else might have manipulated the study or its results to prove or disprove a certain point. Data manipulation can range from dishonest to unethical. If we know that our data is dishonest or compromised, don't use it as "evidence."

- **Was the data generated without following best practices?** If our qualitative or quantitative study was with too few people, or if our experiment was run with too short of a time period, this might not be good "evidence."

- **Is it recent and actionable?** Do we have current qualitative data that helps us understand who, what, where, when, why, and how? Can we create strategies and initiatives that guide our direction from this evidence? Do we look at the data and wonder *what we do about that?*

- **Is our knowledge complete?** Teams sometimes run a study and then realize there's still a lot they don't know. Rather than taking the time to collect proper evidence and conduct a follow-up study, they sometimes go with what they have, and augment it with guesses and assumptions. It's best to hold off on conclusions or actions until we have a complete set of data that answers our questions and replaces assumptions with knowledge.

- **Would it stand up in court?** We are probably not going to court with this data, but we can use this metaphor. Would a highly qualified research expert say that we have factual and scientific data?

Guesses and Assumptions

Some frameworks and models suggest that we can move forward with guesses and assumptions, with or without validation. The assumption about assumptions is that using them will save time. You'll often hear that you will figure out later if guesses or assumptions were wrong.

This assumes that months later, when the outcomes of our project are measured, we will know which guess was incorrect or which conclusion we drew ended up invalid. This *speed over quality* approach imagines that we won't need root cause analysis or to investigate where we went wrong. *We will just know,* and then we can fix that mistake. "Work from assumptions" approaches also downplay the ripple effect of guesses and assumptions.

One example would be personas, which document our target audience archetypes. Personas are an artifact of qualitative research; we can detail target audience behaviors and needs because we studied them. Cross-functional teams can use personas to keep different customer types in mind as we strategize, prioritize, Design, and build. The common mistake here is guessed-at or made-up personas, often called "proto-personas." Rather than researching first, we create proto-personas from what we think we know about customer groups. Teams sometimes create a survey or short research project to validate the proto-personas. We also run into problems when the validation study is specifically designed to validate our work as correct.

> **If research is important, why we didn't research first? Researching first takes less time than guessing first, researching to see if you were right, figuring out where assumptions were incorrect, and fixing mistakes.**

Please do not treat as fact guesses, assumptions, unanswered questions, or hypotheses – even if "validated" by a research study designed to validate them. True concept validation goes way beyond what we often use: waiting lists, fake doors, surveys, and asking some people if they like our idea.

Time and budget spent on validating assumptions could have been spent on the generative qualitative research that would have better informed cross-functional teams and multiple projects. **We will find PSE-market fit by understanding the behaviors of those in our target markets, and then building the PSE that match behaviors and needs.**

Why start with assumptions? Start with research, evidence, and knowledge to avoid the wasted time and effort often invested into assumption lists, workshops, validation, and overconfidence. Guesses and assumptions should not be the foundations of strategies, initiatives, or projects. They are risks we should document. They should inspire us to create generative qualitative research projects that will dispel myths, clear up confusion, and replace guesses and assumptions with facts.

> *"Sign that you're developing software using waterfall: Assumptions are* ***not*** *risks to be evaluated urgently but instead are treated as truths waiting to be disproved."*
> *– Paul Weakley*

If we paid close attention to the costs and time associated with PSE based on cycles of guesses or assumptions – plus the costs and time of failures, root cause analysis, and rework – we should find that it's faster and cheaper to wait for knowledge and work from it than to run with guesses and assumptions.

Try It: Validated and Failed

Think about the ideas that startups and more established companies say they validated. I remember the startup who told me how they validated that surfers need an app to coordinate going surfing. They talked to some surfers, who thought a special app just for coordinating going surfing sounded good. You can Google "failed startup ideas" and "failed Kickstarters" for more.

How many of these validated ideas found no PSE-market fit? How many pivoted? How many failed? How many invented use cases that didn't really exist?

Inventing Use Cases

Finding or inventing a use case doesn't mean that we are working from good data or that anybody will utilize the feature as we imagine. We can create a use case for just about anything. Bad use case advice sounds like, "Just imagine someone in a realistic scenario using your PSE to accomplish their goal." Great PSE is mission critical to our company and should not be based on guesses or imagination.

Even with hindsight, we *could* imagine uses cases for New Coke, Crystal Pepsi, Microsoft's Zune MP3 player, Blackberry's OS, McDonalds' Arch Deluxe burger, and other textbook PSE failures. They all had use cases and seemed like good ideas, but they didn't have PSE-market fit.

Understanding Target Customers' Use Cases

I use a Tractive GPS tracker on Olivia, the dog who loves to roam around the countryside. I can track her, which is especially great when our other dogs escape and Olivia joins in.

We were over the moon when Tractive created a product with two pieces that fit together: one was the body of the tracker, and one was the battery. This meant we could easily keep one battery charging and swap them out. We immediately upgraded Olivia's hardware to this version, and bought the extended-life spare battery that lasts days.

We were disappointed that Tractive's new 2022 version was one piece without a separate battery. This shows that the company mainly envisions one use case: *My pet is safely home at night, and I can take the tracker off them and charge it up.*

However, we have a different use case: *We have five dogs. Four live outside and love to escape at all hours, mainly between midnight and 3am. We want Olivia's daughter Diana to start wearing a Tractive because Diana orchestrates the escapes. But if she's an escape artist 24/7 and lives outdoors, when can we take off the tracker to charge it? We would need a tracker in two pieces so we can swap out Diana's battery as it runs low.*

Tractive might assume that all or nearly all of their customers can charge the tracker at night. Have they researched with current and target customers to learn more about who they are tracking, why, and where that pet lives? Do they understand the spectrum of use cases for their product?

Decisions like only offering one version of your PSE can facilitate customers leaving or never choosing you in the first place because your PSE don't fit their use cases.

Surveys

CX Quantitative Researchers and Marketing use surveys quite often. CX Qualitative Researchers use surveys less frequently, mainly to collect and screen potential study participants. Surveys are often *not* a great way to grow our customer intelligence and deeply understand customers' needs and tasks.

Taking surveys has made you familiar with common survey flaws. You've seen questions that didn't make sense and questions that seemed to answer themselves. You may have sensed that the people who wrote the survey were fishing for one particular answer.

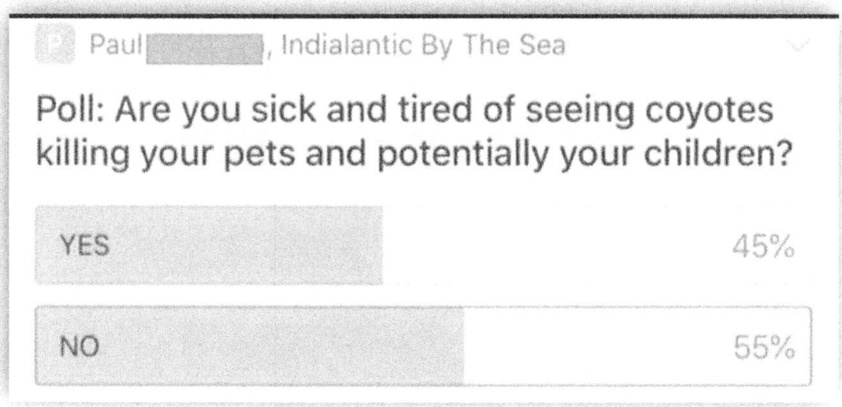

Figure 21: Screenshot of a poll asking if you are sick and tired of seeing coyotes killing your pets and potentially your children, yes or no. Some say this survey was real, and some say it was a parody. But we have all seen survey and poll questions that were fishing for a particular answer.

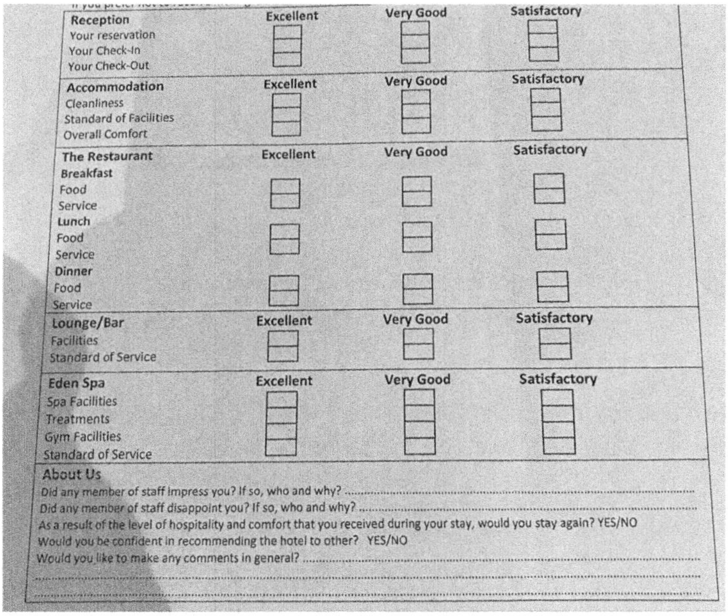

Reception	Excellent	Very Good	Satisfactory
Your reservation			
Your Check-In			
Your Check-Out			
Accommodation	Excellent	Very Good	Satisfactory
Cleanliness			
Standard of Facilities			
Overall Comfort			
The Restaurant	Excellent	Very Good	Satisfactory
Breakfast			
Food			
Service			
Lunch			
Food			
Service			
Dinner			
Food			
Service			
Lounge/Bar	Excellent	Very Good	Satisfactory
Facilities			
Standard of Service			
Eden Spa	Excellent	Very Good	Satisfactory
Spa Facilities			
Treatments			
Gym Facilities			
Standard of Service			

About Us
Did any member of staff impress you? If so, who and why? ....
Did any member of staff disappoint you? If so, who and why? ....
As a result of the level of hospitality and comfort that you received during your stay, would you stay again? YES/NO
Would you be confident in recommending the hotel to other? YES/NO
Would you like to make any comments in general? ....

Figure 22: Miles C. Thomas [https://linkedin.com/in/milesct] shared this photo of a survey he received after a hotel stay. Each parameter's rating is a choice of "Excellent," "Very Good," or "Satisfactory." There are no choices lower than "Satisfactory."

Some surveys use leading wording to tell you what your answer should be.

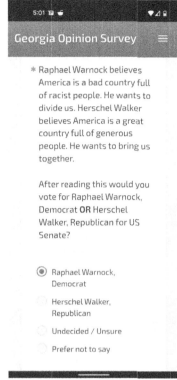

Figure 23: Real survey about 2022 Georgia politics. The survey question states, "Raphael Warnock believes America is a bad country full of racist people. He wants to divide us. Herschel Walker believes America is a great country full of generous people. He wants to bring us together. After reading this, would you vote for Raphael Warnock, Democrat OR Herschel Walker, Republican for US Senate?" My question is: can you tell which candidate's team wrote the survey?

You've seen surveys where you felt that none of the answers matched your opinions. Or the answers you wanted to pick weren't available choices.

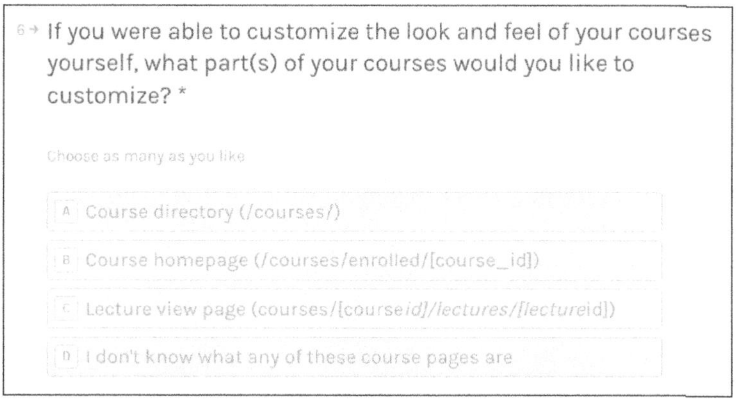

6→ If you were able to customize the look and feel of your courses yourself, what part(s) of your courses would you like to customize? *

Choose as many as you like

A Course directory (/courses/)

B Course homepage (/courses/enrolled/[course_id])

C Lecture view page (courses/[course*id]/lectures/[lecture*id])

D I don't know what any of these course pages are

Figure 24: Screenshot of a survey question asking if you were able to customize the look and feel of your online course, what parts of the course you would like to customize. Your choices are the course directory, the course homepage, the lecture view page, or "I don't know what any of these course pages are." There is no choice for "I don't want to customize any of these" or "it's hard for me to answer this without seeing what you are talking about."

While some try to answer the survey honestly, many survey takers either give up on the survey or answer the questions the way the survey seems to want them to. This can lead to flawed, if not invalid, results.

After a trip with MSC Cruises, I received a survey asking on a scale of 1 to 10 how satisfied I was with each of 12 elements of a cruise. I gave various scores, including a low score for the "onboard experience." I finished the open comments section with a fact: "I returned home from an MSC cruise and immediately booked my next cruise on Norwegian." *Ouch!*

What went wrong for me? Can we tell from the survey? Will anybody read that comment? Will the comment be analyzed by a bot who will see "booked my next cruise" and think this is positive? Will the bot see a competitor's name and think this is a favorable comparison? Will we average up some scores and say we're doing well enough? The survey is unlikely to be actionable unless we follow it up with qualitative research with former cruisers to learn what can be improved.

Surveys also suffer from the flaws of self-reporting. From pride to rose-colored glasses to lack of self-awareness and other reasons, people sometimes do not accurately report what they do or even their opinions. Flawed results used to inform strategies, decisions, or PSE are hazardous. Additionally, if data and analytics don't make your next steps or actions clear, it's a hint that you need qualitative research to give numbers context and bring them to life.

In a LinkedIn post, David Hamill [https://linkedin.com/in/davidhamill/] told the story of a survey run at a former workplace (edited for brevity) [https://cxcc.to/a192]:

"One company I worked with was planning a new feature which asked their users to provide more information about themselves in a process. It was an optional step and there was some internal dispute about whether or not many users would opt to do it. One team decided to survey their users and ask if they would be willing to provide this extra information about themselves. Over 80% of respondents said they would. When the feature was released, less than 0.4% of users actually provided the extra information."

We've looked at poor survey examples and some disadvantages, but surveys aren't always disasters. They can be valid, meaningful, and actionable. But like any other research method, planning, execution, and analysis require time and expertise.

Stepping Stone: Surveys

Stakeholders love how surveys quickly give us tangible numerical data. But what did we learn from the survey, and what do we still not know? After a survey, we are likely to still have unanswered questions or lack details, especially around *why* we received certain answers.

This is our opportunity to raise the need for a qualitative study to answer these questions and dive into *why*. Therefore, while planning surveys, plan a follow-up qualitative research study to fill in the customer intelligence gaps.

Some people suggest that you need a statistically significant quantitative study, such as a survey, to validate the results of a qualitative study, such as interviews. This is not necessary for two key reasons:

1. **A thoroughly planned qualitative research study with the correct number of well-recruited participants is valid.** It does not need further validation.

2. **Surveys are extremely easy to manipulate.** Questions might be biased, leading, clearly fishing for one particular answer, or locking you into a false choice. People hoping to validate or invalidate previous research, an idea, or a hypothesis can twist the survey results to say whatever they want.

Therefore, we should not use an easily distorted method to validate or invalidate anything.

Focus Groups

Focus groups, a type of generative qualitative research, are moderated discussions about a topic or your PSE. As these are done with multiple people in a group setting, you can collect a lot of opinions from the participants in a short time.

But focus groups have a variety of concerns and drawbacks, including:

- **Groupthink**. People are often more comfortable with agreement and consensus. They might not speak up if they have a different opinion or perspective.

- **Fear of judgment**. Sometimes, people are not honest or forthcoming on the assumption that others in the group are judging them.

- **Dominant voice**. One powerful personality in the room can sway the conversation or make more introverted or shy people stay quiet. Sometimes this pseudo leader works to convince others of their opinion, which further flaws the results.

- **Bad questions**. We shouldn't ask a group of people how much they like a concept, how they might use it in the future (they can't predict that), or how their colleagues might use it (they really can't predict that). We shouldn't ask people sales questions like "would you pay for this" (they might not control the budget), "would you pay more if we added a particular feature" (another future prediction), etc.

- **Knowledge gap**. Are we asking people about a topic they don't know much about? Are we assuming they have knowledge or experience that they don't?

- **Wrong method for task performance studies**. We would not ask people in a focus group to perform a task together if they are strangers and would not normally perform this task together. We would not ask participants to perform a task one at a time if others were watching. Spectators will then be biased by how an earlier participant did something. They gain knowledge about the topic or PSE, which changes their perspectives.

- **What people say or predict about themselves often doesn't match what they do**. Thanks to pride, rose-colored glasses, lack of self-awareness, and in some cases, purposeful deception.

CX/UX Research Versus Market Research

According to SBA.gov [https://cxcc.to/a137], market research addresses the following:

- **Demand.** Is there a desire for your product or service? Surveys or interviews might ask people if they are interested in your idea or how likely they might be to purchase a described product or service.

- **Market size.** How many people would be interested in your offering? This is often a statistic representing the total possible population of buyers. For example, our product is for pets, our target audience is families in America who own pets, and there are 90.5 million American families with at least one pet.

- **Economic indicators.** What are your target audiences' income ranges and employment rate? Perhaps we are only looking for American pet owners on a tight budget, who make under $50,000 per year.

- **Location.** Where do your customers live and where can your business reach? Further narrowing the target audience, we might want pet owners making under $50,000 per year and living in or near the 20 largest cities in the USA.

- **Market saturation.** How many similar options are already available to consumers? This is an analysis of competitors.

- **Pricing.** What do potential customers pay for these alternatives? What might people be willing to pay for your PSE?

Market research is often about predicting what people will do or what they will respond to in the future. We use these predictions to adjust our marketing, advertising, price, and other elements. *What imagery should we use so they associate joy with our yogurt? How many people said they would pay for this idea our company has?*

Market research often fuels predictions. We might estimate that it will take us six months to attract 10,000 users paying $10 monthly. We might estimate that six months later, we will retain 80% of that 10,000. **Do we ever go back and check how often our predictions are correct?** How long did it take us to get to 10,000 users paying $10 per month? Six months later, what percent stayed with us? Checking our predictions versus reality might lead to tough but important conversations about our predictions and the market research feeding them.

CX research stays away from predictions, hypothetical purchases, and whether people claim to like a described idea. CX research is typically an investigation into people and their tasks, behaviors, perspectives, needs, and decisions. CX and market research are often very different animals, but some companies prefer market research and don't invest in CX research for the following reasons:

- They believe it is a **duplication of efforts**. If the differences between CX research and market research are not understood, we might imagine that we only need one of them.

- **Confirmation bias.** Market research and CX research sometimes return opposite results. Market research might tell us *we have a good idea people want,* while CX research might indicate that *our idea is not the right match for our target audiences.* Only one of these can be true; thanks to confirmation bias, we would rather hear the former.

    o That's not universal; some market research brings us the cold, unvarnished truth we need to hear. But too often, our market research validates what we were hoping to validate, making it more attractive than CX research.

- **Market researchers say they do CX or user research.** If that is an inaccurate statement, or that research is not being done well (remember our earlier standards for high-quality research), we are missing out on a lot of important evidence gathering and customer intelligence.

- Executing CX research well **requires specialists** you might not want to hire, and time and budget you might not want to invest. You might have staff who can do market research quickly, prioritizing speed over other factors.

- **Our PSE guesses will be "good enough."** If 78% of survey respondents want a better hotel check-in experience, what should we Design to make check in "better?" Do we *know* what "better" means from our customers' perspectives, or are we guessing or assuming what they would prefer? If the market research can't inform these decisions or our Design, we might unfortunately rely on PSE guesses that won't be good enough.

- "500 people responded to a survey" **sounds more impressive** than "we observed 24 people." The assumption is that the method that involved the most people wins, which is not necessarily true.

You can continue using the market research that delivers accurate and actionable business and customer intelligence. Transforming who does your research and how the research is done are fundamental shifts that companies interested in customer-centricity will need to make.

We've All Been in That Meeting

Have you ever been in a meeting where people were surprised or confused that the PSE we built in response to our market research was a failure? *People told us they wanted this thing; we built it, and it doesn't seem to be needed, liked, or utilized! We asked in a survey if they wanted more customization and 72% said yes. We gave them more customization and they aren't using it!*

Meeting attendees are typically shocked and unsure of how this happened. A common assumption is that our customers must have lied to us. The blame should be on the quality of our research. We should not imagine that some or all of our customers are liars. We should take a second look at the research methods we used and the questions we asked. If this is a survey, we must also look at the answer choices.

Do Customers Lie to Us?

When we run focus groups, surveys, or interviews asking people if they like our idea or would buy something like it, we might hear a lot of "yes." "Sure, I'd buy that." "Yes, I'd use it." "Of course, my colleagues would like something like that." But what are people saying "yes" to if they can't try a realistic prototype or live version of this feature right now?

Everybody imagines something that would work fantastically well for them, and they report liking the idea or being sure they would use it. We can't see into their heads. They are all imagining that when we release this feature, it'll be like what they imagined, which means there is a high probability of disappointment. Everybody imagines different executions of different ideas.

This does not mean users should sketch their solutions. People are usually poor at fully understanding their problems, let alone Designing the best solutions. It's up to excellent research to learn their tasks, needs, preferences, and context. We can use that knowledge to Design what works best across target audiences, which might be an even better concept than what each person imagined.

Try It: Did We Imagine the Same Features?

"Would you like your project management software to improve collaboration features?" This is the type of question we might ask in a focus group, survey, or interview. Positive answers help us green light a project we are considering. But when you hear "improved collaboration in project management software," which features or functions do you imagine?

I imagine a system that lets me bring in guests and light collaborators for free. A system that lets me play out different project paths and get feedback from collaborators. A system that facilitates multiple people voting in a prioritization matrix, and calculating results.

Did we imagine similar things? If the project management software company built my ideas but not yours, would you feel like they met your needs or expectations? Despite telling a Researcher *you wanted collaboration features,* might you end up not using the ones you get?

Ask Customers What They Want

A common mistake is to assume that a feature suggestion coming from a customer is a mandate. *Isn't it customer-centric to have the public post ideas and vote them up? Can we find a few customers and ask them what they want or what our PSE are missing? Can we consider that "user research" because we might learn what people want?*

Users don't always understand their problems and rarely are the best architects of their own solutions, especially since they might stay in the "box" of what they imagine is feasible or possible.

When teams review feature requests and suggestions, they tend to do the ones they wanted to do anyway, and ignore the ones that we previously marked lower priority. This is our confirmation bias: our tendency to search for, interpret, favor, and recall information in a way that confirms or supports our prior beliefs or values.

I recommend against any questions that expect the user to be the architect of their own solutions.

Can This Customer Solve Her Own Problem?

I was once near the gate for my flight when the agent announced that all carry-on bags must be gate-checked. A woman went to the agent's desk with her large purse and a wheeled bag. The agent hastily handed her a gate check ticket and turned her attention to someone else. I watched the woman attach the gate check ticket to her purse, which she was not going to gate check. When she reached the end of the jet bridge, she saw all the wheeled bags and left hers without the gate check bar code.

After the flight landed, the announcement told us to wait in the jet bridge to pick up our gate-checked bags. This woman didn't stop. I later saw her at baggage claim without her gate-checked wheeled bag. She might have been waiting for it to arrive on the baggage carousel. I have no idea how she and her gate-checked bag were reunited or how long that took.

What was this customer's knowledge gap? She didn't understand gate checking, and it wasn't intuitive. She didn't understand what to do with the bar code ticket, what to do with her bags, or how to get them later. She might have been a new flyer, not fluent in the language the gate agent spoke, or had never gate checked a bag before and was new to the process. But *she didn't know that she didn't know.* She confidently put the gate check bar code on her purse, and carried on with boarding the flight.

What might this customer request if she were leaving us suggestions? Given that it probably took her a long time to get her carry-on bag, she thinks the airline is slow. She thinks someone tried to steal her bag. She wants our airline to improve the baggage retrieval system. Since she didn't know she accomplished the gate checking task incorrectly, she is unlikely to know how to make gate checking better.

What opportunity might we miss if we take her suggestions at face value and assume this is what our customers "want?" The real opportunity here is around the knowledge gap. While our airline might have room for improvement in baggage handling, we might miss that this problem was a lack of understanding of gate checking procedures.

We might have all the empathy in the world for this customer, but if we don't correctly identify her problem – or we leave it to her to correctly guess her problem and solution – we might never truly solve her problem.

Product Discovery Research Mistakes

Teams in discovery mode typically wonder who would want our idea. They hope to validate that we're going in the right direction. But discovery is not about proving ourselves right and our ideas valid. Discovery must be a quality-focused problem-finding adventure that sets our PSE and customers up for success.

Good generative qualitative research reduces discovery project effort and risk by helping us deeply understand our target audiences, their needs, and behaviors. This allows us to define problems thoroughly so that we can then work on solving those problems.

Discovery isn't "who might want the thing we want to build?" It's "what should we build for the people we want to attract and retain?"

Reducing or skipping generative research sounds fast, but it can add steps later that ultimately make our process slower. Compare the following:

- **Conduct generative qualitative research first.** Unmet needs, insights, and pain points are revealed and prioritized. We understand who our customers are and the problems they need solved. We catalog their needs and create short- and long-term PSE strategies based on this knowledge. Research-informed and evidence-based solutions ensure that we solve the right problems and deliver high quality and value. Designs go through rounds of testing and improvement before Engineering writes code or anything goes to the public, reducing risk and embarrassment.

versus

- **Brainstorm ideas first.** We wonder which ideas are good, who might want or pay for these features, and which experiments will tell us which ideas might create business – and hopefully customer – success. We build our favorite ideas for experimentation. Hopefully, we designed these experiments well and are watching the right metrics for an appropriate period of time. Weeks later, our results are in, and we have a sense of which experiments were successful, though we might now know why. Having validated our early solution concepts, we stick with these ideas and design them further.

  - If our experiments demonstrated that our ideas have little or no potential for success, we circle back and brainstorm new ideas. We may have wasted time and customer goodwill while only being slightly smarter about the best PSE direction. We might be doing a mediocre job solving the wrong problem.

  - If the experiments testing our ideas were flawed, we might accidentally validate a poor idea, increasing the probability of risks and mistakes.

How much time do cycles of guessing and experiments take versus investing in early generative research that would set us up with knowledge and reliable data?

What most teams call "discovery" isn't really discovery, especially where it doesn't start with *discovering* more about target audiences, their tasks, and their unmet needs. Some teams that claim they want to get away from the "feature factory" add research so that they can "build what customers want." Feature factories start with ideas, possible solutions, or guesses and assumptions about target audiences. A feature factory's "discovery" research often aims to find if anybody likes the idea we already have. Accidentally, or on purpose, teams sometimes design the study that confirms the potential market for the idea. **Any research with goals like "find who wants our idea" or "check if customers like this feature we're thinking of building" is likely to be a self-fulfilling prophecy.** We will find what we're looking for, and green light our projects.

These types of "discovery" research goals show that we're using *evaluative* research. Our idea is a sketch or a prototype, and we want to know if people like it. In User-Centered Design, evaluative research is toward the end of the process. Discovery-related research should be at the beginning. Answer open questions and replace guesses and assumptions with knowledge and data as early in the process as possible.

Some trainers demand that product discovery start with generative qualitative research that guides us to deeply understand "the underlying user need." They recommend observational research so we understand what people do now, their workflows, and where those go well or poorly. I agree with these recommendations.

A discovery process should discover everything we can about target customers and their unmet needs, tasks, and the contexts in which they might use our PSE.

Yet despite how often thorough generative research is recommended or required, we rarely allocate the budget or time for this. We listen to the voices calling for *speed over quality* in our research and discovery.

Our "discovery" efforts are too-often a "validation" process disguised as discovery. We want to hear that our ideas are good and likely to be marketable to our audiences. Product discovery should be a solution-agnostic investigation. Put aside the ideas or hypotheses you have, and work with CX Researchers so that the team can have the knowledge and evidence that will drive smarter decisions. The required time and money are worthwhile investments that more than pay for themselves with later customer satisfaction and loyalty.

Hypothesis First?

You will often hear that we need to form a hypothesis and then test or validate our assumptions. This *sounds* right and appears to be from the "Scientific Method." But in our speed-focused world, we forgot that forming a hypothesis, testing it, and drawing conclusions are steps three, four, and five of the Scientific Method.

Step one is **observe**, which utilizes observational and qualitative research methods. This is our full generative research process: planning, recruiting, execution, analysis, and synthesis. Now we have our solid evidence.

Step two is **question**, which is our problem definition and framing.

Step three of the Scientific Method is forming the **hypothesis**, which is our informed best guess at the solution. If the hypothesis is not based on reliable and high-quality evidence and research data, then our hypothesis could be risky and wasteful. Assumptions that can be disproven by existing current research data should be thrown out; do not waste time experimenting or trying to validate these when we already have the answer.

Our hypothesis wouldn't be just an idea, a sticky note, or an entry on a canvas or template. We would have to move through the User-Centered Design process so that we have something to test. This includes designs, prototypes, and Customer Experience improvements, all based on our earlier research and clear problem definitions.

A hypothesis is literally a supposition, which means that we don't know if it's a good solution or not. Step four includes **designing and conducting the experiment** that will test if it's an excellent solution. This is our evaluative research. Note that in most cases, we do not need to release something live to the public to test our hypothesis. We can work from rapid prototypes and early concept models so that we are not burning Engineering's time or the public's trust on a possible solution with unknown value.

Step five **analyzes test data and draws conclusions.** Was our hypothesis correct? Partially or wholly? Our testing should reveal room for improvement, which circles us back to step three of the Scientific Method. The experiment might show that our problem needs to be redefined, circling us back to step two. This leads us to a new solution hypothesis, fresh or updated designs, and another round of testing.

Step six is to **report** on what you found, sharing the knowledge and details with others.

"Start with a hypothesis" can sound Agile or Lean, but is misguided and introduces risk. Don't skip the early generative, exploratory, and discovery research that inform our potential solutions. Guesses and assumptions based on minimal, flawed, or outdated information *could* be called a hypothesis, but should be avoided. **"Hypothesis first" methods often put us in a single-solution box before we have fully understood problems from our customers' perspectives.**

Those who are familiar with User-Centered Design or Human-Centered Design will notice the similarity between them and the Scientific Method. CX practitioners are scientific about problem finding and solving.

Ask the SMEs

A common mistake is to believe that we can skimp on or skip research because we can ask a subject matter expert (SME) for their opinion. The assumption is that someone with extensive domain knowledge would know the right direction and make the best decision. Critical thinking requires us to ask if that person can really speak for all possible users. *Is this person still an active consumer, or might their knowledge be outdated? Do they share current perspectives of our varied target audiences? Can they speak for everybody?*

While asking one person what they think is faster and cheaper than running a research study with a representative slice of our target audiences, we must estimate and document the risk. An SME can be a good person to help us gather domain knowledge more quickly, but they are not a stand-in or replacement for fresh research with our target audiences.

What Would We Like the Research to Say?

Qualitative and quantitative research can be manipulated. To avoid this, specialists must have the appropriate time, budget, and access to participants. They must have the freedom to do their best work and report on it honestly.

Some professional Researchers are asked to provide an "editable" version of their report so that a teammate, manager, or other stakeholder can make changes. This should be seen as dishonest and possibly unethical. It should run against our values and not even be an option. Manipulated data might make a stakeholder "happy," but what are the consequences and risks of utilizing incorrect or manipulated data in our projects?

If we want to validate something, we can design the study that will validate it. To illustrate this point, when I do live training, I like to walk up to someone seated at the front of the room. I ask if they like my shirt (I wear a custom rugby shirt with a Delta CX logo). The person thinks for a second and says, "Yes." I then ask, "Would you like one like this?" Most say, "Yes." *I have just validated that they like my shirt and would like one like it!* But I know that's not true, so I ask, "Do you really?" Then they say, "No." The audience laughs, the tension is cut, and we talk about research mistakes when we ask the wrong questions, the wrong people, or use the wrong methods.

I have seen companies specifically hire the least experienced Researchers they can find, and ask them to do a study that proves the idea or potential solution is a good one. Researchers in their first job don't want to be fired, so they do what they are told, and *amazingly* we prove that our concept is good and people like it. Researchers at all levels might receive this request, but a more experienced Researcher is likely to push back, be solution-agnostic, and request, if not demand, unbiased research.

Do We Want Minimalist, Lean, or the Least Amount of Research We Can Do?

Low effort "research" sounds like a time and money saver, but can be *speed over quality*. Think critically about any methods or approaches aimed at doing lightning-fast research or the least amount of research possible. In many cases, these approaches not only recommend reducing the time or scope of our research, but they typically also recommend that non-Researchers execute specialized research tasks.

If your company insists on these types of approaches, we should be adding the following to our risk documentation:

- We had non-specialists do specialized tasks.

- We knew the best research methods to select based on the open questions and the project, but we selected other methods.

- We understood the correct number of people to recruit, but we chose fewer people.

- We knew who our target audiences are, but we chose people from another population.

- We knew that proper documentation of the entire research project was the right way to set up multiple departments in our company for success. But we chose to create minimal documentation or skip essential artifacts.

There are times when the cheapest and fastest supermarket brand microwave pizza will make a "good enough" meal. You could eat pizza napoletana, handmade by experts using the best imported ingredients, or local ingredients if you are in Napoli, Italy. We might not understand how low-quality the microwave pizza is until we've taken a pizza-eating tour of Napoli.

Figure 25: Photos of Naples-style pizza from Italy (so fluffy and delicious, perfection in every bite) and a supermarket brand microwave pepperoni pizza (factory made, mystery meat, "cheese" in air quotes, speed over quality, eat at your own risk).

It's common to hear, "The stakeholder wants something fast, and anything will be better than what we currently have." We understand the desire to have knowledge and data quickly. Still, we should think critically about the assumptions that *any research is good research*, or that any PSE changes we can create from our superfast research will be better than our current PSE.

It only takes one example to disprove this. Can you remember being stuck with a new version of PSE that was absolutely a downgrade? They removed features you needed, added features you didn't, or made something harder to use. In extreme cases, can you think of a time a company rolled back these changes, and had to return to the previous version of its PSE?

"The importance of research isn't in the frequency. It's in the depth and quality of the study, and synthesizing the information you have – quantitative, qualitative, observational, and contextual – to deeply understand and make informed design decisions. We know that the volume of research doesn't get you to that point, only depth."

– Ovetta Sampson [https://linkedin.com/in/ovettasampson/]

If research sometimes takes weeks or months, why do "innovation agencies" and "research-in-a-sprint" approaches only need days? They are doing minimum viable research, are choosing the fastest methods over the best methods, or they have multiple Researchers working on getting more done in less time.

Here's how you can cut research phases down to the fastest they could go, should you desire *speed over quality*:

- **Use short cycles of evaluative research such as usability testing.** Planning, recruiting, conducting, and analyzing exploratory, discovery, and other generative research thoroughly and *well* would be nearly impossible in short periods of time. Generative research requires *quality over speed*. However, some evaluative research like unmoderated usability testing can be completed quickly, sometimes in days.

  o Therefore, many research agencies or teams offering rolling research or "research in a week" are usually evaluating concepts and existing PSE. You can do this, but it's no replacement from the customer intelligence we need to extract from generative qualitative research.

- **Always use the same methods and templates.** "We always run a survey and then interview eight people." This would create a reliable and timeboxed research unit.

- **Avoid methods that tend to take longer.** Running a survey is faster than conducting observational research. Asking people their task steps is faster than watching them perform the task, or conducting a diary study.

- **Include fewer than the recommended number of study participants.**

- **Recruit from an existing database, often your current customers.** This shortens the time spent finding a more varied population that might include target audiences who are not your customers.

- **Short sessions.** Perhaps 20-30 minutes instead of 60 minutes or longer. Fewer hours of session recordings require less time later to re-watch and analyze.

- **Don't re-watch session recordings at all.** Run with the notes taken while the sessions were conducted, and jump straight to final artifacts and conclusions.

These approaches can be fast, and we *could* call them "research," but we must consider the risks of prioritizing research speed over the insights and knowledge we could obtain when allowed more time. We might *not* have collected significant and unbiased evidence that pushes us in the right direction and toward customer-centricity.

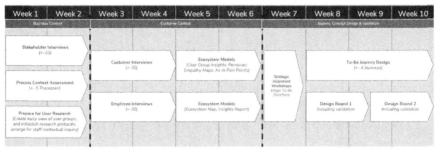

Figure 26: Screenshot of a project plan. Explained below.

There are many risks caused by the Grand Canyon between what agency Salespeople and Account Managers propose to clients and what is good CX. This also happens at our corporate jobs when someone outside CX guesses how long CX needs without understanding the time it takes to do CX work well.

The above screenshot is from an agency. This plan will burn workers out while lowering the quality of the work. Problems include:

- **Week 1 includes stakeholder interviews, but no time was included to plan, recruit, or schedule those interviews.** The project appears to start with unplanned interviews.

- **Thirty interviews are scheduled per week when most people only have the energy to do a maximum of 15 interviews per week.** Thirty interviews in a week *can* be done humanely if you have multiple Researchers moderating sessions, but that's not clear from this plan. This schedule would badly overwork one Researcher.

- **After 70 interviews, this plan has no time dedicated to analyzing them.** Watching videos of 70 interviews, reading transcripts, taking more notes, finding patterns and themes, finding insights and opportunities, etc. can take weeks to do well. This plan doesn't care about that, going straight into artifacts and final documentation of research findings.

- **There are two weeks allotted to documenting insights and creating personas, empathy maps, pain points, and an ecosystem map.** It's wildly rushed unless there are multiple Researchers sharing the work. Some teams bring in Visual Designers to polish the look of maps and artifacts, but this is absent from the above plan.

- **The optimized, desired future state informs Designers, so the order of tasks matters.** This agency's plan shows design work *while* the desired future state is still being decided. The team works on design round 2 while mapping the desired future journey that is still to be designed. *What?* This project needs a time machine.

This is a terrible plan for all involved, including the client, who might not be happy with the quality of the work or the outcomes.

In contrast, here are two research plans from my company. Note that as consultants, we often get more time than corporations like to give their internal teams. But corporate teams should get the time they estimate and request. If you would pay an agency to put two Researchers on a project for eight weeks, consider why you are hesitant to create an internal Research team of two and give them the same eight weeks.

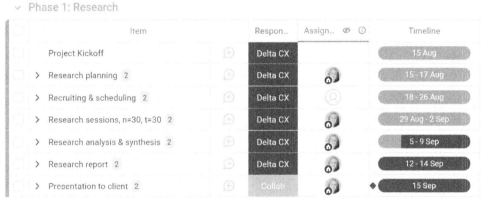

Figure 27: A shorter generative research project for a startup. We estimated two people working 160 hours over 24 working days, roughly five weeks. I use a custom monday.com board for our plans.

∨ Phase 1: Research

Item		Respon...	Assign... ⊘ ⓘ	Timeline
Project Kickoff	⊕	Delta CX		22 Aug
> Voice of the Customer 2	⊕	Delta CX		22 - 23 Aug
> Metrics baseline & success criteria 1	⊕	Delta CX		24 Aug
> Audit of current site 2	⊕	Delta CX		25 Aug - 2 Sep
> Research planning 2	⊕	Delta CX		5 - 9 Sep
> Recruiting & scheduling 1	⊕	Delta CX		12 - 16 Sep
> Research sessions, n=30, t=60 2	⊕	Delta CX		19 - 26 Sep
> Research analysis & synthesis 4	⊕	Delta CX		27 Sep - 11 Oct
> Personas 2	⊕	Delta CX		12 - 14 Oct
> Task analysis & optimized task flow 3	⊕	Delta CX		17 - 19 Oct
> Research report 3	⊕	Delta CX		20 - 28 Oct
> Presentation prep 3	⊕	Delta CX		31 Oct - 2 Nov
> Presentation to client 2	⊕	Collab		3 Nov

Figure 28: A larger research project. Three people (plus a fourth added for just the analysis task) will work an estimated 388 hours over 54 workdays, roughly ten weeks.

One key difference between the above two plans is the length of the sessions, which will impact the time required for analysis and synthesis. For the shorter plan, we cut time by deciding not to re-watch our recordings and only use the notes we took live and right after sessions. Recruiting and scheduling require less time in the larger plan because we primarily recruited people from the client's website, plus some non-customers. The shorter project cut early VOC and metrics reviews, and has fewer artifacts; we did not create personas, task analysis, or an optimized task flow.

We must expect exploratory, discovery, and other generative studies to require multiple weeks if not months. "Exploration" and "discovery" are words we use around longer adventures where we are looking for depth and meaning. These should not be boiled down to the *fastest or shortest research that might be good enough.*

Can longer research be Agile? Let's return to our definition of Agile: "a method of project management, used especially for software development, that is characterized by the division of tasks into short phases of work and frequent reassessment and adaptation of plans." The answer is *absolutely yes.* Research work has clearly defined phases that can be planned, subdivided, and estimated. CX Researchers should reconsider their plans if something learned along the way inspires a shift.

Great research work can be done in less time, but you must change project allocation. We can better balance research quality, desired outcomes, and timeframes if we add more qualified Researchers to the team. *Can we have unqualified or less-skilled people do Research?* We touched on that earlier and will address it further in this chapter.

Chapter 12: Common Research Mistakes

A Researcher from my online community shared this story with me:

"Remember when I told you Marketing is the same in my current company as the last one? That they don't use research?

Because they made a whole mess with our website, our PO pushed them to work with research for a website redesign. I've been so cautious with them because I saw this as an opportunity to build trust with them. I tried so hard not to sound 'know it all' and not to judge them for not knowing anything about research. I suggested starting with stakeholder interviews, and didn't mention anything about user research because I knew considering the time it would take, they'd say no.

BUT I KILLED IT WITH STAKEHOLDER INTERVIEWS. I brought so much valuable, organized data for them. Everybody on the Marketing team was complimenting me and my work after the meeting. They were so shocked. They were like, 'We never did anything like this before. It's amazing how much work you put into this.' Because they started trusting me, when I brought up actual client interviews, even though my anticipated timeline was 4-5 weeks, they were all like, "If that's what you recommend, go ahead. Let's do it correctly this time.' "

Is CX a Skill That Anybody Can Have?

There are some perspectives around tasks and roles that can lead to research and design mistakes. Many Agile Coaches, Scrum Masters, and others (especially in tech) say that CX or UX is not a job, a role, or a specialty. They often say that "UX is a skill that anybody can have." They usually agree that you need this skill on the Agile or product team. But if it's just "a skill," and anybody can have that skill or do those "activities," then we might not need CX, UX, or specialists. This is reflected in statements like, "UX work is easy," "Anybody can make wireframes," or, "Anybody can do research because it's just talking to people."

A variation is to believe that the CX tool or software *is* the skill or work. For example, a belief that anyone who knows how to use Figma or Axure well must be a good CX Designer or well-qualified to do Design work. Would we say that anybody proficient with JIRA or GitHub must be a good Programmer or qualified for a Developer job? Additionally, time with a tool does not mean proficiency with the skills that the job requires. I have been using Adobe Photoshop since 1994, but I am a mediocre visual designer on a good day. When job applications ask me how many years I have used Adobe Photoshop, it's the wrong question.

In mid-2022, I was interviewed on an Agile podcast [https://cxcc.to/a127], and "UX is a skill" came up. I asked the co-hosts, "If UX is a skill, can you please tell me what that skill is?" They started naming standard CX documents and artifacts, including journey maps, personas, prototypes, and screens. While it is correct that those are documents that CX Researchers and Architects create, these are technically not *skills*. **They are outputs and**

documentation of the execution of skills.

As an example, prototyping is the tangible output of skills and proficiencies, including:

- Information architecture and interaction design.

- Studies of human behavior and cognitive psychology.

- Problem finding and solving.

- Critical thinking.

- Deductive reasoning and logic.

- Being able to put your ego and preferences aside so that you are Designing for the target audience and their needs, no matter what you like or prefer.

The *execution* of those skills is tangibly seen in sketches, wireframes, or a prototype. Executing these skills *poorly* might still result in a wireframe or prototype, but that doesn't mean we have a good idea, concept, or design. Therefore, the prototype is not "the skill" since even people without Design skills could create a functioning prototype. Creating a wireframe or prototype doesn't guarantee that they have done good Design work, solved the right problem, or created intuitive PSE.

As another example, some of the skills involved in CX research include:

- Most of what was listed above for the prototype.

- Planning the research.

- Choosing the best method(s).

- Planning the correct questions and the tasks we should observe.

- Choosing the right quantity and types of participants.

- Executing sessions with neutrality and a good interviewing style.

- Observing and noticing things others miss. Being a mini-detective.

- Analyzing the data.

- Bringing it together to report on insights, pain points, and opportunities.

- Delivering actionable suggestions around pain points, opportunities, strategy, and direction.

Someone who lacks one or more of these skills could still "do research," but the research is unfortunately likely to be a junk science study with flawed results. You can "talk to users," but that doesn't mean that you did research well and set the team and project in the right direction.

It's also why creating a customer journey map is about so much more than *did we end up with a document called a "customer journey map?"* Which skills, techniques, or methods were used in making that customer journey map? Customer journey maps start with research and require deep strategic, problem-solving, and other skills. If these skills were not correctly utilized in making the map, you would have a map, but the map might be garbage.

"Democratizing" CX Tasks

Customer intelligence and how we obtain those insights and data are core to improving satisfaction and loyalty. Therefore, who does research work and how it's done will also be key. "Democratization" is a complex topic with people fiercely for and against it, so we need to go through it in detail with our critical thinking hats on. And if we try such a democratization experiment, we must ensure that we have proper success criteria, standards, and governance, which I detail at the end of the chapter.

The most common definition of "democratization" is where anybody at your company can do a particular domain's work, often regardless of their training, experience, abilities, proficiency, or knowledge. For example, democratization assumes that anybody at any skill level can do research or design work now or after some short training.

Some who believe in democratizing CX work want to see the work of non-CX teammates strictly overseen and reviewed for quality so that poor work is not utilized. Some who believe in democratization would prefer to save time by *not* reviewing this work, instead assuming that the work and outcomes will be "good enough."

The pro-democratization movement tends to come from these sources:

- **Trainers and online courses who make money from attempting to upskill your staff.** There's no money to be made in, "Hello, we cannot train your staff to do this work. It takes years to be good at this stuff."

    - Occasionally, a trainer *appears* to be selling democratization but instead does minimal upskilling and tries to teach that CX work really is specialized. Trojan Horse tactic!

    - Typically, the pro-democratization voices and articles come with sales pitches for corporate training, online workshops, and video courses.

- **Software and tools that will make more money when you utilize their system more or need more licenses.** The more research you do with their tool, the more money they make.

- **Workers in non-CX domains who would like to do CX or UX work, but it's not part of their job role.** This causes some people to blur job role lines, sometimes even claiming that their job should require CX or UX skills. Knowingly overlapping your role's boundaries into another role is likely to cause power struggles, morale issues, and conflict.

- **People who don't understand CX work, its specialization, or its importance.** Every worker should understand what their teammates do.

- **Managers of CX or UX teams or departments who are having trouble getting the budget and headcount they need.** They don't want to "democratize," but they have no idea how the work will get done unless they start handing tasks out to random teammates.

- **Newbies lacking confidence.** If you are new to CX work and concerned that you are an impostor or bad at your job, having everybody do your job with you can be one way to avoid scrutiny, responsibility, and accountability.

- **Pseudo thought leaders hoping for social media engagement.** Polarizing online debates can win you likes, follows, and revenue.

Democratization is a sign that you have a bottleneck in a specialty. You need to hire more specialists, not just any breathing human with some spare time. Those who are pro-democratization would say that it solves the bottleneck and more CX tasks will "get done." That's usually the main benefit.

Does it outweigh potential risks and consequences? *Why might democratizing or "anybody can do CX tasks" be a poor approach?*

- **What job exists at our company where the *quality* of their work, outputs, and outcomes doesn't matter?** If we care about the quality of CX work, then we want CX tasks done well and correctly by qualified CX professionals.

- **Which other domains will also democratize their work?** The cries for democratization are nearly always for CX or UX. But any domain could allow anybody to do their tasks.

  o Product Managers are not training and upskilling others to do Product Management work. Nobody demands that Engineering democratize and let everybody do their tasks regardless of skill or work quality.

  o If you want to take on tasks from outside of your domain, expect to help others take on tasks in your domain.

"My new approach is to let people do research and wait for it to fail so they come for help. This is usually at the research planning phase. I'm also demanding to be coached on Product Management in return for teaching people how to do research. Any time I ask them to teach me some PM stuff, they start arguing how complex it is and whether I can do it as a Researcher (I can, by the way)."
– UX Researcher in my community

- **What is the ROI of having anybody or everybody do research or design work?** We will make decisions and create PSE based on the data we have. If that data misleads us, we will find these mistakes much later, probably when customers tell us we suck. We must monitor all of this, and then estimate or calculate the ROI on having "any" research done versus the ROI of **quality** research.

- **When mission critical tasks are in danger of not getting done because of headcount or bottlenecks, we prefer to get the budget to hire a qualified person for that role.** Few specialists in any department would prefer to train someone from outside that department over hiring a qualified person who can hit the ground running.

- **If we're struggling with a bottleneck, the last thing we want to do is stop specialists' mission critical work to try to teach newbies to do mission critical work.**

  - Already-overworked practitioners will be taken away from their work to train or oversee the teammates who are learning.

  - How much time does the overworked CX team spend reviewing, fixing, or reworking poor work? This is adding to CX's burden, not relieving it.

- **You're asking someone to learn some or all of a specialized full-time job.** Becoming proficient at CX work isn't like quick Excel pivot table training. Some CX professionals have master's degrees or PhDs in psychology, sociology, human factors, or HCD.

- **We're assuming the happy outcome that everybody ends up great at CX work.** If the person learning is doing poor work, do we keep that work? Scrap it? Ban that person from future CX work? Allow them to continue doing those tasks? How much risk and waste are we willing to accept?

- **Consider efficiency; experienced specialists will be better at strategy and tactics than any newbie guessing at CX work.** CX efficiency decreases when lightly-trained or untrained newbies are guessing at CX work. Efficiency decreases when specialists' already overbooked time is split between doing the work and running an improvised mini CX school.

- **Did we ask CX leaders what they need so that we can best support them?** We appear to know that we are short-staffed in CX or UX. Ask a CX Manager, Director, Head, or VP what they would like to do about CX being spread too thin, overworked, and understaffed. Few are likely to declare, "Grab some Product Managers and have them do our work," as their first choice. They would want permission and the budget to grow their department and relieve the bottleneck by hiring qualified professionals.

    o Empower and support CX by asking leaders what they need and then giving them what they need.

- **If anybody can do CX work, we wouldn't bother with job descriptions, interviews, and standards.** We wouldn't turn anybody down for a CX or UX job.

    o If teammates from Product, Engineering, Marketing, or Business Analysis were typically great at CX work, we wouldn't even open CX jobs. We wouldn't need specialized professionals if most people trying CX work were doing it well.

    o Your company puts CX candidates through multiple interviews, reviews of past work, and possibly even an exercise to scrutinize how they do their work. If this is how we check if someone is qualified to do CX work, we must check internal teammates and hold them to these same standards for knowledge, skill, and proficiency. CX tasks shouldn't be given to anybody who wouldn't be good enough at them to qualify for a CX job here.

    o Many companies have inexplicably closed the door to entry-level CX candidates, changing Junior-level jobs to requiring two or more years of previous work experience. Yet we are OK with non-CX teammates with zero years of experience doing CX work. **Open entry-level CX jobs.** If we train anybody, it should be the people with foundational CX education who plan to have a CX career.

    o Everybody doing CX tasks should be in the CX department with a CX manager. They should be held to work standards and subject to work reviews.

Before democratization came to mean what it now does, it originally referred to sharing research knowledge and ensuring that everybody on the team and beyond had deep customer knowledge. It was about breaking down silos between CX and others. I would call knowledge sharing and active socialization "collaboration."

"Democratization" is a positively framed word, chosen to make people against it look strange. *Who wouldn't want a democracy?* In a democracy, everybody can vote, we assume those votes count, but few govern. Domains like Product Management and Engineering aren't democracies. Nobody votes, we collaborate where it makes sense, and very few govern. CX should be no different.

Chapter 12: Common Research Mistakes

"Democratization" is a euphemism and the wrong word. The correct word is "dilution." We want more fruit juice but don't have more fruit juice, so we add some water, milk, and olive oil that we happen to have. We could still call this "fruit juice" and hope it tastes "good enough." But if this juice were an ingredient in a larger recipe, that recipe might not come out well.

When you understand the value of a specialty, you respect and grow that specialty. When you don't understand this specialty, it's easy to dilute it – even by accident – because you don't understand what would dilute it and what would support it.

Two common questions during my weekly Office Hours/Ask Me Anything YouTube live streams are from Researchers who are told to democratize research and train non-Researchers. Their questions are, "How do I stop this from happening," and, "Should I quit this job?" That's what your staff or coworkers may be thinking. Are you forcing an approach on people who don't want or agree with the approach?

An interesting angle on this matter comes from a UX leader who posted the following on LinkedIn (edited for brevity and anonymity):

"The worst mistake I have ever made in my career: hiring someone who was simply unable to do the job.

Some time ago, I made the mistake of hiring a designer who didn't quite fit what we needed on our team but was ambitious and curious. Within a short time, it became apparent the designer wasn't as skilled as what was needed at the company. They could "talk the talk" but not "walk the walk" regarding fundamental design tasks.

I worked with the designer as best as possible, making them my single priority for weeks, but after dozens of complaints from peers, the executive team decided the designer had to go.

I failed my team by not rejecting someone who lacked clear skills in the interview process. I failed everyone at the company with that one decision because projects fell behind and team morale eroded."

It's a reminder that putting someone we believe can learn into a role where they are not a fit can be a disaster, even with dedicated coaching. This highly qualified expert was almost desperate not to let this person fail, but still couldn't coach a "Designer" up to an adequate level of Design proficiency.

Cost-Benefit Analysis

If you are considering diluting CX, you should do a cost-benefit analysis of training and oversight versus hiring qualified people as well as the potential Cost of Poor Quality.

For example, I saw a job for a UX Research Coach asking for at least seven years of research experience and three years as a teacher and instructional designer. Let's imagine they are paid $130,000 USD and will coach 20 non-UX workers, who will allocate

10% of their time to UX Research. If the people we train make $95,000 per year, $190,000 of their annual salaries goes to them learning and doing UX work.

Let's estimate that delays, mistakes, lost revenue, and having to fix PSE later – thanks to flawed CX work our non-CX staff did – only cost this company $200,000 in a year. It's possibly way more when you consider what an Agile team of six Engineers is paid for sprints of work leading to a project that partially or wholly fails. There are also costs associated with the work the non-CX role *isn't* getting done in their own domain due to splitting their time with CX tasks.

Our democratization-with-a-dedicated-trainer adventure conservatively costs $520,000 annually. The alternative to this program is to spend $520,000 on one Lead Researcher for $130,000, one Senior Researcher for $110,000 and four Juniors at $70,000 each (note that by the time you read this book, these might not be market salaries; make sure you are paying appropriate current salaries).

We can have 20 people trying to quickly learn and then part-time guess at specialized work, or we can have six qualified staff hitting the ground running and working efficiently. We can have 20 people spending a few hours a week here and there on CX, or we can hire six dedicated full-time specialists.

Looking at this another way, imagine that you offered CX leadership a budget of $520,000. They would want to hire as many qualified CX staff as possible with that money. It's unlikely they would want that budget allocated to the salaries of Product Managers, Developers, and others trying their hands at some part-time CX work.

Looking at costs, benefits, and possible consequences, the disadvantages of "democratization" outweigh the "but we will get more work done" advantages. Giving non-CX teammates specialized CX work is a sign that you need to hire. Later in the book, we'll look at the optimal team structure, including hiring until there are no CX bottlenecks.

What About "Inclusion?"

A common technique to convince CX and UX practitioners that they need to democratize or dilute is to tell them that excluding non-CX roles from CX tasks works against workplace "inclusion." The definition of "inclusion" in the workplace is [https://cxcc.to/a144]:

> *"Inclusion is the practice of providing everyone with equal access to opportunities and resources. Inclusion efforts in the workplace help to give traditionally marginalized groups — like those based on gender, race, or disabilities — a means for them to feel equal in the workplace. Inclusive actions, like creating employee resource groups or hosting information sessions, make the workplace a safer, more respectful environment for all employees."*

Standard definitions of "inclusion" from HR and DEI professionals and organizations center around feelings of belonging and workplace support. Nothing in these definitions suggests or requires that people try or do each other's jobs. Are we demanding this "inclusion" in other roles? Are we telling Engineering that they are not "inclusive" if they don't allow non-Engineers to do coding?

If we care about inclusion, then we must ask: *is the workplace a "more respectful environment" when we tell specialized employees that their specialty essentially doesn't exist, and unqualified people can do their work?* If we believe that the qualified CX professionals we chose to hire are experts, then we should listen when they warn against democratization, refuse to democratize, or quit due to forced democratization.

For those imagining that I'm being dramatic or hyperbolic, I worked at a Fortune 200 that brought in a new VP of UX. This person immediately made decisions and announcements that chipped away at respect for UX work. One announcement was that Product Managers would be allowed to do usability testing after one hour of training. Within what felt like weeks, all four of our Researchers, who had master's degrees and impressive experience, quit and so did their manager. Within months, our department lost most of its 40 Designers. **It was a UXodus.**

CX and UX sometimes allow democratization because they have been bullied into it by being told they are not "inclusive" or "empathetic" if they don't let others share their work. Please don't take that as an approval of the approach; take it as people worn down, bullied, gaslit, or feeling like they can't say "no."

"But Famous Authors Say Non-CX/UX Roles Should Do CX/UX Work"

Authors and trainers from Product Management and Agile are increasingly pushing the idea that Product Managers (PMs) or Engineers should be doing CX or UX research or design. Responding point for point, I wrote a lengthy article, "Should Product Managers Do User Experience Research or Design?" [https://cxcc.to/a130] It says "Product Managers" but it could be any role. The article focuses on research work, but it could be any CX task.

Some key points from my article include:

- **Declaring that Product Managers need CX/UX skills or to do CX/UX work to "have empathy," "understand CX/UX work," "fill in where needed," or have "first-hand knowledge of customers" is a slippery slope.** Will PMs demand to write code? Run QA tests? Build Marketing campaigns? Otherwise they don't have empathy or first-hand knowledge?

  o Nobody should threaten that if Product Managers don't do CX/UX work, they "won't have empathy." Everybody should be capable of customer-centricity without treading into other domains' work territories.

  o If we're worried about PMs having empathy, where is the empathy for their CX coworkers, who nearly never want Product Managers doing CX work? Are we walking in CX's shoes?

- If PMs want to build empathy, why aren't they watching every live or pre-recorded research session CX conducts? They should make time for that as a top priority.

- **The best vantage point for *first-hand* knowledge of customers is from the research observer's seat.** Lower-skilled moderators and interviewers make many mistakes in their questions and interviewing style. They are sometimes more focused on what they are asking and taking notes than being in the moment with what the participant is saying and doing. Being an observer allows teammates to be entirely in the moment and focused on the details of participants' experiences.

    - PMs work from second-hand knowledge constantly and without complaint. They get data and analytics they didn't run themselves. They get information from Support teams without working in the call center.

- **We shouldn't claim that "customers are hurt when we don't democratize" or "customers are hurt when we fight over democratization" without being able to substantiate that.** Are customers aware of our internal staffing, processes, and problems?

    - Did research to learn what hurts customers?

    - VOC data reminds us that we have many customers who are experiencing pain that we caused. If we care about what hurts customers, then there are many fixes and improvements we owe them.

- **PMs don't have to "think like Designers" – whatever that means – to be better at solving customers' problems.** PMs must ensure that CX has been given time, budget, and headcount for the research that will help us understand customers' problems. If that hasn't happened, our "solutions" are probably guesses, whether or not we are "thinking like a Designer."

    - You don't need CX skills or to do CX work to use critical thinking, challenge the status quo, keep asking questions, and focus on user needs.

- **The more people try to tie PM work to CX research or design, the more the tech community might question the need for a PM role.** If our CX roles could easily pick up Product Management tasks, and our Engineers were truly self-managing teams, what would a PM's job be? This is discussed further in a later chapter.

    - I have seen the argument: *if Product Managers are responsible for product strategy and direction, and research informs and guides those, then Product Managers must do research.*

    - This syllogism could easily be turned around: *if CX/UX Researchers do research, and research informs and guides product strategy and direction, then CX/UX Researchers should be responsible for the product strategy and direction.*

It shouldn't take gaslighting, bullying, name-calling, and flawed arguments to make people democratize CX, Product Management, QA, or any other role or task. This is business: if we have a bottleneck and need to hire, hire qualified people instead of hoping any warm body can do world-class specialized work.

There are already companies on the other side of these role-dilution experiments. Articles from these points of view can be harder to find since who wants to publicly admit that they failed, but one such article is, "Undemocratizing User Research." [https://cxcc.to/a142] Some companies saw the quality of their research work go down to an unacceptably low standard. Some companies lost their qualified Researchers when the company appeared to no longer value their specialty or skills. Can you imagine three or six interviews to prove your abilities, and then working in an environment where *anybody can do your job*?

When the author of the undemocratizing article and others with similar experiences push against democratization, are they listened to? Did we defer to an expert's knowledge, experience, and perspective? Or are they told they are "old fashioned," "being negative," or "not inclusive?"

"But I Found a Pro-Democratization UX Expert"

Read enough social posts and articles, and you'll eventually find every angle of every stance hailed as the one true way. Prominent UX voices – some experts and some not – who are pro-dilution tend to provide or more of the following arguments:

- **"Anyone can cook."** *You don't have to be a professional chef to cook. So, we can let anybody do UCD tasks.*

  o In addition to being a logical leap, it doesn't consider PSE quality and outcomes. Anyone *can* prepare food, but not everybody will prepare a tasty or healthy meal. Not every meal would pass a health inspection.

  o Anyone *can* give you a haircut, but you might not be glad they did. Anyone *can* teach children, give medical advice, or design a parachute.

  o Customer satisfaction and loyalty - and our company's growth - depend on us correctly strategizing goals and executing initiatives. This isn't analogous to cooking. If non-Researchers want to try researching for personal projects, they are welcome to try "home cooking research." But while we are a business that needs to make and save money, convert and retain customers, and grow the public's trust for us, we must maintain high standards for our work and its outcomes.

- **"Those against democratization are gatekeepers, elitist, want silos, create**

bottlenecks, and want to block others from having research insights." More examples of bullying and gaslighting.

- o We already had the bottleneck. We made an informed decision to not allocate budget or headcount. We could have fixed the bottleneck and we didn't.

- o If a lack of democratization causes CX bottlenecks, should we solve Engineering or Product Management bottlenecks with the same style of democratization and dilution?

- o Every domain in our company prefers to close the gate. If an Engineer doesn't want to train Marketers to write code, the Engineer *could* be called a "gatekeeper," but they are protecting and preserving their specialization.

- o Nearly nobody would prefer to be siloed. Nearly everybody wants to share insights and customer intelligence. But we don't have to dilute CX's work to accomplish that.

- **"If you have a clear, relevant question, you can do research."** We will need higher standards than that. Clear and relevant questions are a starting point: *what do we need to learn?* But having these questions doesn't imply that research will be planned, executed, or analyzed well.

- **"Design and research are methods we can teach everybody. UX can then influence everybody's decisions."**

  - o How does the understaffed bottleneck-causing domain have time to train or oversee others? Will it be OK if they are doing less work because we shifted them to being trainers or coaches? Does that improve or relieve the bottleneck?

  - o UX is often a misunderstood domain without a seat at the table or an equal voice. It's almost strange to hear a declaration that UX can influence teammates' decisions. If that were happening now, we would be more customer-centric than we are.

Delta CX Governance Model

Pro-democratization views rarely come with a "how-to successfully democratize" guidebook, a set of standards, or a governance model. This leaves the impression that anybody can do any role's work, and monitoring such an experiment is optional. Like any transformation, change, or experiment, governance, monitoring, and assessments are required.

If you want to "democratize" or dilute CX work, then you must set up proper **governance**: *how are we doing this, how are we checking where this is succeeding or* *failing, and who are we holding accountable for what?* The same would be valid for democratizing Product Management, Marketing, QA Testing, or any other work. Note that you do not have to start your democratization experiment with every team and project. You can choose one or two projects and experiment more carefully.

*How do we make sure we're not slipping from **dilution** to **delusion**?* Whether you have already started this experiment or it's something being considered for the future, here are some things you will need to answer, document, and monitor (with CX research as our example):

- **Executive support and an enforcement mechanism are necessary components.** Have we identified the execs or leaders sponsoring this experiment? How will we compel compliance with this model when people might want to "break the rules?"

- **Root causes and problem statement.** What problem are we solving? What do we know about that problem? What's causing the problem? What solutions have we considered? Have we analyzed pros and cons of various solutions?

  o Why are we diluting CX? Is dilution the best solution? For example, if we are diluting CX because "Product Managers would like to do UX tasks," is that a good enough reason, and are we allowing similar experiments in other domains? If we are diluting CX because CX is a bottleneck, and we're willing to burn partial non-CX salaries to "get the work done," wouldn't hiring CX professionals make more sense?

- **Success criteria.** Before embarking on the democratization experiment, we must establish success criteria to know when it's succeeding or failing. Failure signals changing or ending the experiment.

  o Our success criteria can't be any variation of "we did a thing and it got done." Having more people do research tasks might lead to more research tasks being done, but at what quality and cost? Our goal should be outstanding research that brings us closer to customer-centricity and high-quality evidence that will be used in strategies and decisions, not just *any research*.

  o The success criteria should be tied to quality and Customer Experience outcomes. It should use measurable metrics, not opinions or emotions. "People are enjoying doing research" is not a success criterion.

- **Accountability for small or large failures.** If there are no consequences for the people who drove this initiative, then there is no incentive to do better and no reason to reduce, change, or stop a failing program.

  o We said we would hold people responsible or accountable, but what does that look like? Will we block that decision-maker from leading an experiment in the future? Do we reduce their available budget? How about a performance improvement plan and coaching? Could they be demoted? I have seen companies demote managers and leaders; don't exclude it as a possibility.

- **Training.**

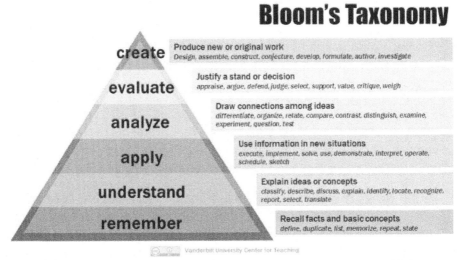

Figure 29: Image of Bloom's Taxonomy from Vanderbilt.edu. Explained below.

o Consider Bloom's Taxonomy, a pedagogical framework visualized as a pyramid. In many cases, democratization assumes that non-CX staff will jump right in at the highest level, which is *the ability to produce new or original work*. Does that non-CX worker *recall facts and basic concepts* about CX, the lowest level in this model? Can they *explain CX ideas or concepts* (the second level) or *use CX knowledge in new situations* (the third level)?

o We cannot expect quality work based on the *application* of extensive knowledge if we are not providing that knowledge and taking people through these pedagogical stages.

o Most companies experimenting with democratization expect a research expert to provide training. Given that the Researcher's full-time job is doing mission critical research tasks, we must create appropriate expectations for the length, breadth, and depth of training.

o Some Researchers are great teachers. Some are not. Have we checked which of our Researchers is also great with training and pedagogy? Let's not also dilute education.

o CX research is highly specialized and, on average, takes people years to be good at. We might see low-quality results through no fault of the trainer, especially since there may not have been a selection process with standards for who will be trying CX work.

o Speaking of which, is there a selection or screening process for non-CX individuals? Can anybody be trained, or do we declare some people not a match to CX work?

o Some students will never be good at research tasks, no matter how much training they get. There will be people who just don't get it.

o How much training will there be? What types of training? Will learners have time to practice on non-urgent projects?

o When does our Researcher have time to shift into Instructional Designer mode and create a training program? Are we sending our non-Researchers to an outside training course or bringing in a corporate trainer? How did we investigate and vet the quality of that course or that trainer?

o Will you utilize formative and summative assessments of the students and the trainer to measure process and effectiveness?

- **Priorities.** Have we codified which work should go to the professional Researchers and which work should go to the non-Researchers? How will we prioritize the incoming work, and match work to practitioners?

  o What are the priorities for the people being **asked to train others**? Which is more important: the work they currently have on their plate or the training and work reviews for those who are learning? Do not say, "They can do both." People with packed schedules need clear priorities.

  o What are the priorities for the people **trying to learn or do** research tasks? Which is more important: the work they currently have on their plate or the training and research work? Do not say, "They can do both."

- **Process.** A good research process includes planning, recruiting participants, executing the sessions, analyzing the data, synthesizing findings, and arriving at actionable insights. Will non-Researchers be required to execute a correct research process? If not, why not?

- **Work and Quality**. Will non-Researchers doing research tasks be required to meet ISO or other standards we have documented? If not, why not?

  o If we find that someone's work doesn't meet our quality standards, what do we do about that? Do we ban them from future research? Do we invest more time and money in trying to train them further? Do we include the bad research or deliver it to a client? Do we scrap the research and pretend it never happened?

- o Some well-paid trainers say that research work done by non-Researchers does not need to be checked. *We can let it go and assume it's "good enough."* If we are not checking this work, that should be documented as high risk.

- o All work that is in progress and completed should be documented and archived. This includes documentation of every step of our research process. We should archive our session recordings, research plans, and artifacts relating to how this data was analyzed.

- **Costs of Time and Salaries**. Calculate the time and salary a Researcher spends training, overseeing, coaching, reviewing work, correcting work, etc. Calculate the time and salary a non-Researcher spends learning and doing research.

  - o Did work have to be redone by someone with higher skill? That took time and salary.

- **Costs of Poor Quality**. Are we monitoring the projects using non-Researchers for research? Have we checked if research quality set a later stage of the project up for mistakes or failure?

  - o For example, was usability testing highly flawed, invalid, or didn't deliver the information Designers needed to improve their designs? Did something that research "told" us turn out to not be accurate?

  - o Did we release something to the public or deliver it to a client, but it's partially or wholly failing? What did that cost us in reputation, stock price, customer trust, Customer Support utilization, negative word of mouth, or customers downgrading or leaving?

  - o Did we make a big enough mistake where we had to roll back a software release, undo a price increase, or negate something we delivered to the public? What are the costs of that mistake and the efforts to fix or undo it?

- **Costs of Attrition and Worker Dissatisfaction.** Did anybody quit our company partially or wholly due to democratization? It would be a serious loss if that knowledge and capability walked out the door.

  - o Researchers might not want to stay in a workplace where anybody can do their job regardless of proficiency. Non-Researchers might not like more tasks dumped on them, especially if they already have no spare time.

  - o Your workers might stay, but are they happy? If you opened a job in their domain, would they recommend that their friends work here? Are they telling their network that this is a great place to work?

We must monitor all of these. And with some effort, we could calculate the time and money spent on most, if not all, of these. We should be able to quantify what this experiment costs, and compare that to the salaries that we could have paid professionals to do this work.

Thanks to Dr. Ari Zelmanow [https://linkedin.com/in/zelmanow/] for his collaboration on this governance model.

Chapter 13: Interview: Accessibility

Sheri Byrne-Haber is a prominent global subject matter expert in the fields of disability and accessibility. She is best known for launching digital accessibility programs at multiple Fortune 200 companies, including McDonald's, Albertsons, and VMware, as well as consulting on government accessibility. Her programs have positively impacted millions of the more than 1 billion global people with disabilities.

Her most recent contribution to the accessibility field is an open-source tool called Crest, which allows users to move some aspects of manual accessibility testing into an automated format. With degrees in computer science, law, and business combined with identifying as a disabled person, Sheri has a complete 360-degree view of all the issues impacting disability inclusion and accessibility.

Sheri is the author of a popular Medium blog called "This Week in Accessibility" [https://cxcc.to/a170], and was named "2020 Author of the Year" from Medium's largest publication, the UX Collective. She was also recently named a LinkedIn Top Voice for Social Impact for 2022. In her blog, which has received over 250,000 views, she summarizes legal cases and issues facing people implementing accessibility programs.

Sheri is a frequent panelist and speaker at accessibility, UI/UX, and HR conferences and is an active member of several accessibility committees and non-profits, helping drive and communicate the evolution of accessibility standards. Her book, entitled "Giving a Damn about Accessibility" is available for free at https://accessibility.uxdesign.cc.

Debbie: How would you define customer-centricity?

Sheri: I would define customer-centricity as putting yourself in the shoes, so to speak, of the customer. That sounds like personas, but I haven't seen anybody that does a super good job at truly intersectional personas. To do it right, you have to think about things like *is my customer a single mother? Does my customer get migraines?* There are all these things that will alter what the customer does without necessarily having anything to do with what the customer's job is. I'm not a big fan of Jobs To Be Done because I think too much of what customers need comes from their personal characteristics and not necessarily their job characteristics.

I'm thinking of anything that will impact how they use the product for either good or bad. Maybe they have Attention Deficit Disorder, so they need things to not be super distracting on the screen. Maybe they have kids running around the house, which is like situational Attention Deficit Disorder because you're getting distracted by what's going on around you without it being a medical condition or a neurodiverse trait.

Debbie: How can we ensure we consider all of our users and not the middle of a bell curve?

Sheri: I always recommend looking at general population statistics. 4.25% of your population is colorblind because that's a general population statistic. That's a given whether or not you've ever met a colorblind user. 5% of your users are dyslexic. These numbers might go up or down depending on the vertical market. If you look at people who work at fast food restaurants, 20% of your users are dyslexic. If you look at prisons, 40% of your users are dyslexic.

You have to think about it not just from the general population but the specifics of the population that you're targeting. If you're targeting 80% men, for example, that increases your colorblindness rate to 6.5% from 4.25%.

Debbie: How can a company learn these things?

Sheri: One of the big failings of people who design software is they don't start with user research. They build a product and then they test the product with the users, maybe right before release, but usually when it's too late to change anything, or at least change anything drastic at that point. I fall squarely in the camp of *do your research first*. There will be less stuff that you have to remediate and throw away when you're done.

Census Bureaus are good sources for these types of statistics. If you're focusing on disability, the Valuable 500 (a nonprofit working on getting disability added to DEI programs) and the United Nations have good statistics on disabilities. It's not difficult to find if you construct a competent Google query.

Debbie: You mentioned "situational" disabilities, which I think of as being from the Microsoft model.

Sheri: I do like the Microsoft model because it makes people realize that there are not that many people who only have one hand as a permanent disability. But there are plenty of people who only have one hand because of temporary and situational disabilities. When our new CEO took over last July, he'd had rotator cuff surgery. He had one of those big things keeping his shoulder at a particular angle while it healed. Situational disabilities also account for people talking on their phones or holding bags of groceries or a laptop bag. I really like the Microsoft Inclusive Toolkit spectrum. [https://microsoft.com/design/inclusive/]

Debbie: Have you had any success convincing people of the importance of research?

Sheri: I've been fortunate in that I was allowed to do some user research in my previous roles. We have an entire user research group at VMware that we can leverage when we want to do specific disability-related research. Smaller companies tend not to do that. Research isn't cheap, but it's definitely worthwhile, and it's cheaper than rewriting your product after your first release. *We don't have enough money to get it done, but we have enough money to do it over.* Invest in the user research up front.

Debbie: *We don't have enough money to take accessibility into account now, but we have enough money to get sued later.*

Sheri: *We can spend a million dollars on litigation defense and settlement payments because we didn't have time to do it right, even though we knew we were supposed to do it from the outset.* I've seen that on multiple occasions.

Debbie: How do we convince Engineering teams or Product Owners that it's worth delaying a release to make sure it's accessible?

Sheri: It's not a matter so much of delaying; I just hate that word because of the negative connotation. It's building enough time in the schedule to do what needs to be done. For example, you need to plan a certain amount of time to test. It's not a good idea to do functional testing and accessibility testing at the same time. If you find functional bugs, they're going to interfere with the accessibility testers' ability to do things. Plus, the code is going to change when you fix the functional bugs.

I always recommend no more than a 25% overlap so that you don't start accessibility testing until you're well into finishing your functional testing. Those methodologies just have to be part of how people build out schedules. When you're doing critical path work, you have to build in those dependencies.

Debbie: We have guidelines saying that you should do generative research with 8 to 12 per persona or segment, and evaluative research (testing) with 5 per persona or segment. But that never seems to include people with various conditions, diagnoses, or disabilities.

Sheri: You have to bring them in at the right time. You can't put a piece of paper or a wireframe in front of somebody who's blind and ask them if they like A or B better. That doesn't work. You have to wait until you have a functioning prototype.

Another important tip that often creates an aha moment is that you need to test with people who have congenital medical issues and people who have acquired medical issues. For people who are congenitally blind, blindness is all they know. Whereas people who have acquired blindness look at it as "I had that ability, and I lost it." There's a totally different psychological perspective, and also a totally different length of time that they've had to learn to use assistive technology.

The 8 to 12 is fine, and I typically recommend individual interviews, especially with people who are blind and use screen readers. It's a lot of noise because they're listening to the screen reader, and they're listening to you. If there are other people in the room, they have their screen readers going also. Individual interviews do work better.

Add screening questions about the length of assistive technology use and length of the disability so you can include some of each. Most companies will need to work with either a specialty agency to recruit those people for them, or they'll need to work with one of the NGOs/nonprofits that specialize in supporting that particular disability.

For example, if you wanted to include people with spinal cord injuries, you would go to the Christopher & Dana Reeve Foundation. If you want to recruit people who are blind, go to LightHouse for the Blind and Visually Impaired because they know how to find these people. Sometimes they rent facilities for in-person testing. Knowbility in Texas and Fable in Canada are really good. Another one I like for recruiting is Helix Opportunities, which is based in San Francisco.

Debbie: Do you have a suggested set of people that tends to represent most disabilities or conditions?

Sheri: Disabilities can come in unpredictable combinations, which will impact the results. I recommend focusing on one type of disability at a time. Focus on low vision first, which are people who use magnification tools. Once you get that all debugged, then focus on screen reader users. Then focus on switch users. I don't typically recruit for Deaf users since they mostly need captions. Then neurodiverse users are another group.

Debbie: People are often unfamiliar with assistive devices like switches. I get a lot of blank looks when I ask companies if people can tab through their websites because some people don't use a mouse.

Sheri: For supporting keyboard use, I always point people to the US government website called 18F. [https://18f.gsa.gov/] You can find things like how a keyboard needs to work in a dialog box, in a menu, in a form, all the interactive stuff.

The other thing I always suggest is for people to look at YouTube for assistive technology videos. My personal favorite, which is the best two minutes of your life you will ever invest, is an Apple advertisement from years ago that has, I think, 13 different pieces of assistive technology demoed in two minutes. [https://cxcc.to/a109] I love that video. There is nothing better to show the impact of assistive technology than that video. Sady Paulson is the woman with cerebral palsy at the beginning of the video where somebody is helping her get dressed. Turns out she was actually the video editor. The Apple video editing software works with a switch so that she can use it. At the end, they show her editing the video.

Debbie: I've seen some short videos from Microsoft on how people with different disabilities were playing Xbox.

Sheri: What you want to avoid are the videos with the sad music and the dark lighting, like the Toyota Super Bowl video from two or three years ago about the adopted child who became a paralympic swimmer. *Oh, sad, sad, sad, sad... Oh, yay, the adopted parents were the saviors of this poor child.* You tend to see this in ads that are trying to sell things that were made *for* people with disabilities but not made *with* people with disabilities. Because if people with disabilities had been included, that type of ad never would have happened.

Debbie: Very often, when you mention accessibility to someone, they say that their product works with screen readers, so we're good.

Sheri: The web is inherently visual. If you look at WCAG standards, more than half of them pertain to working with screen readers because it's hard to make something that's intended to be visual work completely equally for somebody who can't use that visual input. That's why the focus is all on screen readers, and the overwhelming number of WCAG guidelines pertain to screen reader use. There are only two guidelines pertaining to magnification, but there are five times as many users who use magnification as use screen readers. Hearing loss is the most common congenital medical condition. If you're looking at it by numbers of people, you want to tackle some of those other things. But if you're looking at it by *I want to get the hardest stuff out of the way first*, then the screen reader stuff is the right stuff to focus on.

Debbie: In my *Delta CX* book, I interviewed a colorblind musician who had done a video where some company that sponsors him had sent him this guitar pedal thing you stomp on, and it turns different effects on or off. He couldn't tell what states different things were in because it was color-coded. But by the end of the interview, he said he felt like he had more crap in his life from being left-handed than from being colorblind.

Sheri: It's funny you mentioned left-handedness. We had a Disability ERG (Employee Resource Group) event at VMware focusing on left-handedness. If you look at the definition of disability as not a medical condition but a *mismatch between a human state and the environment that they're in*, left-handedness is a disability. The world just wasn't built for left-handed people. It's a mismatch, which makes it a disability.

Debbie: Some companies try to get teams to "experience" disabilities, like *try to use this site blindfolded* and *try to use this site without your mouse.*

Sheri: I'm not a big fan of what we collectively refer to as "empathy-building exercises." People with disabilities have developed coping mechanisms because we had to. We could have chronic pain issues. We could have frustration issues from having beat our heads against a brick wall trying to pay our gas and electric bills. I don't think those things are well represented in the empathy-building exercises.

And at the end of the day, the participants in the empathy-building exercise look at it as a negative experience. *Oh, we tried being disabled, and it's hard.* The no-mouse challenge is the most even-keeled one because if your software doesn't work with the keyboard, it's not going to work for any assistive technology at all.

A better thing to do is to bring in people with those disabilities and share their lived experiences. At VMware, we brought somebody in who had very severe cerebral palsy and spoke through what we call an AAC (Augmented Assistive Communication) device. She was working on her master's degree. Just because people use assistive technology does not mean they're not intelligent. It just means that they have a different way of communicating and perceiving the world.

Debbie: A few years ago, a Fortune 50 did a conference talk with great pride about a project on making one of their internal tools accessible for blind people and others with visual disabilities. They had done the entire project with one blind guy. There was something so hollow about this big accessibility mission, patting themselves on the back, and then only working with one blind person.

Sheri: You need to look at three different groups. You need to work with people who use screen readers only. You need magnification-only users. And you need people with progressive vision loss, who typically use both magnification and screen readers. As the loss is progressive, they are accustomed to using magnification, but occasionally magnification isn't good enough. And as their loss gets worse, they're starting to transition to screen readers. This third group is most rare. And you'll need to separate those groups between the people with congenital disabilities and the people with acquired disabilities, plus your control group of people without disabilities. I usually try for at least 15 total: 5 in the magnification group, 5 in the screen reader group, a couple in the mixed group if I can find them, and then 5 in the control group.

Debbie: What else can we tell the executives and strategists in our company that will help them give a crap about these people with various conditions who have open wallets and would love to be customers?

Sheri: Open wallets is the key. Executives care about money. Make sure that they understand that people with disabilities aren't always beggars. They're not always at the poverty level. We are more likely to be in the lower socio-economic strata, but that doesn't mean we're all there.

We're very loyal customers. Once we find something that works, we don't like changing. There are stats out there, like from the Nielsen group, about what people with disabilities over-index and under-index on compared to the rest of the population. One of the things that they over-index on, interestingly enough, is pet products. They're more likely to have service animals, and they're more likely to want to take care of what they consider to be practically their children. And loyalty is also huge over-indexing.

I'd like to add that in order to attract employees with disabilities, you have to be a disability-inclusive organization. You must have a Disability ERG. You must have the ability for people to be able to apply for jobs and get through the interview process without bias. When you do that, you hire more employees with disabilities. Those employees – and not the accessibility team – are typically the ones that are the subversives in the conference room. They're the ones saying, "Well, what about people with disabilities?"

Even with a huge accessibility team – and the VMware accessibility team is pretty large – we're still only looking at a 1 per 1000 ratio between accessibility team members and Engineers. You need other people talking about accessibility when we're not in the room. If you're not an inclusive organization, you're not going to have those people talking about it.

Look at the tools that you're buying. If 85% of what you're buying is not accessible, you're going to be putting up artificial barriers for your users. For example, I don't know of a single UX research tool that's accessible. Only a few survey tools are accessible.

Debbie: Tell me more about accessibility teams.

Sheri: On the larger accessibility teams, you will have a dedicated Program Manager. They make sure that those tests get staggered correctly and that they're not sitting on top of each other. They assign out testing projects as they come in. There's usually a Manager, and there's occasionally a Strategist; that's one of the roles that I'm currently playing at VMware. Then there's a whole ton of people that test.

A recent WebAIM survey [https://cxcc.to/a139] said that only 30% of accessibility team members have disabilities. You can't have a team entirely of blind people because who's going to test the color contrast? Who's going to test whether or not the magnification ratio flow is working correctly? There are certain things that different types of disabilities can't test. You need to get this mixture of people with different types of disabilities. I prefer my ratios on the accessibility teams I build to be around 60% people with disabilities.

Debbie: Are there multiple accessibility teams that end up connecting with Product, UX, and Engineering? Is this one giant strategic team that has oversight of multiple projects?

Sheri: It depends on the maturity level of accessibility and disability inclusion at the organization. The W3C Accessibility Maturity Model [https://cxcc.to/a140] goes from a 1 to a 5, where 1 is *we don't know what the hell we're doing,* and 5 is *we're brilliant, and everybody wants to copy us.* Level 3 is where you have to have shifted to a centralized organization with experts. But if you're not controlling the information that those people produce to make sure that it's all consistent, you're a level 1 or level 2.

To get to levels 3, 4, or 5, the accessibility organization has to be centralized. My recommendation is always that the budget be centralized also. I've been in a situation where the accessibility team was centralized, but the budget wasn't. That meant that each of the business units was deciding how much to spend on certain types of things. They always wanted to do what was cheapest and not necessarily what was best because it was being charged back to them. Keep the money and the people both centralized if you want to do a good job at it.

Debbie: Speaking of cheap and bad, let's remind everybody why they don't want to use website plugins and overlays for "accessibility."

Sheri: Oh, I could spend a whole hour just talking about that. Plugins and overlays are the epitome of tools that were created *for* people with disabilities without including the people *with* disabilities. They take the assistive technology that users with disabilities have spent sometimes thousands of hours using and fine-tuning to their exact specifications. They yank that out, they put this other thing in its place, and they say, "Oh, hey, we know better. Use our stuff."

I have a friend who has been completely blind since he was 14. He can execute and interpret a Google query faster than I can because he's set his speech rate set at 375%. It sounds like Mickey Mouse to me! I can't interpret it at all. He has a Braille note taker attached to his laptop. Answers come back on the refreshable Braille display. Why take that away from somebody, give them something that they've never used before, and say, "Here, use this instead?"

That's what overlays do. They have some pretty sketchy business practices. They sell themselves as *all you have to do is insert one line of code and pay us $500 a year, and you will be litigation-proof.* That turned out to be horsesh*t. There have been two huge settlements at the end of 2021, one against AudioEye and the other against a company called eyebobs that sold prescription glasses online. Both were forced to make their underlying code WCAG compliant.

Debbie: Can a person with visual disabilities order a Domino's pizza yet?

Sheri: That I couldn't tell you because I don't eat there. I know you can still order on McDonald's. I'm using a screen reader because I had five eye surgeries in the span of 16 days. I had three weeks after that where I couldn't see, so I did everything using VoiceOver. I read my email using VoiceOver. I was hungry when I went for one of my follow-up appointments, so I ordered my Chicken McNuggets meal from the McDonald's next door using VoiceOver, and that worked.

People don't realize it's always been critical. And it's always been about equality for people with disabilities to be able to use these apps and websites. But hello, pandemic. People who are blind can't drive. They'd normally rely on public transportation, Uber, or friends. Especially during the earlier months of the pandemic, the buses were largely shut down. Uber was largely shut down. You weren't supposed to get within six feet of anybody that you didn't live with. Blind people needed to be able to order stuff through websites to have it delivered to their houses. And that just didn't work in a lot of cases.

Debbie: And everybody goes into a workshop and says, "We have empathy!"

Sheri: Yes, exactly. If you want a good definition of ableism, substitute a race or an ethnicity for the disability. Would it ever be OK to say, "I'm going to build software, but people from Mexico can't use it?" You could get fired for saying that. Only 2% of the world is accessible. Many are basically saying, "I'm going to build software, but I don't care whether or not people who are blind can use it."

Debbie: You hear, "Well, if someone's got a disability, they'll ask someone for help." Many people are unaware of the disability community's efforts to be independent.

Sheri: Thinking that somebody with a disability is just going to ask for help is a not-so-small microaggression. If I had to ask for help 30 times a day, 365 days a year, it gets old really fast, and it starts to wear on your self-confidence. You tend to slip into thinking like, "I can't do anything for myself. I always need somebody else to open the door for me." That's really problematic.

At one of my previous jobs, I had to enter all of the travel for anybody on my team who was blind because the travel booking system wasn't accessible. People can sue over that. Unfortunately, people with disabilities are 2.5 times more likely to be unemployed. That was a pre-pandemic number. Post-pandemic, it's actually worse because they were the first to get let go, especially in blue-collar jobs, and they're the last to be brought back. People with disabilities tend not to want to rock the boat by filing complaints because they're thinking, "What if I get fired? I'm not going to be able to find another job." That overwhelming concern about this employment disparity keeps them from filing complaints.

Debbie: People generally don't even sympathize until they or a loved one develop a disability.

Sheri: Exactly. I won't name the company, but there was somebody who was a little thorny about accessibility until he had a detached retina. And then, all of a sudden, it became important.

A couple of weeks before the pandemic really got out of hand, I had made arrangements with an executive to travel with them to India. We were going to check out the new facilities in India because they were being built, hypothetically, to the ADA standard so that American employees with disabilities could travel to India and work there with their teams. The executive said, "I want to see everything you see. I want to be there for the whole thing." And I said, "Do you want to be on the phone with me on hold for 45 minutes every time I have to book with the airline to tell them that I'm coming in a wheelchair?" Her jaw just dropped. She had no idea that every time I traveled, I spent a minimum of an hour and a half on the phone because airlines can't be bothered to store mobility device information with passenger records.

I refer to it as "the disability tax." People with disabilities have to invest time, money, or energy that people without disabilities have no clue about.

Debbie: Any other thoughts around customer-centricity or the employee experience?

Sheri: I subscribe to the Richard Branson rule, which is *if you take care of your employees, your employees will take care of your customers.* The problem is that too many people run fear-based compliance programs. They're more afraid of their customers, who are strangers, suing them than they are of their employees suing them.

Fix your internal house first. Don't forget that invisible disabilities are 70% of disabilities. You see me in a wheelchair, so you know that I have a mobility disability, but you don't know that I'm also a type 1 diabetic. From my perspective, having been in a wheelchair for 56 years, the wheelchair is just a mechanism of getting around. Type 1 diabetes, that's actually my real disability. It kicks my ass multiple times a day.

Get people on board and build a more disability-inclusive environment. And then naturally, with a little bit of steering, things will start to improve because more people will care.

Debbie: My husband's mother has such severe arthritis that her fingers no longer bend. My husband helps his mom with daily tasks like washing her hair or opening a jar.

Sheri: I have pretty bad arthritis. Opening bottles is the worst. Even with the bottle-opening devices, sometimes you just don't have the upper body strength to get those suckers to work.

Debbie: Mamma still drives but was having trouble with the clutch and shifting gears, so we got her a very used Smart Car. It's technically a manual transmission, but there's no clutch, and it has paddles like a racecar. That gave her back a lot of independence.

Sheri: I drive with hand controls. I don't use my feet to drive. It cost me $3,000. That's why people with disabilities frequently don't drive because most of them don't have jobs that allow them to afford $3,000 on something that keeps them mobile.

Debbie: I remember speaking to a woman with MS who is wheelchair-bound most of the day. She said she has to work from home because she cannot get herself in and out of a car. I think we forget that people want to be independent, but some won't be able to move in and out of a vehicle.

Sheri: We don't like the use of the word "wheelchair-bound." We use wheelchairs. Wheelchairs don't use us.

Debbie: Thank you, and I'm sorry. I'm always looking to improve my vocabulary. I still have some bad habits to get out of.

Sheri: VMware has installed an inclusive language module to everybody's Microsoft Word. It will flag if you use a non-inclusive word. "Lame" is an ableist word. "Spaz" is an ableist word. Calling somebody or something "crazy" is not disability-inclusive. There's a lot of language that still shows up every day; it really would be nice if it changed. You don't have to say crazy. You can say wild, bananas, wacky...

● DELIVERY: SENSITIVITY

~~is wheelchair-bound~~ →

uses a wheelchair

is a wheelchair user

Is wheelchair-bound may be considered an insensitive way to describe someone who uses a wheelchair. Consider changing the term.

Figure 30: Grammarly's sensitivity check suggested changing "wheelchair bound" to "uses a wheelchair" or "is a wheelchair user."

Debbie: It sounds like we need HR policies for behaviors, language, microaggressions, etc. Plus, an actual grievance process.

Sheri: It's more than that. It's one thing to have policies, but it's another thing to enforce them. They need to be enforced at the same level that you would enforce a microaggression against a Person of Color or a microaggression against a member of the LGBTQ community.

Chapter 14: Interview: Catering to Everyone

Mei Ke (they/them) is a researcher with an interdisciplinary background in intelligence analysis, government service, and diversity consulting. Their fascination with the impact of storytelling on human behavior drives their relentless curiosity. Their biggest passion is queer and transgender inclusion in research design. Learn more at https://www.meike.info.

Debbie: What is your definition of customer-centricity?

Mei: When I talk about customer focus, what I'm thinking about is: *how can I serve the person who is least served by society*? If I can cater to that one person, everything else is going to fall into line. I'm thinking usually of a Black trans woman who is also disabled and is non-neurotypical, maybe has some learning disabilities, all these things that we would say are edge cases in our society. If I can cater to this one person, then everyone else will be served.

I think that comes from both my personal experience as a queer non-binary person, and also as someone who's done a lot of work in the disability space and the accessibility space. Try to find the edge cases, cater to them, and everyone else will be catered to as well. It's the easiest solution.

Debbie: How do we ensure our leaders, teams, and companies aren't just falling into lazy stereotypes? Like, "A Black person needs this, and a trans person needs this?"

Mei: Everything is a case-by-case basis, but there are themes that are easy for us to follow. That's why our brains automatically go to them. A lot of people think of trans people, and the first thing they might think of is pronouns or bathroom access. Both of those are really important, obviously, but there are also other things that they might not think of like medical access.

I'm doing a case study on dating apps for non-binary people. Almost 70% of dating apps don't allow me to sign up because I have to put down either man or woman before I even sign up for the service. You're not understanding your audience. Non-binary people, like me, date! Surprising, I know! But I am a real human being who's living out in the world. *What are my needs? My wants?* They're usually going to be the same as anybody else. I want stable housing. I want access to food, health care, and access to the restroom. I want people to respect me and who I am and how I identify. Go to that first rather than stereotypes.

Debbie: I've noticed that there is some backlash from some communities, especially more marginalized communities, around the word "empathy." A lot of times when teams say, "We're empathizing with users," there are Black people, POC, LGBTQIA+, and others who are saying, "Are you sure you're really seeing my world through my eyes?"

Mei: It definitely comes off as disingenuous. It's sort of similar to what we call in the trans community the "you're so brave" narrative. Whenever I tell people about my story, they're like, "Oh, you're so brave." No, my life is hard. That's not me being brave. It's me figuring out how to live within the constraints that I have in society.

When we talk about empathy, I would rather have someone who's in the trenches with us, who is there to be an ally. Allyship is not just, "I'm an ally!" Are you out there actively advocating for my rights? When I get misgendered, do you stand up and say, "Hey, you misgendered them, and we need to correct that?" Are you the person who is advocating for gender-inclusive restrooms at every single place you work, whether or not you need them?

There are lots of different things you can do to be empathetic, rather than just saying you're empathetic. Words are really easy. Actions are much harder. You can never label yourself an ally. Seek out people who are in that community and ask, "How can I help you personally?" They will label you as an ally if you do a good job. It's a badge of honor that you should wear, but you have to earn it. You can't just say, "I'm empathetic. I'm an ally."

I can always tell when someone's trying, and I think that's way more important than not trying and just being a jerk. I've had some people who get tangled up in phrasing, and then they just don't say anything. It's much better to just say something and be wrong because then you can learn from it rather than not saying anything and keeping inside the potential wrong assumption that you're making. Say it and then say, "Hey, I think I might be wrong. Can you help me out here?" It could be an educational lesson.

Debbie: A place that I worked at a few years ago created groups, like one for Black people, one for LGBTQ, etc. I felt like I was on the outside of those, not that I should be on the inside of those since I don't qualify for those groups. But how do we give people those spaces and allow others to better understand those groups and identities?

Mei: Over here in America, those are Employee Resource Groups. This is always complicated. I've met a lot of self-proclaimed allies who want to be in the LGBTQIA+ group who are not LGBT. That's always complicated because the A part of the acronym includes allies. But people who are allies take up space in these kinds of groups that are meant for people to be 100% comfortable and 100% who they are. These groups are to be able to talk about microaggressions, discrimination, or just daily life and not have to worry about having to explain yourself or being judged.

When we talk about people outside of those groups wanting to be a part of these groups, what is another way we can do that? Connect with the leader of this group and ask them for any recommendations, maybe people who would be willing to hang out with others for lunch or a coffee. These groups are private, and the resources might not be shared externally, just for privacy's sake. That's a much better approach than saying, "I want to be included in the group because I want to be an ally," because it's the taking up space issue.

As a white person, I would love to help contribute my own perspective to a group about Asian American and Pacific Islanders because I did a lot of my studies around Chinese culture. I feel like I have a lot to say there, but I also need to recognize that while my insight might be interesting to people in the group, is it necessary? Probably not. These people know way more about being Asian or Pacific Islander than I could ever know, as my little white self from Texas.

Even though I feel like I have a lot to say, it doesn't necessarily mean that I have to say it. We should ask how we can support those groups, monetarily or physically showing up. That and shows of allyship are more than just saying, "I want to be included."

Debbie: And that's the route I've taken. I've gone to the leaders of the group and said, "Look, I know I'm not in your group, but I want to support your group. And if there's something you think I can do to express that support, let me know."

I thought about this when I attended a business meeting, and some of the HR staff had their rainbow shirts and their water cups with "I [rainbow heart] [Company]." They had all their rainbow apparel on. My gut reaction was: *this is performative*. How can we distinguish between performative rainbows and doing the right things for our marginalized or misunderstood communities?

Mei: It's always going to be performative until something is done. The rainbow sticker should be the last step. It's not the first step. You should have already done all the steps beforehand. You should be known as an LGBT-friendly and inclusive company before you even consider making your Facebook logo a rainbow. If you're in Silicon Valley and you've changed your company logo to a rainbow, I'm not interested in that, especially if you change it on June 1st, just Pride Month. This is very performative.

Are you making a statement that's like, "We support the LGBTQIA+ community!" and not actually doing anything? For example, Disney says they support the queer community. But then Disney supported a Florida ban on education on queer topics. Disney claimed they got a personal reassurance from the governor that it wouldn't hurt queer people. Oh, now that is a very clear statement that you have no idea what you're talking about! Now Disney is walking back this statement, but they've lost credibility with the queer community. There will be huge repercussions for that, like the financial and other repercussions JK Rowling has been facing from being anti-trans.

Be aware that when your company says something, you have to actually mean it. My community is very loyal, but we're also understanding of and loyal to our own. If you're not going to treat us right, we're not going to be doing any business with you.

Debbie: I remember when the Barilla pasta CEO said he was for traditional marriage, and everyone boycotted him. He had to walk it back within a week, probably because someone saw the sales numbers plummet.

Mei: Exactly. I think people don't understand how intense, loyal, and amazing the LGBT customer base is. I know entire companies that are built exclusively on LGBT customers. One of them that I'm a really big fan of is Tomboy [tomboyx.com]. They specifically make underwear for LGBT customers, a very niche market. But they specifically cater to trans masculine people like me, who have a different body type and have other concerns with finding underwear that is comfortable. Sizes go up to five-XL, and they go super small as well.

You can build an entire business just on trans masculine people. Imagine how much you could do being actually supportive of the *entire* LGBT community. We spread the word around. The whole reason Tomboy is doing so well is because everyone in the trans community spread the word about it. We talk about it, we talk about it on social media, and I recommend this company at almost every single talk I do because they're a great company. Word spreads fast. If you want to get good customers, you need to treat them right.

Debbie: What are some things we can look out for around not living up to our own values or not following through on some of our glossy statements?

Mei: Two things come to mind. First is how easy it is for an employee to change their name in your system. It sounds very simple. But name changes are one of the most difficult issues that trans people face specifically. I've been with a health insurance company for two years, and they still haven't fully changed my name. Some things are in my previous legal name, and some are in my current legal name. There are some prescriptions I can't pick up without bringing in my official court documents.

Can you change your email? Can you change your chat logs? Is your insurance easy to change over? Ask your IT person how easy is it to change an employee's name in the system. If it's not easy, that should be the first thing you deal with. It's such a basic thing, especially as someone who chose my own name, one that's incredibly important and meaningful to me. I want to make sure that people use the correct name for me. I don't want a constant reminder at the bottom of my video chat window of my incorrect name.

Another one is checking in with your healthcare procedures and coverage to check specifically for trans people who want to transition. There are a lot of companies that specifically market on, "We have a trans-inclusive policy, and we will cover all of your surgeries if you come work for our company." That's a huge incentive because my top surgery without insurance cost $35,000 USD.

Also, a company's dress code is important. A lot of people who are in the queer community specifically express themselves through the way that they dress. If your company says, "You're a woman, so you're not allowed to wear masculine clothes," that, obviously, is gender discrimination, and I would argue LGBT discrimination.

Debbie: That makes me think about working for European companies. As an American, it's been interesting to see that the maternity leave in the UK is one year. When I worked for a German company, some new dads took one month of paternity leave. [*Note: I learned after the interview that Germany does allow longer paternity leave, but the maximum monthly salary is quite low, so many people opt for shorter leave. Mei is responding to my original statement that German dads get a month of paternity leave.]*

Mei: If I qualify as the father, do I only get one month off? If I carry the baby, I get a year off. That's a misunderstanding of how gender works. What if the woman in a relationship is the main earner? Maybe she wants to take one month off and then get back to work. Maybe the dad wants to take care of the child the whole time. Plus, assumptions around straight relationships and assumptions that trans people don't exist.

Why can't we just have parental leave? Do we have to make rules because we think people don't know how to take care of themselves? Or they won't know how to act responsibly within the work environment that they're in? I think that's an infantilization of our employees. You hired them for a reason. They're competent people. We need to trust them to be able to do good work, know when it's appropriate to take time off, and when it's appropriate to come back.

Debbie: This might be a little controversial, but I'm saying it anyway. So many companies create a DEI job, but we're not following through on any of that to the rest of the organization. We announce our Black or gay or disabled Head of Diversity, but is that person empowered to make changes and clean up the culture?

Mei: It's so true. It's really frustrating. I'm very tired of people talking the talk and not walking the walk. Companies say they're ready to be diverse and inclusive when they are not ready. They think that you can have a PowerPoint about racism, and racism will disappear. That's not how it works. You have to actually do the work. You have to deconstruct racism in your own life, personally as well as professionally.

Companies say they're ready for that, and they're not. They're looking for that one PowerPoint to check off things for their stakeholders or the board of directors, and then they'll be good. Often, they hire a DEI person who is really good at PowerPoints or knows how to talk about it, but doesn't know how to implement it, isn't willing to, or isn't empowered to. If we're worrying about stakeholders or the board of directors, I call it "catering to white feelings."

This frustrates me because I understand where it's coming from; in some ways, I do the same thing for people who are not queer. I will cater and make things simpler for people who are not queer so they can understand. But that also does you a disservice. It's assuming that you can't understand these complicated subjects.

You have to hire and look for people who are willing to push you and challenge you. You have to accept that challenge, and – even when it's hard – ask how we can do more than that. *How can I go the extra mile?* Not just the metrics or optics of, "We hired one more Black person on our team." Ask how we can completely redo our entire hiring system to be more inclusive of all the people that we can think of. How can we reach out to these people? Can we hire consultants to make sure that we're covering all the bases? Maybe we have a Black woman in a DEI role, which is great, but maybe she's not LGBT. Let's hire a consultant or consult with someone who's LGBT so they could provide additional support here.

Recognize your weaknesses and where you have gaps. Fill them as best you can or outsource when you can't do that. You can't be like, "Alright, what points of diversity does this person have?" They're a human being, and this would be very degrading. You need to see them as a whole person. The points of diversity are just ways that make them more interesting or more fun to be around because you get that diverse opinion and perspective.

Debbie: What can a company do if they wish they were more ready and not there yet?

Mei: The first thing is that you need to have a leader who is committed. But sometimes, the leadership comes last in that process. That's a mistake because you need to have someone at the forefront who has the power and the money to hire the people, get things moving, and make decisions. You need the decision-maker to be the first hire so they can start strategizing this.

Be open in communication. "Hey, we are on this diversity and inclusion journey, and we are not there yet." We want people to feel like they can fail and make mistakes in our environment, recover from that, and be supported in that journey. When we talk about making culture change, you need to create an environment where mistakes are OK, if not encouraged.

However, if people are not going where the company is going, they will leave. If someone doesn't like the company being anti-racist, they might choose to leave. If they are racist and they don't seem to want to change or leave, we need to address that. Provide that room for growth, but also be clear on the boundaries. *We are moving in this direction, and we expect you to move in this direction with us. If you are not willing to make a personal and professional change toward diversity and inclusion, then you're probably not going to be a good match for this company.* You can always work for someone that aligns with your needs and values. Don't just make assumptions that everyone should cater to you if your values don't match the company's.

Debbie: Companies love numbers and metrics and KPIs and OKRs. Part of me says, "Great, make some DEI metrics." And then the other part of me says, "OMG, don't make DEI metrics!" This is not about counting gay or Black people.

Mei: It doesn't matter how many you have. It matters how they feel. Are these people feeling comfortable? Are they experiencing microaggressions? Are they thinking about quitting? Are they thinking about getting a promotion but feel like they don't have access to that because of their identity?

These are way more important qualitative and quantitative things that you can measure. You could send out a survey asking anonymously *how likely you are to leave your job in the next six months. Can you describe the reason for that? Are you happy? Are you experiencing microaggressions?* Then connect that with data like *are you gay or queer.* Doing the metrics based on that is much more telling. Then you can say, "It looks like all of our gay employees are likely to leave in the next six months." That tells me a lot more than, "I have six gay employees." It says *I have these gay employees, and none of them are happy.* Then I can start making these correlations rather than working from percentages and then assumptions about entire groups of people. Talk about stereotypes!

It's also very telling if you have six gay people, but they're all like, "I love this company. I'm not planning on leaving, and I really enjoy the environment here." Then the story is, "It looks like we're pretty gay-inclusive, but what about our BIPOC employees? Are they feeling the same way? What if there is an interaction where someone is Black and also trans?" That impacts the analysis that we're talking about.

Debbie: Anything else on your mind related to customer-centricity or employee-centricity that we didn't touch on?

Mei: Yes. A mistake a lot of people make is they assume that the professional is different than the personal. If I notice that you're surrounded by very diverse people at your workplace, but in your personal life, you are not, that is a red flag for me. You also need to reach out and make personal connections that are diverse and find people that challenge you.

Also, identities are important, but they aren't the whole person. I would rather that someone message me on LinkedIn saying they liked a talk I did or asking me about my interest in video games. Or my recommendation for places to see in San Diego. That's a much more interesting opener than, "What does it mean that you're transgender?" I've literally received messages like that before. You wouldn't go up to a woman and ask, "What does it feel like to be a woman?"

Debbie: As soon as you're thinking, "I have a trans friend," or, "I have a Black friend," you're doing it wrong.

Mei: Yeah, exactly. I know a lot of people who may think we are friends. But I do not consider you a friend. I see you as an acquaintance who likes to use me as an excuse for saying, "I have met a trans person." It's isolating and alienating because you don't actually care about me; you care about my identity.

It's strange how far we've come, and so there's so much farther we have to go.

Chapter 15: Aspirologies

There are trendy approaches that often work against customer-centricity. "Aspirologies" is my made-up term for approaches that don't deserve the credibility of being called "methodologies" since they often hurt processes, morale, and outcomes. Since these are currently popular – and at some companies, beloved – we will need to keep our critical thinking hats on as I ask you to reconsider approaches that you might currently respect, admire, or utilize.

The main Aspirologies you will run into are design sprints, design thinking, Lean UX (from the *Lean UX* book), which is neither Lean nor UX, and democratization, which we covered in the "Common Research Mistakes" chapter. Many of these approaches revolve heavily around the use of group and team workshops, often spanning hours or days.

Aspirologies have several common characteristics you can easily recognize:

- **Co-dependency.** CX or UX seems to require others to do their jobs for and with them.

- **Disrespect of teammates' time.** Coworkers must pause their mission critical work for hours or days to participate in Aspirologies.

- *Speed over quality.* Aspirologies try to make CX or Design work faster, taking hours or days instead of weeks or longer. Aspirologies are less concerned about outcomes and more concerned about timeboxes. But cycles of workshops, guesses, and experiments often take more time and money than using a thorough UCD process the first time.

- **Reliance on assumptions.** Aspirologies increase business and project risk by running with guesses and hoping that'll save time. We should document the risks of running with assumptions and then challenge our assumptions.

- **Giving specialized work to non-specialists.** Aspirologies love giving CX work to those without CX knowledge, expertise, experience, skill, or talent. But where else would we do that? We don't give back-end database architecture to anybody with spare time or an interest in databases.

  o   Non-CX roles never give up power or decisions in their own domains. We don't have the cross-functional team all making Engineering decisions.

- **Team-building theatre.** If Aspirology workshops were great for team building, we would hold these workshops in every domain. We'd have Product, Engineering, Business Analysis, and Marketing workshops. But we don't, because high-performing teams respect each other's specialties and play to each other's strengths rather than trying to turn everybody into a broad generalist.

- **Customer-centricity theatre.** We pretend that we really care about customers and their satisfaction, but we guess who they are and what they need. We don't observe or research the people we're building for.

- **Empathy theatre.** We pretend we have empathy or sympathy, but if we cared about Users' Experiences, we wouldn't rush out garbage that doesn't solve customers' problems and improve their task accomplishment.

- **Innovation theatre.** How many never-before-seen, world premiere ideas came out of these workshops? How many "innovations" were non-viable? How many of our innovations made it to market, and how did they do?

- **Vote for the winner.** We shouldn't pick products, features, or concepts American Idol style. We have UCD to guide us in finding the best solution for our target audiences.

  o We don't all gather together, spend hours or days brainstorming various product roadmaps, and then vote on our favorite roadmap.

  o CX Architects don't hang designs at their desks and invite coworkers to vote.

  o Voting on *our* favorite anything is self-centric.

- **Fun craft time.** Many workshops could instead be a simple meeting where something is discussed or socialized. Why infantilize or distract business discussions and decisions with games, wackiness, or crafts?

  o If your company has a cultural need for fun craft time, schedule that, but ensure that crafts and exercises are not around tasks or decisions in any work domain.

- **Emotional outcomes and no accountability.** We often hear, "Everybody enjoyed the workshop," but where are the actual budget and ROI figures? Does our workshop have success criteria?

  o How will we measure that the original goals and purpose for the workshop were achieved, and it were worth the time and money we spent?

  o When workshops fail us or our customers, how do we ensure that we don't repeat the same errors? Or do we schedule another workshop – possibly with more people – to do another round of guesses and brainstorming?

  o If we believe in continuous improvement and accountability, then we must make sure that we are not caught in cycles of "fun" workshops that burn time and money but produce little or no results.

- **Enough buzzwords thrown in so that it sounds like CX even if it's not CX.** You'll hear about customer journey maps, personas, problem solving, prototypes, and testing.

  o In a workshop environment, these artifacts and documents are often guesses. We prioritize speed and *checking them off a list as done* over the quality of the artifacts. As we learned earlier, making these artifacts doesn't mean they have been made well or will set us up for success.

- **Not accessible.** Many on-site and online tools used in these workshops are not accessible. The very nature of the workshops might be a mismatch for someone with anxiety, autism, memory issues, introversion, shyness, or another trait, condition, or diagnosis.

  o How are we ensuring that everybody is included in ways that best suit them? Are we allowing people to decline these workshops?

- **"Design" or "problem solving" only takes hours or days.** Aspirologies teach leaders and teammates that if we have a problem to solve, just throw some people in a room for hours or days.

  o It sometimes sounds like the more "wicked" the problem, the less time we spend on it.

  o Companies went from believing in full R&D with qualified Researchers, scientists, futurists, etc., to believing that these same challenges can be solved in days with sticky notes, plastic blocks, and pre-defined brainstorming games.

Aspirologies disempower customer-centricity. It's hard to teach the value of *great Customer Experiences* and *thorough CX work* while teaching teammates and leaders that CX can be done quickly in workshops, with templates, and often with little or no research. Aspirologies work against evidence-based Design and decision-making. Aspirologies are hurting ways of working, morale, and the quality of what we deliver to customers. You don't have to take my word for it. You can reflect on the above list, examine the ROI, check on employee and customer outcomes, and decide what's truly working well. Use the governance model from the "Common Research Mistakes" chapter.

Try It: Your Best Ideas

Many people find that they are most creative when left to themselves in a peaceful environment where their brains can make new connections. Harvard Business Review has published multiple articles on how brainstorming alone is more effective than in groups, including "Your Team Is Brainstorming All Wrong." [https://cxcc.to/a183]

In the coming days and weeks, notice when and where you get your best ideas. In scheduled brainstorming meetings? When you first wake up? In the shower? Taking a walk? If you have ever come up with an innovative and fresh idea, where were you, and what were you doing?

Let's dive deeper into the three main Aspirologies we haven't yet covered – design thinking, design sprints, and *Lean UX* – and why they are often customer-peripheric.

Design Sprints

Design sprints are presented as a fast way to solve challenges, design PSE, or innovate in just days. Over a decade ago, they were considered a good way for a startup without CX staff – and usually without research insights – to brainstorm their way to the PSE that would be the MVP.

A design sprint typically involves seven people or fewer, and one is designated as the decision maker. One might hope that this is a CX expert, but it is often the CEO of a small company, a high-level leader, or a key stakeholder. If not facilitated very carefully, the design sprint can be a drawn-out, days-long, extended version of *we'll just do what this higher-paid person wants.* It is not required that CX specialists be facilitators or even present, and executing good qualitative research before the design sprint is often treated as optional.

Professional facilitators started finding problems with design sprints, so they created new versions. This is not an evolution where nobody uses version 1 anymore because newer versions exist. Teams can select which version they prefer to use.

- The original version 1 of design sprints devotes five days to defining the problem, ideating or sketching potential solutions, deciding which sketch is the winner through voting, prototyping the winning concept (often a quick paper prototype), and testing. "Defining the problem" typically includes everybody in the workshop putting together a customer journey map, personas, or an empathy map. We have already explored some problems that can arise when these documents are not based on current data from good qualitative research.

- Version 2 of design sprints does not allow workshop attendees to prototype or test. The design sprint is two days long, and over after picking the winner. Prototyping and testing were deemed too important, so these tasks are done by CX experts, who report later how they went.

- Version 3 of design sprints removed everything relating to defining the problem so that people aren't guessing or going with what they think users do. Facilitators found that the problem the stakeholder presented often couldn't be validated. Version 3 requires experts to do weeks of qualitative research before the design sprint starts. Observational studies, interviews, personas, journey maps, and other artifacts are not done as team exercises. Research data is then shown to design sprint attendees so they can understand customers and the problem.

Figure 31: Visualization of the three versions of design sprints, broken into days. Tasks in orange boxes are given to specialists rather than done by all attendees. The visualization is explained above and below the image.

If we remove what design sprints versions 2 and 3 want done by experts, the only group exercise we have left is "everybody sketch solutions and vote on your favorite." Going back to our list of Aspirology common characteristics, asking everybody to sketch ideas can make it look like your CX Architects or Designers can't do their jobs themselves. The winning idea and its winning execution should be determined through UCD: rounds of information architecture, interaction design, testing, and iteration. This would be more customer-centric, having involved real or archetypal customers, and not our internal team picking their personal favorites.

Design sprints are devolving. Who is making these changes? The facilitation agencies making wild money running design sprints. Like any good capitalists, they want to make money and look good by creating better outcomes for clients. These facilitators appear to have found that better outcomes happen when you take tasks away from the design sprint attendees. One design sprint facilitation company sells version 3 starting with six weeks of research and then four weeks of planning the design sprint before it starts. Ten weeks doesn't feel much like a "sprint." It sounds like we're getting closer to proper UCD, in which case we should just do UCD.

A random email invited me to a webinar about *validating your product roadmap with a 2-hour design sprint*. **If we developed the roadmap through customer insights prioritization and included collaboration between Product, CX, and Engineering, it's a valid roadmap.** How did we previously validate our roadmaps and "get stakeholder buy-in?" How is a 2-hour design sprint better than whatever we do now? Is a 2-hour meeting really a design sprint? Design sprints are not designed for validating roadmaps. Will we be *empathizing* with the roadmap?

The webinar also suggests that you can learn to run multiple design sprints in a week, which makes it sound like the biggest problem with design sprints is that *two, four, or five days were too long*. Are we slapping "design sprint" and "design thinking" on every method and training in the hope that people will attend?

What Is Design Thinking?

An immediate problem with design thinking is its definition. What *is* design thinking? Over the past few years, I have been told that it is a mindset, process, methodology, philosophy, pedagogy, and tool in a toolbox. I've been told that it is the same as HCD, and I've been told that it is completely different from HCD. I've been told that it is a derivative of HCD, and I've been told that it has nothing to do with HCD because "HCD is old-fashioned and out of style."

I've been told that design thinking is something we are all doing naturally because we are all thinkers and we are all designers, whether that be drawing, arranging furniture, or putting together a nice outfit. And I've been told that we are not doing it naturally, and we all need to get training and certification.

The best definition I can provide is: *design thinking is a boiled-down, skimped-on micro-derivative of HCD that has become a cottage industry.*

Design thinking slims weeks or months of mission critical UCD work into stages often called "empathize, define, ideate, prototype, and test." "Ideate, prototype, and test" might sound like UCD, though the design thinking version prioritizes *speed over quality.* "Empathize" varies; in some cases, deep research is suggested. In other cases, we run with what the design thinking workshop's attendees know, assume, or believe about customers. In some cases, workshop attendees guess at customer journey maps, personas, and other documents that are supposed to be the artifacts of qualitative research.

Design thinking is presented as *the* way to solve any problem, especially "wicked" problems. In January 2020, a Fortune article stated that design thinking could solve the coronavirus. [https://cxcc.to/a122] We must have done design thinking poorly since as of this chapter's writing in October 2022, the coronavirus still has not been solved. The article suggested that the entire country of China, which in January 2020 was allegedly wholly at fault for the coronavirus, just needed more "empathy" and "iteration." Never mind those urban planners, epidemiologists, zoologists, sociologists, medical experts, medical lab researchers, and others who might be involved in helping to stop a pandemic. *They all need more design thinking.* This article has not aged well.

Episode 108 of my live streamed video podcast was, "What ISN'T Design Thinking?" [https://cxcc.to/a108] A guest and I walked through multiple definitions of design thinking, and noticed one key thing in common: none of the sources told you how to do design thinking or any of its steps. *What does empathizing look like? What does not empathizing look like? What if we make the wrong type of prototype? What if our testing doesn't recruit the correct number of participants from our target audiences?*

Design thinking has become like religion; *it's anything and everywhere.* It's listening and imagining and making and new solutions. People saying it's a mindset might tell you it's absolutely not a process. People saying it's a process might tell you it's absolutely not a philosophy. Each person believes in their own One True Design Thinking with all others being false.

In addition to the amorphous and chameleon-like definitions of design thinking, its origin story is also troubling. I recommend my article, "Was Design Thinking Designed To Not Work?" [https://cxcc.to/a151] for a look at the history of IDEO inventing design thinking. I examine how IDEO knows design thinking is going wrong and is mostly theatre, but hasn't iterated on design thinking to solve these wicked problems.

Is Design Thinking the Same as HCD or UCD?

A 2022 Senior Lead UX Designer job posted by AT&T says that you will "create new innovative Customer Experiences through modern practices of design and design thinking methods." The job description says, "You're well-versed in user-centered methodologies and design thinking." Seeing a Fortune 50 company clearly delineate between UCD and design thinking helps us understand that these are not the same approach or method.

Some differences between design thinking and UCD include:

- **Design thinking is sold as something you do quickly.** It only requires hours or days of team workshops. When done correctly, a thorough UCD process can take weeks or months.

    o UCD is a *quality over speed* model. And you can be sure when IDEO gets a consulting project, they spend more than five days on it.

- **Design thinking is solution-focused.** The goal of workshops and exercises is to create potential solutions. If we haven't correctly defined problems, how likely are we to come up with the best solutions? If our problem statements are incorrect or guesses, what risks have we created?

    o UCD starts with research aimed at truly understanding people, contexts, and systems so that we can correctly define problems, unmet needs, and opportunities.

- **Design thinking doesn't guarantee that anybody empathizes or defines the problem correctly.** Some teams do little or no research before their design thinking exercises or design sprint. They start with what they assume, guess, or hope about users. You probably know teams who started Aspirology exercises with something they wanted to build anyway, hoping to prove their idea is good.

    o **UCD starts solution-agnostic.** We start with questions and problems without considering yet how they might be solved.

- **Design thinking is attendee-centric.** We choose a solution by having people in the room vote on their favorite. We ask "How Might We" when neither the problem nor the solution is about us.

- UCD chooses a solution by testing over and over with target or existing customers so that we can be sure what we are creating matches real people's needs and tasks.

  - User-Centered Design has customer-centricity in its name.

- **A poor idea or a poor execution of a good idea might be crowned the winner.** If the selected idea isn't five-stars-out-of-five quality, this is very risky for our project and company.

  - UCD is focused on quality, and is unlikely to move forward with a poor concept (when CX practitioners are given the time and budget to do great work).

- **Design thinking seems to have low or no standards for prototyping and testing.** It often sounds like any coworkers you can find or anybody you can grab in a coffee shop is a good testing participant because, *hey, let's do this fast.*

  - UCD would require proper testing planning, participant recruiting and selection, and often a prototype that is more realistic to the experience.

I don't need design thinking because I use UCD and critical thinking. I've never needed a design sprint. Nobody has ever asked me to stop doing my UCD work and just do design thinking instead.

Design thinking is marketed very differently to CX/UX professionals versus those outside the CX/UX profession. Outside of CX and UX, people are sold on the promise that they will think, work, innovate, and solve problems like IDEO's best Designers. Inside CX and UX, we are told that getting our coworkers trained on design thinking and bringing it into our companies will sell the value of CX and UX jobs, Design, customer-centricity, and HCD.

These opposite promises are both false promises. Design thinking does not turn non-CX roles into CX geniuses, even after some training and a certificate. Design thinking has rarely given HCD a real seat at the table, amplified customers' voices, and made teammates understand and appreciate what CX/UX staff do. The opposite has happened. Design thinking has taught non-CX roles that they can do what CX roles do, no experience, education, or talent required. *Just use design thinking!*

I sometimes hear that design thinking is a Trojan Horse: *we'll take a company that doesn't care about users, introduce design thinking, and once they're into it, we'll introduce HCD as the better way to go.* One key problem is that design thinking doesn't present itself as a first step or beginner way to get into HCD. Design thinking presents itself as *the best way* to solve problems, innovate, and create PSE. Therefore, if teammates fall in love with Aspirologies, how will you explain that there is a better way? After all the design thinking fun, who will welcome HCD and its lack of workshops, games, and LEGO?

Some CX or UX experts have told me stories of bringing "design thinking" into the company, but they used HCD, not design thinking. By calling HCD "design thinking," they got interest, support, and buy-in because design thinking is hot and trendy. And since the definition of design thinking is so fluffy, nobody said, "Hey, wait a minute! That's Human-Centered Design, not design thinking!" In these situations, I imagine HCD (under its pseudonym "design thinking") is working, but we should be honest and call processes by their correct names.

Quick Fix Versus Slow Fix: Design Thinking and Design Sprints

If you want to reduce or eliminate Aspirologies, the **quick fix** would be to quit cold turkey. Put your highly qualified CX team in charge of all Design-related workshops. They might decide that they would rather have the time and budget to do their best work and not rush into group solution brainstorming. Instead of frequent workshops and brainstorming sessions, you can also shift toward the product discovery methods recommended later in the book.

The **slow fix** is to continue doing design thinking and design sprints, but you can start reducing the frequency, and you can change their type. Start doing version 3 of design sprints, where qualified Researchers get six weeks to do generative research. Combine that with version 2 of design sprints, where qualified Designers create our prototypes, and partner with Researchers for evaluative research (testing).

Either fix is a good start.

The *Lean UX* Book

Lean UX is another Aspirology turning CX and UX into workshops and Design by committee. For reference, I'm using the 2016 second edition of the book. Core problems include:

- The authors claim they don't want work by committee, but their **definition of collaboration says that all work is a team effort, which sounds like work by committee.** The authors demand that you not give any work to any individual, even if they are highly specialized. CX research and its interpretation should be done by "the team."

- **It's meeting-heavy.** If you thought you were in too many meetings before trying *Lean UX*, look out. Since every CX task is done by committee, Product Managers, Engineers, stakeholders, and others will be involved in multiple daily meetings and team exercises. Everybody is equally involved in research, design, testing, and other important CX tasks, and these all occur in meetings of two or more people.

- **Overreliance on what stakeholders want.** "We've found it helpful to begin with a problem statement. These statements are created by key stakeholders as they begin to address the strategic vision for the business." [Kindle Location 645]

  - We learned from design sprints version 3 that starting with stakeholders describing the problem or what challenge we're here to address was often the wrong way to start.

- o To be customer-centric, we must define problems from the perspectives we have collected from customers, not from a stakeholder looking at business goals. These might not be aligned with or close to real customers' needs, habits, and likely actions. A stakeholder's vision *should* be customer-centric, but if it's not, this is risk we will need to identify and mitigate.

- o *Lean UX* assumes that working from stakeholders' problem statements and team assumptions goes well. The book provides no plan B. What should you do if the stakeholder's problem statement is garbage?

- **Too much time spent on assumptions rather than collecting or using great data and customer intelligence.** Many exercises in the book start and/or end with collecting all of the assumptions everybody on the team has about the customer, the product, how testing went, or something else.

  - o Rather than documenting those assumptions as risks and researching to replace guesses with knowledge, *Lean UX* tells you to move forward with your guesses and assumptions.

  - o This isn't Lean, and runs against Six Sigma's desire to prioritize verifiable data over assumptions and guesswork.

- **The *Lean UX* book recommends nearly zero documentation** because *we were all in that meeting.* It seems unprofessional to rely on human memories of an event so that we can avoid documenting it.

  - o Some documentation is essential. What happens when people quit, are fired, or go on extended leave?

  - o What if someone has a poor memory? What if we all remember that meeting differently?

  - o What if we are onboarding someone new to the team and they want to read existing project documentation? Will we tell them we are "too Lean" to have that?

- **The *Lean UX* Canvas was mostly borrowed from a business model canvas, yet most people are not using the *Lean UX* canvas to decide their business model.** For a full breakdown of why the *Lean UX* canvas is another flawed template likely to create risk and waste, please read my article, "Critical Thinking About The Lean UX Canvas" [https://cxcc.to/a184].

Lean UX is a non-viable model that disempowers CX and UX. Most CX and UX professionals read and then disregarded the book when it was published. Nearly zero CX professionals wanted to see their workplace adopt this approach. But CX and UX practitioners made one critical mistake: they ignored the book and assumed it would go away instead of leaving it bad reviews and speaking up against it. They assumed that if the UX profession didn't adopt or implement *Lean UX*, the Aspirology would be seen as a non-starter.

The word "Lean" on the cover attracted some lovers of Agile. With very few negative reviews of the book, it was assumed that it was somewhere between OK and well-liked, and it was brought into SAFe and Scrum.org. We'll cover this more (plus how to solve it) in our chapter on Task-Oriented UCD.

Some companies say that they are doing "Lean UX." When I ask them to describe the process they are using, it doesn't match what the book proposes. "Lean UX" now means *either* the book or "the least UX work that we can do," jumping off from the incorrect definition of Lean. Lean is about identifying and cutting waste; excellent CX work and customer-centricity are not waste we can or should cut.

"But Big/Other Companies Use [Aspirologies]"

We love to try what big companies do, even when we don't know how well it works for them. Articles announcing "disruptive" and "amazing" methods are sometimes later overshadowed by articles about how those methods didn't work. Sometimes the articles about how those methods failed are *not* being published since who wants to admit a methodological failure? You hear about the company's radical new model or approach, and then you don't hear much about it again.

For example, at one point, people fell in love with Spotify's Engineering model around teams called "squads." We saw a big company doing something that sounded cool. Articles were everywhere about how great this model was. Now, the articles are all about how this model failed, and might only work with serious revisions.

Design thinking, design sprints, and "democratization" are also models we hear big companies using, so we thought we should try that too. But several articles speak out against these methods. They're harder to find since Google searches tend to optimize for positive articles (especially since the Google name is associated with design sprints), but you can find them when searching.

Any time we are trying a new method – for great reasons, or for "that company is doing it!" reasons – we need to utilize change management and governance. You can use and customize the suggested governance model at the end of the upcoming "Strategy and Planning" chapter.

"Design Thinking, Design Sprints, or Lean UX Was Supposed to Transform Our Company"

Did they? Or are you doing the same things as before, but now saying "design thinking" or "empathy" more often, or running more workshops? Have you changed your ways of working other than taking the cross-functional team away from their mission critical work more often to attend workshops? Did we teach everybody the value of customer-centricity? Did the Aspirology deliver or create the desired transformation? Have we rethought KPIs? Are we still a feature factory, driven by velocity and how many features we shipped?

A member of my community told a story about a disastrous workshop. The goal was to get internal staff together to catalog customer pain points despite not having researched them. More than 20 people, mostly stakeholders, were in attendance. One Product Owner declared that they already knew all of the customers' pain points because "we have analytics." The PO said they should be doing the prioritization themselves, and they'll "let Design know when we need something from you." A UX Manager battled this PO for 20 minutes, and asked a different PO for their "top three things," which ended up being the meeting's "takeaway."

Not all workshops go this badly, but I have been at multiple ones like this. I have been at the 50-person workshop run by a Product Manager and a Scrum Master that asked everybody to brainstorm how to make users do what we want them to do, even though we had no research or insights explaining current customer behaviors. I have been at the 20-person workshop that hypothesized that our PSE should be addictive like Facebook, and *can everybody think of ways to make our PSE more "habit-forming."* I was not invited to the workshop where seven visual designers came up with Christmas-themed ideas. They brought these to Product Managers, bypassing CX and UX, and requested that Engineering build and release their sketches.

These are not transformative experiences. If Aspirologies were working well or were transformational, we would see this reflected in both leading and lagging indicators. Are we seeing lower utilization of Customer Support? Is our NPS or customer satisfaction score improving? Is our Cost of Acquisition decreasing while our ease of acquisition is increasing?

Shift away from "workshops are fun" or "we really had a lot of empathy," and make sure that we are using solid metrics to analyze costs versus benefits for Aspirologies.

If Aspirologies Are So Bad, Why Aren't More People Speaking Up?

- **Who wants to say, "Hey, that thing I brought into the company that we spent all that time and money on isn't working, and we need to stop doing it?"**

  - Nobody would have to admit this if we had the right governance and metrics. The people monitoring our processes and internal experiments would see what's working and what isn't, and be authorized to act on their findings.

- **Aspirologies are seen as new, modern, and the cool thing everybody is doing.**

  o The cool thing may be failing and costing you a lot of money. Few companies are calculating what they are spending and how much they are losing by following a cool trend. Forget trends and do the math. Check the Cost of Poor Quality. Check VOC and customer satisfaction scores. We might think we are fast, but how are we really doing?

  o Many of these "skip research, design as little as possible, build, release, evolve" techniques came from books like *The Lean Startup*. Yet statistically speaking, a mind-boggling percentage of startups using this technique fail and go out of business. *The Lean Startup* book requires more critical thinking and challenging.

- **People might feel lost without a replacement.** *If design thinking is an amazing process designed to solve everything, what are we going to do instead?*

  o Your replacement is HCD/UCD.

- **When CX and UX leaders battle Aspirologies, they often hear, "That's not Agile," "Why are you being so negative?" and other arguments that do not debate the pros and cons of Aspirologies head-on.**

  o If we hear insults, negative framing, and gaslighting, we should call them out, hold people accountable for such behavior, and carry on with what we know is customer-centric.

  o Thinking back to the interview about ethics, our company should empower staff to raise red flags and challenge the status quo.

  o "The VP told us everybody can do research. How am I supposed to go up against a VP?" We wouldn't leave lower-level staff to fight leadership if we had governance. It shouldn't be "VP versus staff." CX and UX leaders need to be on the front lines.

Stepping Stone: Remove Voting

One customer-centric improvement you can make to your workshops is to remove voting on PSE ideas, solutions, or features. Brainstorming workshops can be fun and may yield some interesting ideas, but the best idea to work on first is the idea that best matches customers and their tasks, not the idea that happened to get the most popular votes.

Being value-led and evidence-based means that we must work toward what will be the best match for customers. We should not organize our PSE roadmap based on idea popularity contests. Ideas must be moved through the User-Centered Design process so that our CX experts can determine the ones most likely to create customer satisfaction and loyalty.

For groups who don't want to give up voting, have them vote on *customer value*. "Put a dot on the three ideas that have the most customer value." You don't have to use this as your final prioritization, but you can see what your teammates think.

Chapter 16: When Agile Works Against Customer-Centricity

"Agile does not fix: poor leadership, poor management, lack of engagement, company political games, people's ego, command-and-control culture, poor behaviors/culture/mindset, over-allocation of people, lack of focus and commitment, poor customer focus, poor process workflow, poor communication/ collaboration, the lack of collaboration between Business and IT, lack of people's motivation, poor HR compensation. Agile makes it all visible and transparent, but a huge intentional effort needs to be taken by those in the process willing to fix such things."

- Kleber Sotte [https://linkedin.com/in/klebersotte/]

Principle 1 from the original 12 Agile Manifesto Principles indicates that customer satisfaction is our highest priority. Principle 2 says we "welcome changing requirements, even late in development." Principle 5 is about supporting our teammates and trusting them to do their jobs well. Principle 9 is about the importance of good Design. Principle 10 reminds us to be Lean, cutting work we should not do.

Are these really happening on your teams? Are we using retros to identify problems and waste? Do we fix those problems and cut that waste? Can you imagine if we stopped the project when we realized it was garbage or not quite right for the customer? Are your teams welcoming changing designs, even late in development? Are you starting development before you understand what you're building?

Many years ago, we were engineering-led, if not engineering-only. Developers based screen layouts on a set of requirements. If the screens did what the requirements said, we considered that a success, and we shipped that, whether or not it was easy to use or a good Customer Experience. This had flaws including:

- **Engineers didn't always enjoy designing the screens.** For some, it was the worst part of their job.

- **Engineers weren't always good at designing screens.**

- **Engineers didn't always have the time to spend on screen design when they needed to work on coding, testing, or other non-design tasks.**

- **How screens looked was usually based on what requirements documents said to create.** We were rarely working from deep research into customers' needs and behaviors. We researched target audiences just enough to know what we could sell them.

Adding Design work to Engineering tasks made a Developer's day overwhelming and required too many unrelated skills, so we added more roles to our team. This allowed UX as a profession to blossom. Starting in the 1980s, when we had Graphical User Interfaces, big companies brought in psychology and human factors experts to consider how these interfaces could work and make sense to target audiences and end-users. Back in the day, having a "User Interface Architect" or "User Experience Designer" at your company indicated an investment in matching PSE to the realities, needs, contexts, and preferences target customers had.

Fast forward to now, where most flavors of Agile show a complete misunderstanding of – and sometimes disregard for – how we create excellent Customer Experiences. We see the words "customer-centricity" or "design thinking" or a Double Diamond shape on Agile infographics or frameworks. But these don't ensure that we gather the right customer intelligence and use it for risk mitigation and PSE-market fit.

As of writing this, 100% of the articles I have seen published by Agile frameworks on the topics of HCD or UX read like articles compiled based on Googling HCD but not understanding it. Perhaps Agilists enjoy these articles, but HCD, CX, and UX experts can tell that these articles make little sense, are not actionable, and were written by people lacking HCD experience, expertise, and education. Please do not assume that if your Agile framework publishes articles on design thinking, CX, UX, Lean UX, HCD, or customer-centricity that the framework understands these, believes in investing in these, correctly integrates CX staff, or gives CX the autonomy they need.

Before we examine how Agile can be more customer-centric, let's look at some ways it can drag us in the wrong direction.

Speed Over Quality

Many companies want to be "Agile" but implement Agile poorly. Many companies want to be "Lean" but run with an incorrect definition of Lean. These poor implementations and definitions often drop us into *speed over quality* territory. We hear that we should "just ship it" and "Lean is the least we can do to get to the next step." Traditional Lean is about identifying and cutting waste to reduce risk, save money, and be more efficient and profitable.

Speed over quality is a slippery slope. If speed were more important than quality, then we should optimize every process and team for speed:

- **We wouldn't need QA since our code is probably good enough, and why spend more time checking it for bugs?** We'll find bugs later, especially after users report them.

- **We wouldn't need CX or UX.** If our PSE are digital, Engineers will lay out the screens based on requirements like in the old days.

- **We wouldn't need Product Managers.** Teams can self-organize and self-manage, and we can have a Business Analyst tell Engineers what we're building.

- **We wouldn't need Marketing specialists.** Sales will decide the pricing and how to present and sell our PSE.

- **We wouldn't need brainstorming workshops.** We know the features we want to build, and we'll build them fast.

- **Our company would mostly need Salespeople and Engineers, or – if we're service-based – those who push new services live to the public.**

Many companies do not want to compromise speed to improve their quality, even though they claim to want "continuous improvement" and higher internal and external quality. They will compromise quality to increase speed, and will tell you, "We can't slow down!" We must adjust how we judge our staff. If we are mostly or only watching velocity (how much was done in a certain period of time), then teams are likely to make quality secondary.

To be more customer-centric, we must balance working efficiently and creating the maximum possible customer value in every aspect of our PSE. We must start doing the math that will help us know if our drive to be "fast" leads us to efficiency, high quality, or far from them. We can calculate and estimate the Cost of Poor Quality. We can see the effects of poor quality in our KPIs. For example, did we release something hastily and then see attrition, auto-renew being shut off, or customers downgrading?

You rarely hear a complaint that Business Analysts, CX, UX, or Product Managers aren't doing their work well enough or to a higher, world-class standard. But you will often hear that *they aren't fast enough,* and *they slow us down.* We try to solve this by giving them less time to do their work and more rigid deadlines. *What can UX give us in two days?*

This is the wrong question when we care about quality, customer satisfaction, and loyalty. Transforming toward customer-centricity requires us to replace our love of speed with a love of **efficiency**.

**Efficiency balances working at a good pace,
meeting or exceeding customers' expectations and needs,
and reducing or eliminating risks and waste.**

Chapter 16: When Agile Works Against Customer-Centricity

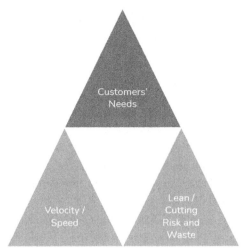

Figure 32: The Delta CX Efficiency model is represented as an equilateral triangle representing the balance between customers' needs, velocity or speed, and Lean or cutting risk and waste.

Think of these as a 3-sided triangle that we want to see balanced.

- **We are inefficient if we work at a good pace, but don't meet customers' needs or improve their satisfaction.** We may have been fast, but we didn't achieve our customer-related goals.

  - We are inefficient if we "get a lot done," but we solve the wrong problem or offer customers the wrong solution for their needs.

  - We are inefficient when we decide to release PSE that are broken or not quite right, and will need to be fixed later. Delaying future projects to fix a previous project undoes whatever velocity you thought you had.

  - We are inefficient when we have used thorough research to know what customers need, but we are ignoring or deprioritizing that.

- **We are inefficient when we get something done "fast" while allowing or creating risk.** Cycles of guesses and experiments can seem "fast," but the full arc of time spent plus the negative consequences we had to deal with ultimately make us inefficient.

- **We are inefficient when we fail to identify, document, or mitigate risk as early as possible.**

**Why do we believe we have no time to do this better now,
but we will have time later to fix it?**

The Customer Is Not in the Conversation

A Product Coach with a variety of Agile and Scrum certifications posted the following to LinkedIn in 2022:

> *"Imagine your CEO asks you for a feature X. You can either say, 'Give me a goal. Is this a feature factory?' or handle it in a better way:*
> *1. Start with WHY. Ask her why she needs X. The first answer may not be satisfying. Keep asking WHY until you understand the problem.*
> *2. Ask about the success criteria. Ask her how she will measure success. How will she know that the problem is resolved?*
> *3. Reverse engineer your goal. Ask her, 'If we had done it differently, would it be okay?' She may answer something like, 'Well, not really. You need also...' Repeat until you are on the same page.*
> *Congrats. Now you have a goal to pursue. And instead of waiting for X, she can hold you accountable for the results she cares about. That's a Win-Win situation. Inspired by an interview with Marty Cagan I watched a few months ago."*

Where is the customer in this conversation? Our key question in this scenario is *why the CEO needs this feature*? What qualitative evidence do we have that this feature is a match to customers' needs? Are potential and current customers pawns we move around a board so the CEO can meet their goal? Problem definitions and understanding should come from researching our target audiences, not from the perspectives of a CEO or stakeholders. I also don't understand how "instead of waiting for feature X, the CEO can hold you accountable for the results she cares about." Doesn't the CEO have to both wait for feature X and then hold you accountable for the desired outcomes and results?

All PSE conversations must include – if not focus on – customers and the recent evidence we have on their unmet needs.

The above conversation appears to be the definition of a feature factory; stakeholders decide features and order project teams to create these features, regardless of the true value to the customer. If we reverse engineer the business goal, we probably also reverse engineer, invent, or assume customer use cases. The feature factory starts with the feature we want to build, and we hope or assume there is an audience who has a reason to buy or use this.

The above scenario sounds like not only do we get feature requests or demands from executives, but they will describe the requirements and possibly the exact mechanism. You ask the CEO questions about feature execution until you have your "goal." If this is how Product, Program, or Portfolio Managers want to work, they might as well get out a piece of paper and have the CEO sketch the screens.

We claim we want to get away being a feature factory, but the advice herein directs you to continue feature factory behaviors and be the CEO's order taker. Product Managers and Product Owners shouldn't be feature secretaries. They should be customer-centric strategists who are critical thinkers. They should be empowered. Challenging the status quo includes telling executives that their feature requests will be considered but will be prioritized based on known customer value.

We're Going in the Wrong Direction

During some of my conference and training sessions, I run a live poll where attendees can drop a dot on a graph showing when they would like to learn that our PSE are going in the wrong direction. Most people place their dots early in the process; the earlier we know, the earlier we mitigate risk and cut waste, the earlier we can course correct.

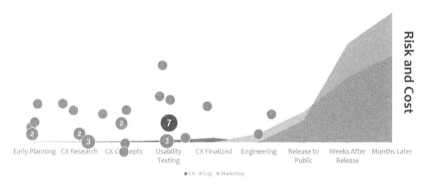

Figure 33: Screenshot of a completed poll. Most people would want to know before Engineering starts that PSE are flawed and we need to change direction. Two respondents wanted to learn this while Engineering was building.

The longer our project goes before we find flaws and customer dissatisfaction, the less Agile and Lean we are. We are slow and reactive, waiting weeks or months to release something to the public, and then waiting again for feedback or complaints.

We know that fixing a technical bug earlier saves time and money later. The blog post, "Cost of Fixing vs. Preventing Bugs" [https://cxcc.to/a160] calculates that for a mid-sized project at Google, 40% of staff time and millions of dollars are spent annually solely on bug fixes. You might see "10x" statements, like a bug that would cost $10 to fix during QA costs $100 to fix after a full build, $1,000 if the bug is found during integration testing, and $10,000 or more if found after that.

What does it cost to fix a *flawed concept* or *Customer Experience bug* before any Engineering work is done? What does it cost to change our solution during QA, after a full build, during integration testing, or after that? Given the size of these changes, the required time, and the number of staff involved, it might be way more than 10x.

CX is your customer intelligence and risk mitigation teammates. A more mature and customer-centric process finds and knocks out CX bugs before we write code or run public experiments.

Feedback from Working Software

Many companies use methods from books and articles suggesting that early research is unnecessary; *just build your idea quickly and get feedback from early users*.

Critical thinking questions include: how will you know what to build? How are cycles of guesses better and less risky than working from customer intelligence and good evidence? If we want to learn early if we're going in the right direction, do we need to publicly release an MVP or real PSE, or can we use User-Centered Design to know this earlier? How soon can we know if we're going in the wrong direction? Can we learn this before Engineering burns time coding bad ideas?

Companies often love releasing MVPs or early versions fast, learning from that, and then working on improvements. This is often flawed or doesn't happen as intended for a variety of reasons:

- **These products are often built from little or no research.** They are often designed based on hunches, surveys, ripping off competitors, or stakeholders' or founders' ideas.

- **If we didn't allow research to guide us up front where it's most vital, will we allow research to guide us after this is released?** Usually not. We are sure that our process was so efficient and working so well that we often don't circle back and include better research. We just keep optimizing small things and making incremental changes.

- **Once the product is released – even if it's only an experiment – the public will see it.** Investors, the media, competitors, customers, stock traders, etc. can screenshot it and discuss it. If we then learn that it wasn't a strong concept or design, and we must rethink it, will that be an embarrassment?

- **Despite the iterative nature of the MVP, we often avoid significantly changing or rethinking our publicly-released MVP 1.** Adjusting or pivoting MVP 1 means we got MVP 1 wrong, and we don't want to admit that. We'll say it's "good enough."

- If MVP 2 looks quite different from MVP 1 because we had to redo it or make significant changes, **the public must learn MVP 1 and then re-learn MVP 2.**

  o This is a negative customer and Brand Experience. The public shouldn't watch the sausage being made; these iterations should be behind the scenes and during the UCD process.

- o Companies typically use this and fear about rolling out more change to customers as reasons to stick to MVP 1 and only make incremental changes.

- **The best time to learn more and improve an idea is before it goes live to the public.** CX has processes and techniques that allow us to test realistic prototypes before we burn staff time and public trust on ideas that could fail in small or large ways.

  - o We don't have to go to market to learn whether we should go to market with this idea. We can use UCD to validate ahead of time, learn that the concept isn't a good solution, and pivot or iterate until we find the best solution.

> **"Working software" must "work" for customers' needs, pain points, and frustrations.**

Looking at this another way, imagine something seems seriously wrong with your health. The equivalent of "feedback from working software is better than early research" would be to guess what illness you have, and try one of the treatments for that condition. After ten days of antibiotics, you don't seem to be better; we learned from actively treating you that antibiotics weren't the right solution. We still don't know what's wrong or how to fix you, but we can try something else. How about we remove an organ? That's a painful and expensive surgery, and you'll need weeks to heal. But then we would have feedback indicating if that solved your original problem.

In the context of a medical example, this approach seems foolish, if not dangerous. It's a slow cycle of guesses where if we guess wrong at any stage, not only have we administered treatments that might make you feel worse, but we delayed the care you needed, all because we didn't want to invest the time and money to learn first.

It's equally foolish and hazardous to believe that we are Agile, Lean, or fast when engaging in cycles of PSE guesses. Every time a cycle goes badly, we have burned time and money on Product Management, CX Researchers and Architects, Engineers, and others. You can research and know the right PSE strategies and direction early. Or you can design an idea, develop it, test it, merge it, release it, wait for feedback or complaints, figure out where it failed, redesign, redevelop, retest, etc. Evidence-based Design costs less and takes less time.

We often end up in a sunk cost fallacy, where we feel like *we've spent this much and worked this hard, so we might as well release this to the public or keep working on it*. It might even be more cost-effective to throw the idea away, but pride and ego block us. Make sure you are guided by research and cost-benefit analyses.

Reframe the MVP

Books about startups made us think that the MVP is a way to determine what customers want. But to do that, Engineering must completely build it, test it, merge it, and release it. You take your chances with real trial or paying customers. The risk is high.

When someone mentions the MVP, this cartoon is often referenced:

Figure 34: MVP cartoon by Henrik Kniberg. [https://cxcc.to/a147] Explained below.

The cartoon shows that you wouldn't build a car by starting with one wheel, then two wheels, then the car's body, and finally, a complete car. The cartoon shows that an MVP would be like building a skateboard first, then a kick scooter, then a bicycle, then a motorcycle, and then finally the car you wanted to build in the first place.

Neither of these is the MVP. Where the MVP is supposedly done right, the cartoon shows a sad face at the first step – the skateboard – and neutral faces at the second and third steps – the kick scooter and bicycle. Why start with PSE that create dissatisfaction? This is customer-periphery.

In both examples in the cartoon, the early PSE you release to users aren't close to what we know customers need. If users need a car, neither a single wheel nor a skateboard will match their needs. Additionally, since most companies are feature factories, the CX team is typically told to design a skateboard, often without knowing if the car will exist or what customers need that might look like a car. We design for the now and the box we were put in. We cannot think ahead or future-proof the project by designing for the ultimate goal or solution. This creates risk and inefficiencies.

Reframe the MVP. If you want to release a slice of something first, make sure that it delivers maximum user value. Instead of a single wheel or a skateboard, it's a small car. The MVP is supposed to be a tiny slice of our proposed complete solution to check that we're going in the right direction. This implies that we designed our complete solution, can break it into pieces, and can prioritize what to build first. We can't know the minimum viable version of something without first designing its full and complete version.

> **Customers don't want Minimally Viable Anything.**
> **Customers want Maximum Value PSE.**

People who believe in "build" before "learn" often ask me how generative CX research can be done before a company has an idea or early MVP. My article, "UX Research Without a Hypothesis and for Products That Don't Exist Yet," explains how that can and should be done. [https://cxcc.to/a154]

"Don't Plan or Design Too Far Ahead"

Lovers of Agile sometimes complain that CX is trying to plan or Design too far ahead. People tell generic stories about a friend whose UX team designed something, and three months later, the design was "outdated." These anecdotes are used as a reason to block CX or UX from starting their work too early. Someone might even suggest that CX working 2-6 sprints ahead of Engineers isn't really Lean or Agile. A later chapter will explain why it is.

Planning ahead is important. Our Corporate Strategists plan now for next year or the following year. Do we accuse them of not being Agile or Lean? Some of the planning that goes into new iPhone models is started three years before the phone's release. [https://cxcc.to/a185] Would we say that Apple isn't Lean or Agile?

A designed solution being incorrect or irrelevant three months after it was created raises important questions:

- **Did we know it was the wrong solution and release it anyway?** Why?

- **What was this project's strategy?** A well-defined problem statement and a CX strategy to address that problem should ensure that our solutions aren't obsolete weeks later.

- **How did we find out three months later that the solution was incorrect?** Did we learn from controlled evaluative research? Or did we release it to the public and then learn that we failed?

- **Who should be held accountable for the design being wrong or immediately outdated?** If CX didn't get the time, budget, headcount, or resources to do their best work, the person who blocked them from what they needed should be held accountable for this waste.

  o Were Designers treated as order takers and told the exact ideas and features to design, but then we blamed the Designers for the solution's failure? The person who dictated the ideas and features should be held accountable.

- **Were these designs guided by current and thorough research?** Generative research insights inform designs, and testing helps us know if they're the right solution for the problem we defined.

  o To be faster, many companies skip generative and sometimes evaluative research assuming that "we'll get the feedback we need from working software." We *could* find out months into our project that we have the wrong solution. This is a risk we should identify and mitigate early.

  o Did we usability test our solution before it went live?

Demonizing Designers is unlikely to solve the root causes of this problem. If you believe your Designers are bad at their jobs, have a Design expert evaluate their work. If they are good at their jobs, then it's likely that something else in your internal process is to blame for this "immediately outdated" design solution.

Is Thorough CX Work "Waterfall" or "Big Design Up Front?"

In a world claiming or trying to be Agile, fewer words invite the anger and strong reactions that the word "waterfall" can. Making speed our top priority – even over PSE quality and customer satisfaction – helps us tell ourselves *we're not waterfall.*

Infographics explaining waterfall typically show phases such as analysis, requirements, design, development, testing and integration, and implementation and deployment. You might think this looks like what our Agile teams do now, and you're not wrong. The difference is that waterfall typically requires an entire project to be coded before it is released. For example, in 2012, I worked on the UX team designing the first iPad app for Wells Fargo bank. This was a roughly 1.5-year waterfall project, meaning the public sees nothing until the entire app is designed, built, tested, and completed. Under Agile, we might have released the foundations of the app and a few core features, and added features monthly or periodically.

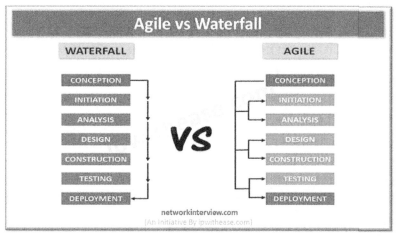

Figure 35: Agile vs. Waterfall infographic from networkinterview.com. It shows waterfall and Agile being somewhat similar, except Agile is more cyclic. Both waterfall and Agile show "Design" done before "Construction."

If you've heard "Big Design Up Front" or "UX is waterfall," it wasn't said by a CX professional. CX and UX wouldn't use negative framing around their own work. "Big Design Up Front" is a term someone made up to make the UX process sound like something we don't want: lengthy, bloated, slow, and risky. Without critical thinking, we could agree, but we would also agree that six or more Engineers on a project for weeks or months is lengthy, risky, and possibly slow. We don't call it "Big Bloated Engineering." Giving each other's work negative names isn't good for processes, culture, collaboration, or outcomes.

Quick Fix Versus Slow Fix: CX Work and "Agility"

One CX practitioner wanting one or two sprints for their work is seen as something to avoid. Ask for multiple practitioners and multiple sprints, and prepare to be laughed at and called "waterfall." In contrast, six or more Engineers working on something for multiple sprints is an excellent Agile approach. It's a double standard that our teams will need to address.

Our typical solution is to tell CX they must get quality work done in less time. *Go faster.* "Be more Agile." Or we request that they lower the quality of their work to prioritize velocity. Considering cycles of work, waiting for customer feedback, and rework that these projects often have, asking CX to skimp on their work is the **slow fix.** Designing the right solutions for customers' needs will take longer when we spend less time understanding those needs, and engage in cycles of live PSE iterations.

The **quick fix** is to hire until you have no CX bottleneck. Give teams the time and resources they need to do great work that won't need to be redone later. More details are covered in the "Designing CX Teams" chapter.

> If it's normal for six or more Engineers to get weeks to accomplish something, it should be normal for five or more CX practitioners to get weeks to accomplish something.

Since the dawn of time, design has been – and should be – up front. We model cars multiple times and in various ways before they roll off factory lines. Wikipedia defines "Big Design Up Front" as "an approach where software's design is completed and perfected before implementation is started." It'll never be perfect, but Design should be completed before we implement it. *How will you implement an unfinished or unknown design?* "Build, release, then Design" doesn't work.

Knowing that Design comes first shines a spotlight on CX's importance as an autonomous domain that can partner with Product, Engineering, Data and Analytics, and others. **Whether or not someone Designs our product well, there will be a Design and a Customer Experience.** Invest in having experts do this as well as possible the first time.

CX doesn't have to design the entire universe up front, but if this is not a small fix, they must design and finalize *a single customer workflow or task*. They shouldn't design a micro-moment from a longer task, assume it's good, and pass it to Engineering for coding. Usability testing should test that whole task or workflow. If we find small or large problems, Engineering will not be happy to get change requests or completely new designs. This wouldn't be efficient, Agile, or Lean. For example, CX shouldn't design *entering your credit card* when it's part of a complete checkout experience. The checkout is the task – a user's single workflow – and should be designed and tested holistically. It's similar to how we shouldn't skip integration testing because we did unit testing.

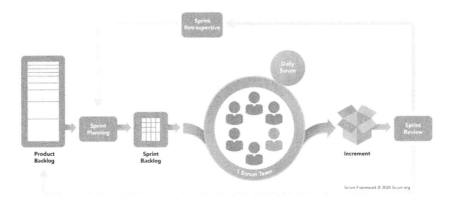

Figure 36: Scrum infographic from Scrum.org. The process starts with a product backlog.

Most Agile and Scrum infographics show the process starting with the product backlog: what Engineering will build and in what order. This might be the start of an Engineering process, but it's not the start of our larger PSE process since it excludes how the product backlog became populated or prioritized. **CX architects and designs what ends up in the backlog.** Design happens so "up front" that it's rarely on Agile and Scrum infographics, but maybe it should be.

Agile Was Meant for Engineering

Agile and everything related to it were invented to make Engineering teams work faster and more efficiently. Agile was not originally meant to apply to non-Engineering tasks. We rarely ask Marketing to plan their work in sprints. We rarely complain that Business Analysts aren't Agile enough, and need to create a predictable continuous deployment cadence.

Nearly zero Agile frameworks correctly understand or integrate CX or UX tasks or practitioners. Superimposing Agile practices on CX work makes as much sense as a CX practitioner complaining that sprint planning isn't using Human-Centered Design. You would laugh at a CX professional who was outraged at Developers not using the User-Centered Design process. Truly empowered teams and good culture require that we not superimpose one domain's preferences or work styles on another domain.

Tri-Track Agile, which we'll discuss later, will help us better separate CX work from Engineering work. This is ultimately about planning; give CX enough time to use their methods thoroughly and do high-quality work. This feeds the backlog without delaying Engineers since the time CX needed was planned earlier.

Chapter 17: Interview: Agile

Michael Huynh is an Australia -based Agile Coach, consultant, speaker, and trainer with SoftEd. He has helped many organizations solve complex problems and deliver value faster for customers by creating the right conditions for smooth delivery, solving the right problem, and faster decision making. He partners with Senior Executive leaders, leaders of teams, and team members to guide the right cultural shifts and processes required to embed and sustain Agile ways of working. [https://linkedin.com/in/mhuynh-cbr/]

Debbie: How do you define customer-centricity?

Michael: Solving the right problems from the customer's perspective. *Is it going to add value?* This means finding new ways to go above and beyond, seeking different ways to delight customers and change their world. How are we making it better for them?

There are no second chances when it comes to a customer's interaction with a company, and customers will consider switching after one or two poor experiences. Steven Denning, a thought leader in the Agile space, described in his book *The Age of Agile*, "The Law of the Customer": *focus on the customers, and be obsessed with delivering more value to customers.* This must be throughout the organization. Everyone must have a clear line of sight to the actual customer, and can see how their work affects the customer. Customers expect delightful experiences from physical service interactions through digital platforms in all industries, including healthcare, banking, hospitality, automotive, and government.

Debbie: Is that approach or definition built into Agile or Scrum?

Michael: Agile embraces a mindset around continuous learning and experimentation. Agility, in my opinion, is the best way to serve the customer. To achieve customer-centricity, Agile acknowledges the need for continuous learning (discovery), continuous improvement, and experimentation to meet customer needs.

The most common customer-centric practice is "user stories," an Agile practice about communication and collaboration. One downside is how this practice is often treated like a requirements specification. "Hey, just deliver me this thing defined in these user stories."

Debbie: I see the Agile Manifesto saying, "Our highest priority is to satisfy the customer through continuous delivery of working software." For me, "customer satisfaction" jumps out as our top priority. Yet I saw someone on LinkedIn who quoted this and said, "Look how important continuous delivery is!" which will feed *speed over quality.*

Michael: Agile frameworks don't describe the discovery processes and the work involved. The first paragraph of the Agile Manifesto includes, "We are uncovering better ways of developing software by doing it and helping others do it," with the key word being "uncovering." The UX discovery process involves researching, uncovering the problem space, and understanding the users and their problems. When we look at a common Agile framework such as Scrum, where does it describe or highlight the customer discovery process?

Debbie: I love all the Scrum infographics that start with "product backlog" as if what we're building magically appeared there and wasn't part of any process.

Michael: There is a whole process that occurs before you build a product backlog. There are lots of questions that need to be answered and outcomes to be achieved in the discovery process. If you're in a large organization that is well established, and you've likely got CX/UX people, why the hell are you not using them? I get that in Agile ways of working, we have a bias towards action, collaboration, and self-organizing teams where everyone needs to be involved in everything. But we need to consider the costs of the meetings and workshops with everyone involved. Trust that self-organizing teams will talk to each other. Bring team members into meetings only when needed.

Debbie: I tend to notice that the Definitions of Ready or Done are mostly self-reflective for Agile teams. *Did I write working code? Congratulations, I'm done.* How do we try to build more customer-centricity into the Definition of Done?

Michael: Agile ways of working take a lot of discipline to ensure quality is baked into the development lifecycle. We can't just inspect for quality at the end because it's too late, causing rework and unnecessary waste. Quoting W. Edwards Deming, the father of quality and management: "Inspection does not improve the quality, nor guarantee quality. Inspection is too late. The quality, good or bad, is already in the product. Quality cannot be inspected into a product or service; it must be built into it."

To bake in quality, we leverage practices like the Definition of Done (DoD) and the Definition of Ready (DoR). The DoR are prerequisites the team agrees on. They are shared "Ready" criteria to ensure the necessary conditions are met before the team begins work. For example, the DoR might include:

- Do we have the X sets/amount of data?
- Did we have a minimum of X people interviewed/observed?
- Has previous research been included?
- Have all the Customer Experience pain points and risks been identified?
- Are recommendations and next steps clear?

The DoD is quality criteria that are agreed upon, shared, understood, and used by the team. It is an evolving, living artifact that grows as teams mature their quality practices. There are multiple levels of the DoD as you move through the hierarchy: story, sprint, feature, release, and product. For each level of the DoD, different stakeholders are involved but must share that same definition.

Debbie: The Definition of Done would include standards for CX process and work output quality.

Michael: Yeah, and then *is content readable for everybody? Is it concise? Has it been proofread? Does it meet WCAG accessibility standards?* These are the sorts of quality criteria that feed into the work.

I've previously worked with UX-specific teams, where we utilized the Scrum framework to organize delivery execution with a cross-functional team. Those UX teams I worked with did a lot of product discovery and user research. They worked hand in hand with the Product Managers to provide recommendations to drive product decisions and validations. They provided Service Design blueprints, CX strategies and reports, gaps in market research reports, recommendations on how services should operate, and designs for how they might look. They were engaged throughout the lifecycle and collaborated at specific points.

Debbie: Have you had any experiences where people didn't get what UX did or why UX was there?

Michael: Several organizations misunderstand what UX is, what UX does, how long UX should spend on discovery, and their remit of responsibility. What I believe is ideal is to get out of the cycle as fast as possible without gold plating so that we can start delivering something, but not to the detriment of the user. Our solution won't work if it is solving the wrong problems to begin with. We want to get to a point where we are at a high level of confidence that our solution is going to work and will solve the right problem.

I've been in organizations where senior executives didn't see tangible outputs and wondered if we were spending too long in discovery. They would often get annoyed. *Nothing is getting delivered, and we've got tight deadlines.*

Another scenario is that UX is too far down the chain in terms of where it sits in the organization. They can be simply overruled by senior executives or by the Highest Paid Person's Opinion (HiPPO). We end up letting things go out the door when they probably shouldn't. That is a problem and hurts not only the organization's reputation, but it hurts the customers as well.

When we bring teams together, we do a kickoff or team liftoff. We bring in all the right people together, set the scene, align on the vision, understand the limitations, define what's in scope and what's out of scope, and do team bonding activities. We come together with a team agreement, a team way of working. *What do we agree to? How are we going to work with each other? How are we going to voice our concerns? What happens if we have opposing views on things? How will we address it?*

The other thing to consider is to have a UX person, Product Owner/Product Manager, and a Solutions Architect/Engineer being a trio. Many teams don't have a UX person in that structure, which is why UX is often overruled. They don't have a seat at the table. In a more structured Agile framework like SAFe, UX isn't part of the leadership team, and they get overruled all the time. Agile frameworks could do with some improvements and iterations.

Debbie: I often hear, "Well, it's good enough, and we'll fix it later." Have you ever had to battle that? Why are we releasing it if we know it needs to be fixed?

Michael: It doesn't matter what organization I've been in. There is always that tension of *when we should release it*. This is where the executives make the decision unless others are fighting and saying that we should not release this. It's a hard conversation.

If we release things, we still need to go back and clean up the technical or UX debt we've incurred. Why would we want to risk the company's reputation and piss off the customers in the process of releasing something we said was "good enough for now?" That's a very dangerous game.

Debbie: What would you say to some of the Agile approaches or frameworks that say you need a UX skill on the Agile team, but it doesn't have to be a UX specialist? These frameworks often say that UX can be decentralized, and anybody can do UX work.

Michael: One of the teams I had the opportunity to coach was building internal software for call center support staff in a large Australian government agency. They did a few iterations, and then it was released to staff. Developers were convinced that their hard work was going to make life easier and solve the challenges the Customer Support staff were having. This was a team that did UX on their own by reading some articles online, no UX qualifications or experience.

When it was released, they went to see it in action and see how well it worked in the field. But they saw the overwhelming amount of clicks it took for someone to find details and information. They saw the jumping from screen to screen based on the nature of the call and the details they needed to find to serve the customer. They saw just how bad the design and their assumptions were. They said, "Oh wow, we really made things worse."

If this software were released externally, that would become an even bigger problem. That's a huge reputational problem and risk. This is where UX work is absolutely important. If you have UX budget and capabilities on your team, use them. They're a skill set that should be leveraged. They're the experts in the field and capability.

Debbie: What do you think about a model where prioritization is more of a shared adventure between the triad of Product, UX, and Engineering?

Michael: I think that's an awesome way to do it. There are lots of prioritization frameworks, but you need to make sure you include scores for desirability, feasibility, and viability. This ensures that critical elements are covered, and there is a healthy balance in our prioritized work.

Desirable: from a UX perspective, is there evidence of the pain points this solves?

Feasible: can we technically do it, and are there enabling capabilities to do it? Viable: from a business perspective, does this have a long-term potential for success, and does it offer value to the business?

Debbie: Desirability is supposed to be from the customer's perspectives based on what we know about them, not based on a stakeholder declaring what they think people will like.

Michael: Yeah, absolutely. Prioritization drives the right conversations. Don't avoid the hard conversation because something got the biggest score, and we say it's the top priority.

Debbie: There's always someone who is sure that they need to just ask a user what they want and then build that. There's always a Product person who wants to sketch some screens because they're sure their vision for the product is the right way to go. They tend to disregard UX or treat UX as, "Oh, you must be the secretary who's here to sketch my idea."

Michael: Yeah, that's a problem. If UX doesn't have a seat at the table, then what hope is there for us to solve the right problems for customers? This is a broader problem, not just a product problem. These are organizational problems that could adversely affect the survival of companies. There is a high price for delivering poor Customer Experiences. Losing customers is expensive.

Everyone's an influencer now. I think about the video where singer/songwriter Dave Carroll did a protest song, "United Breaks Guitars." [https://cxcc.to/a110] The video went viral, and United Airlines' stock fell 10%, costing about $180 million.

Debbie: If I took a two-day JavaScript course, you could tell how good or bad my coding is. I forgot who I heard say this, but the outcomes of UX are so far in the future. If a Product Owner does some flawed research or design, it could take months to learn that they have the wrong "solution." You don't know in the moment the way you know with code.

Michael: I want to tie this back to the Dunning-Kruger effect. It's a super weird phenomenon where people with low abilities tend to overestimate their capability. It's often at the peak of Mount Arrogance where the person has the greatest confidence in the world. You just finished this two-day certification, whether it be UX, Product Owner, or Scrum Master. You get these two-day "experts" that come out after a Scrum or Product Owner certification, saying, "Look at me. I'm a Product person or a Scrum Master now." Yes, you sort of understand the rules of the game. Like a baseball beginner, you have just read the baseball guide, understood the rules of the game, and how to play. You might have watched a few games on television. That doesn't mean you have any real skin in the game, especially if you have never stepped foot on the field and hit the ball before.

You think you can take on the world, but soon enough, you fall off the cliff. You realize, "Maybe I screwed the pooch on this," but it's probably too late. That's where you start on the path of enlightenment. I would caution that anybody trying this type of approach should remember that there are experts out there, and there's a lot to learn from them.

Debbie: And the experts can tell the difference between good and bad work, so please believe them. This reminds me to talk about accountability. There's often no accountability for disaster projects, the Costs of Poor Quality, or the loss of customers. What is your perspective on what we need to do differently for accountability to have some adult teeth?

Michael: What if teams owned their budget and outcomes? They would have full rights to make decisions around who is on the team, what skill sets are needed, and what capabilities they need in the team. That would constrain them to operate like their own business and be forward-thinking. That makes them fully accountable for the budget, the team, and the outcomes. Each role should have a level of accountability. But at the end of the day, the Product person makes many of the final product decisions. That is the job, and that's why it's a hard and often thankless role. As soon as something is successful, the team has a big *hurrah, great work, team*! But when things slip, the Product person is the one that generally gets in trouble because they made the final call and decisions.

What I have observed in different organizations is that they don't put enough accountability on these Product people. This might have something to do with decisions going through multiple layers of decision-makers. Product people should be working with senior executives and ideally the CEO. But in organizations that are even more bureaucratic, the Product Managers and Product Owners aren't the real Product Managers and Product Owners. The decisions are made by executives; they're the real Product Owner or Product Manager. In that case, we can make teams accountable, but at the end of the day, who's accountable? It's probably the executive. If you have more layers in the hierarchy, then perhaps the accountable person is a VP of Product.

This is also where a good Scrum Master or an Agile Coach can help drive that level of accountability back on these VPs and back on teams. They'll help drive the retrospective action items forward. If teams are coming up with their own ideas and solutions to team problems, they will own these ideas and solutions. The Agile Coach or a Scrum Master will hold the mirror, help them reflect on those things, and coach them through it to make sure that there is accountability for these changes.

Consider a futurespective or pre-mortem. Imagine the worst things that could possibly happen to try to avoid risks, address assumptions, and prepare for the worst things that could happen. Those sorts of practices can help us to think forward. Retrospectives are a lagging indicator. It's already happened. The sh*t has hit the fan. Now we're trying to resolve it and remedy it.

We need to look at leading indicators, signs, and signals that might tell us that we are going down the wrong path before risks happen. Small experiments and tests are your best leading indicators. Experiment with small groups of people to get feedback regularly and often. Put the concept into the hands of the end-users. Watch for these leading indicators before going down the wrong path. Use data and facts. Take the emotion out of it. This is probably part cultural and part personality.

I've had my fair share of run-ins with uncoachable people and ones that give the good old lip service. They say, "Yep, yep, yep," to everything but don't follow through. You try to hold them accountable with, "Hey, we talked about this in our last session. Let's go back to what we agreed to last time. What's holding you back from your agreed goals?" It's in one ear, out the other.

I call these people "uncoachable." They don't want to move forward with your advice or commit to the right personal goals. They're happy with what they're doing, and there is no real commitment. Realistically, there's probably not much you can do with them. They do not want to be coached by you. They might resonate with another coach.

You can fight the hard fight, but if a facilitated and structured coaching conversation doesn't go well or doesn't go anywhere, you can try one with an influential peer. Group accountability in front of peers can work well when you have senior leadership all in the same room in a facilitated conversation and agreeing on commitments. You try to get them to hold each other accountable for the things they are going to do and how they are going to move forward. Make those things clear: it's shared, who is accountable, by what date will this get done, and we all agree together that this is the best way forward. If that still doesn't go well, then we have obvious problems with the company culture of accountability. But if people are stepping up and trying to resolve those things, and people are seeing things being resolved, then we are moving forward. We're getting better.

If the same crap gets brought up again in a retrospective, inspect and adapt session, or post-mortem, people will stop bringing it up. Why bother? *We've done this before. We've said this before. Nothing's happened. This sh*t is old.*

PART 4: THE CUSTOMER-CENTRIC PATH FORWARD

Chapter 18: Strategy and Planning

Carefully crafted CX strategies will address everything that touches customers, including how Customer Support is trained, how Marketing speaks to our audiences, pricing, Sales, and more. At the center of all of these is our PSE. The better our PSE, the easier it will be to attract and retain customers. PSE that better match customers' needs allow Sales, Marketing, and Support to reduce effort and expenses.

To keep this book focused, rather than addressing customer-centricity in every business domain, we will look at PSE strategies and how we plan process and other internal changes that will improve our customer-centricity.

Forrester's "Predictions 2023" PDF claims that:

> *"A majority of customer experience (CX) teams lack crucial skills including design thinking, inclusive experience design, survey design, journey mapping, and data literacy and storytelling." [https://cxcc.to/a193]*

In earlier chapters, we debunked the many definitions of design thinking, and we also examined how these listed items are not skills; they are documents representing work done, but not the skills themselves. If you use poor techniques or lack solid evidence from great research, you'll end up with "a journey map," but it might be flawed or not actionable.

The real skills are in strategy, problem finding, and problem solving. Journey mapping and storytelling without these are pretty documents without substance. We know this because companies have been sending staff for customer journey map training and design thinking training for years, yet we don't seem closer to customer-centricity. We still struggle with attraction and retention. We are still feature factories, putting stakeholders' happiness before customers' happiness. Despite all of our journey mapping, design thinking, and storytelling, we are still low on the customer-centricity maturity scale.

Customer-Centricity Maturity Model

If it helps you envision your organization moving through stages of customer-centricity maturity, here is my Delta CX model, with 1 being the highest level:

- **Level 5: Cut Off.** We're building and releasing the PSE that stakeholders and execs like. We assume there's an audience for it, somewhere. Sales and Marketing will have to figure that out. We're not building for any particular target audience or researching them to learn their tasks or needs. We don't pay much attention to satisfaction or loyalty metrics since we'll find more new customers if needed. We might have little or no competition, so we don't cater to customers or worry about their satisfaction.

- **Level 4: Considered.** We think we care about customers, but we research them as far as learning what we can sell them, what they might pay, and other elements that feed Sales and Marketing. We tend to believe that *if we build it, they will come; if they don't, Sales and Marketing will figure out new ways to find and convert them.* We track a few customer-related metrics like NPS but don't always act on them.

- **Level 3: Conversion.** Transition period where some teams are doing better than others. Some teams are more empowered and can raise a red flag when they see customer-peripheric metrics, decisions, or ideas. We take those seriously and then take more customer-centric actions. Other teams are still in the lower levels of maturity. We're building out more of a CX department to handle UCD and CX strategies.

- **Level 2: Coordinated.** Our CX department and teams are in place. They have a hierarchy, including layers of management and leadership. CX has autonomy, and collaborates with all other business units and departments. CX is highly strategic, and not other domains' order takers.

- **Level 1: Core.** Customer intelligence informs all strategies, goals, departments, initiatives, and PSE. We have truly put our current and potential customers at the center of everything we do. We continuously research and test with them to build customer intelligence and ensure PSE-market fit. We rely heavily on observational and interview research, and not just surveys and focus groups. When we learn customers are unhappy, we investigate why. We act on this knowledge and follow through. We leap past what competitors do rather than rip the competitor off. Decisions are ethical and consider customers' perspectives. A CXO leads a CX department.

If your company is low on the maturity scale, or has previously had a CX or customer-centricity program fail, it's time to try again. Your business can't survive without satisfied and loyal customers. If previous attempts to improve CX failed, this should be investigated, and the root causes found. Was there no clear strategy or plan? Was there a lack of allies or too many strong detractors? Are we pretending to want change but blocking it on the assumption that our company is "good enough?"

Whether or not you have "CX" initiatives, and no matter what you are "led" by, there will still be PSE and Customer Experiences. The more deliberately these can be strategized and created, the more success the business will have. Please keep trying to climb the customer-centricity maturity ladder, even during or after CX struggles.

Deliberately Designing Customer Experiences for Customers

I noticed that my TripIt travel organization app showed the layover time between some of my flights but not all of my flights. Since this looked like a bug, I emailed TripIt. The response I received was, "TripIt uses the travel industry standard for determining if two flights are a connection. The airline industry standard rule for determining a connection time to display is less than four hours for domestic flights and less than 24 hours for international flights (from one country to another). Anything longer is considered a stopover and will not display the layover time in TripIt."

This brings us back to our earlier chapter on understanding customers' tasks and designing for the knowledge they have and need. As a user, I have no reason to ever understand or remember airline industry standards for what's a stopover and what's a layover. I do not have a set of mental rules around if the flight is domestic or international, or if the timing between flights is more or fewer than X hours. I'm hoping the app will just tell me what that timing is.

This also ignores the customer's context: *I'm flying from London to Milan, and then from Milan to Olbia, Italy. How much time will I have for a passport stamp, luggage retrieval, check in with another airline for the next flight, re-check my bags, and get through security?* The app doesn't show me because my final flight is "domestic" with exactly four hours in between, which triggers the tech rule to not show me the layover time.

I still want to see that information whether or not the tech rule wants to show it to me. If that information is not shown to me consistently, I assume the app is broken. I might complain. I might say nothing. I might stop paying TripIt and go with a competitor.

Additionally, the TripIt *website* version shows all of the times between all of my flights, and calls them "layovers," even though I just learned that some of these should be called "stopovers". The website appears to be designed for what people need and how people think. The app hasn't caught up. Inconsistent interfaces and workflows can look like bugs to customers.

Great Customer Experiences are created deliberately for how customers perceive their own tasks, the knowledge they have, and the knowledge they need. TripIt could simply do the math for me (*don't make me think!*) and tell me all of the times between flights of any kind. Also note that PSE based on airline definitions could be "product-led" but is unlikely to be value-led using customers' definitions of value and quality.

CX Vision

Consider writing some statements in the following format:

> **Customers will choose us because _____.**
> **We will retain them because _____.**
> **They will grow with us because _____.**
> **Customers will love us because we make _____ easy.**

This helps us get away from canvasses that focus on solving business problems, often by brainstorming what we can push or force people to do. We might be able to optimize that screen until people click a particular button more, but if we can't retain them, our adoption metrics are vanity metrics. How will the customer grow with you? What about our PSE will make them buy more, buy more often, or utilize more?

The challenge with the above statements is to avoid mentioning solutions. If you think customers will choose you for Feature X, and the competitor has Feature X, why would customers choose or stay with you? If you think customers choose you because you release digital products quickly, how do you know that? Does the customer have a sense of fast versus not-as-fast release schedules?

The answers to the above statements are probably not particular features or internal team velocity. The answers will be related to the Customer Experiences you carefully create to meet or exceed unmet needs and invent solutions where customers have been meeting The Four Horsemen of Bad CX: frustration, confusion, disappointment, and distraction.

These forward-looking statements are part of our larger CX vision. They are beacons helping us focus on customers' needs and what inspires loyalty. They showcase how we will meet or exceed customers' needs better than competitors.

Delta CX Impact Map

Traditional impact maps are visualized as a left-to-right tree starting with our key business goal, which might be increasing active users or higher conversion rates. The goal branches out to the next level of the tree's hierarchy, often labeled as "actors." These are our personas, segments, target audiences, or internal teams.

The third level of the tree is labeled "impacts," which are often phrased from a business perspective, such as "more referrals," "increase purchase frequency," or "view more ads." The fourth level of the tree is labeled "deliverables," and appears to be high-level solutions of how we will create these impacts, thereby achieving our goal. Easily-Googleable impact maps show deliverables including better web page layouts, sales promotions, sending more emails to customers, and new content.

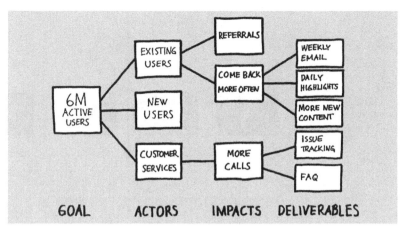

Figure 37: Sample impact map showing how we'll reach six million active users. The impacts are "referrals" and "come back more often." The deliverables are "weekly emails," "daily highlights," and "more new content."

This approach to impact mapping has some weaknesses:

- **We started with a *business* goal.** Our decisions and actions will be driven by achieving that business goal. If the business goal was not influenced by customer intelligence, we might have a customer-peripheric business goal.

- **We built a map based on how we can push customers toward our business goal.** Where is the value to the customers? Why should they increase their purchase frequency or view more ads? Is that what they would choose for themselves?

- **Solution assumptions.** How do we know that a better layout will create the desired impact? How do we know that offering more discounts, weekly emails, or "more content" will achieve our ultimate business goal? Do we know which content types or topics will be most effective?

- **We didn't map customer problems or tasks.** If a template doesn't include customers' problems, pain points, or unmet needs, we are unlikely to find customer-centric solutions.

What if we created an impact map where the goal is something our customers are trying to achieve?

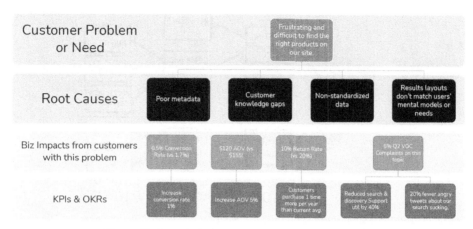

Figure 38: Sample Delta CX Impact Map. Explained below.

Our key customer problem or need is at the top of my Delta CX Impact Map. The example used above is "frustrating and difficult to find the right products on our site." The next level of the map indicates some of the root causes creating or aggravating this problem. For this sample map, these causes are poor metadata, customer knowledge gaps (remember our example from Lush), non-standardized data (sometimes entered by third parties), and the layout of the results not matching users' mental models or needs (they prefer a grid over a list).

We next document the impact on the business. *Customers are suffering, and here is how that plays out for our project or company.* For this sample map, the business impacts are a lower conversion rate (0.5% for customers struggling with search results versus 1.7% for our general population), lower Average Order Value (AOV of $120 versus $155), 10% returning customer visit rate (versus 20%), and increased VOC complaints (5% of our Q2 complaints were about this topic). Include any numbers or estimates you have, especially around lost revenue. Note that visually, the tree breaks between the root causes and the business impacts since there isn't a one-to-one relationship. Many root causes are affecting many business impacts.

Since the Delta CX Impact Map doesn't focus on potential solutions, the final level of the tree indicates KPIs and OKRs that will show when we have improved or resolved this problem for our customers. Metrics might include an increased conversion rate, increased AOV, customers purchasing more frequently than average, and reduced utilization of Customer Support channels related to this problem.

This approach to impact mapping allows us to focus on the customer while considering how the problem impacts both the customer and the business. We can summarize root causes to indicate that we generally understand where we might focus potential solutions, but the map is solution-agnostic. Ultimately, if we can repair the root causes and resolve the original customer problem or need, we will see gains and improvements in both business-related and customer-related metrics. We should aim for these win-win scenarios. Shift away from any maps that might inspire us to be customer-peripheric, only focusing on serving the desired outcomes that stakeholders and the business seek.

Our work is not done if we improve the stated KPIs but do not resolve the root causes or original customer problem. *How can we validate whether the root causes are correct and will resolve our problem?* This is where User-Centered Design can help us know this faster and more efficiently than testing the waters with new publicly-released PSE. At a high level, our process is as follows:

1. **Define the root cause(s)**. We can say that a root cause of poor search results is "poor metadata," but that's not enough information to guide our solution. What's wrong with the metadata? Where does it work well and where does it fall short? The same would be true for the root cause of the "search results layout not matching users' mental models or needs." How do we know which layouts are most compelling and helpful to shoppers? To define the root cause, we need more details and evidence, leading us to…

2. **Refer to earlier research or conduct additional research**. An observational study of how people search on our site and other sites can show us what people expect, assume, and understand as well as what might be a blocker or source of frustration. This would allow each root cause we study to have a well-defined problem statement, plus the insights, actionable suggestions, and other data that qualitative research can provide.

   o Teammates will be tempted to guess to save time, and you might hear resistance to research. Challenge naysayers. Guessing is probably one reason we ended up with a failure we need to fix. Please do not try to fix guesses with newer guesses.

3. **Prototype possible solutions**. For digital PSE, I recommend Axure for realistic prototyping. As of 2022, most CX and UX tools do not allow study participants to interact realistically with prototypes, such as filling in form fields. The problems with evaluative research on "click-through models" was examined in an earlier chapter.

4. **Rounds of usability testing**. Once we have a prototype or two that are strong candidates, one or both should be moved through several rounds of usability testing. Real and archetypal users successfully or unsuccessfully completing their tasks shows us where proposed solutions have room for improvement. We can then iterate and test in cycles – like Engineers fixing code bugs – until we find a usable solution that solves all of the original problems.

   o We can prototype and test concepts that are non-digital products or services by piloting our proposed solution with research participants in the real environment or a realistic but controlled environment. Your Service Designer will know what to do.

- If testing shows that we haven't fully solved the problem or we haven't solved it well, this should not be considered "good enough," and released to the public. This is our opportunity to be customer-centric and aim for five-star quality.

Before Marketing tries to convince customers they want it; before Sales seals the deal; before Engineers code, test, and merge; and before Customer Support has to deal with struggling customers, we can know most of what we need to know through User-Centered Design's learn-build-test-iterate approach. We can understand our root causes, clearly define problems, and iteratively work on improvements and innovations.

CX Strategy

You will need to create a CX strategy in each area of your PSE. It should be solution-agnostic, and focus on how we will meet or exceed customers' unmet needs. This might be through new PSE, innovations, or smaller improvements to existing PSE. Our strategic approach to CX and PSE is based on solid evidence from our qualitative and quantitative research. Keep this strategy *agile*; as we discover new evidence and insights, strategies and priorities might need to change.

For an example of strategy at the project level, let's use a previous problem statement:

- When a customer's credit card expires, Priority Pass closes their account. We create a new account for the new credit card, but the account isn't active until the customer gets a code from Support staff. Our system does not automatically update credit card information, nor do we offer a way for the user to update their credit card information. This creates frustration for customers and taxes our Customer Support teams, who currently walk people through setting up the half-created Priority Pass account.

Imagining that we have extensive research data and insights guiding us, our overarching CX strategy at the project level might be: *simplify credit card updating.* Note that our strategy is customer-focused and doesn't revolve around a business need or goal. We didn't mention a particular solution, feature, or mechanism that would solve this, allowing CX Architects and Designers to be problem solvers.

ProFlowers Sells Occasions

In the late 1990s, Larry Marine was hired to create a fresh website for online florist ProFlowers. Executives suggested that he usability test their existing site, and come up with enhancements. Larry knew that better customer knowledge comes from observational research, so he spent time in brick-and-mortar flower shops observing customers and florists.

He noticed that many customers came in and told the florist their situation. "I need to apologize to my wife." The florist could suggest various bouquets at different price points. Larry realized that nearly zero customers understood the "meaning" of flowers, which flowers went well together, or what is the right bouquet for the situation. They knew *why* they needed flowers, but relied on the florist to know *which* flowers.

At the time, websites expected you to build your own bouquet, which assumed that customers had decent flower knowledge. Larry noticed that customers lacked this presumed knowledge, which highlights a knowledge gap (remember Task Dimensions in an earlier chapter). Larry realized that ProFlowers' overarching CX strategy should be: *ProFlowers sells occasions.*

Larry and his team designed a new website shopping experience that allowed customers to choose by occasion. This not only brought ProFlowers huge success and a conversion rate over 20% for decades, but it redefined online florist websites. It was disruptive. We are now used to online shopping for certain items by occasion, reason, or recipient, but once upon a time, that wasn't a thing.

For the *simplify credit card updating* CX strategy, we know the customers' goals from our problem statement. Our business goals might include reducing Customer Support volume around this topic, longer customer memberships or Lifetime Value, and the percentage of customers with an expired card who were able to self-service. If we have estimates or calculations of saved expenses or increased revenue, we can include those in our documentation or Delta CX Impact Map.

Next, we have initiatives to accomplish these goals and implement the strategy. Improvements and innovations might have been surfaced from our optimized task flow. Using our Priority Pass example, instead of creating a new account that requires further setup, streamlining that workflow might mean a new account isn't created, and we allow users to update their existing account instead.

The strategic choice to change the workflow will require us to redesign the stored credit card page in the account profile to allow card updating or multiple cards on file. We will design and schedule emails to warn customers that their credit card will expire or has expired, and link them to an "update your card" page. We will also need to reprogram the system so it doesn't automatically close accounts with expired credit cards. Don't forget to train Customer Support on these changes. Notice that *the features come from the potential solutions, not the other way around.* We didn't start our project deciding features like "send the customer an email about card expiration." We started with research, which led to evidence around the complete Customer Experience and problem.

Imagine we skipped research and worked from Customer Support letting us know that some people are having trouble completing the new accounts we surprise-created for them. *That doesn't sound too bad! Maybe we can fix that up with some messaging!* With our limited understanding of the problem, we might brainstorm a quick fix: *email the customer the code they need to complete setting up their new account. Now they won't need to call Customer Support for the code.*

We might see fewer Support calls about setting up the newly-created account, and believe we've solved the problem. Would the customer say we solved the problem? They still had their old account closed, which means their Priority Pass card is invalid. If they prefer physical membership cards, we now have to mail them a card with a new account number on it, wasting paper, plastic, and postage. If they are traveling while this happens, they might not be able to use the Priority Pass service because their account expired, and they didn't set up the new account yet.

Band-aids and workarounds might feel like solutions, but dig deeper, past the surface and past the symptoms of the larger problem. Compare *quick wins based on light knowledge* to the more thorough process of gathering qualitative and quantitative evidence, writing well-defined problem statements, and working through your strategy to solve the problem and its root causes.

"What is this project's strategy?" is a question I always ask when I hear stories about executives randomly changing priorities. So far, 100% of people have replied that there isn't one. Teams change what they are working on based on whatever an exec thinks we should chase this week or month. If this sounds like your situation, consider challenging that leader or exec. Create and present a plan to start with the research that will guide the creation of a strategic vision. We can then use that strategy to prioritize problem-solving projects and put teams on a clear path.

Making Decisions Differently

A customer-centricity transformation requires decisions to be made differently than they are now. Changes we will need to shepherd include:

Current State	Desired Future State
What can we convince people to buy?	Learn target customers' unmet needs, and build PSE that fulfill these.
What's the least we can rush out to the public?	Create five-star Customer Experiences in every release.
What can we fake or manipulate to get people to sign our contract?	Define strategies that drive us to create the best PSE so that customers will *want* to sign our contract.
Hey, customer, do you want this idea we have? Would you pay for it?	Conduct generative research to learn target audiences' unmet needs and behaviors.

How do we push or force people to the next step in our funnel?	Create easy and intuitive PSE that facilitate moving through the funnel.
How can we manipulate metrics to make our projects look more successful?	Honest metrics may surface failures, which help us actively work to improve.
Just tell leadership and execs that we're fast and efficient. They don't need to know about our project disasters.	Honesty and integrity are essential and might be among our company values. Being open about disasters means we can learn from them and improve for the future.
What are quick wins we can release to customers?	Ensure that "quick wins" are truly wins for customers and not just the business.
If I can figure it out, it's user-friendly.	You are not the user. Internal workers are always savvier than customers. We must research and test with end-users.
How fast can we get this done?	We work efficiently while being wise about risk and the value we deliver.
"Outcomes over outputs."	Outcomes are important, but *inputs* are how we get there. Don't forget the quality of inputs and evidence.

The key to improved decision-making will be around confidence and risk: *how confident are we that we are going in the right direction? How much risk is acceptable versus when do we press pause to identify and alleviate concerns?*

Make Great CX Processes Part of Compliance

I heard about one company that ensured that research is a part of every project, allowing strategies, decisions, and project directions to be evidence-based. Even when Product Managers or Product Owners don't want to spend time or money on research, they must. *How did this company do that?*

The Head of Design had the legal team add CX/UX tasks such as research into the company-wide development compliance regulations. A team skipping research – or skimping on it, based on how research is defined in these regulations – isn't compliant. In this company, bonuses are attached to compliance. Therefore, even those who are against research are incentivized to *not* block it.

It's important to note that (based on what I heard), the Design leader didn't go to various Product or Engineering stakeholders and ask their permission to include research more often, or, "Can we please add some research to our definitions of project compliance?" It sounds like this leader went directly to the legal team, made a case for why research and being evidence-based is not a "nice to have," and had more thorough UCD processes written into internal compliance regulations.

Writing minimum standards for CX tasks into compliance requirements would certainly inspire teams to meet those standards. Remember that a minimum standard can be a high standard. We do not need to write *the least research we could do* into compliance regulations as our standard.

My suggestions for these standards include:

- **Generative qualitative research must be done before every project** unless we have previous and recent research that answers the team's questions about customers, behaviors, or our PSE. If there are unanswered questions, a knowledge gap, or unchecked hypotheses, we must conduct a study with observations and/or interviews so that we work from knowledge and not guesses or assumptions.

- **Who plans, executes, and analyzes the research.** CX tasks are specialized and must be done by qualified specialists. It shouldn't meet our standards if research is done poorly, the wrong methods are used, or the findings are manipulated to say what we wanted to hear.

- **Content, information architecture, interaction design, service design, and prototyping are done by specialists.** It should not meet our minimum standards if a coworker who wouldn't qualify for a CX job at our company is trying to do CX or UX tasks. That is ultimately not a time saver and can introduce unwanted risk.

- **Designs receive at least two rounds of testing.** Round one tests your concept or prototype for ease of use, how intuitive it is, and how well it solves the original customer problem. It's common to find flaws or Experience bugs during testing, which leads to design changes. We should then test again to ensure that there is no Experience debt that should be fixed *now*, when improvements would cost less and be faster than fixing it later.

- **Diversity, equity, inclusion, and accessibility are baked into compliance**, not something we hope to sprinkle on at the end. We must research, design for, and test with all of our target audiences.

- **CX teams and individual practitioners estimate their required time and resources to do world-class work.** If they will not get what they need to do five-star work, then the person who decided to limit CX is accountable for problematic outcomes. Perhaps this person risks being non-compliant if they are a blocker.

Later in this chapter, we'll look at creating a value-led process playbook. Your playbook includes standards for CX work as well as the guidelines for how CX tasks are done. You might try to have this playbook written into internal compliance regulations or any internal process requirements, especially where bonuses or rewards are part of the equation. Additionally, governance, covered at the end of this chapter, will need to be in place to monitor where we are compliant or not compliant, and how to act quickly to stay compliant.

Attaching customer-centricity and CX processes to compliance or internal requirements or standards would ensure that your "CX program" doesn't fail. CX initiatives can fail where teams and executives see customer-centricity as optional. Additionally, if your CX staff are among the first to be cut in layoffs, then your employees and the public can tell that customer-centricity isn't important at your company.

Take customer-centricity off the "nice to have" list. Make it mandatory. Make it a company value. Connect it to internal compliance and standards. Put it with legal, security, developers, and other teams and processes we see as non-optional.

Concurrent Changes, Obstacles, and Dependencies

Many of the elements and situations that are blocking improved customer-centricity are often intertwined. Since many of our internal pain points feed each other, there will be changes that must happen before some other problem can be solved. For example:

- **You might need to reconfigure departments and hire stronger people onto those teams.** But we might have trouble attracting and retaining key CX staff while our processes around CX strategy and tasks are ugly. Candidates might not want to join or stay in that environment. While we are hiring, we will have to fix other things that are interconnected.

- **You want to improve relationships between teams and the processes they are using.** However, if the KPIs and metrics coming down from the top are customer-peripheric, we could be using new processes but still creating customer-peripheric PSE.

Before you try to create change, break down some walls, and rebuild them, you should map out and consider blockers that could prevent that change from happening. You might be able to predict these, or they might come up as you go. Map these with their appropriate dependencies. I call this a "Change Dependency Map."

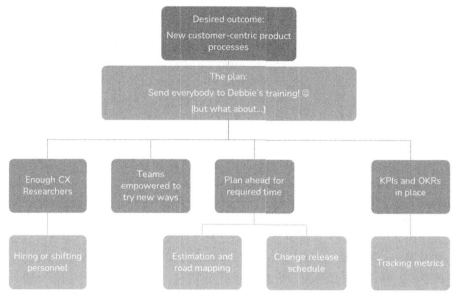

Figure 39: The Change Dependency Map is a hierarchic diagram. Explained below.

For example, we might imagine that training is the main ingredient needed for change. *Let's send everybody to Debbie's training so we will all be ready to improve customer-centricity!* Sure, but there will still be blockers.

- **Do we have enough CX Researchers available to do all of the research that being customer-centric requires?** If not, the change could stall or fail. We will first need to hire some people or shift personnel around so that even just one or two teams are ready to try new ways of working.

- **Are our teams empowered to break out of how we do things now and try new processes, methods, and approaches?** If not, all the training in the world might not produce the desired actions or outcomes.

- **Did we plan extra time to try new ways of working?** It'll probably take us longer than our old ways, especially while new processes are experimental.

  o Did we estimate this time and update our roadmaps? Did we change our release schedule so that nobody is surprised that the new project is taking longer than usual?

  o Forgetting to plan extra time to try new ways of working could block our goal of successfully experimenting with more customer-centric processes. Estimating time, updating roadmaps, and changing the release schedule are dependencies under "planning extra time." This is why the Change Dependency Map is a tree or hierarchy; fixing one or more problems unblocks a higher-level problem.

- **How will we measure if our customer-centricity adventures are starting to work, or where we need to improve?**

  o Do we have KPIs and OKRs in place? Are we ready to track and measure everything that we need to?

  o Does the team believe we are tracking or obsessed with the wrong numbers? Are teams under pressure to deliver customer-peripheric KPIs? We will have to shift or fix these to remove obstacles that can block the change we want.

Some companies bring in expensive trainers assuming that if we train everybody on this topic or method, we can then use this method, which will solve our problems. The example map reminds us that trainers alone rarely solve a problem or create a transformation because we haven't cleared the blockers and dependencies.

Map anything that will block desired changes and outcomes. *What must change before we can create the final or larger change?* Work on changes at the lowest level of the hierarchy first so that teams are freed up and empowered. The lowest level of your map might be root causes blocking other changes. Mapping these out visualizes and socializes obstacles so that we can plan to eliminate them.

The sample map above has a broad and high-level goal of *being more customer-centric*. We can use a Change Dependency Map for a change at any level: project, team, department, or company. Our desired outcome might be very specific or a broader vision.

Beware of Fuzzy Goals

Leadership and executive meetings often result in a to-do list of internal and external improvements. *Improve PSE quality, reduce complaints, be more customer-centric, and increase satisfaction and loyalty.* What are our strategies to accomplish these? What is the plan to get us there? Which initiatives will achieve our goals, and who is leading them? What are reasonable timelines and budgets for these initiatives? What success criteria or metrics will we use to oversee and measure the project and its effectiveness?

Fuzzy goals lead to unclear or no plans, accountability, and actionable tasks. Here's how to make these more actionable and ultimately more successful:

1. **Break it down**. "Improve PSE quality" is too broad a goal. Determine which areas of our PSE need which types of improvements. If we don't know, create generative research projects that will answer these and other questions.

2. **Evidence, data, and knowledge.** Now that we have our issues in more bite-sized pieces, what do we know about what's going wrong for our business or customers?

   o Even if we think we know what is going wrong or why, challenge that. We might have incomplete data. We could be relying on guesses or assumptions.

- o Check our VOC and existing research data and insights. Researchers might know where key pain points and opportunities exist.

- o Try a team exercise where teammates and stakeholders add sticky notes to a virtual or physical whiteboard with four quadrants: unanswered questions, guesses and assumptions, potentially outdated or incorrect information, and what they wish they knew. These may sound similar, but rephrasing things often inspires people to think from different angles and add more notes.

- o This whiteboard feeds generative research goals. One or more studies will be needed to answer questions and replace guesses and assumptions with knowledge.

3. **Problem statements.** Write problem statements based on what our research and data reveal.

4. **Delta CX Impact Map.** Now that we have problem statements, we can map the current negative impact on customers and the business. We can consider root causes, and the KPIs and OKRs we will monitor to measure success and performance.

5. **Delta CX Change Dependency Map**. Map out anything that could block the change you are trying to create. These might be internal processes, culture, deadlines, resources, available staff, or anything that could be an obstacle to accomplishing our goals. Every blocker is a risk to identify and mitigate as early as possible.

6. **Prioritization**. Now that we understand each problem and have an Impact Map and Change Dependency Map for it, we can bring the project team together for a prioritization exercise. We decide which problems we will tackle in which order. Each domain can start planning and roadmapping.

7. **Accountability** – Who is accountable or responsible for what? How will we hold that person accountable if a project fails or shows poor outcomes? What does accountability look like? What is in place to inspire decision-makers to do and be better? Accountability will be discussed in more detail at the end of this chapter.

Whether or not we started with something fuzzy, we now have a more actionable plan.

Prioritization Must Include Customer Perspectives

I heard about a company requiring Product Managers and UX Designers to estimate how much every proposed project will raise a particular (customer-peripheric) KPI. If they want to initiate a project around fixing bugs customers complain about, they have to estimate how much the project would lift the metric execs care about, even if the fixes have nothing to do with that metric. All roads lead to *lift this one metric.*

This is misguided and requires psychic abilities. The company's prioritization framework was based on *how many more clicks on this one button* a project might create. This is another example of an unhealthy focus on lifting KPIs at any cost, and how customer-peripheric KPIs manifest in team behavior, work, and decisions. Additionally, this company had research and data showing that customers wanted to click that button as little as possible. Prioritizing projects that inspire or force people to click that button might make some execs happy, but this is customer-peripheric at its core.

The prioritization matrix must include the impact on customers. Many frameworks use terms like "customer impact" or "user benefits," but they are often from the perspective of the business, such as a "user benefit" defined as someone remaining a customer for a longer period of time. That might be a benefit the business gets from users, but is not necessarily a benefit *to* the user.

Here are some customer impact factors that you can include in your prioritization framework:

- **Self-service**. PSE that allow customers to take care of their own tasks without depending on Customer Support.

- **Customer demand**. PSE that customers are requesting or complaining about.

- **Attrition and deal breakers**. Addressing why we lost customers or failed to acquire them.

You can also try my Delta CX Decision Matrix. [https://cxcc.to/a167] The four criteria for judging are how well this issue relates to our strategies or goals, the number of customers affected, severity or urgency, and the cost to reverse, which estimates the relative time and effort required to redo our "solution" later.

Also note that we are not prioritizing features. We are prioritizing problem statements, pain points, or opportunities. Features, especially if decided before generative qualitative research, are guesses of what PSE to build. They might be solutions in search of problems. They might be stakeholder ego projects or competitor rip-off projects. Having a list of potential features doesn't mean we understand customers, are likely to create the best solutions, or are customer-centric. Even if we try to use good research evidence for feature prioritization, we are still putting the solution cart before the research horse.

Value-Led Process Playbooks

A crucial part of your customer-centricity efforts will be creating or updating process playbooks. *How should we do product or service discovery? What role does Research play? What does CX do? Where are others involved or not involved? When do you need CX? What can you do yourself if there is no CX resource? How does CX work with Agile or Scrum? How do we bake great Customer Experiences, accessibility, and five-star quality into the Definition of Done?* Get it all in the playbook.

Write the playbook for the change you want to see. Don't write anything in here that gives away a domain's power. Watch for anything in the playbook that you might try to undo later with training or evangelism. This is your chance to set the rules.

You will need internal training or other sessions to help socialize these new processes. Make sure the training and playbooks detail who to speak to if there are questions about the new processes or suggestions for improvement. Also, note that there should be one playbook per process. The more playbooks we have for the same process, the less standardized our ways of working will be, which could end up causing inefficiencies, confusion, and conflicts.

Warning: many playbooks you can find online or from corporate trainers were made by Product Managers, often giving a lot of power to Product. They might be product-led or engineering-led rather than genuinely being value-led. This can run against the change you are trying to shepherd. Rewrite these playbooks or create your own.

Make sure the playbook includes details about:

- **Each step of the process, the tasks for this step, and why we do this step.**

    o Create swim lanes or boundaries so people don't overlap each other's jobs.

    o We also want to differentiate between who owns or leads a step versus who is involved or a collaborator. You can use a RACI matrix to indicate who is *responsible, accountable, consulted,* and *informed* in each step.

    o Describe boundaries that will fix some of the problems you're seeing. For example, you might say that only CX decides when we need a workshop, they choose the methods, and are the facilitators. That will stop other domains from running Design workshops.

- **Outputs or outcomes of this step.** Make sure these are actionable so they inform and drive the next and later steps.

- **Tools, templates, or methods we prefer for this step.**

- **Success criteria.** How do we know that this step went well? Can this be measured?

- **Common pitfalls.** What mistakes are typically made during this step? What does failure or having done something incorrectly look like? Again, this is your chance to create some boundaries and undo some bad habits or processes.

Futurespectives and Pre-Mortems

Futurespectives, also called pre-mortems, are exercises where the cross-functional team gets together to imagine the future. *What will it be like when this project is completed?* In imagining our future, we can look at what might block us from the best possible outcomes. It's easy to dream up the "happy path," where the future is bright, if not perfect. *Customers love our PSE. Everything is going to plan.*

But a futurespective is designed to help us now by recognizing what might cause poor outcomes. We can identify and then mitigate those risks. Imagine an ugly, undesirable future. *Our project fails. Support channels are overwhelmed. We're having a higher call volume than normal, please hold. There are angry tweets and social posts, and our stock price drops. Sales reports that customers are leaving or threatening to leave. Offering a discount isn't helping.*

- **How might the unwanted future outcome happen?** What can we envision blocking our project's success or successful customer outcomes?

- **What or who could be a blocker or obstacle?** Are we lacking the time or budget that we need? Is the team being manipulated by people higher up?

- **What potential outside forces might hurt us?** Do we have strong competitors? Is something politically, socially, or regionally going on that might affect this project's success?

- **What's under the tip of the iceberg?** Above the water, it might look sunny and inviting. Beneath the water lies an iceberg that can derail our project or its success. What could that be?

Part of the exercise is to document risks, decide how we will mitigate the risks, and who will be accountable or responsible. If you hold a futurespective, put sticky notes on a board, and then do nothing about risk, you've missed the point. Address and fix *all* of these problems before they become realities.

Possible Outcome: Shoplifters?

While I was a Senior UX Architect at Macys.com, I worked on in-store app functionality that would allow customers to scan their items, pay with their app, and walk out of the store (after having security tags removed). I wanted to use the app's existing checkout flow and screens. The Product Manager and Engineering Lead overruled me, claiming they had a better and "cleaner" app checkout. The Engineering Lead designed what he liked and told his team to build that.

I warned that two different app checkouts would confuse users, especially those used to our current app checkout. The Engineering Lead's design had multiple screens and steps, but could be easily mistaken for a one-screen, one-click checkout due to the layout and wording.

I asked the Product Manager and Engineering Lead to imagine the possible outcome if someone gets the checkout wrong: they won't have completed their payment, but will try to leave the store with merchandise. Our security guards will bring these customers into a back room and accuse them of shoplifting. The Product Manager and Engineering Lead told me I was being hysterical and dramatic, and the checkout would be great.

We piloted this functionality in a special store where Macy's tested new technology. Within days, word came back that people trying this new app functionality confidently scanned their items, went through the first checkout screen, and started to leave the store without paying. They thought it was a one-click checkout that was completed after the big red "checkout" button on the bottom of the first screen. That button started, not completed, the checkout. They exited our app without noticing that the following screen wasn't a purchase confirmation.

Upon hearing this, I suggested to the Product Manager and Engineering Lead that we go back to having the checkout be the same screens the app already utilizes. They rejected that request, and demanded that I "make their idea work." I told them we had just learned in live in-store testing that their idea didn't work, and I couldn't make the wrong solution work. They suggested that I add more text before and during the checkout to explain how to use it. I told them that instructional text, tooltips, and other types of tutorials are considered bad User Experiences; the interface and workflow should be logical and intuitive, and not require explanation, especially help text people are unlikely to read.

They told my manager they no longer needed any UX Architects on the project because they had all the designs they needed, and I was reassigned. This lie quickly unraveled when I received JIRA ticket updates that new designs were being coded and then were ready for release.

This is the Lean sin of underutilized talent when our company is paying for CX or UX specialists, but we cater to the loudest voices or egos on the team. Use the futurespective or pre-mortem, and take possible outcomes seriously. Risks should be documented, understood, and mitigated. Teammates should not be told they are hysterical for reporting potential project and Customer Experience risks.

Try It: Customer Disaster Journey Map

If you are having trouble getting teammates to understand some of the likely risks, try my Delta CX Customer Disaster Journey Map. It's a journey map representing a possible future outcome where things go badly for the customer. Presenting this from the customers' perspective as if it has already happened can help wake up teammates who don't see or care about this possible outcome.

It's another story from my time at Macy's. The beauty subscription box project would send people small product samples to entice customers to purchase the full-sized product. The link from the "what's in my box this month" page to the full-sized product brought customers to a page defaulting to a different lipstick color than the sample we sent them.

Product and Engineering were sure people would notice it wasn't the same shade, and change the lipstick color. Product and Engineering preferred this over coding the link to show the correct lipstick color to people coming from the subscription box page.

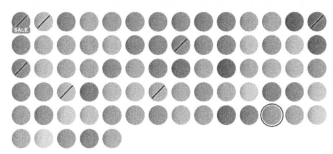

Figure 40: Screenshot of the 75 colors one Sephora lipstick comes in. How easy would it be to notice that the default color isn't the same shade as the small sample you received?

My Customer Disaster Journey Map envisioned the potential future Customer Experience. The customer gets a lipstick sample they like and uses the subscription box link to order the full size. They accidentally order the wrong color because we helped them make that mistake. They call Customer Support, who would be baffled that someone who received the color they ordered is angry and claiming they didn't get the right color. They tell the angry customer to go to the store to figure this out, giving our customer an errand. Our customer takes to social media to unleash their fury at us. Out of frustration, they cancel the beauty box subscription, all because we didn't want to default a page to the color of the lipstick sample we sent.

Once my teammates saw the Customer Disaster Journey Map, it hit them. This risk was unacceptable, so they decided to take the time to write the code that would show the correct lipstick color to visitors from the subscription box link.

Document Risk

Some teams believe that documentation slows us down and makes us less Lean. But a lack of documentation hurts us when team members quit, are fired, or join. Joining a company or team shouldn't feel like an archaeologist trying to figure out a Bronze Age civilization that left no written language. Someone from my online community joined a team that told her they had previous ideas that didn't work, and needed something fresh from her. But they had no record of what happened previously, and nobody wanted to take the time to talk her through the project's history. Decent documentation could have avoided this awkward and risky situation.

"We don't need an accurate document; we need a shared understanding."
– Jeff Patton

"Until everybody with the shared understanding quits, is fired, or laid off. Then we will wish we had an accurate document reflecting the shared understanding."
– Me

In addition to documenting a project's progress and decisions, we should be documenting risks before and after they happen. Document risk in every possible form in which it might appear, including:

- **Team members were not given enough time or budget to do world-class work.**

- **Wasted time and effort by any of the team members.**

- **Guesses, assumptions, or untested hypotheses that we allowed to influence our strategies, decisions, or PSE.** Which of our assumptions, if partially or wholly incorrect, could lead to the failure of this project, service, product, or feature?

- **Continuing with a flawed project, even where team members raised concerns about the quality, value, or benefit to customers.** Moving forward with PSE that we know now will need to be fixed later creates considerable risk and should be documented.

- **Data showing that the solution the team is moving forward with is not the correct solution.**

- **Inconsistent or poor PSE quality, including CX or technical bugs.**

- **Issues related to laws, regulations, security, or privacy.**

- **Bad actors.** What might criminals, abusers, hackers, and people seeking to cause chaos do?

- **Diversity, equity, inclusion, and accessibility.** Are we blocking people who are part of our potential maximum target audience? Are we pretending to know or empathize with communities not represented on our teams?

- **Outside forces.** Which risks are created by competition, consumer demand, the economy, and world events?

The point of documenting these is to identify potential risks and waste early, and then take action to mitigate these. Make sure they never happen, or at least be prepared for what you will do if the potential risk occurs. If someone claims they will be responsible or accountable for decisions, the documentation would indicate who that is.

If your company loves workshops, get everybody together for a "Risk Mitigation Workshop." Brainstorm possible risks in all of the above areas. Document who will own or oversee each risk, and who will be held responsible or accountable, if not the same person. Consider how this risk can be reduced or eliminated as soon as possible. Define metrics we can watch that will tell us if the risk is happening or if a potential risk was eliminated. Use any risk documentation style your teams prefer. You can also use my spreadsheet template. [https://cxcc.to/a164]

Previous failures and disaster projects should help leaders be more open to trying another way. Yet some seem hellbent on making the same mistakes again, often in the same ways. What can we do when those in power don't want to utilize customer-centric processes or listen to warnings about risk?

1. **Document everything that's going on.** Document what you tried to do, what was rejected, and why. Document what leaders decide, how they collaborate, or how they micromanage.

   o There is a slight chance that everything will turn out perfectly. There is a significant chance this project will fail in small or large ways. Document known or predicted risks of taking this path and making these decisions. Try to get the attention of someone lateral to or above you to discuss the risks.

   o If you have suggestions or a plan to mitigate these, present those as well. If nobody wants to talk about risks and mitigate them now, this is the list we bring up after that failure happens.

2. **Make sure there are clear success criteria, KPIs, or other metrics around this project's outcomes.** How can we tell it went well? How can we tell what failed and how? How fast can we know this? Are we going to wait months for a survey? Can we proactively get Customer Support to share tickets as they are created so we can see where the problems are? Check for the Cost of Poor Quality.

   o Be careful of vanity or meaningless metrics being used to show success. At one company I was involved with, magically, every project showed a lift in something so Product Managers could declare it a success. Make sure we have agreed on meaningful metrics related to outcomes, Customer Experiences, or our North Star Metric.

3. **You might have to let them fail.** Sometimes you can't stop someone from making poor decisions. There might be an ego, confidence, or arrogance mountain that we can't overcome. We didn't break this, and we can't fix it, so we might have to let them fail. Of course, we will only know there was a failure if we have clear success criteria and ways of measuring outcomes.

      o   Where a small or large failure was predicted in our risk documentation and therefore avoidable, this could be our future case study helping promote our new, more customer-centric ways of working.

4. **Definition of accountability.** How do we hold people accountable for small or large project failures? How do we hold them accountable when predictable and avoidable risks happen, and now we are stuck with the consequences?

      o   These projects repeatedly happen when there is no incentive to stop them. Accountability means that there are consequences for wasting time, money, or customer trust.

Empowered Teams

Power comes from autonomy, culture, and being allowed to make decisions in your area of expertise. Indicating that staff should work "autonomously" doesn't mean they are empowered. We will need to take a serious look at our teams, and take action to balance power.

Keys to empowering teams and team members include:

- **All members are empowered.** If the Product Manager feels empowered, but CX and Engineering do not, it's not an empowered team.

- **Encourage thinking critically, asking tough questions, and challenging the status quo.** We are disempowered when we are afraid to speak up, or believe that nobody cares what we think. We welcome someone with a concern or warning, and we should pause to address these early, if not immediately.

  - o   Staff must feel safe to speak the truth when witnessing or assessing troubled projects. Your culture must promote trust between employees and management.

  - o   Your teams aren't empowered if you suppress criticism or label the feedback – or the person who delivers it – as unsupportive, not a team player, or negative. The person discussing the problem should not be seen as the problem.

- **Remain open to ideas and possibilities.** If the C-suite or a stakeholder tells a team the exact PSE they must design or build, this isn't an empowered team. These are order takers required to do what they are told. The team should challenge this, and the stakeholder should be open to the possibility that their idea isn't the best or the only one worth considering.

- **Specialists make decisions in their areas of expertise.** If a QA Engineer wants to make an important decision but is overruled, especially by a non-QA staffer, that QA Engineer probably doesn't feel empowered.

- **Specialists now in leadership positions manage those in the same specialty.** This allows each worker to have a manager who understands the work because they came from the work. The manager has experience with what the worker does and needs, and how to best fulfill those needs. The worker has a domain expert to whom they can escalate matters, or get advice on handling tough coworker or project situations.

- **Teams are congratulated as a unit.** Few things are as demotivating for staff as congratulations or rewards for only some team members.

  - I have often seen only the Product Manager congratulated when a feature launches or a project goes well. Engineers, CX staff, and others don't even get a mention.

  - One company told me they only reward and congratulate full-time employees. Contractors and freelancers – even those who had worked there full-time for a year or more – receive no acknowledgment.

  - Another company told me they don't congratulate everybody because "they don't want to send out emails with a long list of names." *Yes, you do.*

  - Congratulate and acknowledge every team member by name or no team member by name. Don't only congratulate the team leader or whomever you think of as the team contact person.

- **Team members stand up for what other members need to do great work.** Product, Engineering, CX, and others on our cross-functional team want to see each teammate getting the time, budget, and resources they need to do world-class work.

  - For example, twice in 2022, I heard about Product Directors giving some of their budgets to UX so that UX could hire more specialists. Product could have kept that budget for itself, but this is an excellent example of one domain on the team taking action because another domain had an unmet need. Ultimately, the team wins.

- **Get rid of your triads and quads.** Many companies go with a "triad" or "quad" model, which typically has three or four roles from the following: Product Owner, Product Manager, Software Architect, QA Tester, Developer, or Scrum Master. Once in a while, though still rare, you might see a UX Designer considered part of the triad or quad, though Researchers and other important CX specialists are excluded. Some companies include Data and Analytics in their quad. These configurations tend to be Engineering-focused since the triad concept is often associated with Agile.

  - **If you want an empowered team, you will need to empower everybody on the team.** We have less-empowered teams when we highlight only a few roles as key members or decision-makers. Crowning a few people in a triad disempowers those who were excluded, and sends clear messages inside and outside the team about who is important or "has a seat at the table."

o "The table" must include all of the roles relevant to the project. We defer to their abilities and skills in their own domains, and we want experts making decisions in their fields of expertise.

o I suggest dropping the triad and quad if you want empowered teams who are collaborative and have a sense of equality. If you're keeping triads or quads, make sure a higher level CX practitioner is an equal voice in decision making.

- **Watch how you use the word "alignment."** It's often a euphemism for catering to the highest level's or most aggressive person's requests.

  o *Won't we need alignment from leaders when we present our CX and PSE strategies?* If we took leaders' requests and concerns into account when we created the strategies, we shouldn't need their "alignment" later. They should naturally "align" because they trust their teams to create the best strategies that take customers and the business into account. If your team's carefully-crafted strategy is shot down by leaders who demand that it be done their way, you don't have empowered teams.

  o *Won't we need alignment when PSE solutions and designs are being finalized?* Our CX strategy took business goals and KPIs into consideration. We then designed the best solution for our original customer problem statement. We can socialize these designs with stakeholders and leaders. But if we are under pressure to change vetted, high-quality designs based on what teammates or leaders request or prefer, this isn't an empowered team.

- **Trust and believe in each worker.** You hired qualified, capable people from the hundreds who applied.

  o Don't wait until you hear the same suggestions from a Fortune 500 leader or a big, expensive consulting company. The specialists working with you now might next work at these places; will you then respect them and take their advice? You can listen to them and benefit from their insights and suggestions now, or you can pay five times what you're paying them when they return as outside consultants.

  o Do we have stakeholders who don't believe in an entire profession? Do we have leaders who don't believe in research, design, or QA, or fail to see the value they have? Are we hiring people and then treating them with disbelief, distrust, or hostility? This is not empowering.

- o If your company doesn't believe in particular roles or professions, it might be best to not hire those people at all. Open those jobs once there is support and trust for the professionals you would hire and their tasks.

"I was interviewing with [famous car brand] for a Senior UX Researcher position. They told me that stakeholder buy-ins are difficult. A lot of stakeholders don't see value in research. They asked what I think about that. I said, 'I'm in a place in my career right now where I don't want to prove my job to anyone else.' I didn't make it to the next interview round."
– Member of my community

Can We Measure the ROI of a Single Person?

What is the ROI of some of the work our staff does?

- **These questions or challenges put staff in very awkward positions.** Did we ask Product Managers to prove their value?

- **You opened these jobs. You hired these people. They shouldn't have to explain their specializations or value.** CX and UX staff are often asked to explain their jobs and the value of their work as part of an ROI conversation. CX practitioners should not show up to a project where teammates don't understand what they do, and then have to deal with that environment or stop their work to teach people what they do for a living.

  - o **If your teams and company don't understand CX or UX roles, get everybody trained on that.** This will avoid later conflicts and confusion, plus the damaged morale of "they hired me but have no idea what I do."

  - o Internal staff should not be expected to "evangelize" their day-to-day work or explain how they deliver returns on the company's investment in their wages.

- **We can know the ROI of a project, but it's hard to know the exact value provided by any one team member.** Who on the Engineering team do we blame for *lowering the ROI* because our new feature has a technical bug? If our new feature performs well, what percentage of the ROI should be attributed to a Product Manager? This is quickly awkward and demotivating.

How Do I Measure You?

A member of my community told me that their new Manager, who had been at the company roughly six weeks, asked them what metrics the Manager can use to measure the Individual Contributor.

A Manager should know how people reporting to them should be assessed and judged. A decent Manager should not be asking a worker anything like, "Tell me what numbers to watch for so I know if you're doing your job well." It sounds like the Manager wanted to hear numbers around velocity, like how much this CX professional got done in what amount of time. We shouldn't measure Developers by the number of lines of code they wrote, regardless of the quality of that code. We shouldn't measure Product Managers by the number of items they prioritize in an Engineering backlog.

If we believe in "outcomes over outputs," and especially if we want empowered teams, then we cannot measure staff like they are factory floor robots. If your company is *speed over quality*, then you will judge people by the amount of work they got done and meeting deadlines. If you are *quality over speed*, then you are measuring shared team responsibility for outcomes.

Accountability

We cannot achieve or improve customer-centricity without both governance and accountability. If people are not held accountable for inefficient processes, culture problems, poor collaboration, disaster projects, wasted budget, and negative Customer Experiences that chip away at customer trust, these issues repeat and grow. Without accountability and a culture shift, this often spirals companies downward toward increasingly poor, customer-peripheric, and even unethical decisions.

The key question for any experiment, process change, or transformation is: what do leaders, stakeholders, or executives need to see to know that something is succeeding or failing?

Without clear success and failure criteria, metrics, and ongoing monitoring, we can tell ourselves we're "good enough," and continue cycles of risk and waste.

We must also consider worker and leader churn. Especially in tech, people stay at jobs for shorter periods than ever, often only 1-2 years. [https://cxcc.to/a165] When the project results come in and you want to hold someone accountable, they might be gone. Knowing they plan to quit, they might be comfortable doing something risky or unethical since they won't be there to deal with consequences and questions. Therefore, accountability, governance, and standards before, during, and after projects are core to raising internal and external quality.

You will need to look at what accountability means to and at your company, how risks are documented and handled, and what happens when people are held responsible for failures. What happens when we document risk, our projects move forward, and the risk happens? How do we hold someone accountable for failing to act on and mitigate that risk?

For example, a UX team I coached struggled with a non-UX Director who only wanted them to design for larger screen sizes. **The risk is known:** *we have X% of users on smaller screens who might not be able to use the product. They might contact Customer Support to complain it's broken and not working on their device.* **The likely outcomes are known:** *UX will have to redesign the product to work for smaller screen sizes. Engineering will have to rebuild it, retest it, and rerelease it. Future projects will be delayed while teams fix this avoidable problem.*

The leader claimed they would "take responsibility" for this decision, but what does that mean or look like? When the company burns time, money, and customer trust because of known issues and risks, what consequences come with "being responsible?" Will the Director be questioned or blocked the next time they try to make a similar decision? Will they develop a reputation for wasting money, and be given less budget next time? Will someone else take the project over because we don't trust this leader to make the right decision? Will this leader be put on a performance improvement plan? How do we hold them responsible if people on their teams are sick of dealing with them and quit?

We must notice the difference between mistakes and informed decisions.

In the above example, there are no mistakes. We know how many people will be alienated or orphaned by not making our PSE work on their screens. This is an informed decision that is high risk. The better we get at identifying and documenting risks earlier, the less that poor decisions will be mistakes; they will be informed and deliberate.

Without stricter governance, risk documentation, and accountability with consequences, our leaders and staff have no incentive to do better. There must be consequences for staff, leaders, and people at all levels who ignore solid evidence or make informed decisions that lead to significant risks and poor Customer Experiences.

Start by documenting these situations. Notice patterns and frequency. Put people – especially repeat offenders – on a performance improvement plan. Give them coaching, monitor what they do more closely, and try to shift behaviors toward customer-centricity and making lower-risk decisions. If this is a C-level Executive or Managing Director, the documentation might have to be presented to the board to determine what action they wish to take.

Governance

Governance over a customer-centric transformation could start with the following framework, which you are welcome to customize:

- **Executive support and an enforcement mechanism are necessary components.** Have we identified the execs or leaders behind this transformation? How will we compel compliance with this model when people might want to "break the rules?"

- **Root causes and problem statement.** What problem are we solving? What do we know about that problem? What's causing the problem? What solutions have we considered? Have we analyzed pros and cons of various solutions?

- **Success criteria are tied to quality and outcomes.** Metrics will vary based on your industry, but you should have separate business success and customer success KPIs. Create metrics and standards for success or failure as the project progresses.

- **Accountability for small or large failures.** If there are no consequences for the people who drove this initiative – or for people blocking the initiative – then there is no incentive to do better. There would be no reason to reduce, change, or stop a failing program, or adjust the behaviors of the people making it fail.

  o We said we would hold people responsible or accountable, but what does that look like? Will we block that decision-maker from leading an experiment in the future? Do we reduce their available budget? How about a performance improvement plan and coaching? Could they be demoted? I have seen companies demote managers and leaders; don't exclude it as a possibility.

  o What could happen to someone who blocks the progress of this project? How will they be held accountable?

  o As an example at the project level, when a design doesn't do well in usability testing or a service does poorly in a pilot test, it fails the success criteria and shouldn't be considered customer-ready. If someone decides it's "good enough" despite this failure, this is an early point where we can hold someone accountable.

- **Training.** What do staff and leaders need to learn to be ready for this transformation? What do they need to learn to execute on new processes, team structure, and other changes?

- **Priorities.** This transformation will require many changes. What will we do first? What changes will be blocked by other changes that need to happen first? Create Change Dependency Maps.

  o Remember that business priorities and customer priorities might not be the same thing. That cool feature the business wants to build may be deemed more important than fixing broken PSE. How was that decided?

And who will be held accountable for continued customer frustration and Support utilization and cost thanks to broken PSE?

- **Process.** We like to say we are Agile, Lean, efficient, and fast. Are we? Are these going well? Are we fast, but customers know we suck? Let's not Congr-Agile-Ate ourselves just yet.

  o Do our processes exclude the customer? Are we claiming to care about customers and empathize with them while avoiding deeper and more qualitative or behavioral research? Are we willing to go beyond surveys and NPS to truly understand what will make our target audiences satisfied and loyal?

- **Work and Quality.** Do we want our fastest or best work? We often can't have top speed and high quality simultaneously. How will we balance working efficiently and intelligently with wanting to have an aggressive release schedule?

  o Teams claim to care about the quality of work. Engineers have QA checking code quality and function. CX has reviews and critiques that help uphold quality standards as well as ways to test concepts with target audiences. We must ensure that we plan project time for quality checks and high standards.

- **Costs of Time and Salaries.** Calculate the time and salary that we are spending on the transformation. This might include new tools and new roles or positions.

- **Costs of Poor Quality.** Did we release something to the public or deliver it to a client, but it's partially or wholly failing? What did that cost us in reputation, stock price, customer trust, Customer Support utilization, negative word of mouth, or customers downgrading or leaving?

  o Did we make a big enough mistake where we had to roll back a software release, undo a price increase, or negate something we delivered to the public? What are the costs of that mistake and the efforts to fix or undo it?

- **Costs of Attrition and Worker Dissatisfaction.** We hope that customer-centric initiatives won't make staff unhappy or quit, but it's possible. There might be a storm before the calm as we take steps to improve our culture or deal with toxic leadership. Toxic leadership might quit or be fired, which sounds like good news, but it will take time and money to replace them. Calculate all costs related to losing or replacing staff.

Chapter 19: Designing CX Teams

Every role at our company should have a customer-centric mindset. Anybody can have ideas, but not all ideas should end up as experiments or PSE. Additionally, not every job shapes customer-centric strategies or initiatives. Not every job is responsible for executing the research, insights, and data that drive strategies and initiatives. Not every job is responsible for information architecture, interaction design, service design, prototyping, and testing our concepts. These and other specialized roles will form your CX department; they strategize, plan, and execute User-Centered Design.

Note that all CX roles should be problem finders and solvers, not order takers. CX staff are internal consultants going beyond CX tasks to also give advice, suggestions, direction, and reasoning. CX practitioners and leaders will likely challenge the status quo, ask critical thinking questions, and raise red flags when they see a troubling process, decision, or outcome. We should welcome this, but many companies would rather suppress this spirit and require CX staff to do what they are told, be quiet, and give stakeholders what they want. The CX department needs autonomy, an equal voice, and support, especially when they have an alternative perspective or want to discuss risks.

To build a strong CX department running strong CX programs and initiatives, we must hire well-qualified CX professionals and empower them to create change. **It's a simple formula: hire specialists, allow them to research processes and experiences, and give them the authority to make improvements, internally for our business as well as externally for customers.**

McKinsey published a report in April 2022 called, "Redesigning the Design Department." [https://cxcc.to/a143] Key points include:

- **Businesses allowing Designers to regularly improve internal business processes are more likely to have better commercial and financial performance.** This is a reminder that when understood and correctly utilized, CX staff are internal consultants. They improve experiences and journeys for potential and current customers as well as for internal teams.

- A quote from an executive: **"We used to tell the Designers what to do, now they're showing us what is possible – and it's so much better."** This highlights CX's roles as problem finders and solvers, not order takers.

- **Welcome entry-level Designers into environments that are organized to support and coach them.** This sounds obvious, but it's a huge problem that will be discussed later in this chapter.

- **Challenges coming from Designers are unlikely to be taken seriously until we give Design an equal position to other roles.** Empower CX practitioners to do their best work and have an equal voice.

One downside to McKinsey's report is that it had a quote recommending democratization, saying that we don't want "diva" Designers. Democratization was thoroughly questioned, if not debunked, in this book's "Common Research Mistakes" chapter. "Divas" is a negatively framed term for a highly qualified specialist, *someone we would want to hire.* Many job descriptions ask for "rockstars" and "ninjas." It's manipulative to try to make readers associate Designers with divas so that people will think, "Yes, we do not want any of those diva Designers." If your company doesn't want "divas" in any role, make sure your candidate interviews check for low ego.

McKinsey's findings sound exciting, but how do we follow through and design the right CX organization?

CX in the Org

Should CX be under Product because CX and UX are tied to our PSE? How about under Engineering because there's a tight relationship between coding and our PSE designs? How about under Brand since the Customer Experience is the Brand Experience? Maybe under Marketing, Customer Support, or Sales? Perhaps we want Service Designers working under Corporate Strategists, Operations, or Digital Transformation?

CX potentially fitting everywhere in the organization signals that it should be autonomous. Placing it organizationally under any of these domains often leads to heavy influence from that domain's priorities. For example, Engineering might value speed more than taking the time to ensure high solution quality. Marketing might value aesthetics more than usability. Product Management might be under pressure to make stakeholders happy, even if those initiatives are customer-peripheric. CX is closely partnered with many departments, showing how it doesn't belong to or under one.

Google what a CXO (Chief Experience Officer) does, and it's all over the place. From "being in charge of call centers" to "you will speak to customers and make a customer journey map," it's clear that this role has not yet been standardized. As a C-level executive, this person is not doing Individual Contributor work. They are not running research, designing screens, creating service blueprints, or talking to customers. They are many levels above that.

The CXO is the key voice and shepherd of positive Customer Experiences and customer-centricity in the organization. The organization under the CXO is focused on the end-to-end Customer Experience, including all target, potential, and current customers' journeys, tasks, and perspectives. These teams deliver intelligence, maps, artifacts, documents, strategies, suggestions, concepts, and solutions that the other domains consume and utilize in their work.

Given the breadth of work within CX and its far-reaching impact, I suggest the following:

- **Where there is no CXO, CX teams should have high-level leaders and executives, and then report to a CPO, Chief Product Officer.** This is an acceptable plan B but can skew the priorities and work of the CX department toward KPIs and business goals.

- o Given McKinsey's indication that Design staff can be great internal change agents, having a CX department without a CXO answer up to an executive responsible for Strategy, Operations, or Transformations might be interesting.

  o I strongly recommend against placing CX organizationally beneath Engineering or Marketing as it can narrow CX's scope and autonomy.

- **Some companies are trying a centralized department that covers all of their research, business intelligence, and customer intelligence.** This would put Data, Analytics, and those tracking competitors and the Voice of the Customer under the CX umbrella.

  o In addition to service design and digital design, our CX department would include research, data, and modeling of all qualitative and quantitative types.

- **Eventually, we will want to grow the CX department to have its own branch in the organization with a CXO at the top.**

Individual Contributors (ICs)

Individual Contributors are staff at levels such as Apprentice or Intern, Junior, Mid-Level ("Medior" in parts of Europe), Senior, and Lead. Some companies have "Principal" as a level above Lead. Your company might use a different hierarchy. ICs do the day-to-day work and usually have no direct reports, though, in some countries, the Lead practitioner is also a line manager.

Some companies are tempted to hire individuals who have expert-level skills across all CX tasks. For example, someone who is great at CX research, interaction design, and visual design. These so-called "unicorns" or "purple squirrels" can be hard to find. The jobs that combine dozens of skills and tasks are a one-way ticket to Burnout City. Priorities are moving targets that change frequently, quality gets sacrificed, and there is ultimately no way for one person to do multiple simultaneous streams of work well. How will anybody get proper research done while under pressure to "get us those screens?" Where will corners be cut, and what are those risks?

Those seeking to hybridize CX jobs are often unaware that the existing "specialized" jobs are already hybridized. For example, there were separate Information Architect, Interaction Designer, and Visual Designer jobs ten years ago. We now often expect all of these skills and proficiencies in one "Designer." Further combining jobs leads us into a territory of asking for an unreasonable combination of diverse and unrelated skills. Someone great at research is not necessarily great at interaction design. Someone great at information architecture is not necessarily a good visual designer. Additionally, "unicorns," especially those with fewer than four years of experience, are unlikely to be experts yet in one CX sub-specialty, let alone many or all of them.

Since our customer-centric transformation requires us to focus on high-quality and high-value work, we will build our CX department from specialists. Note that all roles are expected to be strategic, and all roles are expected to consider diversity, equity, inclusion, and accessibility at every step. The department includes:

- **CX Researchers.** At larger companies, this is sometimes divided into two subspecialties: Qualitative Researchers and Quantitative Researchers.

   - Qualitative research focuses on generative research (researching our target audiences' behaviors and tasks) and evaluative research (testing concepts, designs, and prototypes).

   - Quantitative research focuses on survey data, information from analytics tools, metrics we are tracking, and data from experiments.

   - **Common tasks**: Planning, recruiting, executing, analyzing, synthesizing, and reporting on research findings and insights. Providing evidence-based, actionable suggestions, advice, and direction. Creating and updating maps and artifacts including task analysis, optimized task flow, customer journey maps, personas or user definitions, and problem statements. Collecting and analyzing the Voice of the Customer data. Tasks related to card sorting, tree testing, and usability studies.

   - **Note**: I'm seeing some agencies and consultancies calling this role a "CX Strategist" or "UX Strategist." As all CX roles are strategic and present informed points of view and direction, it's hard to say which role should be called a "Strategist."

- **CX Architects.** This role uses research data to create and refine digital solutions matching customers' behaviors, needs, and tasks. If you don't have separate Service Designers, this role might also work on non-digital solutions.

   - **Common tasks**: Sitemaps, hierarchies, taxonomies, flows (if we don't have an optimized task flow), wireframes, and interactive prototypes. Tasks related to information architecture and interaction design. Visual design skills should not be required or demanded as that specialty has a separate role.

   - **Note**: Some companies divide this role into two subspecialties: information architecture and interaction design. For example, I once met a full-time Information Architect at a retail chain. They focused on the taxonomy (categorization and classification) of the company's products so customers could easily find items in expected categories and subcategories. Some companies still have full-time specialized Information Architects or Taxonomists.

   - **Note**: This is the role a "UX Designer" was before companies mistakenly thought that UX Designers primarily work on visuals, brand, and colors. Depending upon the skills and tasks your company currently gives people called UX Designer, Product Designer, Experience Designer, or UX/UI Designer, your current "Designer" staff might match the CX Architect or the CX Visual Designer role.

- **CX Service Designers.** This role also uses research data to create and refine solutions matching customers' behaviors, needs, and tasks. Service Designers are also often Researchers. Sometimes others have done the research, and the Service Designer is more focused on strategic problem solving.

  - **Common tasks**: CX Research tasks plus CX Architect tasks plus conceptualizing new and improved business and customer workflows. Service blueprints map the current state and desired future state of internal and external experiences. Service design also includes business design and business process improvements.

- **CX Visual Designers.** These specialists might be what we currently call our UI Designers, Brand Designers, and at some companies, Product Designers.

  - **Common tasks**: Working with color, typography, brand elements, mood, symbols and icons, spacing, illustrations, photographs, and anything improving the aesthetics of an interface. Visual Designers are typically responsible for UI kits and design systems.

  - **Note**: If your company has a design system or component library, you still need CX Architects. Design systems are not "anybody can plug and play." Architects design screens and interfaces deliberately based on customer intelligence, human behavior, and psychology knowledge. Having a design system does not replace these skills.

- **CX Content Designers.**

  - **Common tasks**: Strategizing and designing content, media, and text. They are often our writers. Content Designers have their own research and testing they might do themselves or in partnership with Researchers.

  - **Note:** This role has sometimes been called a Content Strategist or UX Writer.

- **CX Data Analysts.** The CX Data Analyst is an up-and-coming role.

  - **Common tasks:** Modeling customer behaviors, loss and demand models, data queries, metrics modeling, and creating dashboards.

  - **Note:** Some companies combine the Data Analyst job with the Quantitative Researcher job.

- **Internal CX Consultants.** These change agents are higher-level practitioners who will help project teams be more customer-centric. They are internal customer-centricity consultants and coaches helping individuals and teams shift from old ways of working to focusing on customer value creation and improved outcomes. We have Agile Coaches and Product Management Coaches; we can have Customer-Centricity Coaches, which I'm calling the Internal CX Consultant.

  o **Common tasks**: Identifying teams needing help, analyzing and documenting their current state and ways of working, assessing collaboration, developing a change plan and initiatives, determining team or project KPIs or OKRs that help demonstrate improved customer-centricity, and coaching the team through the plan and changes. Identifying skills gaps and training opportunities, and providing that training, if qualified. Ensuring standardized ways of working across teams and PSE areas.

  o **Note**: This can also be one or more outside consultants. If you don't create this role, Service Designers are a good second choice if they can make the time to coach internal teams through change. If you have Internal CX Consultants, they can partner with Service Designers to follow through on internal changes Service Designers have recommended.

  o **Note**: The Internal CX Consultant is not teaching CX work to non-CX staff.

For example, Salesforce is one company with a team devoted to this work. The following is from a 2022 job description for "Human-Centered Change Lead," which appears to overlap our Service Designer and Consultant roles:

"The Salesforce Professional Services Human Centered Change team is a group of hard-working consultants who create and complete change strategies through a human-centered approach, enabling our customers to improve value from our Salesforce platform. We take a design-led and appreciative approach to creating achievable strategies to keep users at the heart of everything we do, turning human insights into business impact at Salesforce scale. We work across all industry verticals to help customers fuel the full power of Salesforce through a human-centric approach to organizational change.

As part of Professional Services, our consultants have a strategic mindset, including understanding our customers' business objectives and the challenges they face in achieving the change required to truly transform. We partner with Salesforce colleagues across various engagements to enable a cross-functional team to ensure valuable customer outcomes."

Here are some of the bullet points describing the Lead-level job:

---

* *"Build and execute holistic change strategies for complex transformation initiatives and/or have deep expertise in Enablement Strategies and Management, Education approaches, and Project Delivery.*
* *Integrate human-centered Service Design and the science of behavior change methods and enablement planning.*
* *Facilitate cross-functional partnerships to design and launch new ways of working.*
* *Manage the Change team on customer engagements.*
* *Assist with Pre-Sales as needed.*
* *Drive cross-functional stakeholder alignment, engagement, and buy-in.*
* *Scale new practices focused on human-centered change.*
* *Conduct impact and barrier analyses, maturity level assessments via stakeholder interviews, and review existing processes to identify difficulties and gaps.*
* *Support detailed organizational change activities, including needs analysis, assessment of change readiness, communications, and guiding training teams to ensure an integrated approach.*
* *Engage closely with program management teams and key initiatives to ensure change leadership behavior modeling, change vision and narrative, change enablement activities, and change strategies are coordinated to delivery and execution."*

CX Leadership

CX leaders must have executive sponsors and allies. Too many companies bring in CX or UX leadership, but nobody in the company believes in investing the time and budget required to do world-class work. Without executive sponsors and allies, CX leadership – and therefore the whole department – might be ineffective. Remember that beliefs like "research and design aren't valuable or important" are self-fulfilling prophecies. If CX doesn't have enough budget, headcount, time, and resources, they might be stuck doing the least they can rush out. This work might not be valuable, which will accidentally feed the beliefs that caused it.

As you build or rebuild your CX department, make sure it has at least one leader who is not an Individual Contributor. Consider matching layers of leadership to other departments and domains. For example, if you have Vice Presidents of Product and Engineering, make sure you hire at least one VP of CX.

Like Developers expect to be managed by someone with an impressive background as an Engineering Individual Contributor, your CX Individual Contributors expect to be managed by someone who comes from the work. A certificate in CX or UX is not enough, especially since some of those are short courses with multiple-choice exams. Look for years of experience in candidates' CX or UX specialties, preferably 7+ years for Manager, Director, and higher levels.

Organizing CX or UX staff under management from other disciplines is common but is always a mismatch. ICs whose manager lacks CX experience and expertise can lead to a variety of process, morale, and culture problems, including:

- Managers who don't understand the work their staff is doing because they have never done that work.

- If the ICs have a question about the best approach for something they're working on, their manager won't be able to help them.

- The manager might superimpose their domain's priorities or processes on the IC.

- Managers who don't understand CX work might not budget for CX tools on the assumption that they are unimportant. Managers should support licensing tools that help CX staff be more efficient and collaborative.

We very rarely see QA Engineers directly reporting to Product Directors or Portfolio Managers. Where that might exist, are the QA Engineers happy with their managers? Therefore, as you hire Managers, Directors, Heads, and higher, it's essential to select candidates with years of CX or UX experience at the Individual Contributor level.

Additionally, Individual Contributors want to answer to managers who come from their particular *specialty*. Researchers should answer to someone with an extensive background in research. Architects should report to someone with an extensive background in information architecture, interaction design, or service design. There are often problems with an Architect answering to a Research Manager who has little or no experience with architecture tasks.

Moving up the ladder, there should be Directors and Heads who are specific to CX subspecialties. You might have a Director of Service Design and a Head of CX Research. Eventually, specialized leadership will answer up to a higher-level role bringing everything together; this might be your VP of CX or a Chief of CX. Some companies have a Chief of Design, but since "design" is often mistaken for aesthetics and branding, it's best to use "CX" where you mean CX.

> Researchers I need your help urgently
> The new Director is going to hire a Designer manager and the first
> candidate is a graphic designer that claims to be UX UI with a very
> creative non accessible resume.
> I need to send challenging questions for the director to ask him
> Because I'm 🐺 I can't think. I CANNOT HAVE AnOTHER GRAPHIC
> DESIGNER FAKE UX UI BOSS AGAIN. PLEASE Help

Figure 41: Screenshot from my online community. A Researcher was in a panic because their company might hire a graphic designer as their skip manager. The Researcher was concerned about this candidate's lack of research experience, and asked the community to brainstorm interview questions that would determine if this person were well-qualified or not. The message ends with all capital letters, "I cannot have another graphic designer fake UX UI boss again. Please help." The Researcher quit this job weeks later, despite their Manager trying to convince them to stay.

Management and Higher Shouldn't Be Individual Contributors

Think about your VP of Marketing, your Director of Engineering, or your Head of Product Management. Are they doing day-to-day Individual Contributor tasks? Do you expect them to balance "doing the work" with being a manager, leader, strategist, planner, administrator, and operational change agent?

In CX, we unfortunately see high-level IC jobs given leadership titles as a carrot: *work here, and you will get the fancy title of Senior Manager, Head of, Director, or VP.* But two key hints show candidates that this is more of an Individual Contributor job than a strategic manager or leadership job:

- **Job descriptions say you will be "hands-on" or "roll up your sleeves."** Sometimes they say you don't mind "getting your hands dirty" and doing the day-to-day work.

- **The salary is nearly always at the Senior or Lead IC level, not a Manager, Director, Head, or VP level.**

We want CX leaders respected and not seen as worker bees with over-inflated titles. Make sure that your layers of leadership and your Individual Contributors aren't an overlapping set. Combining an IC job and a management job is an express train to Over-Unicorned Burnout City. Create fair and humane jobs that don't combine multiple full-time jobs into one stressful role. These jobs often set people up to fail, and compromise mental health.

Chapter 19: Designing CX Teams

Nextech

Essential Functions

- Lead development and execution of the Product Design vision for Nextech

- Coach and mentor a team of creative designers

- Actively participate in leadership meetings by providing input towards product strategy and visibility into UX processes

- Lead the team in documenting and refining best practices in Product Design, UX, and our style guide

- Continue to help drive design thinking throughout the organization

- Support the UX team in continuously developing best practices

- Work with clients via onsite and remote interactions to understand in-depth workflows and gain insight into how our applications can thrive

- Create high-quality visual design and interactions of product ideas and workflows

- Create wireframes, storyboards, user flows, journey mapping, process flows, interaction prototypes, and site maps to communicate interaction and design ideas

- Conduct user research, interviews, and tests through a user-centered design process

- Have the ability to understand development libraries and systems to align designs with the development workflow

- Assist in the validation of the design with development teams to ensure the design was followed to completion

- Carry out additional responsibilities as assigned based on business need

Figure 42: A "Director of UX/UI" sounds like a high-level management job. But this job description screenshot shows that responsibilities include creating "high-quality visual design and interactions of product ideas," "creating wireframes, storyboards, user flows, journey mapping, process flows, interaction prototypes, and site maps," and, "conducting user research." Combining the Researcher, Architect, and Visual Designer jobs is ugly. But how will you have time to do three full-time jobs, "coach and mentor a team of creative designers," "participate in leadership meetings," continuously develop best practices, and work with clients on-site? This job seems impossible and sets someone up for failure.

Project Team Composition

Consider the speed and quality of our Engineering work if each project were given to only one Engineer. They would have to be geniuses with front-end, back-end, QA testing the code, and working with API calls, microservices, and DevOps. As much as you might hear that Engineering should be T-shaped or decentralized, we still recognize Engineering specialties and hire into them. We don't open a broad "Engineer" job and tell candidates that what they're working on each day is unknown, so we'll need them to be good at everything.

Consider staffing CX project teams the way you staff Engineering teams. A larger team of well-qualified people gets more done in less time than a single person. You might like the idea of hybrids or generalists who can research and design, but it's slow and risky to have everything relying on one person and their health and availability. We must create a more efficient assembly line rather than waiting for one person to do the whole assembly line themselves.

My updated Delta CX model of **five core CX staff per project** is likely more of a goal than a currently attainable reality. But as we hire to reduce bottlenecks and keep growing the department, it can be part of our CX org's future vision. My suggestions are as follows:

- **CX Architects work in pairs.** Pair someone more junior with someone more senior. If this project is mission critical, pair two higher-level, highly experienced practitioners.

  o They share one seat with the Agile team. Now you have that Design skill on the team, as nearly every flavor of Agile suggests, and you have competent and efficient specialists.

  o If two CX Architects are on the project team, one can do the work if the other is sick or on vacation. If one quits or is fired, the other has 100% knowledge of the project, and can bring someone else up to speed.

- **CX Researchers work in teams of three (or more).** Hire someone with five or more years of specialized research experience, and team them up with two more junior Researchers. This could be two more specialized qualitative Researchers and one specialized quantitative Researcher. CX leadership can adjust each project's team based on the required levels of expertise in particular specialties.

  o Each research team is partnered with a CX Architect pair. This prevents the common bottleneck of project teams or CX Architects not having Researchers available when they are needed. In this model, the Researchers are fully allocated. Dedicated Researchers help us get away from "internal agency" models, where we are waiting for someone from a centralized pool of Researchers to be available to join our project.

- The **"Core Team"** are your Researchers and Architects since they are fully, 100% allocated to their project or team. What I call the **"Satellite Team"** includes Visual Designers, Content Designers, and any other specialists that projects need but not on a full-time basis.

  o As we shift toward utilizing design systems and component libraries more, we still need Visual Designers, but they often do not need to be 100% allocated for the full duration of the project.

- **Service Designers'** work is likely to span across multiple areas of our PSE and multiple departments of our company. They will work with Product Managers, Product Owners, Agile and Scrum teams, and others outside our digital departments.

  o Depending on the project, Service Designers might not be specifically allocated to *one* PSE or Agile team. A Service Designer might be fully allocated to their current project, which might span multiple teams.

- **Internal CX Consultants** will be allocated to no more than two teams at a time to help them with change and transformation. Consultants' work and allocation are not connected to any particular project or PSE.

Open Entry-Level Jobs

There is a worldwide shortage of CX and UX talent at Senior and higher levels (5+ years of experience). Around 2017, employers decided they didn't want to train or support newbies, so they changed Junior jobs to require a year or more of experience. Questions like, "Who will be our Seniors in 5 years?" and "How will people get their first job if their first job doesn't want to be their first job?" went ignored as we mostly closed the door to people looking to start or transition into a CX or UX career.

In 2022, many "Junior" jobs require two or more years of experience, previously the requirement for Mid-Level jobs. Instead of fixing our problem, we are making it worse. It's also strange that we didn't want to train CX or UX newbies, but we have time and money to train Product Managers or the Scrum team when they want to try their hands at CX and UX tasks.

To set ourselves up for the future we want, we will have to open entry-level CX and UX jobs knowing that these people need training, oversight, and support. They will be grateful for the chance.

If your natural reaction to training entry-level workers is, "They will take our training and then leave," you appear to know that your jobs and environment inspire workers to depart. Apprentices, Interns, and Juniors will be loyal and stay only if you create a great job in a positive environment. If you believe that entry-level workers will quit as soon as they feel decently trained, start investigating what it's like to work there so that you can make your culture and processes selling points, not weaknesses.

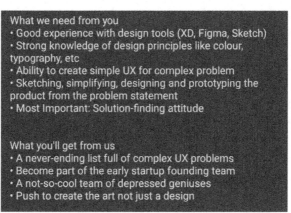

Figure 43: Speaking of culture as a weakness, this is a screenshot of a startup's job description. One of the "what you'll get from us" bullet points is, "A not-so-cool team of depressed geniuses." Whether this was intended to be funny, honest, or both, it sounds like an opportunity to assess and improve the culture. Even startups should do something about "not-so-cool" teams.

Utilize Them Correctly or Lose Them

It's quite common for CX and UX staff to be assigned to a project or team, but then be overruled, minimized, or treated as order takers. If a team doesn't want research as guiding evidence, or doesn't allow a Designer to drive and make design decisions, why allocate that staff to a project that doesn't want them? You probably are short on CX staff. Assign them to project teams that understand what they do and will utilize them correctly.

Some might say that *a dysfunctional team like that is the team that needs CX the most, and we should not remove practitioners.* They suggest that CX staff continue to explain their jobs and the value of their work, which is where you hear that CX or UX must be "evangelized." This sounds like an awful job and environment. Asking CX and UX to explain and evangelize their work – even though everybody working there before them evidently failed at this – is unreasonable. Let's get to the root cause of why so many people don't understand what CX or UX is: profession, processes, and people. And let's fix the root causes.

If these teams' culture cannot be improved, at least let CX professionals walk away from these negative and sometimes abusive experiences. They will be happier on a team that welcomes what they bring to the project. Projects that value CX will benefit greatly by having additional staff and skills.

Allocated Where Needed and Respected

I heard about a company with a Product Director who was against research. They often declared that we can't learn anything from it, and that it would be better to release the product and then learn what people want changed. The UX Research team had planned a sizeable generative research study to inform the project's designs. The Product Director didn't want that either because they were sure their ideas were the way to go.

There were Product Managers nearly begging for a Researcher, their projects being slowed or derailed without one. Why execute a large research project for someone who predetermined that they won't use research evidence and data? If the insights are ignored, the research won't be a strong internal case study showing the value of generative research, which this company needed.

The Research Manager wanted the large generative project to continue. This was a lot of time and money spent hoping that someone with a history of disregarding research data will utilize research data *this time*. They could have reassigned that Researcher to people hungry for fresh evidence.

Hiring Budget

When many departments at our company are fighting for budget, resources, and headcount, where do we get the budget to create or grow a CX department? If your company is new to CX or UX and you are considering your first hire, start with a team of two people. Budget for a Lead-level (often 7+ years of experience) Researcher and a separate Lead Architect. Start by dedicating them to one or two projects. Do not try to put them on every project at the company, especially since lovers of Agile expect these resources to be dedicated to a project or Development team. The more projects they are on, the less time they will have to do projects well, the more priorities will be a moving target, and the more someone will believe that CX is "slow" and "not Agile."

If your company already has a CX or UX team and is considering growing or redesigning it, identify the bottlenecks. Companies rarely open the budget to hire 10, 20, or 60 people at once. Therefore, you should undertake an organizational design project in which you can identify the project teams who need additional CX headcount the most. These teams are easy to identify; they already recognize the need for CX specialists, or they have leaned on Aspirologies because they don't have enough CX practitioners to get the work done. They use workshops, design by committee, or democratization because CX is a bottleneck.

We should also be able to allocate some budget for hiring based on the money saved on the Cost of Poor Quality. CX work will eventually sell itself. As you invest in CX processes and staff, and then tie those to business and customer outcomes and successes, making a case for the budget and expanding the team will be easier.

Some of the hiring budget can come from the following:

- **Reduce workshops.** This saves staff time and budget, but possibly also the cost of external facilitators and agencies.

- **Redirecting the budget currently used to fund non-CX roles trying CX tasks.**
  - This includes the internal and external costs of any mistakes or low-quality CX work the non-CX roles are producing.

- **Being a smarter shopper about outside corporate trainers and consultants.** Some corporate trainers' day rates are what Junior staff make in half a year. Money saved on selecting better trainers and consultants can be immediately reinvested into staffing.
  - I am *for* training and professional development, but companies should be comparing multiple bids and working more closely with trainers to ensure that they deliver the right messages.

Hiring the Right People

If you ask for ten CX or UX skills, but only check for pretty screens, you are not correctly assessing candidates. Additionally, not everybody claiming any particular skill is genuinely good at that skill.

How to hire the right people is a book on its own, so in April 2021, I released a free 8-hour video course, "Attracting and Retaining CX and UX Talent." [https://deltacx.link/hr-training] It's written for HR, recruiters, talent sourcers, and hiring managers. You can take the modules in any order you like, and you are not added to a mailing list.

Start With One World-Class Research Project

We don't have to change our entire organization overnight. Use your culture of experimentation: *try something new, get feedback, measure, learn, evolve, iterate, try an improved version, and cycle through again.* Here's how you might start:

- **Assign three well-qualified CX Researchers to a generative observational research project, something that will answer questions and replace guesses with knowledge.**

- **Give the Research team 8 weeks.** That sounds scary and "not Agile," but try it anyway. It's four two-week sprints, and a good compromise between the more thorough Research and Development companies used to do – and the companies we respect still do – and the rushed or skipped research we do now.

   o CX should not be held to Agile standards for how long "research" or a "research spike" might take since CX processes and work are nothing like an Engineering research spike.

   o We want to see what world-class work looks like. Our company might not have done this before, or not in a very long time. Let's give our coworkers the time, resources, budget, and trust they need.

- **Look and listen for surprises, anything that might inspire teammates to reconsider what they thought they knew or throw away their assumptions.**

   o We might learn that customers' workflows and tasks look little like we imagined. Perhaps there are decision-making and collaborators we didn't consider.

   o We might show that users didn't figure out the thing we assumed they would figure out. We might show that users got through the task, but painfully or with mistakes.

   o We will see where users met The Four Horsemen of Bad CX: frustration, confusion, disappointment, and distraction. Where did users bump into dead ends, popups and interruptions, and meaningless error messages? Did we see Task Dimensions: manually intensive, high cognitive load, error-prone, or knowledge dependent?

- **With fresh and detailed information unlike what we typically have, watch how this changes the rest of the project.** Follow the process suggested in the previous chapter and the next chapter.

   o Define problems, create relevant maps, plan the work, and solve the problems. You'll then monitor that the problem is truly solved, and watch your KPIs and OKRs.

o   Also monitor and measure how our ways of working changed when we set teams up with knowledge and evidence.

Trying real generative qualitative research done thoroughly by experts takes time and money. But it offers short- and long-term benefits and evidence that our company won't have any other way. It will create more interest in and an appetite for research investment, especially early generative research that will inform strategies, initiatives, and PSE.

We're Laying People Off. What About CX?

Whether it's "we grew too fast" or economic concerns, sometimes a company can't avoid laying people off. Every department has reasons why they should be cut as little as possible. Consider risks, costs, and concerns, including:

- **When utilized correctly, CX is critical to your customer and PSE strategies.** CX is generating your most accurate and current customer intelligence. The more you cut them, especially their Researchers, the more likely you will be more out of touch with your customers and their needs.

- **Workload and deadlines must be adjusted.** If your CX team of 20 became a team of 10 due to layoffs, we should not expect 50% of the people to maintain the current workload. We will need to adjust timelines, roadmaps, and expectations so that we are not overworking and burning out the remaining staff.

- **Once the budget allows, try to bring back the staff you laid off.** 2022 saw controversial layoffs where weeks or months later, the company opened the jobs that had recently been cut rather than offering former workers their old jobs. This immediately undoes any of the reasons given publicly for the layoffs, and makes it look like your company just wanted to remove current workers to try to pay new ones less.

- **Try to continue CX efforts.** You might not yet have enough budget to rebuild a team you just laid off. If you cannot get CX budget or headcount, request a budget for temporary staff such as freelancers, contractors, or outside agencies or consultancies.

- **CX isn't KTLO (Keep The Lights On).** Strategizing and Designing Customer Experiences and our PSE can't be a minimum viable effort where we are just keeping the lights on. All you have are your PSE and your customers. You can't afford to weaken your offering or alienate target audiences.

- **It's seed-planting time.** We must continuously strategize what we are doing now and in the future, even during downsizing. We must understand our target customers and what is changing for them *in these uncertain times*. If we are not keeping our CX efforts strong, we will miss opportunities. Our rebound might take longer.

Chapter 20: Task-Oriented UCD and Tri-Track Agile

Very few Agile Coaches and Scrum Masters are experts in CX, and nearly zero Agile models correctly address customer-centricity. Therefore, we will need to examine an approach that can overlay digital and non-digital delivery methods. If you are more of a service business, you can replace "Agile" with the methods and frameworks you use.

> *"You've got to start with the customer experience and work backwards to the technology. You can't start with the technology and try to figure out where you're going to try to sell it."*
> *– Steve Jobs*

We love to quote Steve Jobs, and then we don't *do* anything he advises. *What would it look like to start with the customer and their experiences, and work backwards to the technology?*

Agile Supports Customer Satisfaction and Centricity

Look in Agile methods for anything that supports focusing on Customer Experiences, User Experiences, customer-centricity, value, quality, and user satisfaction. For example, the infographic showing the SAFe Agile process has "Customer Centricity" written in the middle with a "Double Diamond" image, representing a derivative of the User-Centered Design process. Despite SAFE's clumsy and incomplete approach to CX and UX, interpret this as SAFe's blessing for us to be customer-centric and use thorough UCD processes.

Figure 44: Screenshot from part of SAFe's Lean Enterprise framework infographic showing "Customer Centricity," a bowtie-wearing person icon inside a circle, and a Double Diamond. [https://scaledagileframework.com/]

Ultimately, no matter your delivery methods, cross-functional teams are assembly lines. QA Engineers can't perform unit or integration testing until Developers have written enough code to be tested. There's only so much Developers can do when we haven't finalized our solution. CX Architects should be working from what Researchers discovered. There are many stations in our assembly line, and we want both accuracy and efficiency.

Developers will need to strategically decide what can they start when CX designs are not yet finalized. Depending upon the project, they might be able to start work on database architecture, microservices, API calls, and functions our PSE will have, no matter the mechanism, workflow, or execution of the solution. While designs are not yet finalized, Developers might work on a previous project, bug fixes, or refactoring.

Then is customer-centricity anti-Agile? Being more customer-centric is *agile* in that it:

- Prioritizes knowledge over guessing.

- Aims for efficiency.

- Reduces mistakes and rework.

- Truly puts outcomes over outputs.

- Measures customers' experiences and satisfaction.

- Identifies and mitigates risks earlier.

- Feeds knowledge into the system, influencing and informing cross-functional teams.

- Breaks down silos, improves communication and collaboration, and encourages critical thinking.

- Sets projects up for success through estimation, planning, and breaking work into smaller pieces where possible.

Feature-Oriented Versus Task-Oriented

Many teams start with requirements, user stories, or feature ideas. These ideas are often a guess, assumption, or hope based on a desired business outcome. Sometimes these are ideas on how to nudge user behaviors so we can meet business goals.

Ideas around functionality become features we plan and roadmap. We feed features into the Product world and ask UX Designers to create wireframes and prototypes for those ideas. Our solution is based on pre-decided features. This approach is called being **"feature-oriented;"** you decide the features first, and everything is planned around them. If these features aren't a strong match to customers' needs, tasks, or realities, we may create a lot of delay, waste, and risk thinking that we are fast. Hoping to find out later if our guesses were good is reactive and risky. It might be weeks or months until we get survey results or analytics.

Feature-oriented processes are easy to spot because they usually start with *build*, such as "build, test, learn." They might be variations of "idea, quick design, build, test, learn, iterate, evolve." Feature-oriented processes assume that it's not worth the time to try to learn more before just trying your first idea. We assume we will guess well what people need, and we don't mind showing our cards to the public as we go. We will find out later if our idea had any customer value, and we might be surprised.

As an example, situations in which we would never allow a *build, test, learn* process – or *speed over quality* – include:

- **Medical conditions**. We prefer when doctors investigate and learn before medicating or operating. We want to be cured quickly, but we will devote more time to diagnosis, especially if that helps us get the cure right the first time.

- **Vehicles.** We are grateful that manufacturers design, prototype, and test many iterations rather than selling vehicles and then learning where they are unpleasant or unsafe.

- **Buildings and bridges**. We don't start construction on buildings or bridges based on an idea someone has. We have Architects, Structural Engineers, and other specialists learning and designing before anything is built.

Task-oriented design has been around for decades, and is the opposite of being a feature factory. Task-oriented design embodies customer-centricity: what we research and learn about real users' tasks are the starting and focal points. This requires solution-agnostic, generative qualitative research; we are not checking if people like a concept. We are learning who they are, how they do things now, and what their unmet needs are. We have no solution in mind during research. We then write problem statements and prioritize user needs and PSE opportunities.

After prioritization, CX teams can work on concepts and task-oriented User-Centered Design based on our evidence and customer intelligence. Once CX has architected, designed, vetted, and validated a solution, we *now* know the features. **The features derive from the solution.** The solution can be broken into features, stories, JIRA tickets, backlog items, or however your Engineering teams want to do it.

Let's compare a feature-oriented process to a task-oriented approach, where both include some research. *Imagine that we learn from Support channels that customers are unhappy with our dashboard. We're not showing the information people need.*

- **Feature-oriented.** We want to learn the feature people are missing. Product Managers or Marketing run a survey asking if you need bar graph A, line graph B, or pie graph C. Bar graph A wins.

  o We ask UX to design bar graph A since that's the feature we're building. Usability testing might be skipped, but if we tested the design of the new graph, we might find that people understand the graph. Sounds like a success.

  o We believe this solves the original problem, but does it? We might know months from now when we check in with Support and see if their dashboard complaints have decreased.

- **Task-oriented.** We want to better understand the tasks and workflows that relate to dashboard usage. We learn from observational research that our target customers generate certain reports for executives after viewing our dashboard or similar dashboards in competitors' systems. Our users need to make data comparisons that these dashboards currently don't offer, so they export the data into another tool. Some of the work is done by assistants, who must collaborate with their managers. After analysis and internal collaborations, our customers can make informed suggestions to executives.

    o The real task here isn't *to look at a dashboard*. The real task is *to have the evidence empowering our users to advise executives*. The real problem is not only that certain information and functionality are missing; it's also that the data presented isn't actionable.

    o CX starts with research insights and evidence, and doesn't yet know which features will create the best solution.

    o CX can create a possible solution, and use rounds of testing and iteration to check that it's a match to customers' needs and solves the real problem.

    o The vetted and finalized solution can later be broken into features, stories, or whatever Engineering needs for their backlog.

Task-oriented design – starting with qualitative observational research – asks and answers the questions that feature-oriented processes often miss. We take the time to gather more evidence first rather than moving forward with something we hope is "good enough" for customers.

Tri-Track Agile

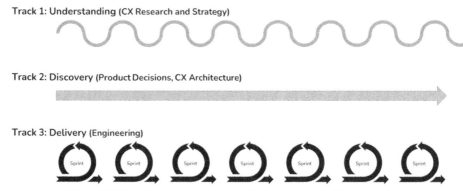

Track 1: Understanding (CX Research and Strategy)

Track 2: Discovery (Product Decisions, CX Architecture)

Track 3: Delivery (Engineering)

Figure 45: Simplified visualization of Tri-Track Agile. Explained below.

Dual-Track Agile separated CX work, called "Discovery," from Engineering and "Delivery." Tri-Track Agile is an evolution past Dual-Track Agile, and is often credited to Dave Malouf. Tri-Track Agile is clearer that within CX and UX, two main streams of work are going on simultaneously.

- **Track 1: Understanding.** The first track works on research, strategies, opportunities, and artifacts from research. This provides foundations in the form of insights, evidence, and strategies. We understand problems and needs, and although we don't yet have the solution mapped out, we can create evidence-based problem statements, and plan the work that will get us to the right solution.

  - o This track is continuously researching something. Generative research – our exploratory and discovery work – is continuously done. Track 1 includes evaluative research, such as rounds of concept and prototype testing. Research, customer intelligence, and strategy tasks are always being planned and executed.

- **Track 2: Discovery.** Informed by the first track, the second track works on roadmapping, architecting and designing PSE, and testing and improving it. Research-guided PSE roadmaps are a hallmark of task-oriented design.

  - o During this stream of work, we create one or more possible solutions and use User-Centered Design to iterate and refine. Evaluative research of prototypes connects Tracks 1 and 2.

  - o This second track includes content, writing, visual design, and other CX tasks that do not happen during the Understanding track.

- **Track 3: Delivery.** Track 2's finalized designs and solutions are fed into the third track. Everything related to Agile, Scrum, and Engineering lives in this Delivery stream. That way, Engineering can do their work with whatever approaches or styles they prefer, and it doesn't affect how Product and CX are working.

Three streams of simultaneous work highlight the importance of specialized CX Researchers being separate people from specialized CX Architects. Some companies try to combine these into one job, but it would be hard, if not impossible, for one person to do two different ongoing streams of work simultaneously and *well*. Customer-centricity requires us to care more about the quality of our work. We want world-class UCD done before world-class Engineering and delivery.

Discovery Stream: Concept and Execution

When we think about PSE, we often think about ideas, solutions, features, and designs. To be more customer-centric, we will need to break this down further. There is the concept or idea, and there is the design and precise execution of the concept.

You are surrounded by examples. The concept is the four-wheeled motorized vehicle that can transport people, animals, and cargo. Executions and designs vary in car styles, sizes, prices, fuel types, offroad capabilities, sound systems, dashboards, etc. Similar ideas, very different executions.

Designing Customer Experiences goes deeper – beyond the idea – to the precise execution of the idea. For example:

- The problem statement is: *customers would like to get purchases faster*. One idea is: *offer express shipping*. That's not the only possible idea. We could also offer faster production or store pickup.

- Express shipping's customer-facing execution and design include:

  o How shipping options are explained on the product page. What is express shipping, how will it be shipped, how long will it take, what does it cost, and what other options do I have?

  o How can shipping options in the cart and during checkout be simple, clear, and intuitive? Plus, how do we make sure people have selected the option they intended to choose? Poor information architecture or interaction design could lead people to choose standard shipping when they need it faster.

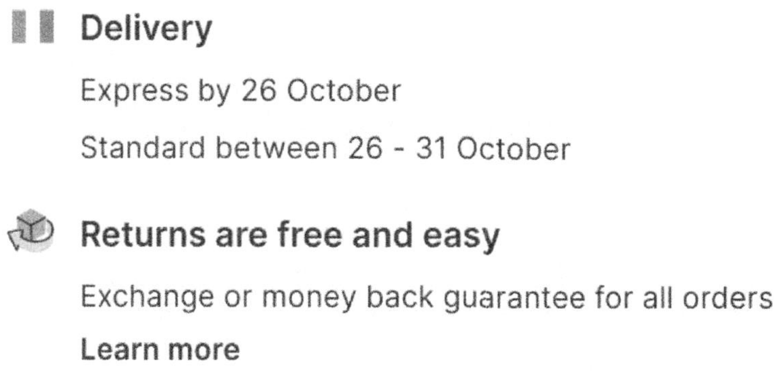

▮▮ Delivery

Express by 26 October

Standard between 26 - 31 October

⬢ Returns are free and easy

Exchange or money back guarantee for all orders

Learn more

Figure 46: Screenshot from an item on Redbubble.com. It understands that I'm in Italy. It offers express shipping that will put the item in my hands on 26 October. Standard shipping will deliver the item during the last week of October. Prices are not stated, but the timing information answers shoppers' questions before they experience doubt or confusion. The layout and information are minimal and clear. This is pretty good!

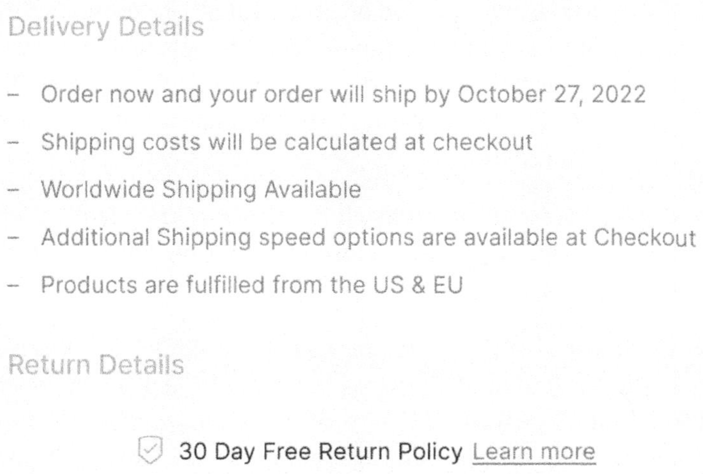

Delivery Details

- Order now and your order will ship by October 27, 2022
- Shipping costs will be calculated at checkout
- Worldwide Shipping Available
- Additional Shipping speed options are available at Checkout
- Products are fulfilled from the US & EU

Return Details

☑ 30 Day Free Return Policy Learn more

Figure 47: Contrast the above to this screenshot from an item on Teespring.com. It's not clear when this item will be in my hands. The Teespring item would ship after I receive the Redbubble order. "Delivery details" are a list I'd rather not read.

Redbubble and Spring (formerly Teespring) are direct competitors offering similar PSE with similar features. The designs and *executions of the same idea* are very different. Different content and information are presented differently. The layout and visual design are different. The experiences are different.

Earlier in this chapter, we discussed designing based on customers' tasks and needs versus working from predefined, predecided features. This comes to life with our Redbubble and Spring examples.

- If project requirements demanded that the product page have a bulleted list explaining policies and how you will find more information later in checkout, then Designers often feel forced to include that, whether or not it's a good design or experience.

- Project requirements may demand that the product page *not* explain delivery times in the hopes that the user will add the item to their cart to see delivery times. This would bump up a metric around the number of items added to the cart, but can be a poor User Experience.

- Customers have various tasks and sub-tasks. The typical task might be to find a cool design, pick an item, and have the vendor print the design on the selected item. In my case, the task is slightly different: purchase an item with my own design on it to examine the quality of the printing and the item.

  o It was easy to tell which website had spent more time on the design and execution of my particular task. Logging into Redbubble made them recognize me as the creator, and the markup was automatically removed from anything I added to the cart from my own shop. Truly a no-brainer.

- A sub-task is my time and brain power spent understanding the many dimensions of shipping and delivery. How much of the behind-the-scenes logistics, such as where the item is produced, should be exposed to the customer? What do customers need to know to feel trust in the company and the purchase?

- Did we invest in the research that gave us knowledge around customers' tasks, sub-tasks, needs, preferences, and concerns? Do we know what increases or breaks trust?

- The Redbubble and Spring post-purchase experiences are different. Despite Spring seeing an Italian shipping address – and the product declaring that they fulfill from the USA and the EU – I received a shipping notification that I have a DHL International package coming from Kentucky, USA. It should arrive in a month.

  - When I checked out, the site said I would get the item in two or three weeks. Would I have decided against ordering if I knew I would have to wait a month?

  - If Spring can produce and ship items from the EU, why is my item coming from Kentucky? Will my package be delayed in Italian customs? Considering I once paid Italian customs $14 on a $25 book coming from America, what will I have to pay on a $20 t-shirt? Does Spring understand that I would not have to pay customs fees if they had shipped from the EU?

  - Spring should have noticed it was me buying a single item from my own shop, and it's my first-ever purchase. This is likely to be someone doing a quality check before they sell the item to the public. Wouldn't you want them to get the item the fastest way possible?

The idea is a start.
The design and execution possibilities are endless.

The User-Centered Design process leads us through trying variations of designs and executions – and then rounds of testing with target audiences – to ensure that we have created the best solution for the original problem or opportunity. Like research, thorough design and testing cycles must not be skimped on or skipped. This is where our customer intelligence comes to life in the form of prototypes and testable concept executions.

When I run brainstorming sessions, I only ask for concepts and ideas. The attendees don't sketch the exact design or execution. They don't draw screens of what offering express shipping looks like. We have specialized CX Architects who can utilize their skills, experience, and application of best practices to design, test, and iterate on detailed and exact executions.

Try It: Ideas Only

If your company likes workshops, you can make them shorter and more efficient by only collecting ideas and high-level concepts.

In a collaborative work environment, teammates would also have access to all customer intelligence. They would have quantitative data and survey results as well as qualitative insights and access to research session recordings. They should be familiar with all of these before the workshop.

The workshop can start with the problem statement, which everybody would already know since we are not siloed, and everybody has access to that information. CX facilitators can lead attendees through brainstorming exercises that utilize our knowledge about target audiences and their tasks, needs, and goals.

Focus on what truly solves the problem for our customers. Any idea that could make the business money or meet KPIs – but is customer-peripheral – should be sequestered with other customer-peripheral ideas, and not done. Remember that you are only collecting general ideas and not sketches, wireframes, or prototypes.

Our Process at a High Level

This book focuses more on research tasks since without high-quality research, you are probably setting projects up for small or larger failures. All of the UCD process is critical and vital. It must not be skimped on, deprioritized, or democratized. Transforming toward customer-centricity means empowering specialists to utilize UCD as your problem-finding and problem-solving process.

Whether you've been calling it "Human-Centered Design," "UX," "CX," "Product Discovery," or "creating empathy," you're talking about UCD and customer-centricity.

Let's walk through our new process at a high level. **Phase 1:** Phase 1 overlaps with the **Understanding** stream in Tri-Track Agile. We start with research. Without diving into people, systems, and contexts, we can't find root causes, needs, workflows, tasks, workarounds, or knowledge (or its lack).

For a PSE discovery project, we wouldn't start with features, ideas, guesses, and the goal of *discovering* if any of those are good. We would start from knowledge about our target and current customers. If you work from qualitative research data, you know where unmet needs exist. You can skip hypothesis-first discovery steps that try to determine if anybody would want a particular feature or idea. Task-oriented design doesn't start with the idea, feature, or a search for who might want either. We start by learning **where** we might need fresh solutions.

As mentioned in an earlier chapter, a great method to use during phase 1 is to create a shared whiteboard, physical or virtual. The entire cross-functional team, including stakeholders, has a deadline by which they must add sticky notes on the board's four quadrants: unanswered questions, guesses and assumptions, potentially outdated or incorrect information, and what they wish they knew. This is what we intend to *discover.*

Rather than moving forward with guesses, assumptions, or outdated information, Researchers use these notes to create and refine research goals, methods, and other study details. This ensures that Researchers will learn the answers to everybody's questions. It's also a great way to collaborate and have more people involved in the research planning.

After a research study is completed, and we have analyzed it along with other relevant qualitative and quantitative data, Researchers map the current state, and represent this with a task analysis diagram, customer journey map, or service blueprint. Researchers construct **problem statements**. They – and Service Designers, if you have them – work strategically and collaboratively on the future state map showing how to make employee, customer, and other experiences more efficient, more intuitive, and better in any possible way.

The future state does not necessarily detail specific features or solutions. It shows where current processes and experiences can be optimized. We are not locked into solutions at this point of the process. Once teammates are aligned around the improved and streamlined future state, we now have a document to guide potential solutions to the original problem.

Note that this "improved customer workflow" could be a fix or change to existing PSE; completely new, innovative, and disruptive PSE; or somewhere in between. Don't let the idea of an "improved" customer or employee workflow make you think that we are focused on small changes or incremental optimizations.

The generative research done in Phase 1 can also create or update:

- Personas, typologies, or user definitions.

- Delta CX Impact Maps.

- Delta CX Change Dependency Maps.

- The stakeholder map.

- The ecosystem map, which visualizes the people and relationships connected to our target audiences.

Research insights, customer intelligence, and actionable documentation set our projects up for successful next phases.

Phase 2: Phases 2 and 3 correspond to the **Discovery** stream in Tri-Track Agile. Product, CX, Engineering, and anybody vital on our team collaborate on reviewing and examining the insights, opportunities, unmet needs, tasks, and pain points discovered during research. They use their preferred prioritization matrices or scoring to determine in which order we will address the issues described in the problem statements. This is not feature or solution prioritization; this is deciding which customer problems and needs will be addressed and solved first.

Now that we've decided on priorities, each domain can create their roadmaps and plans, including time estimation. CX will have its own roadmaps and plans. Engineering has release and sprint planning. Some people roadmap very broadly, like *here's what we're working on now, what's next, and what's more down the road.* Some people roadmap by quarter, release, or month. It's hard to roadmap or plan at a higher level if you don't have a good sense of what can reasonably be accomplished in a day or week. Therefore, I suggest creating detailed project plans that can roll up into roadmaps. As shown earlier, my project plans organize work by the day.

Notice that planning is still not at the "feature" level. None of this says, "Simplifying credit card updating will have these screens," or, "Simplifying credit card updating has a *choose your primary credit card* feature and a *refer a friend* feature." In task-oriented design, we don't have exact features during prioritization and planning. We know the problem we plan to address. Features might change as CX Architects design and test possible problem solutions.

Phase 3: With our work prioritized, estimated, and planned, we can move into content, information architecture, interaction design, service design, and visual design, including testing and improvement cycles. In this phase, we work to solve the original problem statement. We go from "simplify credit card updating" as our strategy to the exact screens, functions, digital or human interactions, services, steps, and customer workflows that best achieve this goal. At the end of this phase, we have vetted and finalized designs, prototypes, and other documentation that move to the next assembly line station.

Phase 4: Phase 4 corresponds to the Delivery stream in Tri-Track Agile. Once CX has a tested and vetted solution, you can break that into features, stories, tickets, or whatever delivery teams prefer. If the company wants to release something less than what CX created, possibly as an MVP, we should check if there is a smaller version of the solution that delivers user value and solves the original problem. If reducing the PSE – just to have an MVP – would remove value, usability, or usefulness, don't strip it down. We should only release what customers are likely to give five stars out of five.

As Principle 5 of the Agile Manifesto says:

> *"Build projects around motivated individuals. Give them the environment and support they need, and trust them to get the job done."*

Beyond phase 4, we are monitoring live PSE for success, failure, metrics, and room for improvement. Then we circle back again to phase 1.

Customers' Definitions of "Quality" and "Done"

Agile typically defines "quality" as "excellent software performance" and "code with few or no bugs that meets stakeholder requirements." Agile typically defines "done" as "completing the work we planned to do" and "our work fit business objectives." "It's coded, tested, documented, and deployable." These definitions of quality and done are self-reflective. *Hey, did I do what I meant to do, and it seems to be working well? Then I declare it quality and done!*

Congratulations on writing working code, but does our PSE match our customers' definitions of quality or done? Does it fit their tasks and needs? Did the system optimize or complicate a workflow? If Engineering's code is high quality and feels done, but the concept doesn't match what customers need, is it still quality? Is it done? Did we waste time and budget building the wrong solution?

We must be careful to not use Engineering's definitions of quality or done as our only definitions. This feature is not quality or done if the customer needs to contact Support, leaves us low ratings, or the feature doesn't solve the original problem or unmet need.

Improve this by:

- **Writing CX definitions of quality and done.** Document and socialize these. If our designs don't meet these definitions, they're not ready, and shouldn't be put in the backlog for Engineering to build.

    o It doesn't match CX's definitions of quality or done if we haven't started with generative research and completed at least one round of usability testing on our proposed solution. Perhaps you require at least two testing rounds to check that your revised solution is a winner.

    o It's not quality or done if CX Architects are treated as order takers and unable to influence the solution.

    o It's not quality or done if DEI and accessibility weren't part of our process at every step. Did we lean on stereotypes? Did we think we could sprinkle on accessibility later? Did we announce that no blind people use our system, so we're probably fine?

    o Definitions of quality and done might be specific to a project, or they could be general principles added to your CX Collaboration Playbook.

- **Including these definitions in Engineering's Definitions of Ready or Done.**

    o It's not ready or done if it's not accessible.

    o It's not ready or done if Engineering got creative with CX's prototypes and built something that doesn't match the designs.

- **Adding a CX review column to your Kanban board, JIRA, or whatever Engineering uses.** While QA reviews for bugs and does their acceptance testing,

CX will review Engineering builds to ensure that they match CX project goals and CX's Definitions of Done. Experience flaws and debt are bugs we want to catch early.

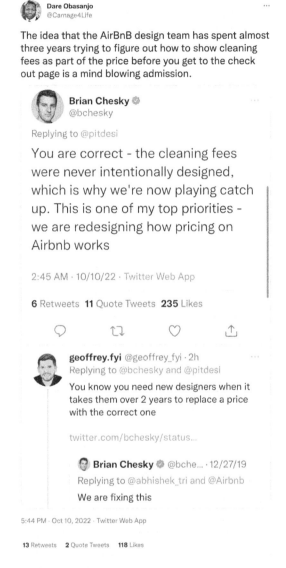

Figure 48: Screenshot of social posts. A tweet from Brian Chesky, a co-founder of Airbnb in October 2022 says that property cleaning fees were never "intentionally designed," they are "playing catch up," and it's one of his "top priorities." Someone else in the discussion retweeted a December 2019 tweet when Brian tweeted that they were fixing the cleaning fees problem. Dare Obasanjo screenshot all of this, and commented that it was a mind-blowing admission that Airbnb has spent three years trying to figure out how to show cleaning fees. It sounds more like Airbnb spent three years ignoring cleaning fees, and they are finally a priority.

Try It: The "Compete Against Yourself" Challenge

It's my variation of an idea Phil Golub [https://linkedin.com/in/philgolub/] mentioned. If you want to experience the power of excellent CX work and try something innovative, here is your chance.

Form a Superstar Dream CX Team of experienced and fantastic practitioners: three Researchers, two CX Architects, a Service Designer, a Content Strategist, and a Visual Designer. Give them six months to work on an experimental and innovative project. If you do not have these workers available, you could bring in freelancers or an outside agency.

Project level 1: The Dream Team will conduct research with current customers as well as target audience participants who are not our customers. The team will have the time and budget to create high-quality research artifacts, task analysis, and service blueprints. After prioritizing insights, the CX Architects can follow the optimized task flow and work on solutions. These solutions would be improved workflows and interfaces for the *same functionality* you have now. Beyond "fresh paint" or "reskinning;" this would be a whole new CX/UX architecture and experience for your existing PSE.

Project level 2: If you have more time and resources to invest, the team can change some functionality based on what they learn in their research, and what an Engineering team (or two) can prioritize. Project level 2 upgrades level 1's fresh workflows, interface, and usability to design sorely missed features and fixes that would add additional PSE value.

Measure: Whether you try project level one or two, you can capture some interesting metrics. Perhaps Sales can offer people both versions and see which potential customers pick or prefer: the current version or your experimental version. Remember, the functionality (for project level 1) is the same; the experience is different. We can measure the conversion rate and Cost of Acquisition for each. We can use metrics from the "Measuring Customer-Centricity" chapter.

Why do this: With project level 1, we can experiment with giving the same features and functions a dramatic User Experience change. You have essentially invented a pseudo competitor with feature parity. As this new PSE is yours, you will be able to track and measure it from Sales efforts through usage through longer-term metrics and experiences. Does the experimental version lead to lower Support utilization, lower Cost of Acquisition, more conversions or sales, longer customer lifetime, etc?

You can also offer it as a "new interface" option to existing customers, giving them the option to revert to the previous version at any time. Track how many users try it and stay with it. Monitor how utilization differs.

If you really want to get creative, you can invent a brand for the experimental version so that people might not know it's your company. Create a website for it and assign some Sales and Support staff to it, training them to use the experimental brand name. For inspiration, consider that Venmo and PayPal have been the same company since 2013, but have different experiences and interfaces.

This experiment is neither short nor cheap, but if you really want to know if investing in significant improvements to PSE experiences is worth it, this would be a clear way to know. You might end up with a design and experience that you eventually transition all users to.

Do We Need User Stories?

As part of a feature-oriented process, some companies write user stories. The format is typically: *As a [user type], I need [thing or feature] to accomplish [goal].* Our solution is pre-decided, so we give these stories to CX Designers and tell them to design what is described.

In a task-oriented, more customer-centric process, CX doesn't need user stories. Perhaps Engineering doesn't need user stories either. User stories are supposed to help Engineers understand our planned features from customers' perspectives. If everybody reviews research videos and artifacts, we have well-written problem statements, and we collaborate with Engineers in every phase, what would user stories give Engineers that they don't already have?

Atlassian's article on user stories includes the following as an example of a good user story [https://cxcc.to/a190]:

"As Sascha, I want to organize my work, so I can feel more in control."

That's a user story, but is it good? What do we really know about Sascha? What details do we have on their workflows and tasks? What does organizing their work mean to them? What does work feeling out of control look like for them? Atlassian's article says that the purpose of a user story is "to articulate how a software feature will provide value to the customer." Sascha wants to "feel in control," but we have to dig deeper to find the real value. Underneath "feeling in control" might be doing their work more accurately, more efficiently, with fewer meetings or interruptions, or something else.

If user stories are supposed to explain customer value to our team, wouldn't this be accomplished with more depth and accuracy by having everybody consume research sessions, or at least research insights and artifacts? A user story will rarely do justice to the complexity of customers' needs and tasks. More customer-centric and collaborative ways of working might make user stories obsolete.

Rethink Sprint Goals

A common template for Agile sprint goals says:

Our focus is on [Achievement or Outcome].
We believe it delivers [Benefit or Impact] to [User or Customer].
This will be confirmed when [Event Happens].

Supposedly, this helps teams focus on users and outcomes. But that's not a guarantee, primarily because of one risky word here: *believe*. Imagine work goals based on something someone *believes*, possibly a guess or assumption. Shouldn't we *know* that our solution delivers certain benefits because it has been evaluated and vetted? Shouldn't we check for customer value before we're planning Engineering sprints?

Every time we notice we are guessing, assuming, hypothesizing, making things up, or working based on what someone *believes*, our CX Researchers should study whatever it is so we can *know*.

I've rewritten Agile sprint goals to be more customer-centric:

Our focus is on [Customer Outcome].
CX has confirmed that it delivers [Benefit] to [Customer].
This benefit will be measured by [KPI or Metric].

In the old version, we're hoping to confirm later that there was a benefit for the customer. There might have been zero benefits, and you will find that out after weeks or months of expensive project team time. That's not Agile or Lean. CX can confirm the benefits and value earlier through UCD. Instead of hoping to find out later if something delivered benefits to customers, we can know this early – and can adjust the solution – if it's low on quality or value.

Time Estimation

Whether you are Agile, waterfall, or something else, projects are virtual or physical assembly lines. We're moving knowledge, CX artifacts, code, and other elements along our (virtual) factory floor. This requires extensive and detailed planning. Assembly line stations don't want to be delayed waiting for something from the previous station. CX Designers don't want to be delayed by Researchers. Developers don't want to be delayed by Designers.

To improve our ability to estimate time accurately, first consider how many work hours there are in a work week. If we require a 45-hour work week – and some companies require fewer or more hours – we should humanely encourage at least 10 hours of meals and breaks per week. We inhumanely often require people in 15 hours of meetings per week. This would leave 20 hours per week to get actual tasks done. For example, if we estimate 90 hours for a particular task, that can't be completed in two 45-hour work weeks; we would need 4.5 weeks, and we might estimate five weeks just in case. I suggest always adding time for what I call "predictable unforseeables:" something will go wrong, but we don't yet know what.

Earlier, we saw my company's plan where we estimated that a project would require 388 hours over ten weeks for three people, plus a little help from a fourth person on one task. Put one Jack Of All Unicorns on this at 100% allocation, and 388 hours of work at 20 real work hours per week takes nearly 20 weeks. *Of course, that's not Agile.* This would take even longer if this Unicorn were allocated to this project less than 100%, as Unicorns often are.

There is often a chasm between what agency Salespeople and Account Managers propose to clients and what creates great Customer Experiences. This also happens at our corporate jobs when Project Managers, Product Managers, or Engineers guess the time CX needs. All of these non-CX roles rarely know the time it takes to do CX work *well*.

The solution is easy: CX must estimate their own time early in planning and at every phase. Non-CX roles should not guess what CX staff will do and how long they need. Make sure that anybody creating the project scope or plan works with CX so that CX can decide which tasks to do, how many specialists are needed, and the required time.

Post-Release Monitoring

Agile requires that we pursue user feedback to improve the PSE and push projects in better directions. Flavors of Agile are not always clear about what types of feedback are most helpful, what types are meaningless, or who proactively or reactively gets this feedback, and how often.

This is one of many areas where your CX department can shine. Qualitative and Quantitative Researchers can monitor metrics and KPIs, and observe and speak to customers to learn what's working, what's not, and why. Getting well-collected, well-analyzed feedback from research professionals brings us actionable evidence more efficiently.

What are we monitoring?

- **Original goals**. We started this project with goals and at least one problem to solve. Did we solve those problems? Did we solve them well? Did we veer off course and fail to accomplish our goals?

- **Metrics/KPIs**. What were our success criteria and KPIs? Have we met or exceeded these? If we fell short and don't understand why, we should conduct qualitative research to reveal the root causes.

- **VOC**. What's the word on the street? What is Customer Support hearing related to our improved or new PSE?

- **Qualitative data.** Researchers should observe or at least speak to some customers. Did we fix one thing and break another? Are there new pain points we should be aware of? How does the new solution work or not work for customers? Where is there room for improvement?

- **Experiments.** Monitor experiments for short- and long-term wins and losses. Are people clicking *that button* less but signing up more? Are people purchasing more items but complaining and returning more than average? Remember to watch for the longer arc of the customer journey. Short-term successes are sometimes long-term failures.

  o   If this is an A/B test, how do we assess which version wins? Can we observe some users to learn *why* B is better or worse?

Reorganize PSE Areas

Customer-centricity and Customer Experiences are holistic across touchpoints, channels, and PSE. Has your organization divided PSE areas, domains, or Product Manager territories? We have often accidentally created silos; we broke the customers' workflows into pieces worked on by separate teams. This typically comes from an engineering-led approach, where we start with the amount of work that one Engineering team can do, and assign a Product Manager or Product Owner to collaborate with that team. We add one or more UX professionals, and we narrow in on the work that team can do quickly.

Companies that have divided their PSE areas this way must watch for collisions and overlaps where one team is accidentally working on something another "owns." It is also sometimes difficult for a team to strategize and execute on only a piece of a solution because one or more teams "own" other pieces.

Imagine teams who are true utility players, able to strategize, research, design, build, and deploy in any area of our PSE or across areas. This also makes sense because even if we wanted a team to focus on and own one small puzzle piece, we would still prefer – if not expect – that they have familiarity and knowledge of our entire PSE. Allowing teams to work on different PSE areas in each project could also keep work fresh for staff, who might find working on the checkout for years stale and stagnant.

How might this work?

- **Generative research delivers insights, opportunities, and actionable suggestions.**

- **We write problem statements.**

- **We prioritize these and create a roadmap or plan of which problems we will address in what order.**

- **We match projects to the availability of a Core CX Team (CX Researchers and Architects).** We will also need to coordinate members of the Satellite CX Team, Service Designers, and others who might be required for this project.

    o Coordinating this can be complicated, and you might want to have a dedicated project or allocation manager overseeing this. Tools will also help; I have used monday.com, but Aha! and others can work.

- **Each specialty on the team estimates the necessary time to do their best work.** This includes research, content, information architecture, interaction design, service design, visual design, testing, iteration, and all Engineering tasks, plus other tasks related to non-digital experiences.

    o This is also a great time to identify any lack of resources, including workers, tools, or budget.

- **CX Leads or Managers, Program Managers, and other high-level Project Managers check for collisions and overlaps.** For example, if one team is working on a project to implement Apple Pay as a payment form, and another team is about to start a larger checkout redesign project, these teams will need to communicate and coordinate. Perhaps the Apple Pay feature can be rolled into the checkout redesign, and one team can move to another project.

- **The project team focuses on the features, functions, or services required to solve the problem.** Each project team member works in their specialty area, collaborating where needed.

- **Engineering can be allocated in one of two ways:**

    o An Engineering team always works on the same area of the PSE. If something needs to be coded in the checkout, Team X always does that. Nobody else touches their code.

    o Or an Engineering team follows their project team. They code various areas of the PSE based on what the project covers. An Agile or Scrum team is connected to a Core CX Team, and they always work together.

Companies with broader PSE offerings won't be able to create project teams that can work on anything in the company. You might need to create some larger product areas where divisions make sense, such as a design system area, an integrations and APIs area, and a few PSE areas.

Two Types of Cross-Functional Teams

Companies often do not want to allocate resources to all of the debt we claimed we would fix later. Customer complaints are unresolved, and broken promises sit in backlogs, iceboxes, and to-do lists. We don't want to delay new features to work on fixing old stuff.

Companies with huge and increasing technical and Experience debt often claim that we don't have enough CX, UX, or Engineering staff to address what we and our customers know is broken. One solution is to create two types of teams. One handles all of the new work: discovery, experimentation, and new PSE. The other handles all of the fixes: CX/UX debt, technical bugs, performance issues, and small improvements.

One of my apprentices got her first job as an Associate Product Designer at HubSpot. Her main job was to design fixes to lower-priority tickets that Engineering had flagged as having UX debt or issues. As an entry-level job, she had a more senior Designer as her dedicated mentor and coach. This is a multidimensional winner.

- A qualified, talented person gets an entry-level job with interesting responsibilities and frequent work reviews.

- Giving these Associates lower-priority tickets means they can take their time, get coaching, and learn how to create the best designs. Associates are not under pressure to deliver five-star work on mission-critical projects.

- HubSpot knocks out some annoying bugs without taking more experienced CX/UX resources off higher-priority projects.

- Customers see HubSpot acting on their complaints and pain points. Problems are being fixed, and improvements are released faster than they used to be.

Improving customer-centricity should create a future with less debt to handle because it never went to market, but there will always be debt. If we don't have enough staff to fix PSE bugs, we will have to hire. We must stop making excuses for knowingly broken PSE that we are ignoring and deprioritizing.

Project and Team Charters

You will need project and team charters that explain what we're doing, why, our success criteria, metrics, and the roles each of us will play so that we don't overlap. Teams often skip this step, leading to conflicts, confusion, inefficiencies, and other culture problems. Project and team charter templates are plentiful and easy to find online. Like any templates, they are *garbage in, garbage out*. No matter which layout or design you use, make sure that you have included information that will set you up for success and help avoid later conflicts, including:

- **How will we address differences of opinion when we make a decision?**

- **Who makes final decisions in which areas?**

- **Who will be held accountable for what?** What does accountability look like?

- **What are our risks?**

- **How will stakeholders be measured or held responsible?**

- **What do stakeholders need, and how will we deliver what they need while also delivering what target users need?** Do stakeholders have to report to people above them? Learn what kinds of data and details they need, in which formats, and how often they need it so that there aren't conflicts or panic later.

If you have standardized how your teams operate, you can incorporate your own templates into your playbooks. Update charters as team members change or team goals evolve. Revisit the charters when people slide into complacency and forget the points that were agreed upon.

Product Management and Product Owner Roles

We need to discuss another elephant in the room: the roles and responsibilities of Product Owners and Product Managers. As we will learn in the next chapter's interview, Product Management historically was well-defined, and covered a variety of strategic and tactical tasks. Over time, many of these tasks were broken off from Product Management and given to roles with deeper specializations related to those tasks. For example, nowadays, Sales and Marketing work on PSE pricing; this is rarely a Product Manager's responsibility.

Some flavors of Agile explain that a Product Owner has the following key duties:

- Communicating the PSE or project goals.

- Defining and writing user stories for Engineers.

- Assisting or leading the Engineering team in prioritizing or planning work for each sprint.

- Validating that stories connect to the Definition of Done (DoD).

- Prioritizing the backlog based on strategies and priorities.

- Validating that completed work meets acceptance criteria, has been appropriately tested, and meets the DoD.

- Acting as a liaison between stakeholders and Engineering teams.

Responsibilities of a Product Manager often include some of the above, plus:

- Understanding customers' needs and the market. Some sources demand that PMs do market research and/or CX research. Some sources suggest that PMs investigate and determine new markets or business ventures for the company.

- Deciding where the PSE need innovations or improvements.

- Translating business goals to our PSE.

- Determining product features. Some sources say this is solely prioritization. Some sources say the PM must create the solution, and then have UX Designers document the PM's ideas through UX artifacts. Some go further to require that the PM execute on CX architecture and design tasks.

- Creating product strategy and roadmaps.

- Aligning teams and stakeholders on product vision and strategy.

- Determining success metrics, KPIs, and OKRs.

- Collecting and interpreting customer feedback after release.

The definitions of both Product roles raise questions, including:

- Can "self-organizing" Engineering teams prioritize their own work?

- Can Engineers and CX Architects work together to create user stories, the backlog, or how Engineering wants to organize their tickets or work?

- Do QA Engineers on a self-organizing team need Product Owners to check that QA has done its job? Could a Project Manager check that the right work has been completed?

- Aren't our market research specialists better than the average PM at market research?

- Aren't our CX Researchers better than the average PM at CX research?

- Given their more strategic roles, could CX Managers or Directors handle most or all of the above Product Management tasks?

- If CX creates an overarching Customer Experience strategy after generative or discovery research, do they need PMs to create the product strategy, which is part of the CX strategy?

- If CX takes business goals into account (in addition to customer goals) during prioritization exercises, do they still need PMs to act as the voice of the business?

- If CX prioritizes its own work, do they still need PMs to create a roadmap? Wouldn't CX create the roadmap?

- If CX understands business and customer goals, wouldn't they be able to create appropriate KPIs and OKRs for projects and PSE?

- If CX has the most knowledge about target audiences, the market, and Customers' Experiences, and has highly qualified Architects, why would PMs design the PSE?

- If CX monitors PSE after new features and services are released to the public – especially where we created a CX department that centralizes all qualitative and quantitative research – why would PMs handle post-release monitoring?

> *"Product management isn't a specific role at Basecamp. While overarching vision and big picture direction comes from a small core team, the teams working on the features/cycles themselves pretty much lead themselves."*
> *– Jason Fried, Founder & CEO at Basecamp [https://cxcc.to/a189]*

While POs in various Agile frameworks are considered necessary and are unlikely to go extinct in the coming years, the PM role is increasingly debated. Many current PM roles and certificate training are moving toward turning PMs into Unicorns, able to do *some* research and design work. Some certificates require PMs to learn some coding. This leads to power struggles, overlapping or duplicated work, and morale issues. [https://cxcc.to/a163]

If PMs continue attempting to hybridize PM and CX work, the likely outcome is that they will find it harder to be hired into their own jobs. If a job requires demonstrable skill and proficiency in CX research and/or design, a qualified CX or UX professional is more likely to be the selected candidate than the average PM, who might have little or no CX education, skill, or experience.

If Product Management is to have a bright future, Product organizations and leaders must identify a clear swim lane that can be the PM's domain without overlapping with other roles.

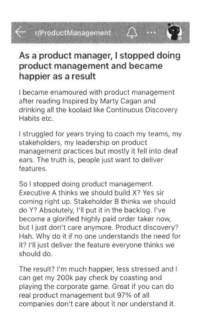

Figure 49: Screenshot from the Product Management Reddit. [https://cxcc.to/a188] The title is, "As a product manager, I stopped doing product management, and became happier as a result." The post is

quoted below. Ask yourself if this person is empowered or part of an empowered team.

"I became enamored with product management after reading Inspired by Marty Cagan and drinking all the koolaid like Continuous Discovery Habits, etc.

I struggled for years trying to coach my teams, my stakeholders, my leadership on product management practices, but mostly it fell into deaf ears. The truth is: people just want to deliver features.

So I stopped doing product management. Executive A thinks we should build X? Yes, sir, coming right up. Stakeholder B thinks we should do Y? Absolutely, I'll put it in the backlog. I've become a glorified highly-paid order taker now, but I just don't care anymore. Product discovery? Hah. Why do it if no one understands the need for it? I'll just deliver the feature everyone thinks we should do.

The result? I'm much happier, less stressed, and I can get my 200K pay check by coasting and playing the corporate game. Great if you can do real product management, but 97% of all companies don't care about it nor understand it."

Chapter 21: Interview: Product Management

Steve Johnson is an author, speaker, and product coach using modern methods to move products from idea to market. His approach is based on the belief that minimal process and simple templates result in a nimble product team.

Steve has been a long-time advocate for Product Management, serving as an executive and advisor to many technical Product organizations and industry associations. In 2020, Steve was awarded one of the first ten 51331 coins for contributing to the best practices of Product Management. Steve's work experience includes technical, Sales, and Marketing Management positions at companies specializing in technology-enabled products.

Steve is a former instructor and vice president at Pragmatic Marketing as well as co-creator of the popular QuartzOpen framework [https://quartzopen.com/]. Today, Steve is a founding partner with Product Growth Leaders [https://productgrowthleaders.com/], a community for experienced Product professionals.

Debbie: How would you define customer-centricity?

Steve: I like to say, "The way to be a consultant is to be from out of town, you have a four-square grid, and be able to quote Peter Drucker." So, here's a quote. Peter Drucker said, "The goal of Marketing is to know and understand the customers so well that the product or service fits them and sells itself." What Drucker refers to as "Marketing" is not promotions and ads; it's what we now call "Product Management." That's customer-centricity.

The failure in so many companies is found in two phrases. "I talked to a guy," which many executives and Salespeople consider a completed research study. And the other one is, "If we build it, they will come." It's so common that we see Developers and Product Managers saying, "OK, we built this thing. Who should we sell it to now?"

Some people say that Marketing or promotion is about "creating the need" for the product, which already tells me you failed. People should need the product, and you should know they need the product because you built the product based on the needs of the market. Verifying and validating that is a key element of the kind of research that UX does and should be doing.

Debbie: We often think that if a Product Manager has a cool idea, we should just get that out as an experiment.

Steve: I don't see that as often from Product Management people as I see it from executives and Salespeople. An executive says, "I was on a plane reading the airline magazine, and apparently this cloud thing is gonna be a big deal. We ought to put our product in the cloud. It doesn't look that hard to me because it was only like a three-page article. So, make it so." There will always be more demands than available resources. Product Managers have to be really good at saying, "No."

Debbie: They have to be strategic gatekeepers.

Steve: Yes. I worked for a company where I was told that the Developers were fundamentally broken. So I went to my Lead Developer and said, "I hear you guys are broken." He said, "It's true we haven't had an official release in quite a while. We've started practicing a thing we call 'requirements aging.' We don't work on anything for a month just to see if it is still a priority a month from now." As we were having this conversation, the VP of Development came in and said, "Stop what you're doing. I'm getting new requirements from the President." The Lead Developer turned to me with this look of "see what I mean?"

The following week, I went to the senior leadership meeting and said, "I found the problem in Development. It's in this room. You need to shut the hell up for a while because one sentence from you is months of work for us. So, I'm going to be the new No Department. I'll take your ideas, and I'm going to write them down. But we're going to finish stuff before we start taking on new work."

Debbie: I like the nice euphemistic name for it: "requirements aging". *Put whatever an executive says in the icebox and see if it defrosts on its own.*

Steve: Exactly. I've worked with teams that have requirements, stories, epics, tasks, or whatever we call them that have been in queue for a year, a year-and-a-half, because there's always something more important. The frightening thing for Product Managers is when they finally realize that we can't do it all. We have to have a way of saying, "This doesn't align with our strategy," or, "This isn't the top priority because there are only so many things we can do with the resources we have."

My recommended prioritization scheme has five factors, three of which are around the value to the customer. Then someone asks, "Who? What customer do you mean?" I mean *all the customers*. The market full of customers.

Debbie: I've seen Product Managers spinning plates, trying to improve a feature or customer task. When they think they're headed somewhere, that VP or executive says, "No, you must deliver against these KPIs." What can the Product Manager do there?

Steve: Product Management is clearly defined in only 20% of organizations. The rest are spinning plates, as you call it, because they have no idea what their job *isn't*. Somebody says, "Hey, Product Manager, we need you to do a wireframe of the UI," and you're like, "OK, I guess that's my job." I saw a Reddit thread about, "What is your favorite prototyping tool?" And I said, "My favorite prototyping tool is a qualified UX Designer." But unfortunately, in many of the organizations I work with, they don't have a UX

Designer, or at least enough UX Designers. So, Product Managers say, "Well, I guess I have to do that."

Then the Salesperson calls and says, "Hey, I'm talking to a super big client. It could be a huge deal. Can you hop on a plane, come over here, and talk to them about the roadmap?" The Product Manager thinks, "Off I go." Product Managers end up doing things that are outside of their responsibilities and usually outside of their expertise. They're doing UX Design. They're doing Project Management. They're doing content creation for Marketing. They're doing Sales Engineering. What they're NOT doing is Product Management.

I was on a speaking panel at a conference, and somebody asked what the job of the Product Manager was. The last panelist said, "Product Managers do everything that no one else wants to do." And I'm like, *if this guy is a consultant, that explains why so many companies are screwed up on the role of Product Management.* And that's why they're spinning all those plates.

Debbie: But it's more than that guy. I've been researching Product Management certificates. Some of them are trying to teach you UX research, market research, and UX design. I even saw one that required you to do coding to get your Product Manager certificate.

Steve: I know that many Product Managers are being told by their management that they need to be UX Designers and Programmers. Their reaction is, "I guess I need to learn how to do UX Design," or, "I guess I need to learn coding," instead of, "Hey, why don't we hire somebody for that?"

Likewise for Sales Engineering. Product Managers are great on sales calls, but it's not Product Management's job. You know who else is good on sales calls? Company Presidents, CTOs, a lot of people are good on sales calls, but that doesn't make it their job.

The real problem is that 80% of companies are defining Product Management based on the holes that they have in their organization. *We don't have enough Sales Engineers, so let's get Product Managers to do it. We don't have UX Design, so let's get Product Management doing it.* Product Managers are living in chaos as a result.

Unfortunately, there is no professional definition of Product Management. All of the training vendors are describing their own flavor. Some trainers are defining Product Manager as Product Owner/UX Designer/Something Else. It seems anybody can define the role through their own lens, and it's a role that almost everyone has misunderstood.

Debbie: Speaking of disputes over job boundaries, should Product Managers be doing interviews?

Steve: I want Product Managers to have the experience of being in the room and seeing problems first-hand. I believe that the interviews don't necessarily have to be done by a Product Manager or a UX Researcher as much as a *qualified researcher*. I teach people that having first-hand experience with customers is critical. Interviewing them is good. Observing them is better. And they should do this with others, such as Product Marketers and UX Researchers or Designers, maybe a Dev Lead. I always recommend customer visits in pairs; the other person will invariably see things you don't see.

In my first Product Management job, my boss admitted that we didn't know what was happening in the market. He challenged me to do ten customer win-loss interviews each quarter. And he based my quarterly bonus on completed call reports. Win-loss analysis is the Product Manager's secret weapon, yet the average high school football team spends more money on win-loss analysis than the average software company. In most of the software companies I visit, the Sales team doesn't want anybody else to do it, but they don't want to do it either. Leadership rarely understands why we lose, but they also don't know why we win! We need to have more kinds of research, one of which is a win-loss interview. Another is observing people who are using your product and competing products.

For a sound business case, we must interview non-customers and competitors' customers, both those who use the product and those who are involved in purchasing the product. I expect Product Managers and Product Marketing Managers to be experts on the market and its problems. If I can get most of that information from UX Researchers, then I'm OK with that.

And that's why I distinguish between buyer personas and user personas. Users actually touch the data or the product. They use your product to get their work done. Salespeople have almost no experience with those people. Salespeople have experience with buyers. The buyer personas or the decision-makers don't get their hands dirty with the product. If you're trying to learn how to build a better product, you need to talk to people who would be using the product. But a Product Manager must also understand the buying criteria or else the product will never get to the ones who use the product. To be successful, we have to understand both the buyer personas and the user personas.

It seems to me that understanding the customer and their problem is the center of everything. I continue to meet people who think, in all honesty, that they are getting statistically relevant feedback from the Sales force. They believe that they are informed about the market. When I point out to them that Salespeople are talking to buyers and not users, it comes as an epiphany, which is good.

Debbie: Given the sources nudging Product Managers toward UX skills, do you ever worry that Product Management and UX will merge?

Steve: No, Product Management and User Experience are entirely different skill sets. People who are merging these two are mistaken. I'm reluctant to say I blame Agile, but I do blame Agile. I love Agile. I can't even fathom doing a nine-month project without doing 90 builds plus check-ins and validation with customers. The philosophy of Agility totally makes sense.

But for many teams, theory never made it into practice. Somewhere related to Agile was the pulling of Product Managers out of their business role into a UX role. I've been in meetings where people say, "I don't see why we need both UX and Product Managers." If you think a Product Manager's job is designing User Experiences and filling out JIRA tickets, then yeah, I don't think we need both roles either. But my perspective is that Product Managers are looking at things through the lens of business. *Is this the right thing for our market full of customers? And is this also the right thing for this business to pursue?* **I like to say that Marketing and Sales teams are responsible for this year's revenue while Product Management is responsible for next year's revenue.**

I saw one of the visionaries of Agile on a stage at Agile World in 2008. He was describing the importance of the Product Owner role. Somebody in the audience raised their hand and said, "But if the Product Manager is also the Product Owner, when are they going to do all the other work of a Product Manager?" The Agile visionary said, "What other work is that?" He didn't see the other work expected of Product Managers, including pricing, business planning, roadmapping, and prioritizing for business value.

If you go back to the original definition per Jeff Sutherland in his book on Scrum [https://cxcc.to/a126], the Product Owner was supposed to represent the business and the market to the Dev team. That would allow the Devs to ask questions like, "Will the user like this? Will this be the right solution for the business?" Product Owner was intended to be a business role, but then it evolved from a role into a title, and now does the job of what we used to call a Business Analyst, writing stories and documenting features.

Debbie: I've seen companies led astray by executive or high-level decisions around KPIs. The KPI might be *we want to see users doing more of this, we want to see users clicking this button more, we want to see users getting to this point of the funnel more.* That's passed down to the Product leader or Product Manager. The message is, "You are under pressure to show a lift in these metrics." The PM now has to assemble all possible troops including UX, Engineering, and Data and Analytics. The PM says, "Stop whatever you were doing. My ass is on the line to show a 2% lift this quarter in users doing this thing."

Steve: Absolutely the wrong way to use KPIs. Metrics were never supposed to be weapons. KPIs should be used to identify where friction occurs. As a simple example, *we're suddenly seeing an incredible increase in abandoned carts. We've been using a KPI to show that we had 20% cart abandonment, and suddenly, we're at 35% cart abandonment.* That's a symptom that we need to drill down to learn what in the world is going on. KPIs were meant to provide insight. It's like the dashboard in your car. The dashboard doesn't say, "Oh my gosh! You're speeding... so I'm going to blow up your car!"

The thing you choose to measure can be absolutely the wrong thing to measure. It reminds me of the old approach for Customer Support, which I hope does not exist anymore, where we want Reps to get the customer off the phone as quickly as possible. Reps would get people off the phone and close the tickets even if they didn't resolve the problem. The measure of success in Customer Support should not be the length of the call; it should be successful customer resolution.

What's particularly funny to me is that we spend enormous sums trying to get Sales and Marketing to be able to talk to customers. But then when customers ask to talk to us, we're like, "Dude, we have no time."

Debbie: I see a world that is *speed over quality*, where it doesn't matter if this product is really suitable for people or has a good product-market fit. *We'll figure it out later, or we'll fix it later. I don't mind releasing something now that I know is broken. We'll just make time to fix it later. It's good enough.* What can a Product Manager do on that team or in that environment?

Steve: The short answer is probably: you're screwed, you'd better leave. But seriously, quality doesn't matter until it does. Then it's too late. Everybody says, "Just get it out there. Just get it out there. Just get it out there." Then they get one-star reviews, and internally, we're asking, "How the hell did you allow this thing to get out there?" The answer is often, "Well, let me read back the email you wrote me two weeks ago where you said, 'Just get it out there.' "

Nobody cares about quality until customers do, and then it's too late. You've already lost a customer, or you've already had your reputation besmirched in the marketplace.

Debbie: I see the MVP as part of the UCD process. We create a realistic UX prototype and then use usability testing and other feedback to determine if we're going in the right direction. We don't have to have Engineering build it since that could be risky and wasteful.

Steve: That's a very, very good point. I wish all companies would embrace this idea of experimentation. Eric Ries said that the most misunderstood point in his book, *The Lean Startup*, was the "MVP," and that he made a simple mistake: *he called it a Minimum Viable Product. MVP should stand for Minimum Viable Prototype.* As Eric Ries talks about it, the MVP is an experiment. It's not supposed to be a product you sell. It's a product that doesn't have a lot of functions yet. *Maybe it just does this one function.* We present it to customers and get their feedback.

Debbie: I guess he didn't feel like creating a new edition of his book to clear that up! What would you say is the optimal role and utilization of a Product Manager?

Steve: There are three roles that are often assigned to somebody with one title of Product Manager, and they're very different roles. There's a strategy role: what products are we going to build for what markets at what price point? I call this "product strategy;" it's the business role.

There's a second role that I call "product planning," which is taking the business rationale to a technical team, which absolutely should include a UX Designer. Describing the problems that we want to solve next and letting the team determine the right way to solve those problems.

And then a go-to-market role that I call "product growth," which asks *how do we find the optimal market segments at the optimum price point? And how do we promote to those segments so that they know that we have solved this incredible problem?*

So, when we say, "Product Manager," that's too fuzzy. What kind of Product Manager?

Strategy, Planning, or Growth? My friend and company co-founder, Grant Hunter, says that Product Management is what connects corporate strategy to product execution.

As much as I love Agile, they did a disservice by creating the Product Owner role because that is Product Management seen entirely through the lens of Development. Those are the things that Developers wanted. That's fine, but that is a subset of the scope of Product Management.

In my first job in Product Management, I went to the Dev team, and I said, "I really want to do well here. How can I be a valued member of this team?" I was a little terrified that they were going to ask me to make better prototypes. But what they said was, "Tell us about what's going on in the market. What are the trends in the market? What are the top three issues facing our target buyers? Tell us about some deals that we recently won. Tell us about some deals that we recently lost. Tell us about what promotions you're planning to run."

It was fascinating to me and a very good experience. My Dev team wanted me to be a business-oriented Product Manager who is sharing all the stuff that is going on with the product. After all, it's their product too. They love their product, or should.

My friend, Rich Smirnoff, says that being a Product Manager is a lot like parenting. I think really good Product Managers – and probably UX Designers and Developers as well – love the product that they work on. They want to see it grow up, become popular with a lot of friends, and have a good life. There aren't that many people outside of that triumvirate of Product Manager, Designer, and Developer that think of the product that way. Everybody else thinks of it as a cog, a widget, or a unit. But for us, they're children.

Debbie: What can Product Managers do differently to help shepherd more customer-centricity?

Steve: I have a phrase I've used for 30 years: *Opinions, while interesting, are irrelevant. You need customer data to offset all of these incredible opinions.* Jim Barksdale, when he was at Netscape, said that, "If we have the data, let's look at the data. If all we have are opinions, then we'll use mine."

Product Management and products should be market-informed and data-informed, not anecdotal, and not opinion-driven. It's too expensive. One customer said they'd like it, and now you're going to build a whole product for them? Seriously? Don't you want to find out if people want this thing before you go any further?

Debbie: *But we ran a survey that said everyone wants it!*

Steve: Ha ha! Yes, data can be tortured into any form you want it to take. I would really want to look at the way you wrote those survey questions. I got a survey the other day from one of the political parties. It was hysterical. It was just one leading question after another, including phrases like, "Don't you agree that...," or, "What do you think about the failed attempts at..." Somebody, somewhere is going to claim that this is good data, but it's absolutely not.

I once visited a customer, and he said, "When are you going to hire a UX Designer?

You have the worst user interface of any product I have ever used." I asked him to say that again into the microphone. He was glad to repeat that he freaking hated our product's user interface. The next day, I'm in a Development meeting. We don't have a UX designer on the team. The Developer was saying, "I know we have some performance problems. But you've got to admit: people are going to love our user interface!" I said, "Hang on. I have a little recording I'd like you to listen to." I played the recording, and the Developers were thunderstruck. Luckily, they took it to heart. They didn't try to dismiss it. They started asking questions about how to improve the Customer Experience.

Our opinions are irrelevant. We need our customers to guide us. I'm not saying *getting our customers to tell us what to build*. Customers are almost always wrong about what feature to build. Instead, I want our customers to tell us the problems they're trying to solve. Or let us observe the problems that they are having, whether they know about their own problems or not. Then we can use our skills to Design a brilliant solution.

Bad Product Managers act like servers in a restaurant. "What do you want? I'll get the kitchen to make it for you." Good Product Managers are like orchestra conductors. They choose the music, but they don't play the music. They choose the venue and the ticket prices, but they don't market and sell the tickets.

Our goal in Product Management is to systematically turn good ideas into successful products.

Chapter 22: Interview: Enterprise Experiences

Stéphanie Walter is a User Researcher and Designer who focuses on building User-Centered, inclusive, and accessible products and services. She spent the last 12+ years helping her clients deliver successful projects in different industries, including banking, finance, automotive, healthcare, press, and travel.

She likes to share her passion for her UX work all around the world. Her successful blog and presentations at conferences and workshops discuss a wide range of topics, including mobile UX, enterprise UX, cognitive biases, inclusive design, design process, and Designer-Developer relationships. You can follow her on social media for curated UX design content. [https://stephaniewalter.design]

Debbie: How do you define customer-centricity?

Stef: Customer-centricity would be making sure that when you build a product that you understand and follow your users' needs. You make sure that those are higher priorities. A customer-centric company would prioritize the things that will benefit the user the most, maybe not the stakeholder(s). But it's a balance between finding a way to bring what the stakeholder needs because, at some point, they want to make money as well. If you're customer-centric, you try to make that money while still building *what the customer needs* as the highest priority.

Debbie: You're our enterprise experience expert. Would you still use the same definition for an enterprise type of environment?

Stef: I would maybe replace "customer" with "employee" in this definition to make it clearer. In Enterprise UX, you usually have two kinds of products. You have the one that you bought. For example, SAP or Microsoft Office. The second kind is products built inside this enterprise for our end-users, who are our employees. Those employees are not paying for the product. It might be an internal budget going from one hand to another.

And since this is for our employees, I would say efficiency is often the key metric. Whenever we are involved in change management, one of the biggest concerns is, "You've changed this. I'm going to waste so much time. I'll be less productive." Enterprise customers' needs and values are a little bit different, maybe a little more pragmatic. They want to be productive. They don't want to waste time.

Debbie: Many companies don't care if workers struggle with the tool or system. They don't care if people are inefficient.

Stef: When I was working for the university, the intranet was a nightmare. So, we created a fun game. My colleague was looking for a phone number on the intranet, and I went downstairs to the reception to ask for that phone number. We found that it was more efficient for me to go downstairs to the reception, ask for the phone number, and go back up to the third floor than for her to find the number on the intranet.

Then they did some real tests and basic task analysis based on things someone might do on the intranet. They checked how long it took them and if they failed or not. A lot of people failed. We then had this weird metric. *How much time does the task take? What is the average salary of the people doing the task?* If the intranet requires double the work, it might cost that much money for you. It's the sunk cost fallacy. *We've invested this much. Why would we change it?* The cost of a poorly designed interface is sometimes hidden.

We have the same issue in banks and other big companies that bought software packages years ago, and they don't want to change them. They're trying to train users on them. Sometimes they pick the cheapest tool in the box, or they choose to outsource to the cheapest company. It might take maybe two or three years to discover that this was a sh*ity package, but they don't care because they're often not at that job anymore.

I get the impression that's why we end up with packages that don't really work. People try to find the cheapest one. Sometimes at the end of the year, the unused budget can be converted into a bonus for people. That's the worst idea possible. People are like, "OK, you mean that I have this envelope of money. If I buy the cheapest stuff, I can split what's left between me and two other people?" What do you think will happen? That person will take some shortcuts, they will compromise on the tool, and they will say, "Yeah, good enough. Anyway, in three years, I'm not here anymore. I've jumped to the next company or to the next position, and this will not be my mess to clean anymore."

Debbie: I once had to put in an official bid to provide software training to an American government agency. I asked if they were going to check for any qualifications since I'm one of the few recommended trainers for that software. They said that their policy says they must look for the lowest bid. Well, good luck getting quality.

Stef: I noticed that in some places you have a Risk Manager and those types of roles. I don't know if they're consulted when it comes to buying software or tools. The people who are responsible for deciding to invest money in either buying or building a tool should be the ones doing the math.

But the problem is that most of the time, they end up with sh*ity KPIs. If the KPI says you need to do something with as little budget as possible, that's what you do. You can't blame human beings for being human beings. It's about helping leaders and managers understand that just because you have an easy-to-measure KPI doesn't mean it's the right KPI.

Debbie: Can you think of some of the bad KPIs you've seen? And why they were bad?

Stef: "How many contracts did we sign?" There's always a certain amount of time, usually one month, where you can say, "I signed this contract, but I want to retract and cancel the contract." What happens when you need to sign that many contracts this year? In December, you have a peak in contract signing. In January, half of the contracts get canceled. Is this reflected somewhere in those objectives and metrics? Do they also measure how many were canceled? Maybe the problem is that the KPI is only measured by the end of the year.

There's some wild stuff that people do with budgets. At some point in France, the army had a budget for gas. If they don't consume the gas, they have a smaller budget next year because they didn't need so much gas. Maybe it's a rumor, but I heard that sometimes they circle vehicles around just to consume gas.

As soon as you have a poorly-constructed KPI, people will try to game the system to keep something or get rid of something. It's human nature. But do our higher-level leaders and execs understand this? Do they care?

Someone presented NPS to me. They took everyone that was neutral and they put them with positives so they could say, "Oh, we only have that many people who don't like the interface." Technically the data was not wrong, but it was the way they presented that data.

Going back to KPIs, a lot of people have yearly objectives. But should it be measured for a year? Or a longer period to remove the temptation to play games? If you have a longer-term objective, that might give you longer-term focus because customer-centricity is not a short-term goal. It's a long-term goal. If you have super short-term goals, how are you supposed to be customer-centric in the long-term?

I heard about a job offer that said your 6-month goal was the growth of how many people signed up for the product. In six months, you have to show at least let's say 10% growth. So you hire someone. It takes them two months to understand the company and products. But in six months that company wanted them to already have more than 10% growth in the people who sign up. Do you know how long it can take to do this? Do the research, design it, have Developers implement it, test it, push it to production. Even some fast and Agile teams need six months for some features because there's other stuff in the backlog. Plus they do heavy testing as well like usability tests and regression tests. I'm nevertheless happy that they put that 6-month goal into the offer because it shows how little they understand the job. You don't want to work for them.

Debbie: What other things can you suggest for enterprise organizations to be more customer-centric or employee-centric?

Stef: The main trick is to try to understand how people in the trenches use your product. I'm pretty sure that if someone in a higher position who makes product decisions spent a whole day trying to work with the tool, they would stop saying it's good enough.

Think about some of the people in our company who are less tech-savvy. If you watch them work, you can understand why they complain about our product. Often, teams don't want to hear those complaints. But we need to see the reality of people who use our product every day to understand how annoying it can be to include the same data in three different systems because there's no communication between the systems. People don't understand how complicated someone else's job might be.

Debbie: I remember an article about a delivery service making everybody, even Developers, spend a day doing bicycle deliveries, and everybody lost their minds and thought that this was terrible and unfair.

Stef: It's complicated because they had to do it for only one day. This one day can help them understand a little bit better what the problems are. I don't like the word "empathy," but at least understanding; that can be a good thing as well. It's easy for Developers to say that it's not a big problem. But then this is only one day. If you are forced to use a company-provided system on a daily basis, just using it for one day might not be enough to understand all the issues and pain points.

I had that happen to me last week. I was teaching, and normally the session is recorded and available automatically as a replay to the students. But we had a technical problem. The assistant called Support. Support acted like, "Yeah, we lost three hours of teaching. That's a super small detail, and it's OK." The assistant wasn't happy: "Maybe you don't care, but now I have three teachers who are paid by the hour who have to re-record the whole lesson. They will not get paid because it's not in their contract. This is not OK! And how do we make sure that it's not going to happen again?"

People demand better experiences. They have "free" tools like Google. They compare Google with the enterprise tools they have to use on a daily basis. They wonder why they have to send a Word document to their colleague, the colleague adds a comment, and sends it back. Compare that to a shared Google Doc, where everyone edits or comments at the same time.

I'm super happy when users report things. Some people say they're just complaining, but I say, "No, that's not complaining. That's feedback." And it means they care. They want to make it better. They want to be more efficient. Doing the same thing often in an inefficient way might drive you mad. *This is a waste of my time. I could be doing other things and more interesting things.* If you have to do the same thing three times instead of only doing it once, you might ask yourself at the end of the day, "What am I doing here? I'm copy-pasting stuff in fields that could be automated!"

It's difficult because in enterprise, most of the time, the tools were built inside the company. They don't really have competitors. But it can still be an argument to say, "If I have to work with that, I will be way less efficient."

Chapter 23: Where to Start

Every page in the book is a place to start: something that can be discussed, planned, and tried. Every conversation you start is a possibility for change. **Did we take a step toward customer-centricity today?** Even one step is a great step. **Are we seeking, welcoming, and acting on the customer feedback that is negative?** Some comments and suggestions can be hard to hear, but we will be stronger and grow more when we take these seriously and follow through on five-star solutions.

Customer-centricity isn't about empathy, delight, and maps claiming to diagram what users feel. Customers will be delighted if we understand their tasks and needs, and build what improves and solves those.

Delight is the side effect, not the goal.

Try It: Have You Ever Never Needed Support?

Customer-centricity is about creating PSE so intuitive – and such a great match to users – that they don't need Support Reps. Can you think of a product or service where **you never needed Support**? You were able to do everything yourself. Nothing was broken or frustrating. I don't mean you tried to get Support, but couldn't reach them or get your problem appropriately resolved. I mean *you never needed help.*

There is poor quality everywhere we look, which means there are always opportunities for improvement, evolution, and revolution. It's never "good enough" for customers.

Target audiences don't care what businesses want or need. They don't care about your goals or initiatives. But that can't be a two-way street. Businesses must care about what target audiences want or need. Without this, you might not have customers. You're leaving money on the table when you treat customers like pawns to push around. You can't give them minimum viable crumbs and assume they will join, stay, be satisfied, or be loyal.

Go beyond "care" and claiming we have empathy for customers. Do we have the necessary information and evidence to make better decisions? If so, we have no excuses for not making better and more customer-centric decisions. If not, we must start focusing on our customers and the high-quality PSE we will need to create to win and keep them. Are we taking customer-centric or customer-peripheric actions? Are we knowingly releasing a guess or broken PSE?

Go beyond building something because an executive or stakeholder requested it. We don't have to be order takers. We can ask a stakeholder why they want the feature, but where is the customer in this conversation? We want to make stakeholders happy, but the consequences of unhappy customers are far worse than a grumpy stakeholder that didn't get their way.

Be customer-centric and value-led, ensuring that we always deliver high customer value. If you don't want to be a feature factory, stop working from features first and "an exec had an idea" first. Where are our problem statements? Are we guessing what customers need? Did we research them well, or just survey them to see what we could sell them?

Resistance to Change

It can be hard to create change when our company got this far doing what it has been doing. Why should we be different or better when we can say this is working for us? We're making money, our stock price is going up, and our HR survey says that 74% of staff are at least somewhat happy here.

We must push past complacency and "it's good enough." Our PSE aren't good enough. Our work environment isn't good enough.

Talk about the projects everybody sweeps under the rug: the disasters and embarrassments. Discuss outcomes and root causes of failed projects that delivered poor Customer Experiences. Showcase these as examples of wasted time, money, morale, customer trust, Customer Support, Marketing budget, Sales efforts, and more. Highlight these as what happens when we aren't customer-centric. Once you have successes from more customer-centric projects, showcase these for contrast and as positive case studies.

Try It: Hindsight

Think about previous disaster projects at your company. Where in the process were the mistakes or poor decisions? Were we wrong about what we thought customers would like? Did we make multiple mistakes along our project's journey?

Now that we see that disaster more clearly, talk about it more openly. Learn from it. Figure out how something like that can never happen again.

Be Who We Claim to Be

If we claim to be *agile* in any form, then we believe in continuously improving our ways of working. We believe in self-assessment and learning how we need to improve our processes and our PSE. We change what needs to be changed once we understand our own problems. We don't avoid that understanding; we dive in knowing it'll hurt a bit before it improves.

If we claim to be *innovative,* then we can correctly diagnose our own problems and invent solutions. We should never say, "We can't do that," or, "But this is how it's always been done." The innovative mindset says, "Let's figure out how we can do that," even if solutions come in phases and evolve over time.

We have company values, but we don't live them. We put them on posters, shirts, and presentation slides. We don't deal with toxic or abusive staff and leaders who behave opposite to our values. Take your culture problems seriously. When results come in from internal surveys, don't just hope that our scores look better next quarter. Investigate and act. Create policies around accountability so that problem-causing staff are motivated to be better.

Empower individuals and teams to be problem-finders and problem-solvers, not just order takers. These are experts and specialists that you hand-selected from hundreds of applicants. Trust them. Treat them like you trust them. Support critical thinking and tough questions. Challenge the status quo. Experiment with new ideas and ways of doing things.

Learn from our failures, but preferably move more of those failures out of the public eye. Catch more of our failures during User-Centered Design processes to reduce the risk and waste of releasing guesses.

Customer-centricity reminds us that the "best practices" for PSE Design and creation aren't hard rules that, if followed, automatically produce PSE-market fit and customer satisfaction.

The best practice *is* research.

Research first, research often, and find solid data and evidence that inform careful decisions. Continuously pursue customer intelligence, and use it in all areas: strategies, goals, initiatives, PSE, and decisions. Most companies we admire invest heavily in generative research to understand target audiences' behaviors, needs, tasks, and perspectives. We can do that too as soon as we stop telling ourselves that research isn't worth our time or budget.

Customers can tell when our PSE is broken or a poor solution. They might not know which team is responsible or how to best describe it. But they know when we didn't give QA enough or any time or resources to find all of the bugs. They know when we didn't give CX enough or any time or resources to understand customers' needs and design the best solution. They know when we rushed it out, half-tried, and thought it was "good enough."

Customers know you suck, but the solution isn't to try to trick them into thinking that we're "good enough." Customer-centricity is about putting customers of all types at the center of our business strategies, goals, initiatives, PSE, and decisions so that we don't suck.

Chapter 24: Interview: You're in the Experience Business

Seth Mbhele is a seasoned Design Strategist who has spent 20+ years collaborating with corporates, start-ups, and nonprofits around the world in diverse Design roles.

He has overseen multidisciplinary delivery teams and driven Design strategy at the four largest Pan-African players in the financial services and insurance sectors. He has led some of the largest and most ambitious transformation and omni-channel re-engineering projects on the continent of Africa.

Seth formed his own agency in 2008, which he ran for a total of 10 years before he became a Design Strategist and Consulting Head at Immersion Group in 2018. He currently serves clients across EMEA as a Design Director at McKinsey Design. [https://linkedin.com/in/sethmbhele/]

Debbie: How do you define customer-centricity?

Seth: An easy but difficult question. Customer-centricity should be about how the organization – from a strategic perspective – is organized around serving its customers. That has multiple implications. *Why should the customer be central? How are we doing things currently? How would this be different? What is the value of doing things differently?* Those types of conversations come to the forefront.

It should be an explicit organizational strategy around putting the current and future needs of the customers front and center. Building that relationship and ongoing value exchange with your customer for the long term.

Debbie: Why do so many companies seem to get it wrong or not be customer-centric?

Seth: Customer-centricity requires a level of transformation. You have to change the way that you do things, and change the way that you are organized to create, capture, and deliver value. **Fundamentally change.** That's where a lot of organizations get it wrong. They still have the traditional pyramid, command-and-control type of structure. The highest-paid person makes all the decisions.

A lot of people in the room who come from traditional business functions like Marketing or Accounting have heard buzzworthy things like *design thinking* and *customer-centricity*, but don't really understand how to get it done and how to integrate it into their way of work. There are customer initiatives being done on the side without much integration back into the way that the organization functions. Things fall short.

Then, typically, professionals like yourself and myself get called in, and it's nearly too late. Strategies and initiatives are already in play. They are using those traditional command-and-control, old-school business ways. When our contribution comes about earlier, it comes in the strategy formulation itself.

Debbie: We keep hearing how design thinking, courses, and certificates will make us really innovative. But it's not changing what's fundamentally going on in the organization. *Hooray, we put a small bandage on a giant bleeding wound. Congratulations, you did a workshop and came up with some ideas, but you really didn't examine or change your ways of working, your corporate structure, or who holds the power.*

Seth: The things you mentioned speak a lot to culture. The structural underpinnings of the organization and how the company is organized have a knock-on effect on culture and the way that things are done.

For example, some organizations have implemented *on paper* a Human-Centered Design approach. They have Designers, they're bringing in the Voice of the Customer, and they're conducting interviews. But there's some missing ingredient, and it relates to the culture. We've missed the essence of what it actually means to be a customer-centric organization.

Transformation, even from a technology perspective, is typically a very expensive exercise. You have to change the way you think about your business, change the way you think about value, change what behaviors are rewarded, and examine the system of capitalism that prioritizes short-term profits and shareholder value. Those are the things that can make a customer-centric push and real ground-up change a bit difficult.

I think that's one of the reasons why companies do the cosmetic stuff. They want to be seen doing the "right" things, making the "right" noises, and designing by committee. But you've put a little layer of icing on a poo cake.

Most of my professional consulting work in the Design space has been largely in financial services focused on South Africa and the continent. The ideas fundamentally still come from the business, who says, "These are the things that we want to do." For example, they want to do a financial education program largely because the state requires them to have a financial education program. They'll put someone in charge of it who isn't empowered or incentivized. You get experts in a room to put the solution together. At the end, someone will call in some Designers and say, "Make this look pretty and speak to some customers."

Debbie: What would it take to make people at executive and decision-making levels more interested in customers' experiences?

Seth: I've been a Designer for twenty-something years, but in different sorts of guises, from a Web Designer to Designing experiences specific to restaurants and theme parks. In the food and beverage industry, you get an immediacy of seeing the thing that you've created, the whole offering: the burger, chips, music, waiters, setting, ambience, etc. You see the entire experience, and you see – in real time – what good and bad experiences look and feel like. You also feel it financially. A partner, owner, or executive in these establishments sees in real time how a bad experience is costly on the bottom line, and how a great experience creates loyalty and drives more spending.

Some types of businesses naturally understand and get it: *they are in the experience business.* Most if not all retail businesses deliver an experience. You walk into a shoe shop. You smell the leather. You see the lighting, the cabinetry, and the person that's helping you. There's an experience that has been orchestrated toward a certain outcome.

The CEOs and the executive layer don't get out of the building enough. This is gonna be harsh, but they don't really understand the business that they are in. If you are a telco executive thinking, "We can throw in a Netflix subscription here or there," I think you've got the wrong idea. *What does our product enable? What is our customer actually doing with our stuff? Who are they calling? Why is it important? How are they consuming data?*

That's where the real the nuggets, the insights, and the real market differentiation come from. Think of someone at the executive level running the organization through spreadsheets and dashboards without understanding *why* things are happening. They may understand the *what,* and that sales are up or down. But they don't understand the *why.*

Debbie: People can go to the shoe shop, watch how the workers treat people, and watch the experience that customers have. People can go to the theme park, watch how the employees treat people, taste the food, and check the experience. But when it comes to digital, so many executives and leaders are not watching the videos of the research that's taking place. They're not exposed to what those digital experiences look like from the customers' perspectives.

Seth: Correct. This is part of the disjointed nature of certain organizations. The one main advantage of a digital business is that everything is infinitely trackable. Of all the organizations that I've worked or consulted with, I don't think that I found one that properly leverages the data that they collect. Or they don't even know what they're collecting. The analytics haven't been set up in a way that is useful or usable.

But you've got mountains and mountains of data, lakes, puddles, and pools of data, and all this machine learning stuff going on. It's still very much that siloed mentality, where you've got these pockets of excellence, and pockets of data and expertise, but it's just not coming together. Data is a type of representation of your customer and their behavior. That should be critical stuff that you look at all the time. But it's hardly ever leveraged in that way.

Debbie: I'm also finding that some executives, even CEOs, who when they receive data that is bad news - like angry tweets or survey comments from unhappy customers - they write that off and say, "Those are mean, deeply bad people." Or, "They're just complainers."

Seth: That's typical. Part of the fundamental transformation that I was talking about earlier is changing *what are we tracking and why. How are we incentivizing staff and customers? Are we incentivizing certain behaviors toward certain outcomes?*

We talk about NPS all the time. It's vague. Organizations tend to leave it at very high-level diagnostic metrics, and it almost becomes conjecture. These metrics are pointing you in a certain direction, saying, "You need to do some work over there." If you've got a well-structured survey, and it starts giving you a trend of negative sentiment, it's probably something to look at.

That's the type of data that should be given to a Customer Experience team. They should have the autonomy to decide what to do with that feedback and how we fix things. This is also where a CEO or manager should not be looking at that data **and making any type of decision**. They should be deferring that to a CX team and saying, "Hey, I remember that we spoke about NPS, and we're getting a consistent score of 6. You told me that's not good. Who in the organization can tell us what this means?"

You need to be open to saying, "I know *this* part of the puzzle, but I need different people to come in and help me figure out the rest." That comes with changes at a personal level, interpersonal level, organizational level, etc. Ego needs to come out of the equation.

Debbie: I wanted to talk about what's going on in Africa because during the time when I worked with you, I was really surprised how many African organizations seemed to be working on spinning up Customer Experience initiatives. They were very interested in CX strategies and the North Star. It seemed like Africa was getting it when other regions weren't getting it yet.

Seth: Are we getting it? Yeah, in pockets. I did a lot of work in financial services, banks, and insurance houses. Within 18 months, I worked on five or six major initiatives or concepts. None of them saw the light of day. The reason is that you've got this *Center of Excellence* type of model, where things are happening next to the organization, almost not in the organization. We may be in the same building, but it's not connected. There's no real understanding unless you've got organizations with quite a flat structure and really empowered leadership.

We get it, but unfortunately, it falls victim to that traditional corporate structure where we incentivize the wrong things. We might do something shiny for a board presentation for this quarter, but when it comes down to getting that initiative funded, there are issues. There's a disconnect in understanding the value. *Why is this initiative being prioritized over business as usual?*

There's always that disconnect in terms of trying to create the Center of Excellence model that is in Agile or fake Agile. It's where things fall flat. You've got very well-meaning, forward-thinking professionals in South Africa, but we very often end up against the wall. Budgets have been slashed for reasons you don't understand. Things have been half-implemented. There's natural movement of people across, in, and out of the organization. As much as we get it, we probably are still a little bit behind in terms of implementation.

Debbie: If you think about the products, services, and experiences that you interact with in your life, can you think of one that is doing a good job with customer-centricity?

Seth: In South Africa, probably no. This could be a very unique South African thing. South Africa has its problems. We've had the highest rates of inequality in the world for many years. For probably close to 20 years, we've been the country with the dubious title of topping the Gini Coefficient [a statistic measuring income and wealth inequality]. It means that we've got very specific problems with poverty and race. The wealth distribution in South Africa is still largely along racial lines.

There's what typical companies do, which is this aspirational, Western lens of how to do business, how to deliver value, and how to create products and services. The Western lens is not necessarily appropriate for the types of specific problems that we are dealing with on socio-economic and cultural levels. Solutions and approaches are not necessarily appropriate.

Here is a banking example. One of the South African banks was working on their financial education initiatives. We had quite a wide research phase, and conducted a lot of interviews with customers and potential customers. A poor person would probably be the beneficiary of the bank's financial education. We expected them to travel on public transportation - which is scandalous and dangerous in this country, plus also expensive - just to get to an interview center somewhere.

They were being addressed by people with no cultural context of where they come from. There's no real depth of understanding of what it actually means to be poor in South Africa. In South Africa, the profile of the typical Designer is a white male, maybe white female. You've got a good sprinkling of Black Designers that are coming up now. But there's that disconnect because of the type of society that we've created: a cultural disconnect between the "experts" that are architecting the experience versus the people that are actually using – or are the beneficiaries of – the product or service. There are disconnects in language and cultural context, and in understanding *what is their life like*.

You're speaking to someone about their financial habits, how they spend money, and how they save money. So, I asked one of the Designers, "Would you be comfortable to take this questionnaire that you've created, that you intend to ask the participants about their financial habits, to Stellenbosch?" which is an affluent, white, predominantly Afrikaans area? "Would you be comfortable to go and ask those people these questions?" He said, "I'm not so sure."

That's the problem. We've got a lack of sensitivity and integration across the races. There's a lot of really shoddy Design work, if I can call it that, which is happening because of that untransformed nature of our segregated society.

I'm doing a lot of work across the continent. When I'm in Ghana, Nigeria, or Kenya, I always insist on having a local person in the room. There are certain parts of the conversation that will probably happen in English as a business transactional language. But it's really important to have a colleague that is able to do the cultural translation.

Debbie: But we keep hearing, "Just have empathy. Just create empathy."

Seth: I don't even understand what people mean when they talk about "empathy." This is where things like diversity and inclusion really matter, especially in a context such as ours, where you've got these very strange structural and cultural differences.

Having a Black Designer in the room really matters. Having Black Design leadership really matters in this country. We're not necessarily seeing it; we're not necessarily getting there. They might feel the same way in the LGBT community. This is why it's really important to have diversity in the team itself. You need to have that community-level voice. The structure of your team needs to reflect the community that you're Designing for. It starts there, and then we can start talking about "empathy," whatever that might mean today or next week.

Debbie: This reminds me of an interesting experiment we ran at my company. When research participants booked interviews with us, they could choose from me or Larry, with our photos shown. We're both white, so there wasn't a rainbow of choices. But you could choose me, Larry, or pick your slot by time, and the system will assign you a person.

We found that every time we did this, including one study where we scheduled 80 people, roughly 50% chose to book by time. 50% chose either Larry or me deliberately. One of the female participants I spoke to said, "I chose you because I got the feeling you would understand me."

If we extrapolate that out, what could it mean to our research participants to be able to choose a Black Researcher or Researchers from different communities? What about the people who are more comfortable talking to someone who looks like them?

Seth: Yeah, 100%. Going back to the South African example, I've run interviews with participants that have literally ended in tears. We got to some really fundamental fundamentals within the interview, off script. But we got to that point firstly by not speaking English. English is a fourth or fifth language for most people in South Africa. For me, it's a third language. English is mostly administrative and transactional. South Africa is 90% Black African with a first language that is definitely not English.

Even the language is problematic if you tried to do that type of research. You are asking people to filter their responses through a couple of filters as soon as you speak English. You just get into a different mode of thinking. It's the same with traveling to interview with us. We want to create an environment for our participants that is comfortable. We are in an office building with aircon and coffee machines, but that could be intimidating for someone that is coming from an informal settlement. It could affect what they share and how they share.

You do a quick 30 seconds of icebreakers, you think you've got *rapport*, and you jump into the interview, but so much was left on the table. It's unsaid and it will never be said because you can't access that stuff. I'm sure there's stuff that I could never access from a non-binary person because I'm clearly binary-presenting. This is why diversity, equity, and inclusion are really important at the level of the team doing the work.

Debbie: This really shines a fresh spotlight on the old, "Anybody can talk to customers! Our Engineers and Product Managers will ask our customers a few questions."

That *sounds* easy to do. But it sounds like it's missing - I don't know if gravitas is the right word - but respect. It points at the importance of that specialized Researcher who really knows how to conduct these sessions.

Seth: Absolutely. Other roles often come into the room and are very myopic. They want feedback about how great we are. They want to validate their own thinking and leave. Do they even know how to receive or tease out potentially unflattering feedback, or the fact that they are probably barking up the wrong tree? They are the proverbial hammer looking for a nail. We need a research phase, but for many, it's a box-ticking exercise.

Debbie: What is the number one thing readers need to look at changing to be more customer-centric?

Seth: A shift in paradigm, even if we're not able to do the structural things like reorganize the organization. At the very least, the thinking needs to change. There needs to be a real shift in understanding why customer-centricity matters, understanding how to achieve customer-centricity, understanding the value of research and design, and really bringing those people into conversations early, before we have a pre-defined hypothesis or even solution.

Let the professionals do their work. I've never seen someone telling an accountant how to balance their spreadsheet. It's unheard of. I would not walk in and say, "Hey, I've done a trial balance before. I can do this. I'll take this from here." On what planet is that happening?

Even when we are including each other and I show you one or two tips, tricks, methods, or techniques here and there, that doesn't make you qualified to do the work.

PART 5: BACK MATTER

Chapter 25: Resources

- **DeltaCX.com**. More info on our coaching, training, consulting, and fractional CX Lead or CXO options. We are also a full-service agency working on CX and UX projects, training, and consulting. We are change agents leading business design and customer-centricity initiatives.

  - Join our email mailing list. I send one or zero emails per month. [https://cxcc.to/email]

- **CustomerCentricity.com**. You love the book; check out the website! Resources and other info are available there, plus updates and new stuff we won't be able to add to a published book.

  - Maps and models from the book plus exercises we do during the live workshop version are available as a Miro board at https://cxcc.to/miro.

- **Delta CX YouTube Channel**. [https://youtube.com/c/DeltaCX] Started in October 2019, we have over 600 hours of video on the channel, which means there is something for just about everybody. Just search YouTube for "Delta CX" and some keywords on your mind, and something should come up.

  - We live stream 2-4 times per week. Shows include "Think Out Loud" sessions where I teach by doing, "Office Hours/AMA" where I take live questions for an hour, "Practicing Critical Thinking," where we dissect and assess articles and social posts, and "Micro Lessons" where we go in deep on one topic.

- **Delta CX Online Communities**. We have free communities on Slack [https://deltacx.link/joinslack] and Discord [https://deltacx.link/discord]. Everybody helps each other, and I'm there daily answering questions, giving advice, and sharing.

- **RBeforeD.com**. Our Medium publication. "R Before D" stands for "Research before Design (or Development)."

- **DeltaCX.Media**. This is the first book in our new publishing imprint, Delta CX Media. More to come! Check out our other titles.

  - This site includes books, authors, video courses, and live workshops.

o   We also have items for sale directly from authors such as signed books.

- **DeltaCX.Shop.** You love the book; check out the merch! This is a shop with clothing, notebooks, mugs, and more.

- **Just tell me what you need.** Email deb@deltacx.com and tell me what's going on. We'll come up with a plan to address it.

Chapter 26: Thanks and Acknowledgments

Thanks to so many people for their work on this book. Some spent hours, if not days, helping with the editing. It was like a giant peer review. I'm eternally grateful for everybody's help in making the book better in various ways.

Thanks to Super Editors

These absolute champions were content editors, structural editors, line editors, copy editors, and proofreaders. Coincidentally, they are all UX Researchers.

- **Jenna Hammer** [https://linkedin.com/in/jahammer/]

- **Linda Hwang** [https://linkedin.com/in/lindahhwang/]

- **Kelene Lee** [https://linkedin.com/in/kelenelee/]

Thanks to Content Editors

- Liliane Abello [https://linkedin.com/in/lily-abello/]

- Roxana-Maria Barbu, PhD [https://linkedin.com/in/roxanamariabarbu/]

- Alexandra Betzler [https://linkedin.com/in/alexandra-betzler/]

- Vijay Bhaskar [https://linkedin.com/in/ckvijaybhaskar/]

- Glen Carrie [https://linkedin.com/in/glen-carrie-za/]

- Alessandra Chazin [https://linkedin.com/in/alessandrachazin/]

- Tiziana d'Agostino [https://linkedin.com/in/tizianadagostino/]

- Julia DeBari [https://linkedin.com/in/juliadebari/]

- Ilaria Fioravanti [https://linkedin.com/in/ilaria-fioravanti-0b50476a/]

- Ines Gomes Rego [https://linkedin.com/in/ines-gomes-rego-a77611b/]

- Bram Govaerts [https://linkedin.com/in/bram-govaerts-ba9a73108/]

- Orjola Kajo [https://linkedin.com/in/orjola-kajo/]

- Chris Lenhart [https://linkedin.com/in/chrislenhart72/]

- Janice Mañalac [https://linkedin.com/in/janicemanalac/]

- Beth Martin [https://linkedin.com/in/bethannmartin/]

- Mehul Mehta [https://linkedin.com/in/mkmehta/]

- Michelle Pakron [https://linkedin.com/in/michellepakron/]

- Myrto Papagiannakou [https://linkedin.com/in/mpapagiannakou/]

- Lynnsey Schneider [https://linkedin.com/in/lynnsey/]

- Maggie Tagoe [https://linkedin.com/in/maggietagoe/]

- Active members of my online community who voted on book cover ideas, reacted to possible book subtitles, and gave a test listen to an audiobook except.

Thanks to Interviewees

- Sheri Byrne-Haber [https://linkedin.com/in/sheribyrnehaber/]

- Trine Falbe [https://linkedin.com/in/trinefalbe/]

- Sarah Freeman [https://linkedin.com/in/sarah-freeman-adkins/]

- Michael Huynh [https://linkedin.com/in/mhuynh-cbr/]

- Steve Johnson [https://linkedin.com/in/sjohnson717/]

- Mei Ke [https://linkedin.com/in/mei-ke/]

- Karen T. Lin [https://linkedin.com/in/karenlin/]

- Seth Mbhele [https://linkedin.com/in/sethmbhele/]

- Craig Sullivan [https://linkedin.com/in/craigsullivan/]

- Stéphanie Walter [https://linkedin.com/in/stephaniewalterpro/]

- Jan Wardecki [https://linkedin.com/in/jan-wardecki-service-designer/]

Thanks for Inspiration

Thank you to people who inspired something in the book:

- Lee Andrese [https://linkedin.com/in/landrese/]

- Tom Bird [https://linkedin.com/in/tom-bird-31356263/]

- Jen Blatz [https://linkedin.com/in/jenniferblatz/]

- Chris Burles [https://linkedin.com/in/chrisburles/]

- Courtney Dunn-Snede [https://linkedin.com/in/cdsnede/]

- Aytan Eminova [https://linkedin.com/in/aytan-emnva/]

- Aaron Esau [https://linkedin.com/in/cohesiveteamsneedaaron/]

- Madalina Galie [https://linkedin.com/in/madalina-galie/]

- Clemens Lutsch [https://linkedin.com/in/clemenslutsch/]

- Larry Marine [https://linkedin.com/in/larrymarine/]

- Piermario Orecchioni [https://linkedin.com/in/piermario/]

- Ralica Parusheva [https://linkedin.com/in/rparusheva/]

- Irena Pavlovic [https://linkedin.com/in/irena-pavlovic/]

- Byron Porter [https://linkedin.com/in/byronporter/]

- Robert Powell [https://linkedin.com/in/uxbydesign/]

- Alessandra Scamurra [https://linkedin.com/in/alessandra-scamurra/]

- David Snodgrass [https://linkedin.com/in/supercreative/]

- Jeff White [https://linkedin.com/in/jwhite-ux/]

- Hang Xu [https://linkedin.com/in/haxuco/]

- My 2022 research apprentices (hire them!):

  - Bobby Bishop [https://linkedin.com/in/bobby-bishop/]

  - Sirocco Fury Hamada [https://linkedin.com/in/siroccohamada/]

  - Uddipta Mahanta [https://linkedin.com/in/uddipta-mahanta/]

  - Janice Mañalac [https://linkedin.com/in/janicemanalac/]

- And to those who wanted to remain anonymous, you know I'm grateful.

Chapter 27: Expanded Table of Contents

Part 5:   Back Matter   319

Index

Your Notes

Made in the USA
Monee, IL
26 March 2023

30553038R00184